THE
SECRET
SCHOOL OF
WISDOM

First published 2015 as hardback
Reprinted 2016
First published as paperback 2020

ISBN 978 0 85318 580 2

Published by Lewis Masonic
An imprint of Ian Allan Publishing Ltd, Shepperton,
Middx TW17 8AS

Printed in England

Visit the Lewis Masonic website at *www.lewismasonic.co.uk*

THE SECRET SCHOOL OF WISDOM

The Authentic Rituals and Doctrines
of the Illuminati

**Edited by JOSEF WÄGES
and REINHARD MARKNER
Translated by JEVA SINGH-ANAND**

Lewis Masonic

Contents

CONTENTS

IV. Appendix

Acknowledgements

All translations from French and Latin are by Paul Ferguson (St. John, Jersey) unless noted otherwise. His contributions during the editing process have been invaluable.

The editors also wish to thank Pantelis Carelos (Große National-Mutterloge 'Zu den drei Weltkugeln', Berlin), Kevin Ditto (Dallas), Hendrikje Henze (Berlin), Tom A. Hidell (Taichung), Arturo de Hoyos (Supreme Council, 33°, S.J.), Hans Koller (Loge 'Zur Einigkeit', Frankfurt am Main), Kornelia Lange (Geheimes Staatsarchiv Preußischer Kulturbesitz, Berlin), Andrew McKenzie-McHarg (University of Cambridge), Pierre Mollier (Grand Orient de France, Paris), Claus Oberhauser (University of Innsbruck), Jacobus Piepenbrock (Cultureel Maçonniek Centrum 'Prins Frederik', The Hague), Helmut Reinalter (University of Innsbruck), Jan Snoek (Heidelberg), Erika Zwierlein-Diehl (University of Bonn), and Peter Hofmann (Loge 'Zur Wahrheit und Treue', Neuwied) for their kind assistance towards this project.

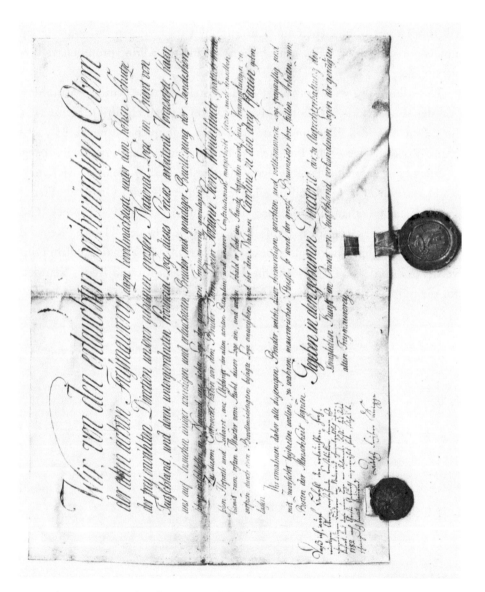

Knigge's constitution for the Neuwied lodge 'Caroline zu den drey Pfauen', 1782.
Courtesy of lodge 'Zur Wahrheit und Treue', Neuwied.

Introduction

THERE HAS NEVER BEEN an exhaustive edition of the degrees of the Illuminati Order before, not even in their original German, let alone in English. By following the series of documents collected here, the reader will trace a path akin to that of a career in the Order, progressing from one stage to the next, ascending through the levels of knowledge and secrecy, and finally reaching those degrees which were meant only for the chosen few. This may leave the impression that all of the degrees of this system were fully developed, and were indeed so since the inception of the Order in 1776. In fact, the whole structure was only rudimentary at first, stayed continually in flux and remained unaccomplished until all activities of the Illuminati ceased twelve years later.

What is presented here is the system as it was practised, or, in the case of the 'Higher Mysteries', still being devised by early 1783, at a time when the expansion of the Order was in full swing and neither internal conflicts nor external pressure had yet reached a point where they seemed seriously threatening. It was a structure developed not so much by Adam Weishaupt, the founder of the Order, but by his most important collaborator, Baron Adolph von Knigge.[1]

Working his way up through the system and its three separate classes, the adept was entrusted in each degree with new doctrines, and with them came new responsibilities and instructions, some of the latter being very detailed indeed. In theory at least, the members assembled in various bodies, depending on their level of initiation, while a continuous flow of information ensured that every individual member as well as every branch of the Order could be monitored by the superiors in charge. By 1783, several hundred members had been initiated, chiefly in western, central, and southern parts of Germany. There were numerous local 'Minerval Churches', reporting to superiors overlooking 'Prefectures', 'Provinces', and 'Inspections'. It was a highly complex and strictly hierarchical system, in fact quite excessively so, and a far cry from the humble beginnings of the Illuminati Order.

---

[1] See his diagram of the system in: Die Korrespondenz des Illuminatenordens, ed. by Reinhard Markner, Monika Neugebauer-Wölk, and Hermann Schüttler, 2 vols., Tübingen 2005 and Berlin 2013 (= KI), vol. 2, p. 366.

I. The Making of a Secret Society

When Weishaupt, then a young professor of canon law at Ingolstadt University,[2] first set out to assemble his most ardent students in a secret society, the organisational structure he envisioned was far less elaborate, while the stated final purpose was just as grand, with no less than the felicity and enlightenment of all mankind supposedly being at stake. Looking back in 1790, Weishaupt explained that a student who had 'arrived from Protestant universities' and brought with him knowledge both of college fraternities and of Freemasonry was the first to make him think of founding a secret society himself. He met this student, 'Herr H.', almost daily for as long as he stayed in Ingolstadt, and talked to him about the subject and recent publications such as '*Compaß der Weisen, Blumenoeck* and others', key books relating to contemporary Rosicrucianism.[3]

It has been possible to identify this 'Herr H.' as one Ernst Christoph Henninger, born in 1745, who had already been enrolled in Jena, Erfurt, Halle, and Leipzig before coming to Ingolstadt.[4] He did not stay for long here either. In November of 1775, he was rusticated from the university for some unknown offence. His own protest as well as Weishaupt's having led to nothing, he went to Heidelberg,[5] where he finally completed his studies and then pursued an inconspicuous career as a lawyer. He never became a member of the Illuminati Order.

Meanwhile, a lodge dabbling in alchemy founded in Burghausen, a town on Bavaria's eastern border, had begun recruiting members among the students of Ingolstadt. With some urgency, a certain 'Baron Cr.' even sought to draw Weishaupt himself into the fold.[6] This student, too, can be identified. It was Maximilian Leopold Baron Cronegg, born 1753 in Braunau, a town just a little down-

---

[2] *A full biography of Weishaupt remains to be written. For his family background see Edmund Hausfelder: 'Die Familie des Adam Weishaupt und seine Schwiegereltern Sausenhofer' and 'Die Familien Ickstatt, Weinbach und Raven und ihre Beziehungen', in: Sammelblatt des Historischen Vereins Ingolstadt 120 (2011) [2012], pp. 195–214 and 215–45. Leopold Engel: Geschichte des Illuminaten-Ordens. Ein Beitrag zur Geschichte Bayerns, Berlin 1906, contains much useful information. Weishaupt's later years, after the collapse of the Illuminati Order, are covered by Hans Schulz: 'Adam Weishaupt', in: Zeitschrift für Bücherfreunde N. F. 1 (1909/10), pp. 194–203.*

[3] *Adam Weishaupt: Pythagoras oder Betrachtungen über geheime Welt- und Regierungs-Kunst, vol. 1 (all published), Frankfurt and Leipzig 1790, pp. 654–55.*

[4] *See Reinhard Markner: 'Weishaupts früher Entwurf einer "Schule der Menschheit"', in: Sammelblatt des Historischen Vereins Ingolstadt (2011), pp. 640–53, here p. 640.*

[5] *See Die Matrikel der Universität Heidelberg, vol. 4: 1704–1807, ed. by Gustav Toepke, Heidelberg 1903, p. 286.*

[6] *Weishaupt: Pythagoras, op. cit., p. 665.*

stream the river Inn from Burghausen.[7] While being inscribed at the faculty of jurisprudence, Cronegg also took courses in science and even edited a volume of essays in mineralogy by his teacher, the professor of chemistry, Ludwig Rousseau.[8] He thus displayed an interest in the study of nature that would have been regarded favourably by his superiors – most likely of the Order of the Golden and Rosy Cross, an organisation spuriously claiming heritage to the mysterious Rosicrucian tendencies of the 17th century.

This was the background with which Weishaupt set out to establish a secret society of his own. His first fragmentary sketch, written around 1775 and entitled 'A School of Humanity', has only recently been rediscovered after more than two hundred years.[9] While not promising its members any kind of 'higher wisdom', this draft already contained a number of features that were later to resurface in some way or another in the Illuminati Order, such as the obligation for every member to keep a journal in which to record his thoughts, feelings, and insights, and to turn over a summary of the entries to his superiors, the plan to establish a collective library comprising of all the members' books taken together, the promise of meritocratic advancement in society, access to medical and other services free of charge, mutual insurance against catastrophic losses, free travel and accommodation when serving the school in an official capacity, and the access to charitable assistance as well as capital for investment. All of these benefits provided to the members in the spirit of fraternal assistance were meant both to make the society itself attractive and to improve the world at large by its benevolent activities.

For some unknown reason, Weishaupt discarded his idea of a 'School of Humanity', most likely before ever completing that draft, and instead wrote the general statutes of an entirely new secret society. Its members were to be called the 'Perfectibilists', i.e. believers in the possible, constant improvement of human nature and society. A handful of his disciples assembled under this banner in May

---

[7] See Das Matrikelbuch der Universität Ingolstadt-Landshut-München [...], ed. by Franz Xaver Freninger, Munich 1872, p. 81; Klement Alois Baader: Das gelehrte Baiern [...], Nuremberg and Sulzbach 1804, vol. 1, col. 201.

[8] Ludwig Rousseau: Nützliche Anwendung der Mineralien in den Künsten, und wirthschaftlichen Dingen zum allgemeinen Gebrauche [...], ed. by Maximilian Leopold von Cronegg, Ingolstadt 1773.

[9] See Markner: 'Weishaupts früher Entwurf', op. cit. – In Pythagoras, Weishaupt referred to even earlier efforts of his to 'strengthen the bonds between men and to gather their dispersed forces', made during his student years and resulting in some 'ridiculous and pitiful statutes' (op. cit., p. 653), but these immature projects cannot have been identical with the 'School of Humanity' fragment which aims at graduates from university rather than fellow students and furthermore refers to 'lodges' and the 'order', thus revealing the influence of Weishaupt's study of Freemasonry and other secret associations.

1776.[10] Only after Weishaupt had briefly contemplated replacing it by 'bee order' or 'bee society' in allusion to the Eleusinian mysteries[11] was the name 'Illuminati' finally adopted in April 1778. It was meant to reflect the members' fight against (the forces of) darkness as being their primary goal.

For future higher degrees, Weishaupt originally envisaged a ritual of fire worship modelled on Zoroastrianism to go along with the light metaphors of 'illumination' and 'enlightenment'.[12] While he did not pursue this idea, which was inspired by his reading of the Avesta,[13] he had the old Persian calendar introduced around June 1778, a decision he later came to regret.[14]

The original statutes of the Perfectibilists have not come down to us in their entirety. They consisted of several pieces, one of which apparently concerned the proper behaviour towards the Superiors.[15] In early correspondence between Weishaupt and his disciples in Munich there is mention of a special 'Instructio pro Carolinis'[16] for wealthy recruits. Two of the texts making up the lowest degree of the Illuminati system as we know it are designated as 'excerpted from the statutes' because they were salvaged from the earlier ones when a reform of the statutes took place, in November 1778.[17] Its original outline (see the Appendix) was written by Ferdinand Maria Baader, a prominent member of the Bavarian Academy of Sciences and Worshipful Master of the Munich lodge 'St. Théodore au bon conseil'. Another document belonging in this context, entitled 'Guiding Idea', apparently represents an intermediate stage between Baader's draft and the final version. The original 'Instructio pro Recipientibus' is remarkable for its explicit provision that no Jews could be admitted. It was dropped from the epon-

---

[10] *See Weishaupt: Pythagoras, op. cit., p. 670.*

[11] *Weishaupt to Hertel and Zwackh, [31 March 1778], KI vol. 1, p. 57; see also Monika Neugebauer-Wölk: Esoterische Bünde und bürgerliche Gesellschaft. Entwicklungslinien zur modernen Welt im Geheimbundwesen des 18. Jahrhunderts, Göttingen 1995, p. 30.*

[12] *See Weishaupt to Hertel and Zwackh, 6 April [1778], KI vol. 1, p. 65, and Weishaupt to Zwackh, 20 March 1778, ibid., p. 46.*

[13] *See Franz Xaver Zwackh: 'Beurkundete Geschichte des Illuminaten-Ordens' (1787), in Engel: Geschichte des Illuminaten-Ordens, op. cit., p. 82. Weishaupt's source was Zend-Avesta, Zoroasters Lebendiges Wort [...], ed. by Johann Friederich Kleuker, 3 vols., Riga 1776/77, or perhaps the original collection by Abraham Anquetil-Duperron this edition was based on. He may also have read Christoph Meiners' treatise 'De Zoroastris vita, institutis, doctrina et libris commentatio prima', in: Novi commentarii Societatis regiae scientiarum Gottingensis 8/2 (1777), pp. 122–56.*

[14] *See Weishaupt to Baader, [c. 18 February 1782], KI vol 2, p. 50.*

[15] *See Weishaupt to Massenhausen, 31 October 1777, KI vol. 1, p. 19.*

[16] *Weishaupt to Massenhausen, [c. October 1776], KI vol. 1, p. 9.*

[17] *See Weishaupt's instruction for Zwackh, Hertel, and Berger, [c. 11 November 1778], KI vol. 1, p. 101, and Weishaupt to Zwackh, 24 November 1778, ibid., p. 109.*

ymous text in the Minerval degree, but the requirement that every member should be a Christian remained in force, as evidenced in the Illuminatus major degree into which elements of the 'Instructio' were later incorporated.[18]

At least superficially, the new secret society had indeed all the appearances of a Christian institution: it was called an 'Order' and its first stage a 'Noviciate' from very early on, thus taking its cues from Catholic religious orders. Weishaupt, who had himself been educated by Jesuits and now taught at a university still dominated by professors who had previously belonged to that order, suspended in 1773 by Pope Clement XIV, abhorred the Jesuits and what they stood for but evidently admired their former might, the foundations of which he examined closely.[19] His study of the constitutions of the Society of Jesus[20] explains why a novice could be accepted without an initiation ceremony, and why there was so much emphasis on reading, the improvement of self-knowledge, and the constant scrutiny of one's own possible flaws. Finally, it also explains why Weishaupt later accepted for himself the rather grandiose title of 'general'. In reality however, his creation still rather resembled a small college fraternity than a fully developed 'order' or secret society, despite branching out to Munich, the capital of Bavaria. The actual degree of sophistication the organisation had reached was mirrored in the recklessly facile substitution cipher that went along with the Noviciate.[21]

In March 1778, Weishaupt was working on the statutes of a 'second class', by which he seems to have been referring to a future Illuminatus degree. He sent a partial draft to his closest collaborators in Munich and promised a further instalment.[22] This took him two months to complete.[23] In November 1778, having received a copy of the 'Statuta Illuminatorum', Weishaupt stated his intention to

[18] *No practising Jews are known to have been among the members of the Illuminati. Joseph Sonnenfels, a leading member in Vienna, had been baptised as a young child.*

[19] *See Adam Weishaupt: Nachtrag zur Rechtfertigung meiner Absichten, Frankfurt and Leipzig 1787, pp. 13–17 and 28.*

[20] *See The Constitutions of the Society of Jesus and their Complementary Norms. A Complete English Translation of the Official Latin Texts, transl. by Carl J. Moell et al., St. Louis 1996.*

[21] *The cipher as printed in Einige Originalschriften, welche bey dem gewesenen Regierungsrath Zwack durch vorgenommene Hausvisitation zu Landshut den 11. und 12. Oktob. etc. 1786 vorgefunden worden, Munich 1787, p. 1, has x and z in their alphabetical order, and both Weishaupt and Zwackh in fact used 24 for z in their correspondence of the early years (see ibid., pp. 169, 207, 235). Later, x and z were swapped, but this made the code only minimally more difficult to crack.*

[22] *See Weishaupt to Zwackh, 13 and 19 March 1778, KI vol. 1, pp. 38 and 43–44, and Weishaupt to Hertel and Zwackh, 25 March [1778], ibid., p. 52.*

[23] *See Weishaupt to Hertel and Zwackh, 27 May [1778], KI vol. 1, p. 75.*

THE SECRET SCHOOL OF WISDOM

write a 'middle degree' that would bridge the gap between the Noviciate and something probably amounting to the earliest incarnation of an Illuminatus degree.[24] After overcoming some initial difficulties, he seems to have accomplished this task by early December.[25] This date matches a later statement by one of Weishaupt's closest associates, Franz Xaver Zwackh, that the Minerval degree was introduced only after the 'Areopagus', a new governing body of the Order, had been established in Munich, i.e. towards the end of 1778.[26]

In March 1779, Weishaupt planned to revise the Illuminati statutes once again.[27] It is difficult to say whether he ever did so, since there is a large gap in his correspondence for the rest of that year. In any case, the structure of his creation was still evolving.

II. Minervals and Illuminati

The Minerval degree was given its name referring to the role of Pallas Athene – Minerva in the Roman tradition – as a patron of knowledge and the arts. When first considering the design of a signet, Weishaupt was thinking of a flying tawny owl[28] before a starry sky, together with the motto 'Quantum est, quod nescimus' (How much it is that we do not know).[29] It would seem that the idea of using a little owl sitting on the pages of an opened book as the sign of the new degree instead was inspired by a page in one of the most famous baroque collection of emblems, *Nucleus emblematum selectissimorum* (1611).[30] Etched by the Dutch artist and publisher Crispijn de Passe, the *pictura* was accompanied by a distich by the German author Gabriel Rollenhagen that might be translated as 'He who carefully studies the words of the wise is deservedly considered a learned man'. The way the Superior, in a passage of the degree where he addresses the candidate, talks of 'nightly reflections' for which the owl is a symbol may have been meant as a pun on the etymology of 'vigilance' in the motto 'studio et vigilantia'.

---

[24] See Weishaupt to Zwackh, Hertel, and Berger, 7 November 1778, KI vol. 1, p. 96.

[25] See Weishaupt to Zwackh, 30 November and 6/7 December 1778, KI vol. 1, pp. 110 and 115–16.

[26] See Zwackh: 'Beurkundete Geschichte', op. cit., p. 84.

[27] See Weishaupt to the Munich Areopagites, 27 March [1779], KI vol. 1, p. 125.

[28] Weishaupt speaks of a 'Nachteule'. This would usually refer to the tawny owl (strix aluco, the proper German name being Waldkauz), though, in line with mythology, he may instead have had the little owl (Athene noctua, Steinkauz) in mind.

[29] Weishaupt to Hertel and Zwackh, 25 May [1778], KI vol. 1, p. 74.

[30] Gabriel Rollenhagen: Nucleus emblematum selectissimorum [...], Cologne and Arnhem [1611].

18

The results of such nocturnal contemplation were to be presented by the Minervals in their regular assemblies. It was here that they regained their voices after having had to remain largely silent throughout an initiation ritual consisting of a series of scripted questions and answers asked by the Superior and answered by the Recipient for the Candidate, as well as the Superior's address. The assemblies provided a forum for moral instruction, for speeches delivered by fellow Brethren, and for participation in essay competitions on questions set by the Superiors.[31] It was even held out in prospect that the best of these papers would be published anonymously by the Order. Earlier, a few pamphlets dealing with the state of Bavaria following the death of the Elector of Bavaria, Maximilian III Joseph, at the end of 1777, had indeed been put to print in Munich, but there is little indication that such activities were being continued.

The establishment of Minerval Assemblies or 'Churches' – the first meeting of one in Munich took place in February 1779[32] – meant that there was a need for instructions for those holding particular responsibilities in their administration, such as the 'quaestor' and the secretary, and a ceremony for

Qui vigili studio Sapientem scripta voludat,
Hic dici doctus, Cur mereatur, habet.

investing the Superior of the assembly with his office. An early version of this, which Knigge deemed 'unsatisfactory',[33] was called 'Constitutio superioris'.[34] On the basis of this, the Munich Illuminati, early in 1781, introduced a new degree of their own and called it 'Illuminatus minor'. This measure infuriated Weishaupt

---

[31] Minutes of the meetings of the Frankfurt Minerval Assembly were published by Wolfgang Fenner and Michael Knieriem: 'Die Praxis der radikalen Aufklärung. Die Protokolle der Frankfurter Illuminaten', in: Quatuor Coronati Jahrbuch 35 (1998), pp. 97–127.

[32] See René Le Forestier: Les Illuminés de Bavière et la franc-maçonnerie allemande, Paris 1914, p. 48.

[33] Knigge to Weishaupt, 16–26 [March 1781], KI vol. 1, p. 268.

[34] See KI vol. 1, pp. 210 and 275.

when he learnt about it because he had not been informed beforehand.[35] In November 1780, he had himself sent an Illuminatus degree to Munich, probably a draft of what was meant to become the Illuminatus minor: hence the confusion.[36] Knigge, too, called the new degree 'ludicrous' yet proposed not to change it but only to downgrade it.[37] In the end, a few cuts were made, the explanation of the Minerval allegories was moved to the Illuminatus minor degree, and a note was added that the Instructions were not a proper degree in themselves. The new version was introduced in May 1781,[38] at about the same time as Weishaupt's degree.

The wording of the Minerval degree was confirmed, with only one minor change, in December 1781, when the leading Bavarian Illuminati convened with Knigge in Eichstätt and Munich to discuss the future development of the system.[39] On the same occasion, the Illuminatus minor degree was accepted without any change, but Weishaupt nevertheless later decided to add further instructions to it.[40] It seems these were not generally regarded as part of the canon, however, which is why they have been relegated to the Appendix in this edition.

Knigge's Preparatory Essay, on the other hand, a text meant to be handed out to potential recruits,[41] gained universal currency. An early version of it (the beginning of which is documented here, for the first time, in the Appendix) is particularly interesting. It expressly alludes to 'the Illuminés, condemned long ago in Spain', as one of the possible precursors of the Illuminati. There is, however, no evidence that Weishaupt ever took a deeper interest in the history of the Alumbrados, also known as the Iluminados, a mystical movement mainly active in Castile and Andalusia in the 16th and 17th centuries and persecuted by the Spanish inquisition.[42] The Essay continues by stating that anyone who had 'read Crata Repoa with some attentiveness' would likely have found 'some kind of

[35] See Weishaupt to Zwackh, 2 April 1781, KI vol. 1, p. 272.

[36] Weishaupt to the Munich Areopagites, 11 November 1780, KI vol. 1, p. 191.

[37] See Knigge to Weishaupt, 24 April and 7/8 May 1781, KI vol. 1, pp. 281 and 284–85.

[38] Knigge to Weishaupt, 7/8 May 1781, KI vol. 1, pp. 284–85.

[39] See Nachtrag von weitern Originalschriften, welche die Illuminatensekte überhaupt, sonderbar aber den Stifter derselben Adam Weishaupt, gewesenen Professor zu Ingolstadt betreffen [...], Munich 1787, part 2, p. 9.

[40] Knigge to Weishaupt, 20 August 1782, KI vol. 2, p. 174.

[41] See [Knigge:] Philo's endliche Erklärung und Antwort, auf verschiedene Anforderungen und Fragen, die an ihn ergangen, seine Verbindung mit dem Orden der Illuminaten betreffend, Hanover 1788, p. 90. (Philo's Reply to Questions Concerning His Association with the Illuminati, trans. by Jeva Singh-Anand, 2012, p. 66.)

[42] See Bernardino Llorca: Die spanische Inquisition und die 'Alumbrados' (1509–1667) nach den Originalakten in Madrid und in anderen Archiven, Berlin and Bonn 1934.

trace' of the Illuminati. And indeed, the fourth degree described in the book of that strange title, written in 1770 by two leading members of the African Builders,[43] a short-lived paramasonic secret society in Berlin,[44] and containing supposed Egyptian mysteries, clearly reverberates in the Minerval degree.

The 'Battle of the Shadows' sees the adept who wishes to advance further and become a 'Chistophoris' being attacked and captured by masked men wielding torches and snakes. When his blindfold is removed, he finds himself in a resplendent hall in the presence of the king and his 'demiurge'. An orator praises him for his resolve but warns him of the tests ahead. He is then ordered to down a bitter drink and handed the shield of Minerva ('also called Isis'), the boots of Anubis ('one with Mercury'), the coat and cap of Orcus, and a sword. Once clad and armed in this way, he does as he is told and decapitates the first person he encounters in 'the cave of the enemy', which happens to be the artificial body of a beautiful woman. The king's demiurge applauds his deed and explains to him that he has brought the Gorgon's head. He is subsequently awarded various privileges and decorated with a medal depicting 'Isis or Minerva in the shape of an owl'. It is explained to him that man at birth was as blind as an owl but became a man by passing through various trials and studying philosophy. He is told that the helmet signifies the highest degree of wisdom, the Gorgon's head the suppression of passions, the shield the protection from slanderous talk, the pillar steadfastness, the water jug the thirst for knowledge, the quiver with the arrows eloquence, the spear persuasion from afar, and the 'palm and olive branch' *(sic)* peace.[45]

This interpretation foreshadowed the one given at the end of the Illuminatus minor degree for one of the two 'Minerval allegories'. In a letter to Costanzo, Baader frankly admitted that 'to tell the truth, our second degree does not contain a lot of things that are unknown to a reader of Crata Repoa'.[46] After a very limited print-run in 1770, the book had become more readily available in 1778, when a second edition was published in Berlin by Christian Ludewig Stahlbaum, himself a Freemason.

[43] *[Carl Friedrich Köppen and Johann Wilhelm Bernhard Hymmen:] Crata Repoa. Oder Einweihungen in der alten geheimen Gesellschaft der Egyptischen Priester, [Berlin] 1770. An English translation was first published in 1882 in The Kneph.*

[44] *On the history of this lodge see Karlheinz Gerlach: 'Die afrikanischen Bauherren. Die Bauherrenloge der Verschwiegenheit der Freunde freier Künste und schönen Wissenschaften 1765–1775 in Berlin', in: Quatuor Coronati Jahrbuch 33 (1996), pp. 61–90.*

[45] *See Crata Repoa, op. cit., pp. 19–23.*

[46] *Baader to Costanzo, 15 August 1780, KI vol. 1, p. 165.*

The footnotes in *Crata Repoa* lead the interested reader to an illustrated description of the chimerical Minerva in an opulent catalogue of Roman antiquities entitled *Le grand cabinet romain*, published in 1706 as a translation of the earlier Latin edition,[47] and it is obvious from the designs on one of the two car-

pets of the Minerval degree that Weishaupt followed that lead.[48] The author of those works, Michel-Ange de La Chausse, a French banker and consul in Rome, presented the engraved gem as a talisman, carved of heliotrope, in his possession. La Chausse, who died in 1724, bequeathed at least parts of his collection, which also included a large number of antique coins, to the French convent Trinité-des-Monts, overlooking the Spanish Steps. There, however, his treasures fell victim to misappropriation and neglect even before the troops of revolutionary France devastated Rome in 1798.[49] Fortunately though, an impression of the engraved gem in question was made by the German diplomat and spy Philipp (von) Stosch and later acquired by the Scottish engraver James Tassie,[50] copies of whose collection of impressions are kept in Edinburgh, London, and St. Petersburg.[51]

---

[47] *Michel Ange de La Chausse: Le grand cabinet romain ou recueil d'antiquitez romaines, qui consistent en bas reliefs, statues des dieux & des hommes, instruments sacerdotaux, lampes, urnes, seaux, brasselets, clefs, anneaux, & phioles lacrimales, que l'on trouve a Rome, Amsterdam 1706, p. 26 (no. 44); original edition: Romanum Museum, sive Thesaurus eruditæ antiquitatis [...], Rome 1690, p. 23 (no. 44). For another, similar engraved gem, made of carnelian, in the same collection see Michel Angelo Causeo dela Chausse: Le gemme antiche figurate, Rome 1700, pp. 70–71 (no. 180).*

[48] *It is conceivable that he consulted a copy of Le grand cabinet romain at the Munich Hofbibliothek, the predecessor of today's Bavarian State Library.*

[49] *See Georges Brunel: 'Michel-Ange de la Chausse', in: Les Fondations nationales dans la Rome pontificale, Rome 1981, pp. 723–47; Isabelle Balsamo: 'La vie intellectuelle à la Trinité-des-Monts au XVIIIᵉ siècle', ibid., pp. 453–78, in particular pp. 463–64; Fourier Bonnard: Histoire du Convent royal de la trinité du Mont Pincio à Rome, Rome 1933, pp. 215–16.*

[50] *See R[udolph] E[rich] Raspe: A descriptive catalogue of a general collection of ancient and modern engraved gems, cameos as well as intaglios, [...] cast [...] by James Tassie [...], vol. 1, London 1791, p. 714.*

[51] *At the (Scottish) National Portrait Gallery, the Victoria and Albert Museum, and the Hermitage.*

Even though the fate of the original engraved gem is unknown, it can be said on the basis of the existing reproductions that La Chausse's description of the piece and thus the foundation of both the interpretation in *Crata Repoa* and in the Illuminatus minor degree was actually mistaken: the chimera has the body not of an owl but that of an eagle.[52] On the other hand, La Chausse had correctly identified the branch in its talons as that of an olive tree, whereas it is confusingly called a 'palm and olive branch' in *Crata Repoa* and finally a palm branch by Weishaupt. Evidently, the complicated process of transmission led to some considerable friction losses. Such was the price to be paid for the fabrication of a secret.

III. Illuminati Freemasons

Although the foundation of what developed into the Illuminati Order had been inspired, at least to some extent, by Weishaupt's interest in Freemasonry, at first the new secret society was no Masonic body of any kind. Nevertheless, Weishaupt was already contemplating the establishment of lodges in Munich and Eichstätt by late 1778, while Zwackh favoured merging Freemasonry and the Minerval Class.[53]

Zwackh had learnt of the secrets of Freemasonry from an unlikely source, the Jesuit *abbate* Giuseppe Marotti, who was later to become the secretary of Pope Pius VI.[54] Zwackh joined the Munich lodge 'St. Théodore au bon conseil', whereas Weishaupt had already been accepted, on 2 February 1777, by the rival and rather more aristocratic lodge 'Zur Behutsamkeit', which adhered to the Strict Observance system. Rarely attending its gatherings, he never got further than the second degree however, whereas Zwackh swiftly succeeded in converting his lodge into an outpost of the Illuminati. It has already been pointed out that the lodge's Worshipful Master, Baader, was even involved in revising the fundamental statutes of the Illuminati Order.

'St. Théodore au bon conseil (St. Theodor zum guten Rath)', founded in 1774, had been furnished with a constitution by the Berlin lodge 'Royal(e)

[52] See *Odyssey* book 3, v. 371–72, and Erika Zwierlein-Diehl: *Siegel und Abdruck. Antike Gemmen in Bonn. 130 ausgewählte Stücke*, Bonn [2002], pp. 27–28.
[53] See *Weishaupt to Zwackh, 6 December 1778, KI vol. 1, p. 113, and Zwackh to Weishaupt, 6/7 December 1778*, ibid., p. 116.
[54] See *KI vol. 1, p. 120.*

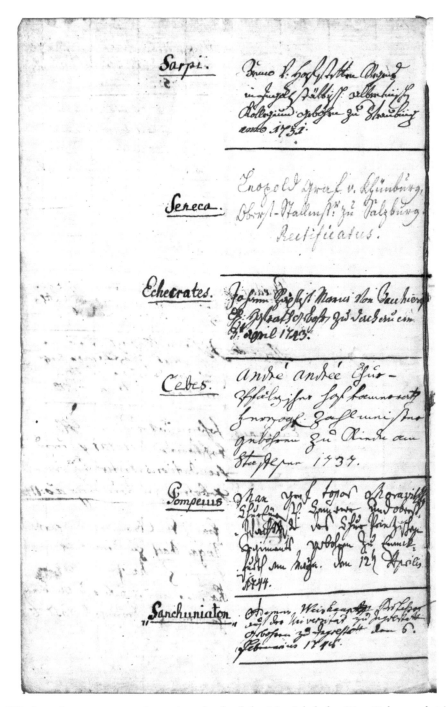

Weishaupt's signature on the register book of the Munich lodge 'Zur Behutsamkeit'.
Geheimes Staatsarchiv Preußischer Kulturbesitz, Berlin.

Yor(c)k de l'amitié' on 29 April 1779.[55] Relations with the francophone Prussians proved to be tenuous, however. The Munich lodge wished to be granted the right to establish its own filial lodges in the south of Germany. After lengthy negotiations, it was finally given the status of a Provincial Lodge in October 1781, but further conflicts and concerns about the financial consequences of the contract led the Bavarians to revoke it only a few months later, in June 1782.[56] At around that time, Weishaupt got hold of a (presumably higher) Royal York degree, which he found unspeakably bad.[57] But the decision to draft a ritual book of their own and to charter lodges under their own authority had by then long been taken anyway.

It proved to be a momentous event for the Illuminati Order that Baron Adolph von Knigge[58] could be won for its cause, in July 1780, by the Italian Marchese Costanzo di Costanzo. Not only did Knigge have unrivalled talents of recruitment and organisation, he was also a well-connected and ambitious Freemason. Following the example of his father, he had joined the Kassel lodge 'Zum gekrönten Löwen' (Crowned Lion) in February 1773, at the age of twenty. Having witnessed its 1778 convention in Wolfenbüttel, he became a member of the Strict Observance, where he was given the name 'Eques a Cygno'. After moving to Frankfurt, he frequented the two lodges operating there, 'Zu den drei Disteln' (Three Thistles) and 'Zur Einigkeit' (Unity).

Knigge was disenchanted with the Strict Observance with its spurious pretensions of unknown superiors and even sceptical as to whether the basic degrees of Freemasonry were worthy of reform at all,[59] but he nevertheless lobbied for a full transformation of the Illuminati Order into a Masonic system.[60] With Weishaupt's consent, he added some unmistakably Masonic elements to the Minerval degree, such as the layout of the assembly room, the use of a tracing board, and the practice of knocking with the gavel to gain the members' attention. In April 1781, he asked for specific instructions concerning the development of a fully-

---

[55] See Vollständige Geschichte der Verfolgung der Illuminaten in Bayern, vol. 1, [Nuremberg] 1786, p. 74 (where the year is misprinted as '1777'), and August Flohr: Geschichte der Grossen Loge von Preussen, genannt Royal York zur Freundschaft im Orient von Berlin, Berlin 1898, p. 91.

[56] See Bernhard Beyer: Freimaurerei in München und Altbaiern. Ein Beitrag zur Kulturgeschichte des 18. Jahrhunderts, Hamburg 1973, p. 122.

[57] See Weishaupt to Zwackh, 14 June 1782, KI vol. 2, p. 134.

[58] Among the many books on Knigge, Karl-Heinz Göttert: Knigge oder Von den Illusionen des anständigen Lebens, Munich 1995, may be singled out as elegantly written and factually accurate.

[59] See Knigge to Weishaupt, 11 [January 1781], KI vol. 1, p. 209.

[60] See Knigge to Weishaupt, [13 January 1781], KI vol. 1, p. 213.

fledged Masonic system. The degrees used by the Frankfurt lodge, he said, were too garbled to be of much help, but he had other sources at his disposal. He also recommended not to worry about supposedly authentic constitutions.[61] At the time, the Strict Observance was the dominant Masonic system in much of Germany, its sphere of influence even extending into Switzerland, France, northern Italy, and Hungary. However, there were grave doubts concerning the central tenet of its high degrees,[62] namely the supposed historical link between Freemasonry and the Knights Templar. The much-anticipated forthcoming convention of the Strict Observance was expected to deal with this and other crucial questions, and Knigge, who was pursuing the plan of a merger of this expansive yet ailing system with the Illuminati, initially wanted to wait for the results of the congress before working on an entirely new body of Masonic degrees.[63] The convention was due to be held in October 1781, in Frankfurt. When the news reached him that the date was postponed, Knigge immediately set out to write his own version of the three basic Masonic degrees. He also suggested that Weishaupt should finish both the Illuminatus major and dirigens degrees which he could then cloak in the manner of 'Scottish' degrees.[64] Some three months later, in late August 1781, Knigge had finished work on the Masonic degrees and an accompanying book of constitutions.[65]

The result was deliberately eclectic, and since Knigge did not divulge any of his sources, a meticulous comparison of all the degrees he may have had at his disposal, in printed or manuscript form, would be necessary to fully appreciate it. Suffice it to say that some elements are typically German, such as the three lamps and rapier lying on the altar, some are taken from the Strict Observance rituals, such as the Master of Ceremonies carrying a sword rather than a baton, some are of English origin, such as the office of the Stewards, and some are French, such as the cardinal directions to be found abbreviated on the two *tapis*: O[rient] – M[idi] – O[ccident] – S[eptentrion].

In the Apprentice oath one sees a distinct deviation from regular Masonic ritual. The penalties for violating the oath are combined with the penalties of the

---

[61] *Knigge to Weishaupt, 7–10 April [1781], KI vol. 1, pp. 275–79.*

[62] *For an English translation see Collectanea: Official Transactions of the Grand College of Rites of the United States of America vol. 21, part 1: The Rite of Strict Observance and Two High Degree Rituals of the Eighteenth Century, trans. by Alain Bernheim and Arturo de Hoyos, Fulton, Miss., 2010, pp. 1–106.*

[63] *See Knigge to Weishaupt, 10/11 May [1781], KI vol. 1, p. 292.*

[64] *See Knigge to Weishaupt, 13–19 and 24–27 [May 1781], KI vol. 1, pp. 302 and 314–16.*

[65] *See Knigge to Weishaupt, 27 August 1781, KI vol. 1, p. 358.*

original Fellow Craft and Master Mason obligations. In addition to the symbolic act in which the candidate's throat is cut, the body is also to be pierced, his vitals torn out and burnt to ashes, scattered to the four winds and then cast upon the rough sands of the sea. The reason for combining these penalties lies in the fact that the oaths are later waived in both the Fellow Craft and Master Mason degrees.

The ceremony for a Table Lodge described as part of the Apprentice degree is standard contemporary practice with one notable exception. Typically, the first toast is to the Sovereign, whereas here it is to the Superiors, namely to the Provincial Grandmaster, if present. The following three toasts are to the Craft and Order. The head of state is not honoured until the fifth toast.

Knigge also rearranged the catechism questions for the three degrees, thus making them peculiar to the Illuminati system. Noteworthy is an exchange contained in the Fellow Craft degree. When the Brother is asked if he can write, he responds: 'Yes, the Master has taught me'. He is then asked what he writes with, and he responds: 'With the square.' This is emblematical of the pigpen cipher subsequently given to the Brother as it consists of angular signs. This cipher was the standard cipher used in French ritual of the period. There is no indication, however, that it was ever used by an Illuminati Freemason when dealing with business of the Order.

Breaking its bonds with the 'Royal York' lodge in Berlin, the Munich lodge 'St. Théodore au bon conseil' began adopting Knigge's ritual in the summer of 1782.[66] So did another lodge taken over by the Illuminati, 'Caroline zu den drei Pfauen' (Three Peacocks) in Neuwied on the Rhine, which Knigge in person provided with a new constitution.[67] In December 1782, the Wetzlar lodge 'Joseph zu den drei Helmen' (Three Helmets) followed, and in early 1783, the ritual was translated into French by a member in Munich.[68]

These developments came about even though Weishaupt himself was dissatisfied with Knigge's creation. He complained to Zwackh that the three Masonic degrees had 'almost no connection with the preceding and following degrees' of the Illuminati system proper. There was no real progression; instead, the Masonic degrees, while nominally higher, had less content and were less demanding

---

[66] See Beyer: *Freimaurerei in München und Altbaiern, op. cit., p. 123.*

[67] See *KI vol. 2, p. 148.*

[68] See the reports on their respective provinces by Count Stolberg-Roßla for December 1782 and Marchese Costanzo for January 1783, in: Staatsarchiv Hamburg 614-1/72 Gr. Loge no. 1350.

than the ones of the Minerval Class. Furthermore, the unity of design was clearly lost.[69] As a possible solution to the problem, he thought of merging the Illuminati degrees with their Masonic counterparts one by one, for instance the Minerval with the Entered Apprentice. This would of course have amounted to a complete revision of all degrees. Weishaupt therefore decided it would be better to leave them unchanged for the time being. Instead, he resorted to demonstrating his dismissive attitude towards the Masonic degrees by recommending fast-track promotions: all three Masonic degrees in three days.[70]

Knigge responded to Weishaupt's criticism by pointing out that there was little room for manoeuvre. Those men who had already belonged to other lodges, which was certainly true for most of his own recruits, were fond of the 'old and venerable customs' they were used to practising there. He pointed out that many of the prospective members of the Illuminati lodges were not destined to become members of the Order itself anyway. The lodges themselves were merely an outward form in which to hide from the world.[71]

As a matter of fact, the Munich lodge operated quite openly. In July 1782, the wealthy industrialist Franz Karl Arnhardt spent 6000 guilders on a centrally-located house sizeable enough to hold its gatherings. According to Zwackh, this put an end to adverse gossip, and the citizens of Munich began treating the Freemasons in their midst with great respect.[72] They remained unaware, however, that the same house was being used by a society still maintaining a secret existence.

IV. Scottish Brethren

It was customary, one might even say strictly required for any high degree system of the eighteenth century to have one or more 'Scottish' degrees. Whether or not these degrees originated in France, as is often believed and sometimes questioned,[73] they were definitely practised in Berlin from 1742[74] and soon spread to

[69] Weishaupt to Zwackh, 8 March 1782, KI vol. 2, p. 74.

[70] Weishaupt to Zwackh and the Munich Areopagites, 25 [June] 1782, KI vol. 2, p. 144.

[71] Knigge to Weishaupt, 20 March [1782], KI vol. 2, p. 97.

[72] See KI vol. 2, p. 83.

[73] See the sceptical remarks by Alain Bernheim, 'Did Early "High" or Écossais Degrees Originate in France?', in: Heredom 5 (1996), pp. 87–113.

[74] See Pierre Mollier: 'News from the "Russian Archives". About the Early History of the High Degrees: The Scottish Order in Berlin from 1742 to 1752', in: The Chain of Union n° 2 (special issue), 2003, pp. 59–64.

other parts of Germany as well. It was only natural, therefore, that the Illuminati Order, having been transformed into a Masonic system, should also have its Scottish degrees. Knigge suggested as much as early as May 1781, when he envisioned the Illuminatus major and dirigens degrees as future 'Scottish' degrees (he was then thinking of a Master and a Knight degree, respectively).[75]

A little earlier, probably judging from an early draft, Knigge had called the Illuminatus major 'a masterpiece'.[76] In June 1781, he urged completion of the 'marvellous' degree.[77] This proved to be time-consuming task: a few weeks later, he was already working on a revised and clean copy, making a number of additions in the process, but in September, he was still busy giving the degree a Masonic form.[78]

The focus of the degree lies on the 'study of man', a recurrent theme throughout the Illuminati system. Using a handheld mirror as a simple prop, the candidate is taught that he must not content himself with following the Delphic maxim of 'knowing thyself'. It is also the knowledge of others that he has to aspire to, benefiting from his heightened self-awareness and employing an elaborate catalogue of questions appended to the degree.

There is not much evidence as to how the provisions of the degree were put into practice. Count Johann Ludwig von Cobenzl tried to do so in Eichstätt and reported that 'everything went perfectly well'.[79] It is fairly obvious, however, that the task of assessing each and every candidate for promotion according to the immensely intricate catalogue of questions could easily have led to an overburdening of the superiors. Perhaps in response to this danger, Knigge devised a simple scheme of grading the members' discipline and diligence. It was circulated, in January 1783, among the Illuminati tasked with the supervision of Minervals.[80]

Weishaupt himself hoped that the first 'Scottish' degree would help to convince leading members of the Munich lodge that the Illuminati did in fact possess their

---

[75] See Knigge to Weishaupt, 13–19 [May 1781], KI vol. 1, p. 302.

[76] Knigge to Weishaupt, 24 April [1781], KI vol. 1, p. 282.

[77] Knigge to Weishaupt, 15–22 June [1781], KI vol. 1, p. 327.

[78] See Knigge to Weishaupt, 11 July, 20 July, 24 July, 2/3 September 1781, KI vol. 1, pp. 342, 351, 353, and 368.

[79] Cobenzl to Weishaupt, 4 October [1781], KI vol. 1, p. 401.

[80] See KI vol. 2, p. 388–91, and Monika Neugebauer-Wölk: 'Praktische Anthropologie für ein utopisches Ziel: Menschenbeobachtung und Menschenbildung im Geheimbund der Illuminaten', in: Zwischen Empirisierung und Konstruktionsleistung. Anthropologie im 18. Jahrhundert, ed. by Jörn Garber and Heinz Thoma, Tübingen 2004, pp. 323–38.

own brand of Masonry, which would then induce them to fully support the cause of the Order.[81] Which in fact they did only a few months later, when they chose to break free from the Mother Lodge in Berlin, though their decision to do so was probably largely based on other considerations.

In March 1783, Count Johann Martin von Stolberg-Roßla, writing from Neuwied, suggested a makeover of the catalogue of questions, which he regarded as excessively long and needlessly repetitive.[82] The surviving manuscripts show that some revisions were indeed made, though it is impossible to ascertain when and by whom. At any rate, they were slight, and the degree stayed largely unchanged.

Plans to add an Illuminatus dirigens degree to the system date back to early 1781.[83] By September of that year, Knigge was eagerly waiting for Weishaupt to complete his draft.[84] Cobenzl, too, pressed him to get a final text ready before Knigge's upcoming visit to Bavaria,[85] yet to no avail. During his negotiations with the Areopagites, which took place in early December, it was only Knigge who presented a draft of the degree, which was duly approved. In Weishaupt's opinion, however, the issue was not yet fully resolved. He kept hinting at a version of his own, thus causing some confusion,[86] but Knigge narrowly managed to avert an open conflict by suggesting that Weishaupt's 'marvellous thoughts' would find a more fitting place at the next level, in a future Presbyter degree.[87]

Knigge's Illuminatus dirigens has a distinctly Christian character throughout. The Table Lodge held by the Scottish Knights, the *agape*, or love feast, in particular amounts to a re-enactment of the last supper. It was meant to resemble the celebration of such ceremonies among the earliest Christians. In contributing this part of the ritual, Knigge followed the example of a 'Scottish' degree in his possession. He guaranteed Weishaupt, who was sceptical towards the idea, that the effect would be most exhilarating.[88]

Knigge had promised to deliver a 'sensible' elucidation of the so-called Mason-

---

[81] See Weishaupt to Baader, [c. 18 February 1782], KI vol. 2, p. 53.

[82] See Stolberg-Roßla to Weishaupt, 29 March 1783, KI vol. 2, p. 543.

[83] See Knigge to Weishaupt, 11 [January 1781], KI vol. 1, p. 209.

[84] Knigge to Weishaupt, 19/20 [September 1781], KI vol. 1, p. 382.

[85] See Cobenzl to Weishaupt, [c. mid-October 1781], KI vol. 1, p. 407.

[86] See Cobenzl to Weishaupt, [c. end of December 1781] KI vol. 1, p. 440.

[87] Knigge to Weishaupt, 8 [February 1782], KI vol. 2, p. 42.

[88] See Knigge to Weishaupt, 1–5 [February 1781], KI vol. 1, p. 232.

ic hieroglyphs.[89] He believed that interpreting them in the light of Christianity would also be a means of coming to a more rational understanding of the 'Christian customs and mysteries' and, at the same time, a contribution to the weakening of popular superstitions.[90] With this aim in mind, he wrote an explanation of the Masonic symbols that culminates in the revelation of the secret that Hiram is actually Jesus, that Freemasonry is a vessel for communicating his secret teachings, and that taking heed of his great yet unaccomplished revolution is the true task of every Mason. Knigge seems to have been less than proud of his product. In a letter to Weishaupt he called it, in May 1782, his 'galimathias on FreeM[a-sonr]y',[91] but this was not as self-deprecating as it might seem. After all, Knigge had only elaborated on ideas first laid down by Weishaupt himself.[92]

Others were no less critical when confronted with the Dirigens degree as a whole.[93] Turning himself immediately to the Order's General by writing a message labelled 'Primo', Johann Georg Heinrich Feder confessed that reading the new degree had 'greatly bewildered' him, causing him to reject his promotion and to remain an Illuminatus major instead.[94] He specifically criticised the religious elements of the text, which in his view contravened 'the pure philosophical spirit' of the Order that he, as a professor of philosophy, had come to cherish.[95] Johann Benjamin Koppe, another member of the Göttingen assembly and a theologian himself, concurred and added that Feder had also found 'traces of hard despotism' in the degree.[96]

Weishaupt, who was anxious not to alienate the Göttingen members for whom he had the greatest respect, immediately reacted by ordering Zwackh to halt further dissemination of the degree. He ordered new copies to be made, in which the obligation, the love feast, and what he called Knigge's 'gibberish, half-theosophical address' with its explanation of the Masonic hieroglyphs should be omitted.[97] His own alternative text, which had been shelved for some months,

---

[89] *Knigge to Weishaupt, 7–10 April [1781], KI vol. 1, p. 276.*

[90] *Knigge to Weishaupt, 10/11 May [1781], KI vol. 1, p. 291.*

[91] *Knigge to Weishaupt, 15 [May 1782], KI vol. 2, p. 117.*

[92] *See [Weishaupt:] 'Erklärung der maurerischen Hierogliphen', in: Nachtrag von weitern Originalschriften, part 2, pp. 121–35.*

[93] *See Mieg to Weishaupt, 29 March 1783, KI vol. 2, p. 541.*

[94] *Feder, Primo, 30 August 1782, KI vol. 2, p. 184.*

[95] *Ibid., p. 185.*

[96] *Koppe, Quibus licet, 30 August 1782, KI vol. 2, p. 186.*

[97] *See Weishaupt to Zwackh, [c. mid-September 1782], KI vol. 2, p. 194.*

would take its place after all. Or so he thought, but Knigge was having none of it. Some 'great controversies and divisions', in Weishaupt's own words, ensued.[98] In the end, Weishaupt wrote a new lecture as a replacement, which he completed in the spring of 1783.[99] This solved the problem with regard to the degree, but it did nothing to mend his relations with Knigge, which by then had ended in bitter acrimony.

V. Mysteries

As early as March of 1778, Weishaupt announced that he wished to save all his 'imagination, philosophy, and eloquence' for future 'mysteries' with which to crown his degree system. He intended to make them attractive in their 'solemnity' and conceal the fact that they would not be honoured by tradition but newly-written texts.[100] When Knigge became involved in the creative process, he suggested fully revealing the Order's doctrines only 'in a priest-magi-sages degree or whatever one might call it'.[101] His deliberations with Weishaupt and the Bavarian Areopagites led to the resolution that the future 'higher mysteries' of the Order would be comprised of three degrees yet to be written. The members promoted to them would be called Priests, Magi, and Regents, respectively.[102]

Having returned home from Bavaria in January 1782, Knigge began working on the first of these degrees and had an early draft ready by May.[103] In the meantime, Weishaupt had formulated some questions to be put to the candidates, which Knigge thought to be rather too critical of conventional Christianity.[104] His work on the degree was greatly hampered by the fact that his drafts, once sent to the Areopagites for comment, were neither copied nor returned to him.[105] Knigge had similar reasons for complaint, too.[106]

For the key element of the Presbyter degree, the lengthy 'Lesson in the First Chamber', Knigge drew upon the text that Weishaupt had originally written

---

[98] Weishaupt: Nachtrag zur Rechtfertigung, op. cit., p. 73.

[99] See Mieg to Weishaupt, [19 April 1783], KI vol. 2, p. 583.

[100] Weishaupt to Zwackh, 19 March 1778, KI vol. 1, p. 44.

[101] Knigge to Weishaupt, 6–10 [February 1781], KI vol. 1, p. 236.

[102] See Nachtrag von weitern Originalschriften, op. cit., part 2, p. 14–15.

[103] See Knigge to Weishaupt, 2 May 1782, KI vol. 2, p. 108.

[104] See Knigge to Weishaupt, 15 [May 1782], KI vol. 2, p. 116.

[105] See Weishaupt to Zwackh, 16 February 1782, KI vol. 2, p. 47.

[106] See Knigge to Weishaupt, 21–30 January, 8 [February], and [15/]16 [March 1782], pp. 29, 43, and 85.

with the Illuminatus dirigens in mind. As an essay in the philosophy of history, the 'Lesson' is an unmistakable product of late Enlightenment thinking and follows the cues given in earlier seminal contributions to the field such as Rousseau's *Discourse on the Origin of Human Inequality.*[107] It is stated that mankind was once free but has become the victim of subjugation as a result of its own weaknesses. The power and control exerted by a few men over the multitude are derived from the fact that men are invariably in need of one another. However, the dialectics of progress will eventually ensure that mankind finds the path to restoring its natural state of liberty. This basic structure of the argument has justly been called a 'plain three-phases doctrine'.[108]

It is expounded to the future Priest of the Order that the teachings of Jesus Christ have been misunderstood and distorted, and that their true purpose was to return humanity to its original dignity and freedom by tempering men's passions and curbing their needs. These intentions were supposedly preserved in a *disciplina arcani,* esoteric doctrines kept alive over the course of centuries by 'secret schools of wisdom' and inherited by Freemasonry. As evidence for these claims, a great many quotations from the Gospels are presented, as well as several examples taken from patristic texts that are meant to illustrate the similarity and continuity of the forms and ceremonies of baptism in the early Church with initiation into Freemasonry.[109]

This was essentially bogus theology. By contrast, there is no question that the idea of organising a secret academy of sciences was put forward in all earnestness. The *Instructio in scientificis* incorporated into the Presbyter degree, Weishaupt's answer to the *Ratio studiorum* of the Jesuits, was originally written, in May 1781, as an instruction for the Provincial Superiors.[110] Now it was envisioned that the Priests would be the overseers of the Order's scientific endeavours. In the context of a narrative repeatedly stressing the historical importance of 'secret schools of wisdom', the idea of establishing an academy hidden from the prying eyes of the public may have been appealing enough, and no member is known to have questioned the uses of scientific knowledge exclusive to the Illuminati Order. Never-

---

[107] *See Weishaupt to Zwackh, 20 March 1779, KI vol. 1, p. 125.*

[108] *Reinhart Koselleck: 'Adam Weishaupt und die Anfänge der bürgerlichen Geschichtsphilosophie', in: Tijdschrift voor de studie van de verlichting 4 (1976), pp. 317–27.*

[109] *See Weishaupt's earlier draft 'Erklärung der maurerischen Hieroglyphen', in: Nachtrag von weitern Originalschriften, op. cit., part 2, pp. 121–35.*

[110] *See Weishaupt to Zwackh, 26 May 1781, and Knigge to Weishaupt, 24–27 [May 1781], KI vol. 1, pp. 310 and 315.*

theless, there is no indication that the founding of such a secret academy, neatly divided into classes just like its counterparts in the exoteric world, was ever actually attempted.

The final element of the Presbyter degree is a ceremony for the initiation of a Deacon in the higher class of Priests. The entire proceedings are in Latin and can be identified as a variation of an old Roman Catholic ceremony called the *scrutinium serotinum*, or late (i.e., final) scrutiny of a bishop following his election yet preceding his consecration.[111] This section of the degree was furnished by Knigge at a time when his well-known fondness for elaborate ritual, Latin liturgy, and splendid costumes contributed to the emergence of rumours of his conversion to Catholicism, a charge he strenuously denied.[112]

When the completed degree was handed out to a few meritorious and trustworthy members, in October 1782, it was once again Feder who urged restraint.[113] Years earlier, Feder had given Weishaupt the gnomic advice 'moderata durant'.[114] Eventually, Weishaupt came to the conclusion that he had indeed been rather too stark in his first sketch of the address. He decided to make some changes to it with the intention of leaving out those passages that some had found offensive, mending any corruptions of the text that Knigge might have caused, and incorporating new insights.[115] When he was done with this, he was convinced that the result was more correct, more complete, and much more substantial than his first version. Indeed he became so carried away by his own train of thought that he half-jokingly confessed to Zwackh that he was 'almost' beginning to believe in this interpretation of Christianity himself.[116] Knigge, for his part, had merely regarded it as a *pia fraus* to be unveiled as such at a later stage in the higher mysteries.[117]

Another example of such tactical deception can be found in the next higher degree, the Regent. Here, the Provincial Superior delivers a short lecture addressing the future Regent in which he makes it clear to the candidate that he is now

---

[111] See *Josephus Catalanus: Pontificale romanum in tres partes distributum Clementis VIII. ac Urbani VIII. auctoritate recognitum, vol. 3, Rome 1740*, pp. 278–96.

[112] See his memorandum on the matter, *KI vol. 2*, pp. 197–200.

[113] See Feder, Primo, 30 October 1782, *KI vol. 2*, p. 226.

[114] Quoted by Martin Mulsow: "'Steige also, wenn du kannst, höher und höher zu uns herauf". Adam Weishaupt als Philosoph', in: *Die Weimarer Klassik und ihre Geheimbünde*, ed. by Walter Müller-Seidel and Wolfgang Riedel, Würzburg 2002, p. 34.

[115] See Weishaupt to Zwackh, 28 January 1783, *KI vol. 2*, p. 396.

[116] See Weishaupt to Zwackh, [c. early February 1783], *KI vol. 2*, p. 407.

[117] Knigge to Zwackh, 20 January [1783], *KI vol. 2*, p. 365.

free from his obligations to the Order, since he has become fully capable of governing himself. Consequently, all the existing files on the candidate, including his signed oath of allegiance, are returned to him. The candidate is still not given the full truth, however, and the obfuscation concerning the Order's beginnings continues. He is told once again that the Order is ancient and has adopted many forms over time, of which Freemasonry is one, to protect the hidden treasures of wisdom and virtue. He is made to believe, if indeed he is gullible enough, that the men who founded the Order have long resigned and that it is now in the hands of others, with all the original records having been burnt.

The chief purpose of the Regent degree was a rather technical one, namely to provide those in leading positions within the Order with instructions on how to perform their duties. Already in May 1781, Knigge contemplated that a future Regent degree should contain 'some sort of political system, the ceremonies, and the various instructions for Provincial Superiors, etc.'[118] Early drafts of the latter had in fact already been in his hands since the beginning of that year,[119] probably similar in kind to the lengthy fragment that came to be printed in the second volume of *Originalschriften* in 1787.[120] When Weishaupt later made some changes to the degree, he sought to eliminate everything that did not immediately serve its main purpose.[121] It was probably on this occasion that an instruction for the National Superiors was added, complete with a striking musical cipher (see the Appendix).[122] This cipher, too, was never put to use.

It had been decided during Knigge's stay in Bavaria that the development of the highest degrees of the Illuminati system should be a collective effort. As it turned out, the attempt to give the Areopagites a say in the matter was a bad mistake. The Eichstätt Illuminati, Baron Friedrich Joseph Roth von Schreckenstein in particular, at first did not respond to repeated requests to return the documents they had in hand. Worse still, when they finally were returned, after no less than seven months had passed,[123] it became apparent that the manuscripts

<hr/>

[118] *Knigge to Weishaupt, 24–27 [May 1781], KI vol. 1, p. 314.*

[119] *See Knigge to Weishaupt, 11 [January 1781], KI vol. 1, p. 208, and Knigge to Weishaupt, 1–5 [February 1781], ibid., p. 228.*

[120] *See Nachtrag von weitern Originalschriften, op. cit., part 2, pp. 17–43.*

[121] *See Weishaupt to Bode, 24 July 1783, KI vol. 3 (to be published).*

[122] *For a concise history of this method of cryptography see Eric Sams: 'Musical Cryptography', in: Cryptologia 3 (1979), pp. 193–201.*

[123] *See Weishaupt to Zwackh, 24 January 1783, KI vol. 2, p. 372.*

had been the subject of some heavy editing.[124] Knigge regarded this as sheer vandalism. He was particularly appalled by the prospect that copies of the Presbyter and Regent degrees that he himself had authenticated might be withdrawn from circulation.[125] He felt betrayed by the very man whose disorganised little fraternity would never have flourished without him. Livid with rage, he wrote a lengthy letter to Weishaupt in which he even threatened to expose the origins of the Order and its supposedly dangerous principles.[126] While it did not come to this, Knigge's relations with Weishaupt were beyond repair. After some two years of a most intensive collaboration, all communication ceased between them.

Weishaupt had come to rely on Knigge to provide the degrees, for which he himself delivered the essential ingredients, with the necessary ritualistic structure to support them. Having alienated and subsequently lost Knigge, Weishaupt was now left to his own devices, which proved to be lacking. There is no indication that he even tried to complete the 'greater mysteries', the two highest degrees of the system, on his own. He had shied away from such tasks before and may have been further discouraged by calls from within the rank and file of the Order to do away with all ceremonial trappings. As a result, only the lectures for the two final degrees were ever written. It has even been speculated that Knigge never got to see them, but this can only partly be true, since he had been given an early version of the Docetists degree to read as early as January 1781.[127]

This degree is in fact a philosophical lecture reflecting Weishaupt's brand of sensualist idealism. It was originally meant to be called 'Magi', but the cryptic title Docetists, as it stands, refers to the adherents of an early Christian current which maintained the belief that Jesus did not really have a physical form and therefore did not actually die on the cross. Surprisingly, this particular gnostic heresy is not even mentioned in the body of the text itself. It would seem that it was used symbolically in the heading to indicate that all perception, as mediated by the senses, is inevitably flawed and restricted.

In dramatic fashion, Weishaupt begins by doubting whether the words even exist to express his daring ideas and whether there is any audience capable of grasping them. But of course he was not the first thinker to claim that there are

---

[124] See Weishaupt to Zwackh, [c. 21 February 1783], KI vol. 2, p. 475.

[125] See Knigge to Weishaupt, 18–22 December 1782, KI vol. 2, p. 289.

[126] See Knigge to Weishaupt, 25 February–31 March 1783, KI vol. 2, p. 549.

[127] See Knigge to Weishaupt, 11 [January 1781], KI vol. 1, p. 202; see also Stolberg-Roßla to Weishaupt, 21 May 1783, KI vol. 2, p. 625.

no innate ideas and that all human knowledge is derived from perception. Where Weishaupt's text does indeed veer off the high road of the empiricist and sensualist tradition, two rather incongruous influences can be discerned: the death of his beloved first wife Afra in February 1780, after a prolonged illness, and a philosophical treatise by Charles Bonnet, the Genevan scientist famed for his discovery of parthenogenesis.[128] Like all other phenomena, Weishaupt interprets death as a matter of perception. While it puts an end to human perception in this physical form, it also means a transition to modes of perception in a different form. From this it follows that the departed loved ones are therefore not irrecoverably lost to those left behind but remain part of the universe, and everyone will eventually be reunited on a higher plane of existence. Death itself is to be understood as an initiation into a new life in some other shape or form forever incomprehensible to man. By developing these ideas, Weishaupt was consoling himself for the loss he and his surviving little daughter had experienced.[129] He was clearly following the lead of Bonnet who, in his *Palingénésie philosophique,* published in 1769 and thereafter almost immediately translated into German, had also argued that death leads to a higher state in which the soul is capable of sensual perception unattainable by man in his worldly existence.

On the basis of his earlier drafts, Weishaupt was working on the essay in February and March 1783 and, while doing so, sent it off in instalments to Johann Friedrich Mieg. The Heidelberg churchman was quite delighted by it overall but insisted that the number of five human senses should indeed be regarded as finite. Failing to do so, and even hinting at the possibility of acquiring further senses, would open the gates to irresponsible enthusiasm. Mieg also doubted Weishaupt's claim that his system really amounted to a refutation of materialism.[130] These were quite sensible remarks; however, judging from the only two existing manuscripts, Weishaupt chose to ignore Mieg's criticism and left the incriminated passages unchanged.

The final and highest degree of the Illuminati system had the working title 'Rex', but the only two manuscripts extant (one being a mere copy of the other) carry the headline 'Philosophi. Sages' instead. Indeed it might be called the

---

[128] *See Martin Mulsow: 'Vernünftige Metempsychosis. Über Monadenlehre, Esoterik und geheime Aufklärungsgesellschaften im 18. Jahrhundert', in: Aufklärung und Esoterik, ed. by Monika Neugebauer-Wölk and Holger Zaunstöck, Hamburg 1999, pp. 211–73.*

[129] *See Mieg to Weishaupt, 29 March 1783, KI vol. 2, p. 539.*

[130] *See Mieg to Weishaupt, 27 February and 12 March 1783, KI vol. 2, pp. 481–83 and 506–07.*

degree of the philosopher king. There is not much that constitutes a link to the preceding lecture, except for the invitation to the candidate to find a vantage-point from which to see the world from a new perspective.[131] Once again, it is the perspective of the philosopher of history who is able to predict future events by studying the past and comparing it to the present.

Weishaupt presents both a dialectical and a perfectibilist interpretation of his-tory, which is shown to be a history of changes in wealth and poverty, in power and weakness, reflected in the blossoming and wilting both on the individual level and on the level of entire nations. He claims that history shows that there is a correlation between the population of a nation and its level of culture, morals, and form of government. Despite adverse factors such as celibacy, wars, and childhood illnesses, mankind has continually increased in numbers, thus illus-trating the progressive realisation of nature's design. Man has nothing to fear, as nature is keeping watch. Having children and increasing the population is there-fore a virtue and a blessing to mankind as it progresses towards perfection, in a patriarchially organised society. Humanity in this light is in fact nature's tool to achieve these ends.

One of the most striking details in this panorama is Weishaupt's argument that the memory of the great flood left a collective scar on mankind in the form of superstitions which restrained its growth at first. This was borrowed from Nicolas-Antoine Boulanger, the author of the entry on the 'Déluge' in Diderot's *Encyclopédie*. Weishaupt had only recently discovered his works. In late 1782, he made them recommended reading for the Presbyters.[132] In France, several of Boulanger's books had been confiscated and publicly burnt at the stake, with only *L'Antiquité dévoilé* being tacitly tolerated.[133] In Germany, by contrast, a translation of this book made by Johann Carl Dähnert, a well-respected Greifs-wald professor of philosophy and Freemason, was freely available,[134] but even Johann Gottfried Herder, a man not generally averse to daring hypotheses, had dismissed it as partly whimsical, partly impudent nonsense.[135]

---

[131] See Mulsow: 'Vernünftige Metempsychosis', op. cit., p. 253.

[132] See Falcke to Stolberg-Roßla, 3 January 1783, KI vol. 2, p. 343, and Feder, Quibus licet, 1 February [1783], ibid., p. 411.

[133] See Paul Sadrin: Nicolas-Antoine Boulanger (1722–1759) ou avant nous le déluge, Oxford 1986, p. 135.

[134] Nicol[as] Ant[oine] Boulanger: Das durch seine Gebräuche Aufgedeckte Alterthum. Oder Critische Untersuchung der vornehmsten Meynungen, Ceremonien und Einrichtungen der verschiedenen Völker des Erdbodens in Religions- und bürgerlichen Sachen, tr. Johann Carl Dähnert, Greifswald 1767.

[135] See his fragment 'Zur Geschichte der Wissenschaften aus Boulanger', in: Herders Sämmtliche Werke, ed. by Bernhard Suphan, vol. 32, Berlin 1899, pp. 153–56.

The division of the higher Illuminati degrees into lesser and greater mysteries followed the example of the Eleusinian mysteries as described by Feder's colleague at Göttingen university, the philosopher and polymath Christoph Meiners, in an essay that Weishaupt never tired of recommending.[136] This meant that only the two very highest degrees of the system would contain the truly esoteric wisdom of the Illuminati. Mieg in Heidelberg and Count Stolberg-Roßla in Neuwied were given the *Philosophi* address to read in early April 1783, and their response was enthusiastic.[137] Over time, only a few other high-ranking Illuminati were let into the secret. Both the fact that there was no ceremony to go along with it and the mounting problems the Order was facing ensured that this degree and the one preceding it truly remained the exclusive knowledge they had always been designed to be.

However, when the Illuminati came under attack in their homeland Bavaria, Weishaupt briefly contemplated publishing the two highest degrees, i.e. the two lectures he had written for them, as a means of vindicating his creation and refuting its critics.[138] Alternatively, he thought of handing handwritten copies immediately to the Elector.[139] Weishaupt was confident that this would lead to a favourable turn of events, presumably because he reckoned that Charles Theodore, if judging on the basis of first-hand knowledge obtained in this way, would come to the conclusion that the Illuminati posed no threat to public order or indeed his rule. These expectations, which turned out to be overly optimistic, were in line with the arguments Weishaupt had put forward in his earlier essay 'Preparation for Those Who Are to Participate in Governing the Order' (see the Appendix).

Eventually, the two degrees were in fact published by their author, though not in their entirety and not in their original form. Nor did they avert the fate that the Illuminati Order suffered at the hands of the Bavarian authorities. In 1786, without referring to the suppression of the Order, Weishaupt expanded upon the Docetists degree in his 'philosophical fragment' *Ueber Materialismus und Idealis-*

---

[136] See Christoph Meiners: 'Ueber die Mysterien der Alten, besonders über die Eleusinischen Geheimnisse', in id.: *Vermischte philosophische Schriften*, Leipzig 1775, vol. 3, pp. 164–342, and Weishaupt to Hertel and Zwackh, [29 March 1778], KI vol. 1, p. 55.

[137] See Mieg to Weishaupt, 2 April 1783 and 6 April 1783, KI vol. 2, pp. 559 and 561, as well as Stolberg-Roßla to Weishaupt, 9 April 1783, ibid., p. 572.

[138] See Weishaupt to N. N., 18 December 1784, KI vol. 4 (in preparation).

[139] See Weishaupt to Hertel, 18 December 1784, KI vol. 4.

mus (On Materialism and Idealism).[140] In the following year, he presented a lengthy excerpt from the Philosophi degree in his book *Nachtrag zur Rechtfertigung meiner Absichten* (Supplement to the Justification of My Intentions).[141] Finally, in 1788, he reused other fragments in his *Geschichte der Vervollkommnung des menschlichen Geschlechtes* (History of the Perfection of the Human Race).[142]

In the second of these three books, Weishaupt stated in self-defence that his 'history of the development of mankind' given in the Philosophi degree had superseded the earlier one given in the Presbyter degree. That is plausible enough with regard to their respective place in the hierarchy of knowledge imparted to the Illuminati. There is no evidence, however, to support his claim that the 'Instruction in the First Chamber' was actually withdrawn or 'abolished' as he said it was.[143]

While *Ueber Materialismus und Idealismus* went to a second printing at a time when the public took a great interest in the persecution of the Illuminati, the ambitious *Geschichte der Vervollkommnung des menschlichen Geschlechtes* was left unachieved. What led Weishaupt to abandon this project may never be known. His offerings, just like those of any other writer, faced stiff competition on Germany's marketplace of ideas. No longer profiting from the appeal of the secret and the scandalous, they failed to make a lasting impression.

MUCH OF THE ENDURING NOTORIETY of the Illuminati Order can be traced back to the fact that it was probably the first secret society ever to be comprehensively exposed by the publication of its rituals as well as correspondence between its leading members. At the time, the reading public in Germany was both thrilled and appalled by these insights into dealings that were meant to be forever hidden from the uninitiated. Little did the contemporary observers realise, however, how much was still obscured from their view. It is only now, after more than two centuries have passed and despite the loss of many precious documents, that a fuller picture of the Order's inner workings is emerging.

Reinhard Markner and Josef Wäges

---

[140] See Adam Weishaupt: *Ueber Materialismus und Idealismus. Ein philosophisches Fragment*, Nuremberg 1786, pp. 29 ff.

[141] See Weishaupt: *Nachtrag zur Rechtfertigung*, op. cit., pp. 89–109.

[142] See Adam Weishaupt: *Geschichte der Vervollkommnung des menschlichen Geschlechtes*, vol. 1 (all published), [Nuremberg] 1788 (passim).

[143] Weishaupt: *Nachtrag zur Rechtfertigung*, op. cit., p. 71.

A Note on Sources

MANY OF THE DOCUMENTS assembled here were first published after the Illuminati Order had been suppressed in its native Bavaria in 1785. Weishaupt and his followers on the one hand, and his detractors on the other both had a selection of them printed.[144] Then, in 1788, the 'lower edifice' of the Order was presented to the public almost in its entirety. A book entitled *Der ächte Illuminat* (The Genuine *Illuminatus*), anonymously edited,[145] assembled the Preparatory Essay and the Novice, Minerval, and Illuminatus minor and Illuminatus major degrees. In 1793 and 1794 three of the higher degrees, Illuminatus dirigens, Presbyter, and Princeps, were published, again anonymously, in two books, *Die neuesten Arbeiten des Spartacus und Philo* (The Latest Works of Spartacus and Philo),[146] along with the complementing volume *Illuminatus Dirigens*.[147] To this day both serious research on the Illuminati as well as publications designed to denounce them have all largely rested on this foundation.

To a varying extent the text of the degrees as presented in the above books is corrupted, with obvious consequences for their interpretation. It does make a difference, to give just one example, if the printed text has 'Fremde' (strangers) where it should have 'Freunde' (friends).[148] The surviving manuscripts are not flawless either, but a diligent collation of the material can arrive at much more reliable, unadulterated versions than were available until now. A full documenta-

---

[144] *Grosse Absichten des Ordens der Illuminaten, dem patriotischen Publikum vorgelegt von vier ehemaligen Mitgliedern, Munich 1786; Vollständige Geschichte der Verfolgung der Illuminaten in Bayern, Frankfurt and Leipzig 1786; Einige Originalschriften des Illuminatenordens, op. cit.; Thomas Franz Maria Freyherr von Bassus: Vorstellung denen hohen Standeshäuptern der Erlauchten Republik Graubünden in Ansehung des Illuminaten Ordens auf hohen Befehl vorgelegt, [Nuremberg] 1788.*

[145] *Der ächte Illuminat oder die wahren, unverbesserten Rituale der Illuminaten, Edessa [i.e. Frankfurt] 1788. This book is generally ascribed to Johann Heinrich Faber (1742–1791), then a free-lance journalist in Frankfurt, probably because he was the editor of a monthly (and very average) review called Der Illuminat. However, the preface to the book is signed 'H. v. L.'*

[146] *Die neuesten Arbeiten des Spartacus und Philo in dem Illuminaten-Orden. Jetzt zum erstenmal gedruckt und zur Beherzigung bey gegenwärtigen Zeitläuften [ed. by Ludwig Adolph Christian von Grolman], [Frankfurt] 1793, ²1794.*

[147] *Illuminatus Dirigens oder Schottischer Ritter. Ein Pendant zu der nicht unwichtigen Schrift: Die neuesten Arbeiten des Spartacus und Philo in dem Illuminaten-Orden, [Munich] 1794.*

[148] *Die neuesten Arbeiten, op. cit., p. 28.*

tion of the existing textual variants can of course only be presented in a future German edition.

For most of the texts presented here the translation relies on a series of manuscripts kept at the Secret State Archives (Geheimes Staatsarchiv Preußischer Kulturbesitz) in Berlin as part of their masonic holdings, deposited there by the *Große National-Mutterloge Zu den drei Weltkugeln*. They were neatly copied by the same scribe, using the same paper (bearing the watermarks of a paper-mill in Hof[149]). While they are not dated, by all appearances they were written within a relatively short period of time, and no earlier than 1783.

A General Idea of the Society of the Illuminati: Our translation relies on a copy of this text with the shelf-mark FM 5.1.4. no. 3589,[150] which has been compared to another one preserved among the archives of the Frankfurt lodge 'Zur Einigkeit' (shelf-mark no. 6040). There is a shorter version of the 'preparatory essay' with a different beginning. This can be found in the Appendix and was translated on the basis of the manuscript FM 5.2. D 34 no. 1828.

Noviciate: This first stage of the Order's system was published, with its parts in a somewhat different order, in *Der ächte Illuminat*. Our translation is based on the manuscript FM 5.1.4. no. 3590. The 'General Statutes' were also published in *Vollständige Geschichte* (pp. 119–34), which has superior readings in some places, and later additions in others. The former have been taken into account here.

Minerval: Our translation is based on FM 5.1.4. no. 3591. Some amendments have been made by following the older manuscript FM 5.2. G 39 no. 107, doc. 3. The illustrations are taken from the same source. (It would seem that the unknown draughtsman mistook Medusa's head for the sun.) The 'Correct Pronunciation and Spelling of the Persian Months of our Calendar' is a later addition to this degree. The oath to be taken by the Minervals was the first excerpt from an Illuminati degree to be made public. It was printed and critically commented upon in a denunciation of Freemasonry published in late 1784.[151]

Illuminatus minor: This was the first degree to be printed in full, in early 1786.[152] Our translation is based on FM 5.1.4. no. 3592. Once again, a number of superior readings have been lifted from *Vollständige Geschichte* (pp. 154–221).

[149] *'Harfenpost', manufactured by the company of Johann Albrecht Wunnerlich.*

[150] *Unless stated otherwise, all shelf-marks are those of the Geheimes Staatsarchiv in Berlin. 'FM' stands for 'Freimaurer und freimaurerähnliche Organisationen'.*

[151] *See [Joseph Marius Babo:] Ueber Freymaurer. Erste Warnung, Munich 1784, pp. 29–48.*

[152] *See Schreiben an den Herrn Hofkammerrath Utschneider in München. [...] Nebst Instruction für den Obern der Minerval-Kirche wegen Ertheilung dieses Grades, [Nuremberg] 1786, pp. 59–136.*

Ritual Book for the Three Symbolic Degrees: The texts of the masonic degrees used by the Illuminati have never been published before, with the exception of a brief excerpt in Leopold Engel's history of the Illuminati Order.[153] Our translation rests on the manuscripts FM 5.1.4. nos. 3602 (Entered Apprentice), 3603 (Fellow Craft), 3604 (Master Mason Degree), and 3601 (Improved Constitution Book for the St. John's Lodge).

Illuminatus major: Our translation is based on the manuscript FM 5.1.4. no. 3596, which has been compared to FM 5.2. G 39 no. 107, doc. 16, as well as a recently digitised copy held by Bonn University Library (shelf-mark S 444).

Illuminatus dirigens: Our translation follows the manuscript FM 5.1.4. no. 3596. It contains a number of later additions, particularly in the Address, which are inserted here in square brackets. The Address, including these additions and a few further ones, was published in *Vollständige Geschichte* (pp. 222–50), somewhat corruptly but offering superior readings in a few places, which have been taken into account. The illustrations are taken from FM 5.2. G 39 no. 107, doc. 18.

Presbyter: The manuscripts of this degree differ significantly from the publication in *Neueste Arbeiten.* When Knigge edited the degree he used Weishaupt's 'Anrede an die neu aufzunehmenden Illuminatos dirigentes' as the foundation for the 'Unterricht im ersten Zimmer'. This lecture, revised and enlarged, was first assigned a place at the end of the degree (as Addendum A). Later, it was revised once again and reintegrated into the degree itself. However, the manuscripts where this was done are all incomplete. Some of the more noteworthy late additions to the degree, extracted from one of the two manuscripts in FM 5.1.4. no. 3598, can be found in the Appendix to this volume. For the bulk of the text our translation relies on FM 5.2. G 39 no. 107, doc. 20. This manuscript does not, however, contain Addenda B and C. For these, our translation relies on the other manuscript contained in FM 5.1.4. no. 3598.

Princeps: Our translation is based on a manuscript kept at the Hamburg State Archives (shelf-mark 614-1/72 Gr. Loge no. 1347), written by the same scribe as the Berlin manuscript 5.1.4. no. 3599 but containing some paragraphs deleted in the latter, which have been put into square brackets. Both manuscripts differ somewhat from the publication in *Neueste Arbeiten* (pp. 113–72), though not nearly as much as the preceding degree. The illustrations are taken from FM 5.2. G 39 no. 107, doc. 22.

---

[153] *Engel: Geschichte des Illuminaten-Ordens, op. cit., pp. 359–62.*

Docetists: This degree was first printed as such in 1994 by Hermann Schüttler, who wrongly believed it to be highest of the entire Illuminati system and did not realise that Weishaupt himself had published it, in a revised and expanded version, as his essay *Ueber Materialismus und Idealismus*.[154] Our translation is based on Johann Joachim Christoph Bode's copy (FM 5.2. G 39 no. 107, doc. 26). A few errors on his part have been rectified by comparing his manuscript to the only other one extant (ibid., doc. 27) as well as Weishaupt's later book.

Philosophi. Sages: In its entirety, this text was also first published only in 1994, virtually simultaneously, by Hermann Schüttler and W. Daniel Wilson,[155] based on the only two manuscripts extant, FM 5.2. G 39 no. 107, doc. 25 (in Bode's handwriting) and doc. 24 (copied by Duke Ernest II of Saxe-Gotha-Altenburg himself from Bode's copy). Once again, our translation mainly relies on Bode's manuscript.

The Appendix comprises of a number of texts that, for one reason or another, were not part of the main sequence of degrees.

A School of Humanity: Weishaupt's first sketch of a secret society precedes the foundation of the Illuminati Order by a few months or possibly years. The significance of the eponymous document was first recognised by Friedrich Ludwig Schröder, the influential Hamburg Freemason who was one of the pioneers of masonic historiography. Unfortunately, the original manuscript appears to be lost. Schröder received it in 1804, along with other Illuminati materials, from Duke Frederick Christian II of Schleswig-Holstein-Sonderburg-Augustenburg, who had obtained them, in return for financial support, from Weishaupt himself, some twenty years before. Schröder immediately had the text copied and circulated among the *Engbund* circles. Drawing on two of the surviving copies,[156] the text was first published, along with remarks on its importance and on the discussion it elicited within the *Engbund*, in 2012.[157]

Some Early Documents: The texts comprised under this heading were printed in 1787 *Einige Originalschriften des Illuminatenordens*, the first of two volumes containing a selection of materials published by the government of Palatinate-

[154] See *Johann Joachim Christoph Bode: Journal von einer Reise von Weimar nach Frankreich. Im Jahr 1787*, ed. by Hermann Schüttler, Munich 1994, pp. 395–414.

[155] See ibid., pp. 361–94, and W. Daniel Wilson: "'Der politische Jacobinismus wie er leibt und lebt'? Der Illuminatenorden und revolutionäre Ideologie. Erstveröffentlichungen aus den 'Höheren Mysterien'", in: *Lessing Yearbook* 25 (1993) [1994], pp. 133–84 (here pp. 150–84).

[156] GStA Berlin FM 5.2. D 32 no. 76, pp. 60–98, and FM 5.2. B 113 no. 828.

[157] See Reinhard Markner: 'Weishaupts früher Entwurf', op. cit., pp. 643–53.

Bavaria to justify its persecution of the Order and its leaders.[158] The original manuscripts were destroyed, along with other Illuminati materials and innumerable other files pertaining to the Bavarian State Archives, during an Allied bombing raid on Munich in April 1944.[159]

Supplement to the Illum. min. for the Better Instruction of the Superior: This text was intended by Weishaupt, according to the heading of his own handwritten sketch, for 'Br. Diomedes' – i.e. the Italian Marchese Costanzo di Costanzo, a leading member of the Order in Munich. A marginal note by Knigge indicates that he wished to see the text inserted at the beginning of the 'Instructions for the Education of Useful Collaborators'. However, it was never put there and instead circulated on its own. This is the only Illuminati degree text still extant in Weishaupt's own handwriting (FM 5.2. G 39 no. 117 doc. 37), which was difficult to read even for his contemporaries. The copy authenticated by 'Campanella', Count Stolberg-Roßla (FM 5.1.4. no. 3593), does not contain the last segment of the text and several later additions to it, again by Weishaupt himself, in the margins. Our translation presents the unabridged text, with the additions put into square brackets.

Preparation for Those Who Are to Participate in Governing the Order: Our translation of this unpublished text is based on the manuscript FM 5.1.4. no. 3597 and, for the two Addenda, on FM 5.2. G 39 no. 111, doc. 63, a manuscript partly in Knigge's handwriting, probably dating from early 1781.[160] To this, Bode added the following note: 'According to Philo's assurances, these two papers, A & B, are by Spartac[us]'.

Instructions for the National Inspectors: These are a late addition to the *Princeps* degree. They were neither printed in *Neueste Arbeiten,* nor are they included in most of the manuscripts of this degree. Our translation is based on the manuscript FM 5.2. B 113 no. 803, a manuscript formerly belonging to the collections of the Brunswick lodge 'Carl zur gekrönten Säule'.

Reinhard Markner

---

[158] *See Einige Originalschriften des Illuminatenordens, op. cit. (pp. 12–26, 26–38, 38–43, 57–60, 61–64, 67–70).*

[159] *See Reinhard Markner: 'Zur Überlieferungsgeschichte', in: KI vol. 1, in particular pp. XL–XLI.*

[160] *See Knigge to Weishaupt, 6–10 [February 1781], KI vol. 1, p. 235.*

Preparatory Essay

A GENERAL IDEA OF THE SOCIETY OF THE *ILLUMINATI*

There are certain truths, holy truths, that enlighten man about his past, present, and future condition. – They most certainly exist. – Call them revelation, or what you will. – Whether they are the results of thorough research or communications from the hands of higher beings – enough! any intelligent man is bound to feel that he requires them, because he remains in doubt about so many things in nature. – Can he see these doubts removed, or can he not? Are those explanations that the various nations have received from priests, philosophers, and scientists true, or are they not? – The investigation of this question is no ordinary task. Their passions, their social and economic circumstances and many other obstacles make it impossible for most people to fully devote themselves to these higher subjects; furthermore, given the current state of the world, it would be very unfortunate for mankind if all men were to devote themselves to the speculative sciences, thus withdrawing their hands from the commonwealth. In times past, it may have been otherwise. When our needs were not as manifold, our relationships not as interwoven, our passions not as vastly divided and excited; when people regarded their civil bonds only as a secondary goal and not as the main purpose of their existence: in those days, a man's highest aim was the fulfilment of his destiny. He viewed himself primarily as a link in the chain of creation, next to being a citizen of the world. But, gradually, true wisdom and a genuine insight into human destiny became increasingly rare: more and more interwoven with human statutes determined by the spirit of the age, it became falsified and ultimately the monopoly of a small number of men who, removed from all distracting obstacles, preserved the unadulterated truth, bequeathing it to their descendants. But since these men never forgot that they were also citizens of the Earth, their main purpose always and unmistakably remained to provide a direction for the masses who were being swept away by the cultural currents, so that this stream would never, as much as world events and the resulting circumstances permitted, rise too much above its banks.

To this purpose, in each century they veiled their teachings, the pure principles of truth, in whatever garment best suited the age. They never forgot that man lives in the world not only for speculation and for his own happiness and serenity, but that he also owes his fellow men a debt of succour and consolation.

Without a doubt the Order of Freemasons also belongs to the various mystery schools that have taken on the responsibility of teaching the holy truths, preserving them from corruption, and to using them for the welfare of all. However, although its Inner Sanctum has remained pure, its outer form is wholly corrupted. And yet this order could achieve so much! And now is exactly the time when the world most needs such a school, for the world has strayed so far from the path that, presently, one would truly have to start backwards and tune people to a different pitch, make them receptive for [truth], before one could teach them greater wisdom.

The society about which we speak understands this and is in a position to restore what has been desecrated. In its ranks are men of great understanding, men who were educated in more than one school of wisdom, men who are acquainted with persons at the helm of all secret societies and all Freemasonic systems and who thus know with certainty what is good, real, and useful, and what is not. However, they do not demand that one take them at their word, but only that one should judge them by their external organisation and their effect on the world.

To act is therefore their first purpose, to make the world better and wiser. – One should completely forget that they are in possession of secrets and only consider what they do for the welfare of mankind in general. All sciences and all worldly establishments are in need of reform, but such a reform must not be conducted publicly and cannot take place quickly: neither can this be a reform that tears down more than it builds up. Instead, it must be general and encompass everything, and must busy itself not with theoretical speculations but with active endeavours, in order to raise humanity to its original dignity. When better men unite to control the corruption and clear those obstacles standing in the path of wisdom and virtue, then these persons must not only know all obstacles but must also possess the most powerful means to remove them. This, however, cannot be found in such secret societies and especially not in contemporary Freemasonry, because

1. it consists partly of men who do not rise above the crowd at all.

2. These men are not enlivened by a *common spirit;* for since they have not been trained for this purpose from an early age, everyone walks in his own path and follows his own reasoning as his passions lead him.

3. One does not know the members well and does not know what each of them may be good for:

4. And yet all are led in the same way and examined, if they are examined at all, by the same tests, which themselves are quite uncertain.

5. And they finally arrive at a point where they have learnt nothing, because not only does Freemasonry lack a solid system for the most common truths, nothing at all is taught of the higher wisdom; and how can people of such diverse temperaments, who have not even been introduced to the most basic knowledge, possibly be in possession of supernatural wisdom? Indeed, most of them are unfamiliar with the history of Freemasonry and its actual purpose.

6. Contemporary Freemasonry is not concerned with the obstacles opposing wisdom and virtue; thus it will never do anything for the world in this way.

7. Prestige, power, and all passions are flattered grossly or subtly, and selfishness, ambition, vanity, private hatreds, and favouritism, vain enthusiasm, deceit, and ignorance all have an opportunity to play their part in this.

8. Everyone seeks to learn only for his own sake, without doing anything for the general good, and yearns to harvest fruits he has not sown.

In our society, however, all these issues are resolved:

1. Only those who have been thoroughly examined are accepted and promoted.

2. They are educated gradually and indescribably artful so that, by and by, they see all human matters with the same eyes. Therefore we prefer young people, since they have not yet been much infected by prejudice and demand less at once. The adults, however, must pass all these examinations. We are unconcerned about their impatience, and if they resign, we let them go.

But he who demonstrates his devotion by persevering and by holding nothing in low esteem that concerns the ennoblement of the human race will certainly find with us what he has always sought.

3. We have the surest means to get to know our members down to the smallest detail.

4. Since there is some diversity among our members, no one is treated exactly the same as the other, but everyone is led and motivated according to his direction and skills. Therefore, it is almost in every member's own hands if and to what extent he wishes to participate in our plans.

5. No one is promised any secrets, because one cannot know if this is a promise that can be kept for everyone. Instead, everyone receives enlightenment about

whatever can help him in this world and in his situation. If he has any doubts, these doubts shall be removed. If he believes he may find more and better things faster in other societies, then he is allowed to seek them.

A person who is not a Freemason of the 3rd degree cannot even easily advance with us. Our systems are solid and unwavering, the result of proven experience and research.

6. We are able to tear out any obstacles to goodness by the root, and we have chosen the best as well as the safest means to provide tangible rewards for virtue, to be fearsome to vice, to fetter malice, and to combat prejudice [courageously], yet prudently. This is a labour worthy of the holy legion of better men.

7. We do not take any notice of social class, reputation, etc. The wiser and the better man rules, but without anyone knowing that he rules. The inner constitution bridles every harmful passion. Since we only know one another by quality, not by name, we never become entangled with private favour or hatred. Ambition can never find a foothold, and curiosity and envy can spoil nothing. Idle gossip finds its prompt punishment, and vain enthusiasm, ignorance, and deceit are quickly exposed.

8. Each member is shown a perspective from which he can contribute to the greater whole.

He must be willing to work in such a manner that only distant generations may harvest the fruits of his efforts. He must value his insights only to the extent that they allow him to further the general welfare.

He who is such a man, someone to whom these things seem important, he alone is welcome to join us: for we do not sell the truth; we are paid nothing; and where we hold Assemblies, it is for the members themselves to decide if they want to contribute a little on a monthly basis to cover postage and similar small expenses. Furthermore, we do not recruit for our own benefit. One must seek entry with desire and complete trust.

The society has only recently begun to think more about its proliferation, because this diseased world requires help more urgently, and perhaps this is why its achievements have been less visible of late. But it has already achieved quite a few great and well-known successes, which the unknowing have attributed to luck or happenstance.

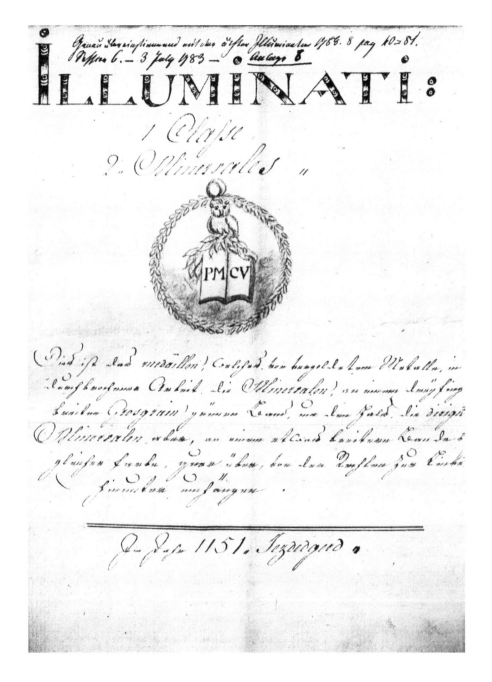

Title page of a manuscript of the Minerval degree from the archives of the 'Zur Einigkeit' lodge in Frankfurt am Main. At the top of the page a note by Georg Kloß, the famous Masonic historian and collector.

Table composed by N. N. concerning his Insinuates.

Christian and surname, age, outward appearance.	Class, office, place of residence, financial circumstances.	Moral character, inclination, way of thinking, religion.	Arts, sciences, language, favourite study.	Parents, siblings, patrons, friends, enemies, correspondence.	How he can be of use to the Order.

First table composed by N. N. about himself.

Christian and surname, place of birth, day and year.	Class, office, place of residence.	Arts, sciences, languages.	Favourite study.	How he intends to be of use to the Order?	Correspondence.

Second table by N. N. about his relationships.

Parents.	Siblings.	Closest relatives.	Patrons, friends, enemies.	Persons he would like to bring to the Order, and why?	Persons [he] would like to see excluded from the Order, and why?

I. Minerval Class

1. Noviciate

OBLIGATION. LETTER OF A CANDIDATE.

I, the undersigned, obligate myself by my honour and my good name, without any secret reservation, never to reveal to anyone, not even to my most intimate friends and relatives, neither by word nor gestures, glances, nor in any other conceivable way, anything of the matters entrusted to me by Herr … concerning my acceptance into a certain secret society, whether I am accepted or not. This even more so as I have been assured prior to my acceptance that in this society nothing is done that is against the state, religion, or good morals. I also promise to immediately return the documents which will be communicated to me for this purpose or any letters I may receive after having made the necessary excerpts in a manner unintelligible to others. All this, as I am an honest man, and intend to remain one.

Signed in … on the … day of … in the year …

(L. S.[1])

INSTRUCTIONS FOR THE *INSINUATI,* OR *RECEPTI.*
(EXCERPTED FROM THE STATUTES)

From the moment someone has submitted an Obligation he is committed to observing the following:

I. Everyone must keep a *diarium* in which he keeps an exact record of everything he receives from or sends to the ☉[2] and [which he] submits upon request.

II. He must faithfully complete and submit the 1st and 2nd table presented to him prior to his acceptance.

---

[1]   *Locus sigilli, place of the seal.*   [2]   *Order.*

III. From time to time he renders an exact account of the skills and character of those persons he would like to see accepted by the Order or those he would like to see excluded from it.

IV. It should be noted that the subjects suggested for membership must have a good heart, a desire to learn, and a love of hard work. If they are not knowledgeable in the sciences then the ☉ can aid them with instruction. Artists may also be suggested, as well as skilled and respectable craftsmen.

V. Everyone must set aside special individual sheets of paper dedicated to the following rubrics; he must add new ones after completing them.

> 1) A collection of the characters, actions, and modes of thinking of learned and respected men in ancient and modern times.
>
> 2) Noble thoughts, sentiments, pithy sayings by these men and from books prescribed or recommended by the ☉. These must be submitted when requested as proof of his diligence.
>
> 3) At the end of every month each member hands a sealed sheet of paper, headed *quibus licet,* to his Recipient, in which he states:
>
>> a) How his Recipient treats him, diligently or not, mildly or harshly.
>>
>> b) Whether he has any complaints against the ☉, and what these are?
>>
>> c) Whether money has been demanded from him, and how much?

In case someone has a special complaint or a secret request, he includes it under the title *soli* in the *quibus licet* slip, and if he does not wish even the Highest in the Province to read it, he adds the word *primo.*

VI. Every man receives a name from the ☉, and in order to make use of this for the benefit of learning he shall collect data on the history of his namesake so that in future he will be able to write it.

VII. Matters of the ☉ are to be kept in a special container including a sheet of paper inscribed 'to the Recipient or Superior'. It must be sealed in case one contracts a severe illness.

VIII. Summary copies must be kept of everything submitted to and received from the ☉, including all models, tables, instructions, etc. Original orders and letters must be returned.

Note.

Young persons who do not know a convenient way of taking notes can be instructed that this is best done on separate sheets: the subject, e.g. *Love,* is stated at the top, and any information gathered about it is written below the title. These sheets are kept in alphabetical order.

INSTRUCTIO PRO INSINUANTIBUS SEU RECIPIENTIBUS.[3]
(EXCERPTED FROM THE STATUTES)

I. Everyone is permitted to suggest or introduce new members.

II. Thus, if a member wishes to suggest a suitable person he must compose a faithful and elaborate description as prescribed in tabular format or *punctatim*[4] and submit it to the ☉ through his Recipient or include it in his *quibus licet*.

III. If the *Insinuator* then receives the *facultas recipiendi*[5], he must very carefully commence his work, report all events with the utmost precision and await further instructions.

IV. He must guide the Candidate, according to his own experiences and the instructions of his superiors, in such a manner that the desire to join such a society is stimulated gradually rather than suddenly: this is achieved through conversations which can subtly proceed to the subject of social bonds or by reading to him suitable passages that elevate the soul. Ancient and modern works of literature alike can serve this end. Seneca[6], Plato, Cicero, Isocrates[7], Antonine[8], Epictetus[9], etc. Anyone can suggest newer books, according to the Candidate's inclination and need, for instance Abt on merit,[10] Meiners' philosophical writings,[11] several works by Wieland[12], etc. Generally this Class includes any books that are rich in imagery and moral maxims. In the course of these conversations and actions the *Insinuatus* must display zeal and submit a request if he wishes to be accepted. However, he may only submit his Obligation after continued persistence.

V. After his acceptance he must declare in writing to which art or science he wishes to devote himself.

---

[3]   *Lat. Instruction for 'Insinuators' or Recipients.*

[4]   *Lat. Point for point.*   [5]   *Lat. Capacity/faculty to receive.*

[6]   *Lucius Annaeus Seneca (c. 1–65), Roman stoic philosopher.*

[7]   *Isokrates (436–338 BC), Greek rhetorician.*

[8]   *Marcus Aurelius Antoninus Augustus (121–180), Roman Emperor.*

[9]   *Epiktetos (c. 55–c. 135), Greek stoic philosopher.*   [10]   *Thomas Abbt: Vom Verdienste (1765).*

[11]   *Christoph Meiners: Vermischte philosophische Schriften (1775/76).*

[12]   *Christoph Martin Wieland (1733–1813), German poet, novelist, translator, and journal editor.*

He is asked to complete and submit the tables. These are forwarded to the Superiors along with a small fee, suitable to his circumstances, to cover any expenses (this is customary in some places). But even this amount is remitted to him if he wishes to resign prior to his initiation, as he is free to do. Elsewhere only small monthly dues are collected, and no initiation fees.

VI. The *Receptus* then receives an ☉ Name and a *pensum*[13] which he must complete to demonstrate his skills. This main *pensum* has to be handed in prior to the end of the probationary period.

VII. So that the ☉ can evaluate the industry of the *Receptus* as well as his growth in knowledge and delivery he is required to submit a moral essay once a month, at least a folio in length, or a small *pensum de nexu sociali*[14] which he may be assigned, depending on the circumstances.

VIII. During the probationary period the *Recipiens* presents to his subordinate the essence of the General Statutes of the ☉, point by point, and explains them to him.

IX. He also hands him a simple ☉ cipher, shows him how to take notes, how to write his diaries, the *quibus licet,* etc. He gives him copies of these instructions if necessary. He reads good books with him, reviews his excerpts and generally endeavours to enlighten and prepare him.

X. The *Recipiens* must see to the exact execution of the Statutes and report everything to his immediate Superiors, but he himself should not give reprimands too easily.

GENERAL STATUTES OF THE ORDER.

To reassure and assuage the doubts of prospective as well as actual members of this society and to anticipate any unfounded suspicions and fears the ☉ declares first of all that it harbours no harmful sentiments nor engages in any actions harmful to the state, religion, or good morals, nor does it approve of such among its own members. Its whole purpose and all its efforts are designed solely to make the improvement and perfection of his moral character interesting to man, imbue him with humane and social sentiments, thwart malicious intentions, come to the aid of an harassed and suffering virtue against injustice, further the promotion of worthy persons, and make useful knowledge which still remains largely

---

[13] *Lat. Task.*   [14] *Lat. On [the subject of] social interactions.*

hidden more generally available.

This is the unmasked purpose of the ☉. It stands for nothing else. Should members encounter something they do not expect from time to time, then this should help to convince them that we, compared to the practice of other societies, make fewer promises but fulfil more of those that we do make. A member who has been moved to join the ☉ by the prospects of great power and riches will, however, not be the most welcome.

I. Since mutual assistance, good concord, and unbreakable commitment are needed to maintain such a purpose, the members should never lose sight of the ☉'s ultimate goals. They should keep in mind that everything they seem to be doing for the ☉ actually furthers their own welfare and that all members must unite their forces to bring about their mutual felicity.

II. Therefore, they must look upon one another as their most faithful friends, set aside all hatred and envy, guard their hearts from all harmful selfishness and conduct themselves in such a manner that they win over not only the hearts of their Brethren but also those of their enemies.

III. They must cultivate a dignified, cordial demeanour in dealing with others and generally strive for the greatest inward and outward perfection.

IV. Philanthropy, virtue, and righteousness are expected of all members, as are accomplishments in the arts and sciences by those who have been gifted with them by nature or as a result of their own diligent efforts.

V. Therefore, every member must promote industriousness, sociability, and virtue; those who are able to do so must also promote the arts, sciences, and good taste and seek to remove all obstacles opposing them.

VI. In addition, the ☉ emphatically recommends the golden mean, domesticity, satisfaction with one's status, respect for elders, superiors, principals, and state servants, friendship and love towards one's Brethren and courtesy and compassion towards all men. He who demands respect from others must also treat others with reverence and respect.

VII. Manage your offices in civil society with faithfulness, zeal, and steadfastness; preside over your families as good fathers, husbands, and lords; or be obedient as sons, servants, and subordinates. He who neglects the duties of his status or of his office will also neglect his duties towards the ☉.

VIII. Although all differences in status found in civil society disappear inside the Order, it is still necessary to remain within the boundaries of proper decorum and show due respect, especially in the presence of the uninitiated.

IX. Older members have acquired more knowledge and more honours and, consequently, have received higher degrees. They may indeed be Superiors; therefore, they are met with the kind of reverence that shows one's true respect and esteem, but without slavish cowering.

X. The more courtesy a brother shows you, the greater the respect you must reciprocate. Never indulge in too ostentatious a familiarity; you must love one another, and experience has taught that nothing severs the strongest and closest friendship as easily as excessive intimacy *(familiarity).*[15]

XI. Superiors are our leaders, guiding us in darkness and in error, leading us away from treacherous paths. Thus submission and obedience become duty and then gratitude itself, for no one will refuse to follow him who labours for that which is best for himself.

XII. The ☉ thus requires of its members a sacrifice of personal freedom, not necessarily immediately, but always when it is a means to the great end. One should always assume that the Superiors' commands serve this purpose, as the Superiors see more clearly and have deeper insight into the system, and it is for this reason and no other that they are Superiors.

XIII. They know human nature, know with whom they are dealing, and thus they will never abuse their status; nor will they forget that they should be good fathers. Still, the Order has taken the following measures to protect its members from all oppressors, from conceited and tyrannical persons, etc. At the end of every month every subordinate submits one or several sealed sheets to his Superior or Recipient with one of the following titles, depending on the circumstances: *quibus licet, Soli, or Primo.* On this sheet, he indicates:

1) How his Superior approaches and treats him.
2) What complaints he has against the ☉.
3) What orders the Superior has given him this month.
4) What monies he has paid this month.

XIV. Everyone must submit such a slip each month irrespective of whether or not he has anything to report or complain about. So that this can be done with a minimum amount of effort, every member prepares one sheet at the beginning of each month, recording every event he thinks should be noted there, and seals it at the end of the month.

---

[15] *English in the original.*

XV. This order concerning the sheet to be submitted is in force throughout all degrees, and no one is exempt. If it is contravened, the subordinate as well as his Superior who has failed to demand or submit it in a timely manner are subject to an appropriate monetary fine. The subordinate must submit his sheet on the last day of each month.

XVI. So that all members are ensouled by a single spirit and are of one will as much as possible, they are to read certain books by which they must educate themselves. Superiors and Brethren alike will have the opportunity to evaluate their presentation as well as diligence and increase in their knowledge from their monthly reports, at least a folio in length[, and from lectures during the meetings].

XVII. The books are made known to [each member by his Superior]. In general, no book that educates the heart is excluded. To prospective members we recommend authors of fables and other writings that are rich in images and moral maxims. We especially approve of seeing the members draw nourishment from the spirit of the ancients and, especially, *when they come to reflect and observe more than they read.*

XVIII. Each Candidate's Recipient is his respective Superior; everyone who reveals the ☉'s existence to another person and thus has stirred in him the desire to join it, must await further instructions from him who has brought him into the ☉, i.e. his Recipient.

XIX. Everyone has permission to suggest and introduce new members; therefore all members must maintain certain documents for [all persons] they would like to see accepted into the ☉ as well as for those they desire to be excluded, in which they record those speeches and actions that provide insights into their souls, especially the smallest details which a man may believe are not observed[. Since all opinions uttered and all actions give us away], there will never be a lack of material for such notes.

XX. These notes are the basis for all future proceedings. Therefore they must be taken very precisely; they should be more narrative than speculative. These notes provide the immediate Superiors with the Candidate's character when a man is considered for acceptance or exclusion.

XXI. Since every person has two sides – one good, one evil – the ☉ demands that the members do not acquire the habit of only observing and describing one of them; our humanity demands that we also seek goodness within our enemies; righteousness demands that we credit even our enemies with it. One must seek to judge the whole man from his character, not from a single action and not merely from his relationship with us.

XXII. To see whether the Candidates are following the directions above, whether they wish to expand their knowledge, shed and dispute their prejudices, perfect their moral character, in a word, if they wish to become worthy members, the ☉ demands proof of loyalty, discretion, diligence, and obedience.

XXIII. Therefore, the ☉ has set a certain time for the Candidate to prove himself in: three years for young persons, two years for others, and only one year for others still. It is the Candidate's industry, zeal, maturity, and dedication that can shorten this probationary period.

XXIV. During this time the Candidate reads the prescribed books, researches his fellow men, records everything diligently, sets it down according to his own method, seeks to understand what he has read and to express it in his own words.

XXV. An abundance of notes, commentaries, character sketches, recorded conversations with men who were speaking in the language of zeal, as well as compliance with the ☉'s statutes and obedience towards the Superiors are the surest way to promotion.

XXVI. Among these notes, physiognomic observations and any rules discovered for evaluating the human character are of great merit; above all, however, we recommend viewing these matters not from another person's perspective but from one's own.

XXVII. In addition to the whole range of practical philosophy, the ☉ occupies itself with natural history, with administration and economics, and with the liberal arts, humanities, and languages.

XXVIII. During his initiation, the Candidate declares which art and science he wishes to study; he must acquaint himself with the books of this discipline, make succinct excerpts from them, present them as proof of his diligence to his Recipient and send them in on demand.

XXIX. Among the first proofs of his ability is the task everyone must complete and submit at the end of his probationary period.

XXX. During his initiation, the Candidate also changes his name to a different name. He must read, collect, and note everything about his namesake that he encounters.

XXXI. Since the Candidate is to acquire the habit of being especially cautious and secretive he will not be told who belongs to the ☉ and will not get to know a single member during the whole of his probationary period:

1) So that he cannot dissimulate himself and, therefore, is under constant observation.

2) If he were to gossip he would run the risk of gossiping about members of the ☉ and thus violate the statutes in a way he could not deny.

XXXII. For this reason, and because one never knows whether he with whom one is speaking is of a higher, a lesser or the same ☉ degree, it is not permitted to speak of one's date of initiation, of degrees and dispensations, not even with members of the ☉ one has met in the Assemblies. But most of all, it is not permitted to say the least thing of ☉ matters to those one only surmises to be fellow-members.

XXXIII. Absent members must write to their Superior every fortnight, postage paid. Present members must visit their Superior at least once a week. If the Superior has the time, he divides the number of days between his people. He reads, takes notes, and has instructive conversations with them.

XXXIV. The Candidate copies those materials he receives from his Superior as necessary and in a manner intelligible only to himself, always returning all originals, personally or by mail, immediately. In general, the Order seeks to remain secret as much as possible. Everything secret is more enticing and commands more loyalty. Thus, Superiors have more opportunities to make observations. Furthermore, the ☉ is thereby safe from intrusions by incompetent yet powerful persons and from the speculations of curious meddlers. The noble intentions are less likely to be thwarted, and any outbursts of power-hungry and divisive persons can be suppressed more easily.

XXXV. To cover various expenses and support destitute Brethren, the ☉ demands of every member who has signed the Obligation a small contribution, commensurate with his ability to pay; this provision, however, is not yet in place everywhere.

XXXVI. Other than that, the Candidate does not have to pay any dues during his probationary period, and even this small amount is reimbursed if he wishes to resign, as he may at any time, prior to his initiation. In any case, he will very quickly convince himself how little we are intent on monetary profit.

XXXVII. Truly destitute members not only have their membership dues waived; to the contrary, they receive aid from the ☉. With others, the small dues are deferred until their situation improves.

XXXVIII. However, since these are only nominal, whereas the entry alone to other associations costs 100 guilders or thalers[16], or more; we would hope that since it is easy to understand that such a large enterprise requires tremendous sums of money for travel, correspondence, etc., most of which are contributed by the generosity of some of the Superiors, one will not complain about having to pay a trifling amount for the upkeep of the whole edifice. No money is ever sent to the Superiors.

AN EASY CIPHER FOR READY USE.

m.	=	1.	d.	=	9.	r.	=	17.
l.	=	2.	c.	=	10.	s.	=	18.
k.	=	3.	b.	=	11.	t.	=	19.
i.	=	4.	a.	=	12.	u.	=	20.
h.	=	5.	n.	=	13.	v.	=	21.
g.	=	6.	o.	=	14.	z.	=	22.
f.	=	7.	p.	=	15.	y.	=	23.
e.	=	8.	q.	=	16.	x.	=	24.

---

[16] *A Reichsgulden had two thirds of the value of a Reichsthaler.*

2. Minerval Degree

This is the *medallion,* an open-work piece made of gilded metal, which is worn by the Minervals around the neck on a ribbon, [grass-green and] three fingers wide, while the Directing Minervals wear it on a slightly wider ribbon of the same colour from right to left.

The sign is made by holding the hand flat over the eyes, as one does when blinded by a light.

The grip is given by taking the other man's hand and softly tapping it three times with the little finger.

Each year two watchwords are given, the name of a place and that of a man. One might ask, for example: 'Where does the light shine brightest?' Answer: 'In Sagunto[17].' Who sees it the brightest? Answer: 'Hanno.'

STATUTES FOR THE MINERVALS.

It has already been stated, in the opening remarks of the general Statutes of the Order, that the ⊙'s purpose is directed to the propagation of human felicity in general, but especially to the improvement of the moral character and the infusion of noble and worthy sentiments. However, since the improvement of the intellect and increase of knowledge are an indispensable means for this purpose, they are the Order's main pursuit *in this Class.*

---

[17] *A city to the north of Valencia.*

Thus, this Class is the school, as it were, in which some members are educated to provide the necessary instruction to others and where everyone has resources made available to him that he would never find on his own. This is the reason for the name *Minervals*. Members are either apprentices *(minervales),* or they are instructors *(minervales illuminati).*

The provisions and regulations to be observed by the former are the following:

I. As is known from the Statutes, the Order concerns itself with all the arts and sciences, theology and jurisprudence (in the general sense) alone excepted. Therefore, over the course of his life, every member must gather everything he can find in *his* art [or science to which he committed himself during his initiation], especially its rarest and most difficult aspects, presenting his findings to his Recipient at least once a year or more frequently if requested, as proof of his industry and obedience.

II. Conversely, every working member is entitled to demand, within his Province *(co[u]nty)*[18], contributions and tools for every art and science that he has chosen for his main course of study. If he lets the Superior of his Assembly announce an important and difficult matter on which he has worked for a long time and in which he would like to deliver something exhaustive, all members in the district are required to report to him everything they have already collected about the subject or, in case they have not collected anything, they must expressly gather such information and submit it to him within one year. Everyone must therefore arrange his notes accordingly. The method of taking notes has already been explained.

III. In larger places where there is more than one Assembly, specific regulations and orderly registers of the arts and sciences are issued and the members divided into separate classes according to their chosen art or science, where they are given instruction in each subject.

IV. The Order further collects information pertaining to libraries, objects of nature, antiquities, and diplomatics; every member must endeavour to gain insights into these subjects and make them available for general use.

V. Every local Superior has a *catalogus desideratorum*[19] listing what is missing or hard to come by, and every member is requested to look for those things and deliver them. Conversely, any resources that the members are lacking can be placed among the *desiderata* and then announced within the district in order to

---

[18]   *English in the original.*   [19]   *Lat. Catalogue of desired information.*

obtain them by trade, purchase, or loan.

VI. To encourage the members to work harder and to reward their efforts, the ☉ proposes one or several prize questions every year. Anyone is free to participate, while the prize and date of submission are set beforehand depending on the difficulty of the question.

VII. The essays must be fair copies, and everyone must submit them to his Recipient or his Assembly's Superior, who processes them from there.

VIII. These essays as well as other ☉ works, e.g. tasks, discourses, [monthly] pursuits, collections regarding the ☉ name, remain the property of the ☉, so that whereas the author may never publish them, the ☉ can do so, provided this does no harm to the author.

IX. Since it is not feasible to standardise the book trade in the English fashion in all Provinces, and so that prospective authors especially do not have to depend too much on booksellers, the ☉ itself will take care of all suitable works by its members, print them at its own expense and let the members handle distribution, subscription, or advance orders. It must be understood that this does not apply to mere trifles, excerpted brochures, invective diatribes, and the like, and that every author will have to submit to sensible and modest censorship. Manuscripts requiring too harsh a censorship will not be accepted, but will be returned to the author.

X. It has already been stated that in order to defray the ☉'s expenses, especially the costly correspondence, every Minerval makes a monthly contribution, the amount of which can be negotiated if necessary.

XI. If someone wishes to travel or visit foreign countries, he must report to his Superior beforehand so that he may enjoy his due share of the benefits usually meant for the higher degrees, such as acquaintances, support, and the like.

XII. If a Brother falls ill, the others take turns in comforting and entertaining him and providing him with aid and succour. If the illness is life-threatening, his ☉ documents are collected and returned to him only when his health has been restored. Should the Brother die, his Brethren pay him their last respects, and his memory is hallowed with a speech at the next Assembly.

XIII. The rules concerning the diary, sealed monthly complaints, character sketches, etc. described in the general Statutes remain in full force in this degree as well.

XIV. Among the primary duties that everyone must observe in this degree and in which anyone who wishes to be promoted swiftly must excel are:

THE SECRET SCHOOL OF WISDOM

1) Satisfaction with one's status and fate.

2) Good housekeeping.

3) Respect for all authority, of the ☉ as well as the state.

4) Respect and love for one's parents.

5) Reverence and high esteem for old age.

6) Respect for all institutions of learning, especially schools, learned societies, and universities. Also, helping them to flourish and prosper.

7) Recommendation of worthy, known Brethren and defence of them against slander and libellers.

XV. In general, everyone must lend a helping hand to the other and provide him with resources that will ease his way to illumination.

XVI. In this Class, the ☉ wishes to be regarded only as a learned society, where example and instruction better the heart and guide the mind.

XVII. Therefore read diligently and think about what you have read. Above all, use your own mind, not someone else's. What others have said and thought, think and say in your own way. Do not accept an opinion without having examined its origin, its author and foundations. Practise solving the assigned tasks; read works that elevate the soul and move the heart; share this with others; contemplate the practice and execution of what you have read and thought. Most of all, explore human nature not so much from books as from within yourselves. From the observation of others and from conclusions drawn from similar circumstances abstracted onto others.

INITIATION CEREMONIES.

The following must be present:

The Superior or some other delegate as *Initians*.

The Secretary or someone else as *Actuarius*.

The Candidate's Recipient as Godfather, and the *Recipiendus*.

The initiation takes place in the evening in a room with closed windows and lit [only] by three lamps. A lamp of white glass stands on the table at which the deputies are seated. The superior *Initians* is still concealed by a [green] screen. Two other lamps of yellow glass stand at a distance on two console tables or similar furniture.

Those present wear their Order jewels. As soon as the Recipient arrives with the Candidate at the house where the ceremony is to be held, the Superior informs the latter or, depending on the circumstances, reads to him the order that permission has been granted to initiate him and then asks him whether he still, in all earnestness, demands to join the ☉; and if the answer is 'Yes', he asks him to put down his rapier and lets his Recipient then escort him to a dark, unlit room. There the Recipient bids him sit down and says: 'Here you may reconsider once more whether or not you remain resolved to join the ☉!' Then the Recipient departs, leaving the *Initiandus* to his thoughts.

After 10 to 15 minutes have elapsed, the Superior gives two knocks; the *Recipiens* does the same on the door to the dark room in which the *Initiandus* sits, then enters the room and asks the Candidate if he has given the matter due thought and is still ready to take the step. If he answers 'Yes', the *Recipiens* enters the Initiation Chamber after two knocks, answered by the Superior, and delivers the answer, whereupon the *Initians* says: 'Then bring him here.' The Recipient ushers the *Initiandus* in and directs him to stand at a distance from the table where the others are seated; now the *Initians,* wearing a hat, asks him,

I. 'What is your desire, (☉ Name), why have you come here?' The *Initiandus* is allowed to answer at first, but he is then told that it is customary for his *Recipiens,* who has assumed the role of his Godfather in these proceedings, to continue answering in his stead; he should always declare afterwards if or to what extent he agrees or disagrees with the answer.

Recipiens. Noble member of this Illustrious Order, after the preceding due examination (if the Initiandus has been dispensed from this, the *Recipiens* adds: for the abridgement of which O. N. is immeasurably grateful) and having thoroughly considered the matter once more, O. N. demands and requests to be accepted, if indeed he is found worthy in the eyes of the ☉.

II. *Initians.* You have been found worthy to become one of us on account of your qualifications reported to our Illustrious Superiors and the required examinations to which you have submitted yourself. I wish you luck with this endeavour, and I admonish you to obey exactly everything which will be demanded of you, unless you wish to resign from the ☉ and forego the benefits of a fraternal coalition and the full purpose of the ☉. Tell me, O. N., what is your understanding of this Order?

Recipiens. O. N. knows from the Statutes and from conversations that the ☉'s true, unadorned purpose is brotherly support, aid to oppressed virtue, and the improvement of heart and mind.

III. *Initians*. This is a true and right understanding of our Illustrious ☉. You will have learnt through reflection, personal encounters, and the information communicated to you that it is truly thus. You will have seen for yourself that our goal is neither power nor wealth, nor that we endeavour to usurp the rule of the world or overthrow ecclesiastic or secular governments. Thus, if you envisioned the ☉ in this manner, you have deceived yourself; and so that you penetrate no further into this honourable Sanctum with your deceptively bold expectations, the ☉ fully dismisses you through me, if you so desire. You have no obligation other than complete silence. You are as free as you were before. Unless you insult or betray it, you need not fear the least from the ☉. – Do you wish to resign, or do you persist in your previous decision?

Here the Candidate alone answers, and this answer is logged, as are all others.

IV. *Initians*. Have you also considered thoroughly that you burden yourself with new obligations, that you limit your natural freedom in this manner?

Recipiens. O. N. has considered everything thoroughly. He is the true sovereign of his will; he is convinced that without the assistance of others man is impotent, that indeed he is nothing; that complete independence would be harmful to him; that instead, man requires guidance and support from others under all circumstances. Therefore, O. N. has joined this Illustrious ☉, so that through his membership and initiation he may obtain further degrees and be more thoroughly connected with the honourable members of the same.

V. *Initians*. Have you thoroughly considered that the ☉ demands the strictest obedience under certain circumstances? That you must keep silent and be obedient in matters of the ☉, and that you may also receive inconvenient orders that may be in conflict with your passions?

Recipiens. O. N. knows that there must be superiors and subordinates in every well-ordered society; he knows that this is indispensable because of the individual's weakness and the necessity of social organisation. He has already obligated himself to silence and obedience when he joined the ☉. Why should he not follow those in matters of the ☉, of which he is convinced that their intentions are good, do honour to humanity and are useful to the whole as well as individual members? Should O. N. eventually be given a task he would consider inconvenient, not understanding the reason behind it, he will still complete it, because he knows that not everything which is unpleasant is truly evil for man, just as not everything which is pleasant is truly good. He is convinced that he will not be given tasks without good cause, but only for his own or the ☉'s good.

VI. *Initians.* Indeed! Never will you be given any orders other than those which are useful, which serve your improvement and enlightenment; no tasks other than those which serve the general purpose. One more thing, however, I must ask you to consider. You might also find among the members of the ☉ persons whom you dislike or those who may even be your enemies. Such personal hatred might tempt you to become lukewarm and inactive or perhaps even disobedient towards the Superiors and to perjure yourself against the entire ☉.

Recipiens. O.N. will extinguish such hostilities and regard all members as his Brethren; in his eyes, everyone whom the Illust. ☉ has deemed worthy to become its member will appear to deserve his esteem.

VII. *Initians.* These statements are sufficient for us. However, before I can grant you further entry into the ☉, I wish to hear under which conditions you seek to enter the ☉. Therefore, do tell me in turn: what do you demand of it?

Recipiens. While O.N., through his submission, grants the worthy Plenipotentiary certain powers over him, and through him grants these to the Illust. ☉, he also expects that the ☉ can ensure his safety and best interests, as long as these can be in harmony with the general welfare and help him in all good things. He in turn binds himself to obey, to honour all members and to use his powers for the best of the ☉.

VIII. *Initians.* This desire is just and reasonable. I (now the Plenipotentiary states his O.N., removes his hat and stands up), authorised to do so by the sublime ☉, promise you, in the name of our Illust. Superiors and in the name of all members of the entire Order, protection, justice, and assistance. On the other hand, the ☉ never stands for misfortunes of your own doing or which may come about by insisting on the power and assistance of the ☉. Furthermore, I once again solemnly assure you in the name of the whole ☉ that you will find nothing with us that opposes religion, the state, or good morals. [However, (here, the Candidate is called by his O.N., and the rapier is placed on his breast), should you become a traitor or perjurer, all members would be called to take up arms against you.] Do not believe yourself to be safe; wherever you might flee, shame, the accusations of your heart, and the vengeance of your unknown Brethren will haunt and vex you to the core. (The rapier is put back on the table.) If you persist in your decision to be accepted, then give the following oath. (The *Initiandus* is bid to kneel, place his right hand on his head, and repeat the oath verbatim. An opened Bible is on the table, and when the words 'So help me God!' are spoken, the Candidate removes the hand from his head, placing three fingers of that hand on the Bible.)

'I, O. N., confess here, before God Almighty and before you, the Plenipotentiary of the Illustrious Order to which I seek admission, that I recognise my natural weakness and impotence, that with all the advantages of rank, honour, titles, and material goods that I may gain in civil society, I will always remain a mere man among men; that just as I have attained all this through my fellow men, I can also lose it through them, that the approval and respect of my fellow men is hence indispensable, and that I will seek to earn such by all means. I will never use my present or future respect and power to harm the common good, but I will certainly resist the enemies of the human race and civil society according to my powers and circumstances. Furthermore, I promise and swear that I will eagerly seize all opportunities to serve mankind, improve my knowledge and will, and apply my useful insights to the common good, inasmuch as the welfare and the Statutes of the present society require this of me.

I also swear eternal silence in inseverable faithfulness and obedience to all Superiors and the Statutes of the ☉. In matters of the ☉, I faithfully relinquish my private insights and obstinacy, as well as the [un]limited use of my powers and abilities. I obligate myself to see the best of the ☉ as my own, and I am ready to serve it with my wealth, honour, and blood for as long as I am a member. Should I ever act against the Statutes and welfare of the Illust. Society, out of precipitance, passion, or even malice, I submit to all penalties and punishments placed upon me by my Superiors.

I further promise that in matters of the ☉. I will act and counsel according to my best knowledge and conscience, sacrificing personal advantage. I shall view all friends and enemies of the ☉ as my own, but will refrain from exacting vengeance against the latter and will act towards them as ordered by the society. I am equally willing to concern myself with the expansion and proliferation of the Order by any permissible means, and to use my powers to this purpose as much as this is possible.

To this end, I waive any secret reservations and promise all this according to the true intentions of the society which has placed this oath upon me and true to these words:

So help me God!'

He then signs the minutes, and the Superior tells him the following:

1) That he will not yet have an opportunity to meet all the members of the ☉. but only those of the same Class who congregate in Assemblies under the same chief. But he will be given means by which he may discover some members he has never met. Here he is given the sign, grip, words, and the watchword, which is changed every year.

2) Within the space of one month, he shall submit a register of his important or rare books. His Recipient will advise him what format this catalogue should take.

3) In this time, he shall also compose his thoughts about the following questions:

A) What would he wish to be the ☉'s ultimate purpose?

B) Which means would he employ to attain this purpose?

C) What in particular would he not wish to find in the ☉?

D) Which persons does he hope not to find therein?

In this way the ☉ sees how deeply he tries to understand the entire system and is able to study people who have often been recommended too warmly by some from a perspective from which others have failed to, or could not, properly observe them.

FORM FOR INITIATION MINUTES FOR ABSENT, ADULT CANDIDATES WHO WOULD OBJECT TO BEING INITIATED IN THE SAME MANNER AS VERY YOUNG MEN.

Minutes of the Initiation of Brother O. N.

From the documents of the ☉ that are now in your hands it will become apparent to you that this degree of the ☉ is primarily concerned with the education of young persons and, therefore, it should not surprise you that the Illustrious Superiors not only

1) have set a long probationary period for these young men, but also

2) require of them a high degree of submissiveness and complete reliance on the ☉; because they also assume the place of teachers and parents of these young pupils, and as they have pledged to them protection and good counsel, it is important for the ☉ to be certain that every step that these young men take is in accordance with the principles of our holy and close association.

In essence, admission to the ☉ should be viewed as a mutual contract. With each Candidate the ☉ only gains a man of whom one cannot yet be certain, whether or not he will be entirely suited for our lofty purposes; the entrant in turn joins an association of upright and tried men: the ☉ can expect from this new addition nothing further than perhaps another industrious collaborator; the Candidates, on the other hand, can hope for all the benefits of this solid and widespread association. And since these prospects are revealed to them in a most altruistic manner, and since all obligations, except silence, expire as soon as they choose to resign, which they are at liberty to do whenever one demands of them something they cannot do, it is only fair for the ☉ to try to ascertain that in admitting you, it does not acquire an inactive member that may destroy the unity of the entire project.

The Illustrious Superiors have shortened your probationary period. You will now be accepted in our association. But first tell me:

1ˢᵗ question. What is your understanding of this Order?

2ⁿᵈ question. Have you considered that, by accepting an obligation, you limit your natural freedom?

3ʳᵈ question. Have you further considered that, in certain circumstances, the ☉ requires the strictest obedience, and that an order's underlying reasons cannot always be explained to you, which may prove inconvenient?

4ᵗʰ question. What would you do if you happened to find persons whom you dislike, or who may even be your enemies, in the ☉?

5ᵗʰ question. Now you know what we expect of you; but what do you require of us in return?

The proceedings up to this point are written down and sent to the absent Candidate, together with the files of the Minerval degree. He reads everything, writes his answers in the spaces provided and on a separate sheet completes the form for the oath if he wishes to swear it. He then sends everything back. If the Superiors are satisfied, the following is written below the request:

This request is just and reasonable. I, the undersigned, authorised by the Illustrious ☉ to do so, promise you on behalf of our Illustrious Superiors in the name of all members and the entire ☉ protection, justice, and assistance. However, the ☉ will never stand for any misfortune you may suffer through your own fault or may incur through insisting on the might and assistance of the ☉. I further solemnly assure you again and in the name of the entire ☉ that you will find among us nothing contrary to the state, religion, and good morals. If you are still resolved to join this ☉, please copy the attached written oath in the space below.

(O. N. of the *Initians*.)

Then the proceedings are sent back to the Candidate. He writes his oath underneath it and signs it.

INTRODUCTION CEREMONIES.

He who has received permission to attend an Assembly for the first time is called an *Introducendus*.

When entering the Assembly, the youngest Minerval is obliged to say that there is a Brother in the ante-chamber. (The Godfather or the Censor must have told the *Introducendus* that he may not enter the Assembly until he is fetched.) As soon as the last Minerval has announced this, the Superior delegates the Brother Censor to investigate whether or not it is a true brother.

The Censor holds the hand before his eyes, as if blinded by a bright light, exits, demands from the new arrival the word and sign, enters the Assembly-room after the customary two knocks and their answers, and states he has proven himself a true brother by word, sign, and grip. The Superior commands: 'Let him enter', whereupon the Censor fetches him. When entering, the Censor and the *Introducendus* give the blinding sign. All members present, except the Superior, answer the sign and then approach the pyramid, bowing before it, then stand by the Superior's table.

After the Superior has demanded the word and sign from the *Introducendus*, he asks him if he will fulfil everything he has sworn during his initiation obediently and without any secret reservation? If he answers ['yes'], the Superior bids him kneel, place three fingers of his right hand on his heart and repeat after him: 'I swear to God, the Superiors, and all my dear Brethren that I will fulfil everything I have sworn during my initiation and in the Obligation, faithfully and without any secret reservation.'

Now the Superior lets him stand up, kisses him, requests the Order ribbon with the jewel from the Br. *Quaestor*,[20] places it around [the *Introducendus*'] neck and explains it to him in the following manner:

'We place this jewel of the ☉ on every member of this Class, not for them to seek greatness and respect therein or that the Brethren become accustomed to

[20] Lat. *Treasurer*.

73

ribbons and tokens of honour, but rather so that they learn to realise that only virtue and science may bestow a right to nobility and benefits, and that the outward symbols will never blind an enlightened mind without the soul's inner worth, and that they should never wrest wishes and desires from him. A truly wise man must always seek out the beauty of the soul and rise above common prejudices, neither despising outer appearances, nor devoting himself slavishly to them.'

The ribbon to which the jewel of the ☉ is attached has a twofold meaning; first, the bonds of prejudice which had bound our reason from an early age and, second, the formation of friendly and social bonds which enable us to join forces to break the shackles of folly more easily and to jointly rise to a spiritual height that individual men have only rarely reached. Left to his own devices, man has neither the strength nor the power for this, and at every turn he senses that the connection with others and their support are necessary, if not indispensable.

Minerva's bird, the symbol of wisdom and nightly reflection, must remind us of labour and activity, without which nothing great can be achieved.

Whenever a Brother dons this jewel, he must resolve never to commit anything that would shame him as a human being, a Brother and a wise man. Whenever he hangs it around his neck, he must examine himself to see whether or not he has committed any actions that might render him unworthy of this jewel or this society. So that everyone might examine himself in this manner for a few moments, all the Brethren do not enter at the same time, but one after the other.

Following this, the Superior recites a maxim either of his own choosing or one that has been prescribed to him, and the Br. Censor directs the *Introductus* to his seat.

STATUTES AND CEREMONIES FOR THE MINERVAL ASSEMBLIES.

The dates for these Assemblies are marked in the calendar. Extraordinary Assemblies are determined by order of the Superiors or as compelled by circumstances.

Date and hour of the Assemblies depend on local conditions. The Superior alternately announces them to as many Brethren as necessary. If the number of members in a certain location has grown too large, more Assemblies are held by the same or another Chief.

The Assembly room must be secured by a locked ante-chamber. Entry to the Assembly room is through the ante-chamber; other entryways must be barred and secured against eavesdroppers.

There are three small tables in the room: one at the back, where the Superior and guests are seated at a distance; the second at the opposite end with a wax light, where whoever has something to read out will sit; the third stands at a distance to the side of the Superior: a wax candle is placed on it, and the chancellery officials are seated there.

On the Superior's table stands the small white lamp with the shade; behind the [shade], the image of Pallas is fixed, next to which are two tinted glass lamps.

From this table and all the way to the other table, chairs for seating the members are placed on both sides. The pyramid lies on the floor in the centre of the room. An empty chair stands to the right of the presiding Superior. In the beginning, the room is lit only by three lamps.

The members gather in the ante-chamber or in another room and remain there until the Superior summons them, one after the other, with a sign. If the Superior is not already in the Assembly room, he says to the members in attendance: 'Dear Brothers, the hour of our labour has come.' He then enters, his head covered, and takes the Order jewel. But if he has already been in the room, he makes a sign with two knocks, and the Censor replies: 'Dear Brothers, the hour of our labour calls us.' After two knocks, which must be answered by the Superior from within, he enters, head uncovered, bows before the pyramid, and makes the blinding sign before the Superior, who remains covered and seated; hereafter, he goes to his seat at the Superior's right, the first chair in the row, and hangs the Order jewel around his neck. After the knock (which must always be answered from without and repeated from within), the *Cancellarius*[21] or, if none is present, the *Quaestor*, follows him in the same manner. The *Cancellarius* takes his seat at his table, and the *Quaestor* at the back to the left, on the first chair. Now follows the *Secretarius,* who takes his seat at the chancellery table. Next, the other members enter, in order of seniority. The last member locks the door. If an Introduction is taking place, it is the Censor who locks the door. The knocks are given with a key.

Now the Introduction is performed, if such a ceremony is scheduled. Once all members are quietly seated, the Illustrious [Superior] rises and greets the mem-

[21] Lat. *Chancellor.*

75

bers in attendance by removing his hat and passing it across his face down to his chest. He then puts it on again and asks: 'Dear Brother Censor! Is the Assembly tyled?' The Censor bows and makes the blinding sign, verifies and corrects the locks on the doors, then returns and says, bowing and giving the sign: 'Illustrious Superior, the Assembly is tyled.'

The Superior: Dear Brother Censor! It is not enough that the Assembly is tyled. Commence your work; see to it that no son of darkness is present. Remove all the profane!

The Censor goes forth, bows, gives the blinding sign, and says: 'Br. *Quaestor,* give me the watchword.' The *Quaestor* does so, and all others follow suit, giving the watchword to the Censor, who goes from one to the other, letting him whisper it in his ear.

This watchword is: 'ἑκάς, ἑκάς, εστὲ βέβηλοι.[22]

Once this is corrected, the Censor says to the Superior with the customary ceremonial: 'Illustrious Superior, there is no son of darkness in this Assembly.' Following this, the Censor also gives the watchword to the Superior, who receives it standing and bareheaded.

However, should it happen that someone cannot give the watchword, the Censor says to the Superior: 'Illustrious Superior! There is a son of darkness among us." The Superior replies to this: 'We know him not, as long as he does not make himself known to us.' He demands the watchword from him once more and has him punished. The Censor does this and fines him e.g. to pay a monthly fee for his negligence. However, if he still cannot give the watchword, all present shout: 'ἑκάς, ἑκάς ὅστις ἄλιτρος!'[23] The erring man is required to remove himself immediately from the Assembly upon this call. With the Superior's approval, a contribution to the poor box may return him to the present Assembly.

Once all this is corrected, the Superior gives the appropriate two knocks, removes his hat in the manner described and, after he has covered himself once more, removes the shade from the lamp and asks aloud:

'Dear Brothers, who among you can see the light?' The Brethren give the blinding sign until the lamp is covered again with the shade.

The Superior: You want to see the light, but your eyes are weak. He who wants

---

[22] Gr. 'Away, away, ye profane.' From the Eleusinian mysteries.

[23] Gr. 'Away, away, ye who are sinful.' From Callimachus: Hymn to Apollo.

to see the light, his heart must be pure, and so must his mind, his thoughts, words, and works; he must observe our holy Statutes. – Dear Brother Censor! Have you no complaint against the present Brethren? Are they pure in thought, word, and works?

The Censor (standing:) Illustrious Superior! I am to judge others, but am I, in your eyes, pure in thought, word, and works?

If the Superior has a complaint against the Censor, he gives him the reproach slip[24], adding: 'Better yourself and others.' If, however, he has no complaint, he says to him: 'I find you just, but are the other Brethren also?' Now the Censor hands out the reproach slips. But if he has no complaints, he says: 'Illustrious Superior, all is just.' Thereafter, the Superior gives his two knocks and summons the *Quaestor:* 'Dear Brother *Quaestor,* if the Brethren are pure in heart, ensure that they pity the poor Brethren.' The *Quaestor* then rises, takes up the poor box, bows, and presents it to the Superior, saying: 'Have pity on the destitute Br.!' He holds his hat over the box so that he cannot see what every member puts into it, and so the box is passed around. It is up to everyone how much he wishes to give, but everyone must give something. It must be noted that, when in Assembly, everyone must be addressed by his ☉ name or the title of his office. While the *Quaestor* walks around, two wax candles are lit, and after the work of love of collection is completed, the Superior opens the Assembly with two knocks. Unless someone has been specifically designated to do so, the youngest Brother must then read an uplifting ode. Here is one which has been translated and first chosen for his purpose:

Ode to Wisdom[25]

The solitary Bird of Night
Thro' the pale Shades now wings his Flight,
   And quits the Time-shook Tow'r:
Where, shelter'd from the Blaze of Day,
In philosophic Gloom he lay,
   Beneath his Ivy Bow'r.

---

[24] *Unsigned responses to the quibus licet slips submitted by the members.*

[25] *Elizabeth Carter: Poems on Several Occasions, London ²1766, pp. 85–90. First published, anonymously, in 1747. A German translation was made in 1756 by Johann Peter Uz. It underwent several revisions; the version copied by the Illuminati was that of 1768. See J. P. Uz: Sämtliche poetische Werke, ed. by A[ugust] Sauer, Stuttgart 1890, pp. 141–45.*

With Joy I hear the solemn Sound,
Which Midnight Echoes waft around,
  And sighing Gales repeat:
Fav'rite of *Pallas!* I attend,
And faithful to thy summons bend,
  At Wisdom's awful Seat.

She loves the cool, the silent Eve,
Where no false Shows of Life deceive
  Beneath the lunar Ray:
Here Folly drops each vain Disguise,
Nor sport her gayly-colour'd Dyes,
  As in the Glare of Day.

O *Pallas!* Queen of ev'ry Art
'That glads the Sense, or mends the Heart,'
  Blest Source of purer Joys:
In ev'ry Form of Beauty bright,
That captivates the mental Sight
  With Pleasure and Surprize!

To thy unspotted Shrine I bow,
Assist thy modest Suppliant's Vow,
  That breathes no wild Desires:
But taught by thy unerring Rules,
To shun the fruitless Wish of Fools,
  To nobler Views aspires.

Not *Fortune*'s Gem, *Ambition*'s Plume,
Nor Cythérea's fading Bloom,
  Be Objects of my Pray'r:
Let Av'rice, Vanity, and Pride,
These glitt'ring envy'd Toys divide
  The dull Rewards of Care.

To me thy better Gifts impart,
Each moral Beauty of the Heart,
   By studious Thought refin'd:
For Wealth, the Smiles of glad Content,
For Pow'r, its amplest, best Extent,
   An Empire o'er my Mind.

When Fortune drops her gay Parade,
When Pleasure's transient Roses fade,
   And wither in the Tomb:
Unchang'd is thy immortal Prize,
Thy ever-verdant Lawrels rise
   In undecaying Bloom.

By thee protected, I defy
The Coxcomb's Sneer, the stupid Lie
   Of Ignorance and Spite:
Alike contemn the leaden Fool,
And all the pointed Ridicule
   Of undiscerning Wit.

From Envy, Hurry, Noise, and Strife,
The dull Impertinence of Life,
   In thy Retreat I rest:
Pursue thee to the peaceful Groves,
Where *Plato's* sacred Spirit roves
   In all thy Graces drest.

He bid *Ilyssus'* tuneful Stream
Convey thy philosophic Theme
   Of Perfect, Fair, and Good:
Attentive *Athens* caught the Sound,
And all her list'ning Sons around,
   In awful Silence stood.

Reclaim'd her wild licentious Youth,
Confest the potent Voice of Truth,
   And felt i[t]s just Controul:
The Passions ceas'd their loud Alarms,
And Virtue's soft persuasive Charms
   O'er all their Senses stole.

O send her sure, her steady Ray,
To regulate my doubtful Way,
   Thro' Life's perplexing Road:
The Mists of Error to controul,
And thro' i[t]s Gloom direct my Soul
   To Happiness and Good.

Beneath her clear discerning Eye
The visionary Shadows fly
   Of Folly's painted Show:
She sees, thro' ev'ry fair Disguise,
That all, but *Virtue*'s solid Joys,
   Are Vanity and Woe.[26]

After the ode has been read, the Brother who has read it returns to his place. Then the Chancellor or the Secretary announces any orders, assignments, requests, etc. After that, the Statutes are read, first the general ones, then the ones for this degree; sometimes only one or the other, depending on the circumstances. Then the Superior says: 'The Statutes of our wise founders charge us, dear Brothers, to better and illuminate our spirits in our Assemblies. Thus, first hear the teachings of wisdom with which I have acquainted myself, and then tell me how you have nourished your spirit.' Now the Superior reads some beautiful passage from the Bible or from Seneca, Epictetus, Marcus Aurelius, Confucius,

[26] *The thirteenth and fourteenth stanzas do not appear in the German version recited by the Illuminati. They are:*

'Thy Breath inspires the Poet's Song,   *No more to fabled Names confin'd,*
The Patriot's free, unbiass'd tongue,   *To Thee! Supreme, all-perfect Mind,*
* The Hero's gen'rous Strife:*   * My Thoughts direct their flight:*
Thine are Retirement's silent Joys,   *Wisdom's thy gift, and all her Force.*
And all the sweet engaging Ties   *From Thee deriv'd, unchanging Source*
* Of still, domestic Life.*   * Of intellectual Light!'*

etc. This passage must be selected in such a manner that it applies to any flaws that have occurred and which must be remedied. When the lecture is over, the Superior says: 'I have nourished myself and you with the spirit of the Ancients (or the Bible). Is there not someone among you who would like to educate us with his own works?' Now the Brethren read, one after the other, either their own works or those submitted by others.

After a knock is given, one after the other rises and is asked:

1) What book he is reading?

2) What he has chiefly read in the meantime?

3) What new things he has discovered therein that strike him as especially useful?

4) What work he is doing for the Order?

Now the speaker chosen for this day delivers a speech or treatise that ought to be of practical relevance and must not consist of empty compliments. On special holidays the Superior delivers the speech himself. In general, he often reads out a short address before the Assembly is closed. When all this is concluded, the Superior gives the customary two knocks and says: 'Dear Brothers! My eyes and spirit are brightened; can you also see the light as I can?' He then takes the shade from the light. The Brethren rise, view it, and give the blinding sign; so does the Censor, but not the Superior. The latter says: 'Your eyes see more brightly, your spirits are clearer; you have taken another step towards the light; but darkness and stupor have not yet fully retreated from you. Go forth now and further prepare yourself for the great day of light.'

He then blows out the light, rises, greets the Brethren with his head bared, and says: 'Brother Censor! Teach us a maxim.' The Censor recites one. The Superior then signs the minutes and takes them and the other documents into safekeeping. The Assembly is thus closed. Afterwards, the members may enjoy a small meal at this or another house, but the following should be observed:

1) That it may not be financed from the Order's coffers.

2) That no meat dishes of any kind and no beer should be consumed, but

3) only fruits, bread, and wine (which must however be mixed with water).

4) And that strict temperance and morality must be observed here.

A.

B.

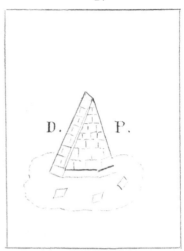

A. Description of the painting hanging above the Superior's chair.

B. Drawing of the carpet lying on the floor.

CALENDARIUM.

According to our calendar the year begins on March 21st. The 10 remaining days are rolled over to the following month.

1st month. Pharavardin, from March 21st to the end of April, has 41 days. Of these, the following are holidays: 1) the first of the month, that is March 21st, and 2) *every new moon.*

2nd month. Adarpahasht, May; holy are: 1) every new moon, 2) the 7th day.

3rd month. Chardad, June; holy are 1) every new moon, 2) the 24th.

4th month. Thirmeh, July; here, every new moon is holy.

5th month. Merdedmeh, August; here, every new moon is holy.

6th month. Shaharimeh, September; holy are 1) every new moon, 2) the 23rd.

7th month. Meharmeh, October; holy, every new moon.

8th month. Abenmeh, November; holy, every new moon.

9th month. Adarmeh, December; holy: 1) every new moon, 2) the 21st and the 27th.

10th month. Dimeh, January; holy, 1) the first, 2) every new moon.

11th month. Benmeh, February; holy, every new moon.

12th month. Asphandar, March; has only 20 days, holy are: every new moon and the last day, or the equinox.

Holy days are primarily those days which are dedicated to smaller and greater ☉ Assemblies and on which the Brethren of the ☉ mainly dedicate themselves to work for the Order. The numbering of the years, as well as the accompanying term Jezded[ger]d,[27] dates from a remarkable epoch in the Order's history. Thus one would count, for example, the year of our Lord 700, from the beginning of spring, as 70 Jezdedgerd. The true and original chronology stretches out over much longer periods of time, as will be proven in due course.

Note. If spring begins before or after March 21st, one begins the year on the day the sun enters the sign of Aries, adding the extra days to our first month.

Benmeh 16th, 1150 is the same as February 16th, 1781.

$$
\begin{array}{lr}
 & 700 \\
\text{minus} & 70, \\
\text{equals} & 630 \\
\text{add} & \underline{1150} \\
 & 1780.
\end{array}
$$

CORRECT PRONUNCIATION AND SPELLING OF THE PERSIAN MONTHS OF OUR CALENDAR.

Pharvardîn	April
Ardibehesht	May
Chordâd	June
Tir	July
Mordâd	August
Shahriver	September
Meher	October
Abân	November
Ader	December
Dey or Dee	January
Bahman	February
Esphendarmad	March

Meh is sometimes suffixed to the name; however, it is not strictly a part of it, but just means 'month' and can therefore be omitted.

---

[27]   *The Zoroastrian calendar, still in use today, begins with the accession in 632 of Yazdegerd III (†651), the last king of the Sasanian dynasty.*

3. *Minervalis illuminatus,* or *Illuminatus minor*
(the Lesser *Illuminati* Degree)

The O. medallion is the same as that of the Minervals, only it is worn with a wider ribbon over the right shoulder, down to the left side.

INSTRUCTIONS FOR THE SUPERIOR OF THE MINERVAL CHURCH CONCERNING THE ISSUING OF THIS DEGREE.

In the lowest Class the Minerval has worked on purifying his intellect. In order to be further promoted he must become a Freemason, but he may still obtain this degree without being a Freemason, and in such a case, the ritual will be modified accordingly.

If he wishes to become a Freemason, he must contact the ☉, which will provide him with proper instruction how to join a sister Lodge, so that he is not led astray elsewhere.

If the Minerval has received the authentic three symbolic degrees of Freemasonry, which provide him with the means to consider higher matters; if his heart and mind are properly prepared; if he yearns for higher knowledge and increased agency; if he has thus given proof of:

a) Morality,

b) enlightenment,

c) loyalty:

then, and only then, will he be accepted into this degree. While still frequenting the Minerval Assemblies as before, he is now entrusted with supervising and observing a small number of Minervals about whom he frequently reports to the Superiors, either in writing along with his Q. L. or orally, when the Superior calls together the Lesser *Illuminati,* which happens as often as he deems necessary.

The *Illuminati minores* must also accept that they are tasked with correspondence and other work for the Order.

It is in this degree that the main education finally begins; if the Superior wishes to suggest someone for this degree, he must therefore choose the best, most dedicated, and most industrious man from among the other Minervals.

Having received permission from the higher Superiors, he sets a date for the initiation. The following must be observed:

1) The Candidate must not know that he is about to be promoted.

2) The members gather without any ceremonial. Present are the Superior, the Secretary, and a Deputy who is appointed [beforehand] and who has to deliver the following address (Addendum A.). However, all other members may also attend the initiation. The initiation address is seen here as a text containing some obscure and not yet fully elaborated passages on which the members of this degree offer their comments and present practical speeches, the topics of which are given by the Superior.

This discussion is then followed by Addenda B. and C. Instruction D. is not read out; instead, a written copy is handed to the new Initiate immediately after the initiation.

After this, the wide ribbon is placed around his neck, and he is given the grip which is done by gently pressing with one's thumb the back of the other's hand three times when one grasps it. The *sign* is described below. The words are the same as in the Minerval degree.

Then the Minerval symbols (Addendum E.) are explained to him, and he is told which Minervals he must supervise from now on.

Ordinary Assemblies are often held on the same day as the Magistrates Assemblies, right after the conclusion of their business, since the *Illuminati minores* enter at this point.

Since the ultimate purpose of this degree is to train people who will properly guide and lead the Minervals in the spirit and principles of the Order; and since they are to refine themselves by educating others:

1) Every *Illuminatus minor* must supervise two Minervals or more, according to his circumstances and the approval of the Superiors, who will [either assign them to him or] let him choose for himself those over whom he has more influence than anyone else.

2) He must teach these people all the principles of this degree, educate them according to these, and devote all his energies towards this purpose; they must become the chief object of his studies; he must practise his knowledge of human nature upon them.

3) He must visit them, or they must visit him, daily if possible, and he must take note of all their opinions, utterances, gestures, flaws, and virtues.

4) During the Assemblies he reads out the observations he has made throughout the month. He indicates how he has applied to them the maxims he has learnt here, what results this has had; how he intends to treat them, and in what respect they must still be changed.

These observations must not be made casually or in passing; instead, attention must be focused on the finest detail. It would not be acceptable to excuse oneself by saying that one has not noticed a single thing in the whole month. Since every man must speak and act throughout the whole month, it is obviously a sign of the observer's careless laziness if he cannot report anything at all, and the Superior must not suffer such negligence. Everyone takes these observations back with him, keeping them for future use.

5) When in doubt on how to conduct oneself towards one's subordinates one may request the other members' advice, and in this case each of them takes his turn giving his opinion.

After this work is completed, the tables are presented, examined, and corrected, person after person, and then submitted to the higher Superiors. There should be no Minerval who has not been referred to an *Illuminatus minor* for instruction and about whom a full report has not been given in this Assembly.

In his reports the Superior notifies the higher Superiors to what extent the *Illuminati minores* have fulfilled their duties.

In addition, minor matters of the Minerval Class are included, decided, and expedited here.

Except for the Lesson attached (Addendum D.) and the *Instructio pro recipientibus* the *Illuminati minores* are not handed anything for safe-keeping. Anyone can read Addenda A., B., and C. in his Superior's chamber as often as likes, but he may not take the least part of them home.

Since the fundamental education begins in this Class, the ☉ cannot emphasise strongly enough to each and every Superior the importance of the most exacting precision and punctuality in his subordinates. Too much indulgence and kindness or even negligence and laziness would be such a crime that it would have a most detrimental effect not only on all of the lower degrees but on the higher ones as well. The highest degree of vigilance over the subordinate flock is therefore necessary. This is why the Superior and his Censor alone must complete the tables for the members in this Class in the greatest detail, most carefully noting therein to what extent his men's conduct towards others conforms to the regulations.

Do not think, ye Superiors! that one can lead men and educate them permanently, and still indulge in one's own convenience. Men are reared by constant, sensible, and timely encouragement, by good example and by persistent diligence. The flock thrives by the shepherd's eye, and the providence of good, watchful, and tireless men creates other good men in turn. Thus if you seek to harvest, first till and cultivate your field, and then wait until the time for harvest, your reward, is at hand. Do not weary of your labours, because by improving others you will also improve yourselves.

[Addendum] A. ADDRESS DURING THE INITIATION OF AN *ILLUMINATUS MINOR.*

As has been previously stated, a Deputy steps forth without the Candidate's knowledge and petitions his promotion.

The Deputy. Illustrious Superior! I am submitting a petition.

Superior. What is it about?

Dep. A member of our Illust. ☉'s Minerval Class wishes to be promoted.

Sup. Promoted? That depends on him and upon whether he has done what is necessary for his promotion.

Dep. He is a man of much experience, with whom this anxious caution is unnecessary.

Sup. He may have experienced much, but he has not yet experienced what he needs for our purpose. He may have seen as much of the world as he will, yet with regards to our purpose we still view him as someone in need of our guidance. He may have experienced many good things, but also much that is evil. Who will vouch to us that he has not been lured away by evil? Experience *in the world* is good, but it is not yet experience *in the Order.* Every class needs its own instruction, its own teachers; he who is not willing to submit to our instruction is of no use to us.

Dep. He is not only experienced in the world, he is also a Mason, and he has experience with secret mystery schools.

Sup. If this is so, he will also have learnt that these often make many promises and keep only few. But if he has found satisfaction in Freemasonry or another secret society, then why does he not remain there? What does he seek from us?

Dep. He seeks better instruction from us, but he believes we might deliver just as little.

Sup. These are the words of a man who has often been deceived in great expectations. But can he judge us before he has reached the end?

Dep. He still cannot see any decisive indications of the importance of our cause. He wishes to see proof.

Sup. This we do not give, nor do we promise anything, and this must be proof enough for the wise. We would have to reveal to him that which we must carefully hide from him if we were to [prematurely convince] him of our [institutions' greatness. If he does not trust our] righteousness and prudence[,] he may think what he will. If he is too impatient to wait for its unfolding, if he wishes to do nothing to accelerate its development, then let him remain where he is and judge us as he will. Our foundation is laid in such a manner that the cautious preparation and education of our fellow Brethren would be laughable, were it not the groundwork for great things to come. We do not care whether we have many followers or few. We ask no one to remain with us. We are concerned neither with money, nor with power and prestige. No man is useful to us if he has not been trained according to our intentions. If all of this does not speak for us, he shall hold to the purpose shown in the General Statutes of the Order: if he does not believe that everything we do surely leads to this purpose, he may resign.

Dep. But in this manner we shall have few members indeed.

Sup. Neither do we desire and seek many. The crowd does not make the ☉. A single man who submits to our intentions is worth more than a thousand wilful men, and a single man who does not act according to the Statutes can hinder and destroy the entire structure by his poor example.

Dep. But how can one achieve great intentions without many collaborators?

Sup. What we seek is not accomplished by the throng. It is better to labour for centuries but with safe steps than destroy the work of millennia with a single misstep.

Dep. But we still see no fruits from our labour. The world is as bad as before. Illustrious Superior! these are not my doubts; I speak the words of another.

Sup. Perhaps the fruit of our labour is that the world has not grown worse. *He who wants to do everything at once will accomplish nothing. Great endeavours are brought about by infinitely small changes. What we achieve must be enduring and permanent,* and for this, time is needed. As long as you do not know this, as long as you wish to enjoy fruits before they are ripe, you are not yet the man who should ask for more. What use are all his experiences, if the man does not know *that nothing yields later results than goodness, if these fruits are to be permanent?*

Dep. But nowhere does one hear of our association.

Sup. Nor should one. *Part of our strength lies in our secrecy.* And yet, one knows us all too well, *having sought us out too fervently.*

Dep. This secrecy might lead my friend to suspect that the Order may perhaps be new.

Sup. Let him believe that, too; let him think *we* have founded it ourselves. He who seeks us out of his attachment to antiquity, who is not enthralled by the goodness of our cause, is not welcome among us. Anyone may view himself as the founder of this society, since we must not offer any explanation in this matter anyway! *May he regard himself as the first benefactor [of the human race]! It requires more greatness to plant a tree for posterity even though one will not live to rest in its shade than it does to enjoy the fruits of our forefathers' labours without reproducing them. Our Illust. Order is good not because it has come down to us from antiquity. Furthermore, very little has been achieved compared to that which still remains to be done.* Your Candidate, however, seems to eschew work. Does he like taking his seat at the set table to enjoy the work of others?

Dep. He does not, but he despairs of his advancement in the ☉ if only perfect persons are of use in it.

Sup. If this were the case, we would be long extinct. Human we shall always be; and among us there may be some who are very weak. We are content if the flaws decrease over time. But we can take pride in the fact *that our society has been preserved as flawlessly as is possible for a human institution.* If he has found immoral men in our midst, it was certainly only among the lower degrees, where such risks must be taken to see what may become of these people, and when they fail, it is not always prudent to exclude them; but these can never harm the ☉, *and with all their might and all the riches of the world it is still impossible for them to rise to higher ranks.* The higher the degrees, the purer and more refined are our members, but they are also fewer in number. In the highest degree there are never more men than are necessary to preserve certain secrets that were intended for the very few. Before he can reach it, a man must undergo all kinds of purifications, and we are told: *'The angels rejoice when such a man is found, and in him one may see what heights human nature can reach.'*

Dep. But how long does it take to reach this stage? Life is almost too short for this.

Sup. As long as it takes to remove the dross – longer for some, faster for others. *It depends on each individual, how soon and with how much zeal he begins to work. One can say that every man promotes himself.* The ☉ can only give pointers in this matter. If he does not follow these pointers, if he does not pay attention to every detail, if he carelessly passes up good opportunities, regards himself in too bright a light, underestimates the flaws in himself, does not seek to improve them, suppresses the ideas and inclinations that the ☉ subtly attempts to awaken in him, then he cannot blame the ☉ if he falls behind, turns grey or even passes away without having reached the goal. *This is our way of proceeding, and it has not been introduced by us, but it was established in the nature of things by the Creator Himself. Our hands are tied. But all who teach true wisdom proceed as we do, and he who does not reach the goal with us will not find the true goal elsewhere either.* But here is consolation for the weaker ones: he who does not reach the end despite his honest industry will find that none of his labours go unrewarded. Every degree has its own important lesson; every member can contribute to the perfection of the whole; each of our steps is a step closer to perfection, to elevation; every degree provides new insights, a new perspective to endeavours worthy of a sensible man; each of these labours is an essential part of our felicity, better enables us to affect others and to bring about good things, not to mention material benefits. *He who merely seeks the latter and to satisfy his passions with us seeks in vain: but he who demands greater enlightenment, who is concerned with the improvement of his heart and the appreciation of his nature can find with us as much as he can bear throughout every period of his life.*

Do people really think this is such an easy task, a day's work, that we can change them thus at once? They, whom we have taken into our care, in the midst of the world's clamour, with all their harmful inclinations, passions, propensities, surrounded by miserable examples, poorly raised, and encumbered with a thousand prejudices? How much effort does it not require to even instil a doubt, inspire the thought that they might become better, to change their perspective, to weaken their old propensities, implant new ones and strengthen these, to give them full control over these harmful ones, to prevent the old ones from stirring within them again and to encourage them to pay attention to themselves, to teach them to mistrust themselves, even where they appear in the brightest light? Is it the ☉'s fault that nearly all of them are still children in this respect, that they are ill, and the more so when they seem to be feel most healthy? Honour even to him whom the ☉ admits to only the lowest Class; it is proof that he is a better man and that, with all his flaws, he has at least the potential and ability to become excellent under our guidance! Thus, even our lowest Class is ennobling – judge for yourself what the higher ones accomplish! – *And he to whom this does not seem important, let him sink back into the abyss from which we lifted him for a while.*

And now, worthy Brother! who is this malcontent who so bitterly complains, who wants to harvest where he has not sown, who so greatly enjoys how other heads and hands have paved his way and laboured on his behalf, who only seeks pleasure and does not want to do anything for others, who demands so much and gives nothing, who claims to have unearthed all of nature's secrets but does not know his own self, he who wishes to see without eyes – what is his name? (The Deputy takes the Candidate by the hand, lets him rise, and leads him to the Superior.)

Dep. Illustrious Superior! I know not if these are his thoughts, but he himself is present. Let him present his own case. It is N. N. who stands before you. Maybe he has not thought all these things, but perhaps he has. Others may offer him these objections, and therefore he must be instructed what to say to them in reply. Your instruction will have assuaged him if he had any doubts. Illustrious Superior! once again I petition his promotion.

Sup. Thus it is you, N. N., who demand promotion and further insights? But if you think what Brother N. (name of the Deputy) has stated in your name: I cannot grant your wish. *Grumbling, impatience, and discontent are not the paths by which one gains it.* No degree can be extorted by force, nor can it be purchased in any way. We do not impose ourselves upon the malcontents. No man has the right to complain about the basic foundations, since anyone may shake off this yoke at will and at any time, and seek satisfaction elsewhere.

However, you may be in the wrong or perhaps not know yourself well enough, or you may not have weighed your own interests against [those] of the society. Thus I will teach you a lesson that everyone of this degree in the ☉ receives. It is my hope that this lesson will assuage you; may you be satisfied now or not. Now take your seat and give me your complete attention.

(The Candidate seats himself on a chair close to the Superior, which has been placed there for him, and the Deputy seats himself in his usual place.)

[Addendum] B. INSTRUCTIONS FOR A BETTER UNDERSTANDING OF THE ORDER'S ORGANISATION.

When men form an association for specific purposes it is a sign that they do not yet have everything they desire, that they are still searching for something, and that they place in this something they seek and yet still lack a part of their felicity, which remains imperfect until it has been found. *Thus, a member of any society must first of all be filled with love for its purpose.* And the greater the love, the more indispensable to our felicity we believe that which we are seeking to be, the more tightly knit is this union.

Not every man [seeks] the same from a society. Diverse opinions make for diverse wishes; *thus, a society that could satisfy every honourable wish would also be the most perfect.*

However, there are certain general deficiencies in the world which the wise and just men of any epoch would like to see remedied. When we see that every man could be happy in this beautiful world but that our own felicity cannot be permanent because it is often disturbed by the fate of our brothers and the malice of those who have lost their way, when we see that evil men are so powerful, more powerful than the good, that the allure of vice is so strong that any solitary struggle against it must be fruitless, that a truthful man's honesty barely goes unpunished: it is only natural that the desire arises for nobler, more worthy persons to enter into a durable alliance with one another, an alliance that can never be severed nor desecrated, one that will strike fear into the hearts of the evil, assist all good persons without distinction in gaining tranquillity, contentment, and security for themselves, will first shackle vice and then curb it by the strongest means, by means that promote virtue as well as goodwill and make the hitherto weak appeals to righteousness more palpable, powerful, and attractive by means founded on a higher understanding of human nature. Such a purpose of a secret association would not only be most innocuous, surely it would be the most noble purpose a sensible, reasonable man could desire.

But where is this excellent society, this foundation, this foretaste of heaven on earth? Where is this order which intrudes so little upon the domestic and other affairs of its members, which stirs and nurtures so few deceptive desires and passions, which labours only for the edification and improvement of man and possesses securely-founded institutions for this purpose, where political conditions can effect no change? The order that judges men only by their true goodness, their inner worth, where dissimulation is powerless and even the [most] artful deceiver stands exposed, where all artifices of evil men are rendered ineffective, where every virtue, where the smallest moral deed shall find its certain reward without fail, where one conducts oneself only according to grand and general principles, where one is numbed against all baser interests, where one is stirred only to affect the grand and the general, where one's soul is inflamed with noble enthusiasm towards every grand design; where is the society that will solve the hitherto unsolvable problem *to ensure the victory of good over evil?* Where is the society that gathers the most capable minds in every class, which encourages them when their courage has failed them, to labour and to become grand; which pulls every thinker out of the dust, making his ideas shine again, which increases the paths to knowledge with the increase of its membership, multiplying them infinitely, thus uniting the greatest intellects with an unbreakable band; where everyone works hand in glove with the other, where even the weakest becomes the teacher of the greatest, where the individual's insights become the insights of all, where the unknowing can begin where the knowing have left off, where no insights are lost but are preserved from one person to the next among the elect? Where do you find this source of all knowledge, all ancient and new wisdom, this abode of peace, this refuge for the unhappy, this sanctuary from persecution? – What if our Order were this society? Would it be deserving of your membership[? Not only of your membership], but also of your greatest efforts and activity? Yes! You have found this society. It is the very same, if we do not desecrate it: *However, not words are required [here], but deeds.* You had never heard of this society before? Then commiserate our fate with me, for we have to keep secret while pursuing our great and unselfish work; or do you not yet know how powerful evil men are, and how easily virtue can become a crime? We have not always been what we are now, we did not always labour as we do now. The time of completion [has not yet arrived], and our toils and struggles are far from over. Do not imagine our cause as an easy one or as one already accomplished! Imagine yourself as the founder of this alliance. Do you have the courage to fight for the good cause, not to allow any false lustre or passion to lead you from the straight and narrow path? Do you know how much is required for this and that you must begin by working against yourself? Have you thoroughly considered what such a society, composed of the best, most unselfish and enlightened persons, can and must accomplish? Are you fully prepared not to be a useless member, and do you intend to place yourself in our care? Do you see in our incipient establishments the first foundations that promise the fulfilment of such great purposes, or do you find fault with them? Would you have set them up differently? Or does their goal not seem noble or general enough to you? We shall spare you the trouble of answering these questions, and we are convinced that a man of your heart and mind will not carelessly view such a prospect to fulfil his holy purpose. Decide now whether or not we promise too much when we say our endeavours enable us to know and achieve more than other men. *Where else shall be the seat of wisdom, where shall a man make his discoveries, where can one achieve great things, if not where the most insightful men labour with joint forces and use tools unavailable to the rest of the world, and where one is furthermore led by the short[est] route?* However, should you have found greater efforts elsewhere that are more useful to the world, we tell you once more to return thence. We do not wish to deceive you with false expectations. *You should judge us only by our efforts, rather than believe that we have already accomplished any of our goals.*

But do you not think, my friend! that one requires certain extraordinary resources for such *great purposes?* Do you believe that every man is immediately capable as soon as we have picked him from the crowd, the way he is? Do you think that his preparation is a day's work? Or that we possess the panacea that will turn all evil persons or even only mediocre ones into saints? Do you believe that every man can act according to his instinct here? *In our association, everyone must have the same purpose before his eyes, doing only that which certainly leads to the goal, and must refrain from doing anything else.* All members must be filled with enthusiasm for this goal: and if this address has inclined you towards our purpose, *then our spirit rests and hovers above [you,] he who has looked into your heart [will not abandon you], and you are called upon to do what has been predestined. But it would be better if he who remains cold and indifferent, he in whom the desire to become great and good cannot be awakened, had never been born. He is lost to us, and we to him!* Grieve and wail, ye noble ones, that there will always be those who remain cold and immovable towards their sense of destiny and the dignity of their own nature! You have lost a soul on its way to purification. In this respect, there must only be one will amongst ourselves. From your actions it should never be apparent that there are more of you; all must be united in a single interest, or you will never reach that which you seek, that which is so dear to you. Not every man is suited to this task. Even a better man does not attain greatness of the soul and power over his passions all at once: This self-abnegation, often so essential, only arises when love for the purpose becomes weightier, and without this preponderance, without this direction towards the general, this difficult purpose remains mere speculation. Therefore, do not trust everyone who claims to have the general good in mind; his deeds must speak for themselves. Our smallest actions must lead towards the great goal; only thus can we create concordance, the tight bond, without which every society is powerless. Not all deeds lead to the goal with equal certainty, least of all those that satisfy our private interests. Their relation to the whole must always be observed. It is obvious that in such a society not everyone can do as he pleases; from time to time he must sacrifice his freedom. If he wanted to act as if he had no one to answer to but himself, and if everyone were to act in the same way, the goal would be missed. There must be Superiors, and they are only Superiors because they oversee the entire system, because they have passed every examination and undergone all preparations. They have made laws, but he who obeys them does not obey the whims of other men, but acts in his own interest, which is none other than to see this dear purpose fulfilled. The Superiors know best which actions safely lead to this goal; therefore it is proper to obey them. Thus, if we are taken no further, if we are not promoted as quickly as we desire, we can be sure that this is so because we are not yet arrived where we should have, that we are not enlightened enough, because we have not risen far enough above our prejudices, passions, and private interests. The Superiors can have no other reasons. They would like to see the whole world on the uppermost tier! In addition we are often only held back to test our dedication, our steadfastness, and our patience: that is a real test, when intimate wishes are not always satisfied and curiosity, ambition, lust for power, sensuality, and routine are combatted. Few persons endure it, but those few who do gain happiness, serenity, and immortality. And what a comfort [it must be] to belong to the few noble souls who have elevated themselves above so many that were too weak to reach the goal! It makes us truly cherish the small circle of Brethren who have also resisted those false temptations and persevered.

It is true that no struggle is harder than the struggle against oneself, but then no victory is more glorious. It is by this self-denial that you must prove that of which you are capable. It is toilsome indeed, but toil is the price of honour. The gate to our Sanctum is barred to those who succumb. You will be tried in many ways. At times the O. may show you the very opposite of your desires. – Behold (he makes the sign of the degree, raising the right-hand index finger in a warning gesture) and mark this well. You may not hear this voice of warning again so soon. But you will see this sign when the danger of succumbing seems greatest. Remember then this hour of your initiation and these words of warning: *Take heed that you do not fall*. This is the motto of this degree: *Cave ne cadas*.[28]

Your fall would be all the more shameful and dangerous since I am here to entrust you now with the guidance and leadership of others. It is your responsibility to lead them by your example, because their eyes are upon you. Look after these young pupils diligently and carefully. Do not think that this Class is insig-

---

[28] *Plautus: Mostellaria v. 324.*

nificant because your thirst for secrets has [not yet] been stilled here. This Class is the foundation of the ☉. In it, you work on the foundation of an edifice that shall endure for the unity and benefit of the human race. This Class leads *to the greatest of all secrets, one that so many have ardently desired and which they have often sought fruitlessly: the art of governing men, leading them to goodness, transforming them into good men and then to achieve with them everything which until now seemed a dream to most and possible only to the most enlightened.* This then is the great art: to execute everything that is good without resistance, to eliminate flaws, remove obstacles, to pull evil out by the root – in short, to accomplish that which all institutions, education, morals, state constitutions, and even religion itself have hitherto failed to bring about.

Now follows:

[Addendum] C. INSTRUCTIONS FOR THE EDUCATION OF USEFUL COLLABORATORS.

I. Take careful note of every one of your subordinates, observe him during occasions where he may be tempted to act differently than he should. This is the moment where it becomes apparent how far he has progressed: observe him where he believes to be unobserved; where the desire for fame and applause, fear of reprimand, shame, and punishment cannot influence his actions. Record everything carefully. This will be immensely helpful both for yourself and your men.

II. Your passions, inclinations, or aversions must not, however, influence your observations. Do not believe that a man is thoroughly good only because he has one excellent quality shining forth; or, by the same token, that he is evil because one all too noticeable stain tarnishes him. Many judges of human nature make this mistake and are immediately captivated.

III. Do not allow yourself to be seduced by persons who demonstrate brilliant powers of intellect either, even though one might expect them to have risen above the general opinion. All too often they disappoint once one becomes more familiar with them, being proud, too unrestrained, vain, and quarrelsome; and because many of them know and are able to prove the most wonderful principles but only few truly feel that which they are wont to tell, they often lack the noblest quality of all: a good, kind heart. Further, you should not allow yourself to be seduced by someone who agrees with you. There is a difference between being convinced of a proposition and applying it in practice. Today, they may agree with you on everything, and tomorrow they may do the opposite of what they held for true; or someone may agree with you because he was swept away by your eloquence at the time, or because he was courting your favour, or out of fear, or to probe your mind. Only his deeds will tell if he was truly convinced of and permeated by the truth. Most dangerous is the approval someone gives you for a truth that runs counter to his own interests or contradicts his favourite passions and skills. It takes time to defeat these; the proof that these are completely eradicated must be established in practice, and this is where most men fail.

IV. Do not readily trust the wealthy and those of noble birth. Their conversion is always slow. The former are too unfamiliar with suffering and need; the latter are encumbered with the prejudices which come with their status, and they always want to be first. This is not quickly cast off, and it shines through at the first opportunity.

V. Above all else, it is a good heart which you must search for in your men and which you must educate with the greatest care. However, it is not the one who boasts of having a good heart who actually has one. It is the same with good health, which one never notices while one enjoys it. *He who does not close his ears to the suffering, who does not harden his heart against gentle compassion and is a friend and brother to the wretched; he who loves all creatures and does not even trample the worm writhing underfoot on purpose; he whose heart is inclined towards love and friendship, who is steadfast in adversity [and tirelessly carries out a good work he has begun, undaunted by the difficulties he may need to overcome]; he who does not mock the weaker; he whose soul is open to grand designs, desirous of rising above all base interests and of distinguishing itself through great benefactions; he who eschews idleness; he who does not consider any insight that he has the opportunity to gain as useless but keeps pursuing the knowledge of man as his main study; he who has the courage to rise above the approval of the crowd and great men alike where truth and virtue are concerned, following his heart instead – this is a man for us.* And this is the measure by which you must teach your subordinates, enlarge their souls, and divert them from everything base. He who clings too much to petty things, whose perspective is too narrow, he who cannot rise above his narrow circumstances – he is useless to us.

VI. Read good books with your subordinates, books that are easily understood, rich in images, and that exalt the soul. Speak to them often, not from the head, but the heart. You must be ablaze if others are to be warmed by your fire.

Therefore your words must be lively; but let an innocent and simple heart do the speaking where eloquence is lacking. You must understand how to awaken lively desires and resolutions. Your men must yearn for the hour when they can bring all these things to fruition. You must demonstrate that you are serious, that you are permeated by the truth and goodness of the cause, that this is no idle speculation, and that you truly feel what you say. But be careful that your deeds do not speak the opposite. Furthermore, no watery declamations, no sapless morality, no subtle and useless metaphysics that do not make man any better. Everything must be vivid, full of images and examples, immediately applying a proposition to specific instances, demonstrating its results, importance, and usefulness.

VII. Above all, awaken a love towards the cause, describe it as grand, important, and bound to their own interests and to each individual's favourite [passions]. *Everyone must believe to find what he is seeking.* Describe the suffering in the world; vividly demonstrate what men are, what they could become, what they should do, how they [can perceive] their own true interests, [to what great extent the Order promotes this,] and how much its foundation shines through [even] in the lowest Class; and what they can further expect.

VIII. Earn their love and trust, but also their respect and reverence; avoid familiarity and the opportunity to show weakness in the presence of your subordinates.

IX. Always speak of the ☉ with earnestness and majesty; it certainly deserves this.

X. Infuse the subordinates with fondness and respect for the Superiors. Help them [understand] the necessity of subordination in well-ordered societies: the military and other organisations will provide examples of this. The best method of teaching others how to conduct themselves towards Superiors is by honouring them yourself, even if you had the inclination and occasion to be dissatisfied.

XI. Your subordinates must work, read, think, feel, and act. Practise with them, awaken their courage. Show them the benefits of all their labours. Work is easy when one can see the benefits, when the matter is not made difficult for us, when what is interesting about it is demonstrated in detail, when the matter is not presented too dryly, trivially, or speculatively. You will discover in time where your men are lacking, but you must deal with each of them in his own manner to make the subject attractive to him. *One can do anything with men if one can use their prevailing inclinations to one's advantage.*

XII. *Man's foremost study is the knowledge of man.*[29] Make this especially interesting for your pupils. Whoever develops a liking for it is not lost to us. He will learn the art of *evaluating others, leading them, and of conducting himself in such a manner that others think well of him. He learns to be prudent, he becomes aware of himself, thus becoming a better man.*

XIII. Begin with small experiments. Casually ask your men easy questions that are oriented towards exploring the nature of man, regardless of any pretence. In the beginning these questions must be easy, so that they can be answered immediately and orally. Even if your knowledge is superior, let your pupils' answers appear better than your own at first. This will encourage them, and you will find an opportunity to express your opinions soon enough. Speak to them on an equal footing and share your observations about physiognomies, gait, voices, and the like. Praise your pupils; tell the first he has the potential to become an excellent judge of human nature, that he only lacks practice; praise the next in front of a group of people, so that he may come to learn about it; refer to him young, curious persons who seek to be instructed by him and who admire him. He will then want to show more of himself and, by teaching, will learn more himself.

XIV. And since you now realise how much effort is required to bring men to where one expects them to be, you must miss no opportunity, anywhere and as much as you can, to spread healthy principles and awaken courage and resolution. But when doing so remember this: it is impossible to cope with the many. He who wishes to change all will change no one. Therefore, share this work with the members of this degree in your location. Choose one or two Minervals, three at most, with whom you enjoy the most respect and credit, and whom you can best measure up to. Invest [all] your efforts and care in these men. *You will certainly have accomplished something great if you have educated three good men over the course of your life.* These then must be the subject of your observations and the focus of your constant attention. If one kind of treatment fails, try another until you find the right method. You must know what your man is inclined to do at any time, how much he expects, and which intermediate propositions he still lacks in order to applaud the main propositions. *It requires great skill to take advantage of the true and right moment.* Often heated passion is needed, and at other times composure. Yet your people must not ascribe their transformation to you, but to themselves. You must be the invisible tool. Do not act in the heat of

---

[29] *Allusion to Alexander Pope's dictum 'The proper study of mankind is man' (in his Essay on Man, 1734).*

THE SECRET SCHOOL OF WISDOM

the moment, do not contradict: hear him out, even if he is wrong. *Never dispute the conclusions, only the underlying principle!* Anticipate the moment when this can happen, at which you can introduce your thoughts without giving the appearance of contradiction. Preferably, you can arrange to have the same dispute in his presence with another person in whom you are less interested or with whom you have arranged this, in a setting where he is only a listener, not taking sides. And then present all reasons in their full strength!

XV. [Never] present those errors and flaws that you would like to see changed in him as his own. Tell him what he has done as if a third person had done it. Ask him for advice on the matter. *He must become his own judge* and cast his own verdict.

XVI. All this takes time, however. Do not regret the effort and time you spend, even if years should pass; no time is wasted, and the foundation must be solid. Do not hasten anything. Your subordinate must develop consistency and skill. By often reading, thinking, and hearing the same things, one gradually acquires the skill and ultimately the habit of thinking in this and no other way. Therefore, this must be your craft: to put their duties and the principles they are to adhere to before their eyes frequently, so that everything reminds them of that which they are to become.

XVII. Therefore, do not demand too much at once. Treat your pupils carefully, fatherly, and studiously.

XVIII. Never despair of their improvement. *Men can be changed into anything.* Most are only evil because they find no interest in being good. This ambition must therefore be awakened in them. The mainsprings of actions stemming from experience and education, as well as their principles, must be explored, and if they are found to be useless, they must be weakened, so that they do not resist. But for this, a deep wisdom is required.

XIX. Looking at various religions, state constitutions, sects, and societies, we see how easily men can be so enthralled by matters with which they have been born and raised, even if they are truly worthless and are despised by all others, that they will take steps that are evidently counter to their interests and sacrifice their lives, possessions, and blood to the most foolhardy systems. If some dull monk can induce the most prudent man to entrust him, in his enthusiasm, with his most intimate thoughts, one has to concede that men can indeed be moved to anything if only one understands their weakness, and that reason and consideration guide their steps less often than habit and prejudice. If enthusiasm for folly can be ingrained in us, the reason for our failure to tilt the scales in favour of truth and virtue must be found in our approach. Success will be certain *if one uses the same means to enforce good that deceit uses for evil. Evil men only have their way all the time because the good are too quiescent and fearful.* There are occasions when one must show gall to protect the rights of man.

XX. Ensure that your men are loyal to the ☉ only because of the goodness of its cause, and that they are indifferent to its antiquity, proliferation, power, reputation, and wealth. They must only look to the goodness of the matter, the organisation, the use of resources, the selection, treatment, instruction, and behaviour of the members, order, interconnection, subordination, the reputation of the Superiors, their prudence, the varying of their behaviour to suit different cases, difficulty of advancement, unselfishness, equality of social classes, freedom from prejudice. *A thinking man will soon discover that nothing under the sun is impossible in such a society.* He will also easily foresee that in such institutions his ambition, love of power, his desire for [serenity and security] and his thirst for secret knowledge and hidden insights will certainly be taken into account and not forgotten. *But he must not imagine all these things to be the main and final purpose; they are only natural consequences of that for which he has been prepared,* results that are never manifested if everyone does not work with all his might to first bring about their causes. He must first learn the fine art of cultivating sensible desires.

XXI. Tell your people without hesitation or reservation that the ☉ asks no one to join or stay. It does not care how few or how many members it has, whether they are rich or poor, sons of princes or craftsmen. High-born and wealthy persons it seeks the least because they seldom succeed. They should deem themselves fortunate if they are accepted. Usually, their good fortunes and circumstances prevent them from understanding just how much men need one another, and for this reason they are rarely good persons. But we do not summarily exclude them if they comply and do not seek to assert their worldly status. They must learn the meaning of true nobility and be prepared to accept a man they may deem far inferior to them in civil life in a much higher position. He in whose mouth this leaves a bitter taste may resign, and may even become our enemy: we do not fear him; he will hurt himself by missing the opportunity to become, with our support, that to which his station and birth have doubly called him, and in which he has now been surpassed by the lowest member. Incidentally, we begrudge no one the satisfaction to arrive at their goal faster and more securely in another society;

we only regret we do not know of a society in which this more rapid transformation can be brought about, and where one knows the art of using lowly and mediocre people for great purposes or of teaching higher insights to men who have no solid understanding of even the most lowly truths. Meanwhile, should such a miraculous society exist, we are convinced that it would approve of our more cautious approach and not favour the man who did not find it to his liking. Meanwhile, we keep to ourselves, obey the honourable regulations of the Superiors, work in peace and persecute no one. – If you follow these instructions and train just two persons according to these principles, you will have done much for the world.

XXII. Carefully seize those moments when your pupil is dissatisfied with the world, when things do not go as he pleases. Such occasions, where even the mightiest feels how much he needs his fellow man, and how many better institutions could still be made, are the times you should use to sensitise his softened disposition even more. It is here that you must demonstrate to him the usefulness of a secret association of proven men. You will not fail to encounter such moments even with the mightiest men, when you are able to penetrate their weak side.

XXIII. Do not rush to believe that if your subordinates obey your will and orders in one instance, they will certainly do the same in another. It requires much more time to form a habit. Perhaps their compliance was brought about by fear, hope, or the satisfaction of a passion: men do not become good this quickly. It is better to assume the worst. The careless heart is only too fickle.

XXIV. Never nurture deceptive hopes in anyone; promise little, so that you can achieve even more. Encourage the downcast man; seek to confront the boisterous with doubtfulness and the prospect of danger in order to curb their excesses. *A reasonable man should hope in bad fortune, and fear in good.*

These, then, are our lessons for becoming a good and safe guide of promising men. Increase the host of the noble and elect in this manner, and if you have ever valued your own felicity, then be resolved, according to our instructions, *to rescue so many thousands of men who so easily could and would be good from the fatal necessity of being evil.* Most people are only evil because the preponderance of evil men holds all the power to make people happy or miserable, and because, with this evident imbalance, nothing seems to be left for virtue but to be silent, to suffer, to bow, or even to succumb to vice. Believe [us]! because we know it from experience: *divest vice of its strength and tilt the scales in favour of virtue, and all will be well with the world. Vice is only so powerful because the good are either too idle or allow themselves to be separated, because they console themselves with visions of the future without making preparations for such a revolution; because they wish time to accomplish everything while in the meantime, they would rather yield than take action against the realm of vice.*

However, these men, highly praised for their goodness, are only good in the negative. While abstaining from all insults, they never curb evil due to their fear, timidity, and idleness, even though doing so may well be in their power[;] if they were convinced that virtue lay not in mere patience but mainly in action and work, and not in tranquillity and insouciance, they would awaken from their slumber. They are weak because they pass up every opportunity to strengthen themselves. They lose courage and they despair when there is still hope for victory, and for this precise reason are they overcome and led into servitude, because they pay homage to vice themselves, neither contradicting nor ending it, because they even honour it outwardly despite their inner revulsion. They take the villain under their wing, providing him with room and board, flattery and caresses in the hope that this will prevent further losses, and even go as far as handing him weapons to use against them. They prefer to align themselves with vice in quiet collaboration before they make the effort to seek out noble men to unite against malice. What moral code can justify this shameful behaviour, unworthy of a man of resolve and honour? Everyone should walk the path of virtue, far removed from such base politics, and courageously step into the way of vice! Close ranks, ye faithful, and you shall be strong and invincible. If you are too weak alone, then suffer until you are stronger, but miss no opportunity to strengthen yourself. Look to your Brethren for help: they will not abandon you, if you are the man you are meant to be. Trust the ☉ faithfully. It can accomplish anything if only one follow its instructions. *We work to repay the deserving whose wages have been wrested away unrightfully, to give strength to the weak, to give the fallen the means to redeem himself, to bind the villain, and to return mankind to its high dignity.* This is the second, promised Canaan, the land of plenty and of blessing, which sadly so many see only from afar. Flee, ye unholy, no one unprepared shall approach the Sanctum, guarded by the Legion of the Elect!

But come, ye nobler ones! with reverence and fear! Receive our blessing even from afar, come ye who are sick and suffering! Despair of your cure if your ailments are not healed here.

[Addendum] D. A LESSON THE *ILLUMINATI MINORES* RECEIVE IN WRITING.

Since this degree of the Illust. ☉ is entrusted with the direction of the lower Class, we cannot overemphasise to its members just how important their office is. The Minerval Class is the ☉'s foundation. If the base is poor, one cannot contemplate achieving lofty goals.

Everything depends on four components, namely:

I. The manner of proliferation.

II. The education of the Minervals.

III. Maintaining zeal, and

IV. obedience and subordination.

Under the supervision of the *Illuminati* new members are introduced to the ☉; it is therefore necessary

I. *to give them instruction in the principles followed by the Illust. Superiors with regard to its proliferation.* While it is certainly in their interests to see the ☉ being spread further, the greatest caution must be used in doing so. The zest for expansion that leads other societies to take many harmful measures has no place here. Our society is not right for everyone, and only the elect may partake in this bliss, but of these there are still only a few in the world, and in future, the human race will have our efforts to thank for the increase in the number of nobler persons through our education. Therefore, although the ☉ has members scattered throughout all parts of the world, there are actually very few of them, especially in the higher degrees. The lengthy training in any case makes the business of proliferation more difficult; hence the ☉ only desires it if it can be achieved safely.

A. These principles the *Illuminati* should

1) thoroughly ingrain in all their subordinates.

2) Only choose those men for recruiting efforts on whom they can fully rely.

3) Explain and recommend to these persons what has been prescribed only briefly in the Instructions for Recipients.

B. When selecting the Candidates one must look at

1) *the heart;* they should be upright, sensitive, good-natured, earnest, moral, and obedient men.

2) *The mind.* They must be capable, scientifically-minded, inquisitive, and attentive.

3) *Temperament and education.* They should be active and lively, well-mannered, not proud but discreet, modest, magnanimous, satisfied, sociable, moderate, and generous; they should also be good hosts.

4) *External circumstances.* One shall recruit young persons as much as possible, and those who in future may have to thank the ☉ for their employment, but not too many destitute men who might become a liability to the ☉, unless they have extraordinary qualities. One must also consider their relatives and other civil connections. If, however, the man is truly excellent, all of this does not apply.

C. The Superior concerned shall thoroughly investigate each of these characteristics in every prospective recruit and instruct the Recipient accordingly. Once the Candidate is accepted, the second main point will be:

II. *His further education.* This includes:

A. The most intimate knowledge of the subordinate's ways of thinking. It is gained

1) when the Superior treats his subordinate in such a cordial manner that the latter develops a child-like trust in him and is willing to divulge every thought to him.

2) When he observes him thoroughly and has him thoroughly observed by others. This is why the *Illuminati* must share in the supervision of the Brethren and keep diaries containing the minutest notes on their subordinates' seemingly most insignificant actions. They must compare these diaries later during their Assemblies and compile the *conduite*[30] lists they have to submit on this basis.

3) The allotted *pensa* serve this purpose. If, for example, one would like to know someone's opinion on a certain topic, the man is asked to write an essay about it. This not only provides him with the opportunity to think about the topic more thoroughly, but the Superior will also see the full force of his reasons, which he must refute if they are unsound.

4) The Superior should, from time to time, seize the opportunity to test the subordinate, e.g. his general sophistication, his ability to keep silent, etc.

Once one knows one's own people, all that matters is

B. how to further treat and guide them. Here, of course, one must consider

[30] *Fr. Conduct.*

temperament and other circumstances: therefore, this cannot be discussed in general terms. However, it is possible to point out the techniques that should be used. Among these, most of all

1) setting a good example in any kind of virtue and skill.

2) One's treatment of subordinates, which must combine seriousness and severity with gentlemanly benevolence and friendship. The Superior, even the unknown Superior, should distinguish himself with a certain respectability and dignity when dealing with his subordinates.

3) Diffusing the spirit of the Order, so that all of its members are ensouled by a noble enthusiasm and only speak about the ☉ in one way. To achieve this, one should

a) never speak about the ☉ without reverence and enthusiasm.

b) Use every opportune moment to extol the unselfishness of its purpose, its glorious institutions, the advantages enjoyed by its members, and the difficulties involved in achieving these great benefits in such a manner that they stir a new desire to gain such happiness by fulfilling one's duties.

4) Teachings, lessons, and warnings. Cold declamations, watery, repetitive moralising, and tedious lectures cannot serve this purpose. One should not so much [prescribe] good deeds as prevent evil [ones]. Powerful speeches suited to the occasion, a word spoken at the right moment when a person is in the right mood to receive it and, finally, the reading of inspiring literature and interaction with refined society must play their part here.

5) Punctiliousness in all affairs.

6) Finally, practical guidance in all the required virtues.

Once the members have been thus educated, if one has successfully shown them how much the application of each virtue serves their own interest, then all that matters is keeping them faithful to the Order.

III. This *allegiance* is achieved

1) by not neglecting subordinates, by gathering them together often, keeping them active, seeing them, speaking with them, i.e. always renewing their impressions and making the ☉ their favourite subject.

2) By removing any doubts that might arise within them so that they fully trust in the goodness of the matter. Where one's own knowledge is insuffi-

cient, higher Superiors should be asked for advice.

3) By stirring great expectations without promising anything. Only here and there should a word about future disclosures be dropped, as if spoken in passing, and always very mysteriously when doing so, thus stimulating curiosity and allure by means of secrecy.

4) By the Superiors' conduct, which must always be commensurately cordial or reserved, depending on the subordinate's demeanour.

5) By the Superior's efforts to exemplify those qualities that the subordinate especially values.

IV. *Thus, it will be easy to gain reverence, obedience, and loyalty. Especially*

1) by exemplifying these things in one's conduct towards one's own Superiors.

2) By only giving few orders and never arbitrarily, while strictly enforcing their observance.

3) By rewarding the obedient and mercilessly punishing transgressors.

4) By skilfully removing recalcitrant persons.

5) By issuing few, but firm reproaches.

6) By avoiding familiarity with subordinates.

7) By avoiding all opportunities to receive favours from them and by thus solely and unselfishly acting in the interest of the whole.

8) By never flaunting one's own greater insights and by avoiding to abuse one's standing to force one's opinion onto the subordinates; by thanking the ☉ for all one's knowledge and by ascribing all one's orders to the Superiors.

It would lead too far to deliberate all the other cases that might arise, but we place our trust in the *Illuminati*'s own judgement and in the counsel they receive from their Superiors.

[Addendum] E. EXPLANATION OF THE MINERVAL ALLEGORIES.

You are now entrusted with the care of young pupils who shall be enlightened under your leadership and educated by wisdom. This work requires vigilance, industry, and energy. Let the letters inscribed on the Order's seal, P. M.C.V., remind you of this; they stand for: *Per Me Coeci vident*[31].

---

[31] Lat. *Through me the blind see.*

Now take a look at the pyramid you can find depicted on the carpet of the Minerval Church and around which lie scattered here a number of separate stones! This is the symbol of our Illust. ☉, which takes large steps closer to its goal only if the members join forces in working towards its attainment for the honour of the Supreme Architect and the happiness of the world; which is why you find written here: *Deo Proximo,*[32] D. P.

The image of Pallas[33] and the owl signify wisdom and vigilance. These must make us into men first, and then the spirit drawn forth from the darkness binds the prejudices and raging passions, just as Pallas holds fast the Gorgon's head.[34] Only then do we raise ourselves from the class of animals to the highest step, where we learn to get to know ourselves, the world, and the Most Supreme Architect, and we reach this step through our efforts to gain wisdom and virtue. For this, however, one requires courage, zeal, and a brow that radiates honesty, just like the helmet on Minerva's head.

A clean conscience withstands ridicule and slander, just as the shield is impenetrable to any weapon. The spear is the symbol of steadfastness and resolution. The pitcher indicates moderation, the pillar steadfastness, the quiver with the arrows signifies the power of eloquence when it springs from the fullness of the heart, while the palm branch symbolises peace, patience, and serenity. The three lamps point to the three main divisions of the Illust. ☉. Two are unlit, but they lead to the greater light in the higher Class; at the same time they are a symbol of nightly diligence, of sacred darkness, secrecy, and reservation. Our light shines quietly, without any ostentatious gleam. The Brethren must never flaunt their knowledge, must tolerate the weaker just as they do the enlightened ones, and always be inwardly happy and content.

The three feet of the lamps stand for silence, obedience, and moderation. Their foundation and focus is industriousness, and this is what we now primarily expect of you in this new career. Take your place among the ranks of collaborators.

Following this initiation, other matters are dealt with, if time permits.

---

[32] *Lat. Close to God (or God is with us).*

[33] *Athena, also known as Pallas Athena, the Greek goddess of wisdom and warfare, identified with Minerva in Roman mythology.*

[34] *According to Greek mythology, Medusa, one of the Gorgons, a family of monsters, was beheaded by Perseus, a son of Zeus, who gave her head to Athena, his half-sister, to place it on her shield.*

4. Initiation of a Magistrate of the Minerval Church

A rough sketch of the Minerval Magistracy signet. The meaning of the letters is as follows: Sigill. Eccles. Minerval. E[des]s.[35], and so the last letter is changed according to the name of the place in question.

INTRODUCTION.

This is not a degree of the Order but only a ceremony devised for the Lesser *Illuminatus* once he is called upon to serve as a Magistrate in the Minerval Assembly; from then on, he takes part in the Magistrates Assemblies.

CEREMONIES FOR THE INITIATION OF A MAGISTRATE.

At a table the other Magistrates are seated, along with any other higher ☉ members who might be in attendance. The *Magister constituens* is at the head, while two Assessors sit at the opposite end. All are dressed in black and wear the Master Mason's apron, as well as the O. jewel. The Superior and Assessors carry [small] gavels. The Superior knocks twice ♪♪, and the two Assessors answer in kind.

Then, after the Superior has briefed the Assembly about the reason for today's gathering, a member is ordered to bring the *Constituendus* to the door. The *Introductor* goes forth, divests the *Constituendus* of hat and rapier, and leads him by the hand to the door after he has passed on the hat and rapier to the Superior by means of a Serving Brother or a Chancellery clerk who has accompanied him; ♪♪.

The *Constituendus* is also dressed as a Mason.

Jr. Warden or Assessor. ♪♪ The knock of a Minerval.

---

[35] Lat. *Sigillum Ecclesiae Minervalis Edessensis, Seal of the Minerval Church of Edessa (i.e. Frankfurt).*

Sr. Warden. ♪♪. Illustrious Superior! The knock of a Minerval.

Superior. ♪♪.

Introductor. ♫♪.

Jr. Warden. ♫♪. The knock of a Mason.

Sr. Warden. ♫♪. The knock of a Mason.

Superior. ♫♪.

Introductor. ♪♪♪.

Jr. Warden. ♪♪♪. The knock of an *Illuminatus*.

Sr. Warden. ♪♪♪. The knock of an *Illuminatus*.

Superior. ♪♪♪. See who is there.

Sr. Warden. See who is there.

Jr. Warden (goes to the door.) Who is there[?] (Meanwhile, the members all rise.)

Introductor. An *Illuminatus* and Master Mason, who is led here on the orders of the Illust. Superiors, so that he may be initiated into the Magistracy of the Minervals.

Jr. Warden (repeats this.)

Sr. Warden (likewise.)

Superior. What is the Candidate's name?

Introductor (states his ☉ name.)

Jr. Warden (repeats it.)

Sr. Warden (likewise.)

Superior. Let him enter. (He is led in and stands to the side of the Superior, who asks him:) Brother N. N., are you a Minerval?

Constituendus. Yes.

Superior. Prove yourself as one to Brother Jr. Warden, N. N.

Constituendus (goes over and does so with signs, words, and grips.)

Jr. Warden Illust. Superior! The Brother N. N. is a Minerval.

Sup. Brother N. N., are you a Freemason?

Con. Yes, my Brethren, etc.

Sup. Prove yourself as one to Brother Sr. Warden, N. N.

(*Constituendus* does so.)

Sr. Warden Illust. Superior! The Brother N. N. is a true Master Mason by the radiance of the light.

Sup. Brother N. N., are you an *Illuminatus*?

Con. Yes, Illustrious Superior!

Sup. Prove yourself as one! (*Constituendus* does so, and the Superior continues:) If you are truly illustrious, you must surpass your subordinates not only in virtue but also in wisdom. The Superiors are satisfied with your zeal to attain it as well as your conduct, and you have been led here on the orders of the Illust. Superiors (he removes his hat), as a reward for your diligence, to enter the Magistracy of the Minerval Class. Maintain this zeal of yours. We entrust you with the office of a ... for the Minerval Assembly in ... . Here you receive your instructions, and I remind you to follow them strictly. (He hands him a copy of the instructions for the entire Magistracy as well as the addendum for the specific office he is to hold.) I so appoint you to your new office; in the name of our Illustrious Superiors (he takes off his hat) receive from me the kiss of peace (he kisses his right eye), the kiss of wisdom (now the brow), the kiss of the bond (he kisses his left eye). (He puts his hat back on and takes the *Constituendus'* rapier in hand.) This rapier is an outward sign of your dignity, but only the Superior wears it during the Assembly. Draw it in time of need, only in the defence of your rights, for the aid of innocence distressed, the punishment of perjurers and the protection of the distressed. (With the gavel he gives the ♪♪ on the rapier's pommel.) Make your Brethren worthy Minervals! ♪♪♪. See to it that they ever become more illustrious. ♫♪. Remain a true Mason, and in your Assemblies, allow not that the Royal Art be disparaged. (He puts the hat on his head.) As the hat covers the head, so shall virtue and wisdom cover the Brethren enveloped therein. Now take your seat.

After this ceremony, everything which normally occurs in the Magistrates Assemblies is conducted, and the Assembly is then closed.

Other than on such solemn days, the Magistrates Assemblies are held without any ceremonial, without aprons, sashes, lamps, etc.

INSTRUCTIONS FOR THE MINERVAL MAGISTRACY.

The Magistracy proper consists of the Superior, Censor, Quaestor, and Secretary. Every member must follow precisely the specific instructions for his office.

In order to ensure that the proceedings are always conducted in an orderly manner, we wish to clearly define the tasks during these meetings.

I. It is understood that the Magistracy meets at least once a month.

II. It is primarily the Superior's responsibility to look after the members in his Assembly and the Recipients residing in his Parish, to maintain good order, and to care for their proper instruction; however, we also wish to assign to the other Magistrates the task of supervising the stated subordinates and would like to urge them to ease the Superior's burden of work in this respect.

III. At the Magistracy meetings the events that have occurred during the month are reported, and the Secretary enters these into the minutes.

IV. To ensure that everything is reported, every member of the Magistracy must keep a detailed diary.

V. At least once a month the Superior files a report on his Assembly's growth, specifically: the Initiates, *Recepti, or Insinuati* with their initiation date as well as their conduct, unless he has received special orders in this matter.

VI. All Obligations and minutes of the initiations and Assemblies are attached to the Magistracy minutes, and the Superior then sends them to the *Illuminati* Assembly. The same goes for all *quibus licet* slips; they are handed over at the end of each month to the Superior, who in turn dates, numbers, and labels them with the sender's name. Members who have not submitted a *quibus licet* are listed in the minutes.

VII. The Superior counts the votes and, if the vote is unanimous, he makes his pronouncement. He must sign all the minutes.

VIII. The Public Censor reports on the conduct of the members as well as the *Recepti.* Only particularly noteworthy items are entered into the minutes; the Censor must however go into greater detail when compiling the tables, which he then submits to the Superior for correction.

IX. The Quaestor reports what dues, alms, or fines he has collected during the month; this is why the poor-box, the key to which is in the Superior's possession, is opened during the Magistrates Assembly.

X. The Quaestor submits a financial report every quarter, and every six months he hands over the remaining cash balance to the Superior against a receipt, as stated in his instructions.

XI. The Magistracy's other duties shall be:

A. To make provisional decisions in urgent cases.

B. To assign the day, hour, and participants for the initiations and meetings.

C. To determine the fines as prescribed by the Statutes.

D. To add opinions to the reports.

E. To have the Secretary enter the bibliographies submitted by the Initiates into the general catalogue maintained by this Magistracy, and to see whether the *desiderata,* if these are submitted, can be acquired.

F. To become thoroughly acquainted with the Statutes and to have them read out at the Magistracy meetings from time to time.

G. To distribute amongst themselves and assess the monthly essays written either by the Magistrates themselves or received from their subordinates.

XII. All orders not addressed to the Minerval Assembly as a whole are opened by the Magistracy, and the necessary actions taken to execute them. Thus, the Magistracy must send the necessary notifications to all the absent Brethren within its jurisdiction and ensure that these are promptly drawn up by the Secretary.

XIII. Dispatches are signed by the Secretary alone and are formalised with a signature along with the Minerval Assembly's seal, which is held by the Superior.

XIV. In general terms this Magistracy is wholly subordinate to the *Illuminati* Assembly, holds no powers other than those conveyed by this Assembly, and must report all proceedings to it.

XV. The archive will be entrusted to that Magistrate who can offer the best and most secure place for them; every quarter, after an index has been compiled, it is sealed and, with the exception of those documents that are still in use, handed to the Superior for further delivery.

INSTRUCTIO PRO SUPERIORI.

As with all other Magistrates, the Superior of the Minerval Assembly is appointed by the Provincial Superior and installed according to the ritual. His office and duties are primarily the following:

I. As he holds the highest rank among his Brethren, he shall strive to surpass them all in virtue and wisdom. Examples are more potent than orders. The earnestness of a sage, though without any rigidity, fatherly kindness and, lastly, a judge's strictness shall earn him his Brethren's love and admiration.

II. He must endeavour to gain and keep his subordinates' full trust.

III. Thus, he must not only follow the statutes and by-laws with the utmost precision himself but must also be diligent in ensuring that they are strictly observed by all others.

IV. He provides proper instruction to the Recipients on how to conduct themselves towards their *Insinuati* or *Recepti* and shows them the required books, as well as the method of annotating them.

V. From time to time he reads and takes notes with his immediate subordinates, encouraging them to do the same with their respective subordinates.

VI. In general he must endeavour to keep his people occupied, to as far as possible accustom them to and encourage them in the habits of work, industry, silence, and obedience, and to ensure that all members are nourished and imbued with the spirit of the society.

VII. He shall expect to receive letters from absent members within his jurisdiction every fortnight with strict regularity, and will reply to them as swiftly as possible. All subordinates must return his replies with their next letters, as no subordinate may keep a handwritten document by his Superior.

VIII. Furthermore, he must require timely submission of the slips headed *quibus licet* from present as well as absent members and forward these to his own Superiors unopened.

IX. If these Superiors are not located in the same place, and the entire Assembly is subordinate to one that is located in a distant town, he must write to that Assembly every fortnight, submit reports, and wherever these members are allowed to make autonomous decisions, he should expect a most expedient reply.

X. However, if he is answerable to an *Illuminati* Assembly in the same town, he must submit everything there and await the Assembly's decisions. When so ordered, he meets with the Superiors of this *Illuminati* Assembly to consult about necessary actions.

XI. Furthermore, he gathers his Magistracy at least once a month, makes all the necessary arrangements for meetings and receptions, etc. He duly and calmly listens to all viewpoints while weighing up the arguments and counter-arguments, and then makes his decisions according to just and equitable principles and sends the minutes to his Superiors for review and ratification.

XII. If they have something special to report, other members may also be invited to these Magistracy meetings or demanded to give their assessments.

XIII. He holds the counter-lock to the treasury for his degree and, at the end of each quarter, submits the balance statement which has been reviewed in the presence of the Magistracy and signed by all. Every two years the funds are sent to the treasury of the higher degree against a receipt; the funds are also used for justified expenses of the lower degrees on request.

XIV. However, the primary duty of the Superior of any degree is to know his subordinates very well, and he must be so thoroughly familiar with their character that he is able to describe them in the smallest detail.

XV. For this reason he must keep his own records for his subordinate members and enter this information in the respective rubrics, according to the forms.

XVI. He may admit no one to his meetings unless so ordered or if the person to be admitted carries *literae pacis*.[36]

XVII. Everything else is to be found under the specific headings, e.g. 'On the Ceremony', etc. Without special permission he may not communicate anything to a member in writing, the sole exceptions being the *Instructio insinuatorum*[37] and the *Methodum notandi*.[38]

DE OFFICIO CENSORIS.[39]

The Censor is a Magistrate who has been appointed by the Provincial Superior to monitor the Brethren's morals. His office is either public or secret. The *Public Censor* is chiefly responsible only for the gatherings and Assemblies. There, he ensures good order and obedience, prevents outbursts during votes, as well as chatting, arguing, joking, and the like; he censures wrongdoing, records any offences, punishes these with fines appropriate to the circumstances and hands the monies collected to the Quaestor. He also ensures that the meeting is adequately housed and secure, ushers the other members in, hands out the reproach slips, ensures good order, etc.

The *Secret Censor* is unknown to the Brethren and can be changed from time to time; he does not proclaim his charges publicly and has no punitive powers, but discloses his observations solely to the Superiors.

His duties are the following:

I. He must strive to know all the members well and, in particular, he must keep a close eye on the *Insinuati*.

II. Consequently, he must examine his fellow Brethren through close personal contact.

III. When portraying their characters, he must examine both their good and their evil side.

IV. He must focus his attention especially on their minor habits, manners, willingness to serve, and conduct towards the Brethren and the profane.

V. He must discover if they are proud, jealous, wasteful, talkative, lustful, miserly, unaccommodating, crude, intemperate, etc.

VI. He must strive to discover their opinions of others and of the ☉, and whether they are zealous or negligent, loyal or [indifferent].

[36] Lat. *A letter of recommendation.*
[38] Lat. *Method for note-taking.*
[37] Lat. *Instructions for 'Insinuation'.*
[39] Lat. *On the office of the Censor.*

VII. He must observe them in moments of passion, e.g. ascertaining if they remain gentle when their anger has been roused.

VIII. He investigates his subordinates' reputation in the eyes of various [persons].

IX. He must exercise the greatest care to ensure that the Statutes are observed, and report any abuses, conspiracies, and the like to the Superiors.

X. He keeps a detailed log about all these things, which he surrenders to his Superior upon leaving office; he provides excerpts whenever they are requested.

XI. Most of all, he is required to note all good deeds by his fellow Brethren, e.g. self-restraint, growing perfection, kind-heartedness, loyalty, etc., because promotions to the higher degrees mostly depend on these reports.

XII. It goes without saying that the Censors must never base their conclusions on their own inclinations or hatred, but only on the unadulterated truth.

The Public Censor may also be the Secret Censor.

DE OFFICIO QUAESTORIS.[40]

The Quaestor belongs to the Magistracy, and he manages the funds. Therefore he must:

I. Enter all income and expenditure in a separate ledger,

II. not allow any outstanding balances to accrue but must diligently bring any payment notices to the Superiors' attentions and forward these to them.

III. Attach receipts for all payments made.

IV. Collect itemised receipts when someone else advances monies to the ☉ at certain occasions or on the orders of the Superiors.

V. Not incur any major expenditure for himself without prior request or unless so ordered.

VI. And, in general, maintain accurate accounts and endeavour to discover the exact amounts for all expenditures.

VII. Render account every quarter to the Magistracy of this degree, whereupon it is signed by all and submitted to the assigned Superiors.

VIII. The monies must also be sent there every quarter, except for those funds required to cover the expenses. He issues receipts for all money received.

IX. The Assembly's Superior holds the counter-lock.

[40] Lat. On the office of the Paymaster.

DE OFFICIO SECRETARII.[41]

I. The Secretary must possess all the qualities of a privy secretary:

a) Good penmanship,

b) neat, regular handwriting and, evidently,

c) confidentiality.

d) He must have the Superiors' trust.

II. He records the minutes during all initiations (if no other person has been assigned to do so) and writes down the Candidate's answers precisely; he reads the oath to him as well as the minutes, whereupon the Initiate signs them with his ☉ name. Following this, the minutes are put into an envelope and sealed thrice. To the right is the Secretary's signet, to the left that of the Recipient and in the middle the signet of the Plenipotentiary or Superior. He then writes *quibus licet* on the envelope and hands it to the Plenipotentiary.

III. During the Assemblies he announces any orders, reads out the Statutes, records the minutes, enters therein the names of those present, briefly summarises the proceedings and then presents them to the Superior for signing.

IV. In the Magistrates meetings, too, he records the minutes, including any decisions made; he may also vote in these proceedings.

V. All tabular records not under the auspices of the *officio Censoris* or another are also his responsibility.

VI. He must pen all essays and copies but he may not issue anything that has not been revised by the Superior.

VII. He furthermore keeps the archive in good order where he keeps the essays, or at least copies thereof, organised in sections.

VIII. The office clerks, if there any, are subordinate to him, unless there is a Chancellor.

IX. He must be at the Superior's disposal at all occasions in the ☉, and he must submit all original manuscripts and copies wherever appropriate or put them *ad acta*.

---

[41] Lat. *On the office of the Secretary.*

FORM THAT THE SUPERIOR OF A MINERVAL ASSEMBLY CAN USE TO ESTABLISH HIS *CONDUITE* LISTS.

Half year tabular report, on the subordinate Brethren, the month of … until … Year …

	1. N. N.	2. N. N.	3. N. N.	4. N. N.
Character.	A good heart, generous, noble, a little too ambitious.			
Enlightenment.	Full of talent and knowledge, but frequently takes odd paradoxical sentences without due inquiry to be true.			
Degree in the O.	For the past six weeks a Novice.	For the past year a Minerval		
Service to the Order through recruitment, discoveries etc.	He has enlisted the head of the Normal School in …	He has found in … an old important manuscript on …		
Loyalty, Diligence, Obedience.	When one lets him play a role in the Order, then everything will be expected of him. Furthermore he will not easily be won to disloyalty.			
Contributions of money.	He paid all the ordinary monthly dues and has given to the library …			
Civil relationships.	Respected, rich, visible, but persecuted by envy, which yields him too little flexible opportunity.			

II. Freemasonic Class

A) Symbolic Freemasonry
I. Ritual Book for the Three Symbolic Degrees

a copy of which must be before every Worshipful Master and each of the Wardens so they can perform their duties accordingly.

INTRODUCTION.

The egregious abuses and falsifications to which true Freemasonry has been subjected in this century, by which the Royal Art has been desecrated, its hieroglyphs distorted, mingled with false embellishments, and explained carelessly and incorrectly, and which finally, its true perspective having been lost, have made all of Freemasonry become a meeting-place of indolent and vile men, gathered together without discrimination – these abuses have moved our Masters in the East, who until now have quietly watched this dreadful state of affairs and have revealed themselves, for good reason, only to a few Brethren in Germany, to give the small band of true Freemasons instructions by which they can perform their labours in the three symbolic degrees of Freemasonry according to the ancient custom and tradition without being led astray by false doctrines. Here follow the instructions for the Entered Apprentice, Fellow Craft, and Master degrees. May the Supreme Architect of the world bless the small circle of the true followers of the Royal Art, so that it may flourish while the Brethren prepare themselves for higher knowledge and the kingdom of truth becomes great and mighty by the sacred number.

1. Ritual for the Entered Apprentice Lodge.

Place. Every Lodge shall have at least four chambers, these being

1) *the Lodge room,* which is used for initiations, workings and, on occasion, also for Table Lodges.

2) *The dark chamber,* which is wallpapered entirely in black; on a small table are a skull and a small lamp, also a bound book, containing only virgin paper. There are also shackles and chains on the table. The more gruesome this chamber can be made to appear without resorting to childish trifles, the better.

3) *The preparation room.*

4) *The gathering room,* where the Brethren gather before the Lodge is opened.

Time. Lodge should never be held before noon, and it should never be open after midnight, neither for Table Lodges or others.

The ornamentations of the Lodge are blue and gold.

Carpet for the Entered Apprentice Lodge.

Floor Plan of the Lodge Room.

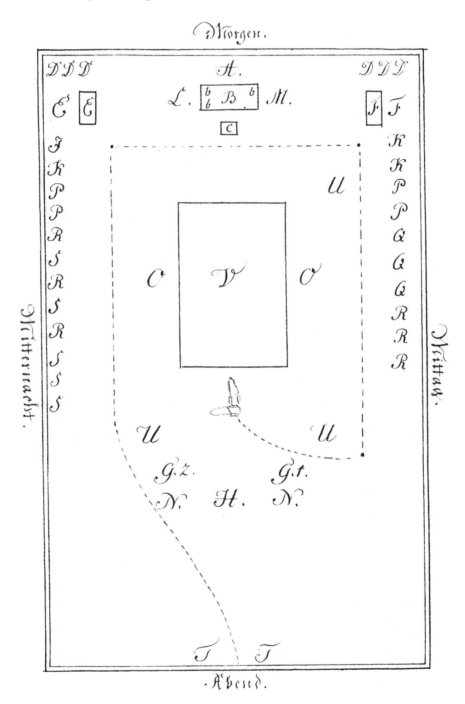

Key.[42]

A. Chair of the Worshipful Master under a celestial canopy.

B. Altar with three lights b.b.b. On the altar lies an open Bible covered by a compass, a tracing board, a rapier, the ritual book and, if initiations are to be made, the aprons and gloves. The Worshipful Master and the Wardens hold gavels in their hands and, like the other Officers, wear the jewels of their offices on a blue ribbon around the neck. Every Lodge has a membership jewel, and every Brother who belongs to it must acquire one and wear it on a blue ribbon suspended from the third button-hole.

C. A padded footstool for kneeling and on it, a square.

D.D.D.D.D. Seats for higher Superiors.

E.E. Chair and table for the secretary. On the table, a light, an ink-well, the minutes, a register of the Br.Br. and the constitution book.

F.F. Chair and table for the Orator. On the table, a light.

G1.G2. Chairs for the Senior and Junior Warden.

H. Master of Ceremonies, who carries a sword.

I. Treasurer.

K.K. Other Officers, Almoner, etc.

L. Deputy Master.

M. Visiting W. Masters, or past W. Master.

N. N. Deputy Wardens, if any.

O.O. Stewards.

P.P.P.P. Visiting Brethren.

Q.Q.Q.Q. Masters.

R.R.R.R. Fellow Crafts.

S.S.S.S. Entered Apprentices.

T.T. Serving Brethren, if they are not otherwise occupied.

U.U.U. The three great pillar-lamps.

V. Carpet.

---

[42] Ger. *Morgen, Mitternacht, Mittag, Abend: morning, midnight, noon, evening.*

BEFORE THE LODGE IS OPENED.

Before a ▭ is opened, the Worshipful Master enters the room with the Wardens and the Officers and, if everything is in order there, asks for the Masters to be called in; he then asks and lets the Wardens inform him if there is strife among the Brethren. If indeed there is a disagreement among some of them, they must make peace publicly or in the side-room and in the presence of an Officer before the opening of the ▭ ; but if they persist in their ill-will towards one another, then both, or the defiant party, must leave the Lodge, and the matter is subsequently reported to a higher authority. The Fellow Crafts are then called in, and among them also all disputes are settled; finally the Entered Apprentices are called in according to the same procedures, all of which must be done by the Master of Ceremonies, who also ushers in the visiting Brethren, after having examined them, leading everyone to his proper place. He must also ensure that everyone is properly attired.

OPENING OF THE ▭.

Worshipful Master. ♪. To order, my Brethren!

Sr. Warden, ♪. To order, my Brethren!

Jr. Warden, ♪. To order, my Brethren!

W. M. Worthy Br. Junior Warden! What is the duty of the Junior Warden?

J. W. To see that the Lodge is tyled.

W. M. Very well, see to your office.

J. W. (draws his rapier, goes forth to lock the doors, and then returns:) Most Worshipful Master, the doors are locked and the profane have been removed. The Lodge is tyled.

W. M. Worthy Br. Senior Warden! What is the time?

S. W. It is high noon.

W. M. Worthy Brother J. Warden! Is it the proper time to open this Entered Apprentice ▭?

J. W. Yes, it is the proper time.

W. M. Then I now open this Lodge in the name of our Illustrious Superiors with this sacred number ♩♩♪.

S. W. ♩♩♪.

J. W. ♩♩♪.

W. M. My Brothers! This Entered Apprentice ☐ is now open.

S. W. (repeats this.)

J. W. (likewise.) (All Brethren draw their rapiers.)

INITIATION INTO THE ENTERED APPRENTICE DEGREE.

Note. The Serving Brethren are initiated in the same manner, except that they are given neither the embrace, nor the hat and rapier.

When the Candidate is led to the Lodge house by his friend, he is not allowed to see any of the Brethren. He is led to the preparation chamber, where his friend may stay with him. He is not locked in the dark chamber earlier than about half an hour before his initiation. Everything should imbue the man with reverence, but nothing may induce terror, reluctance, or boredom. The door of the dark chamber is slammed shut behind him and locked. After the Worshipful Master has indicated to the Brethren that Herr N. N., having been recently chosen for initiation is to be accepted this day and in fact is already waiting in the dark chamber, the Preparer and another Brother are sent to him; both keep their hats on as they enter the preparation chamber, to which they have him brought from the dark chamber by a Serving Brother. After the preparation is complete, they divest him of his hat and rapier and bring them to the Worshipful Master. During and after the preparation various Lodge matters can be conducted and discussed. Soon thereafter, the Worshipful Master sends out the Treasurer to collect the reception fee from the Candidate. When he has returned and given report, the Master of Ceremonies is sent forth to properly divest the Candidate of his clothing and all metal: his right knee bare, his left shoe downtrodden and the left breast bared; the Serving Brethren may help with this. In the meantime sundry matters may be discussed. Once the Candidate is properly prepared and hoodwinked, the Master of Ceremonies leads him to the door and gives three strong knocks with his fist. •. •. •.

J. W. ♫♪. It is the knock of a profane.

S. W. ♫♪. It is the knock of a profane, Most Worshipful Master.

W. M. ♫♪. See who is there.

S. W. (repeats this.)

J. W. (walks to the door, where he remains the entire time until the initiation.) Who is there?

THE SECRET SCHOOL OF WISDOM

M[aster of] C[eremonies]. A free man who wishes to be accepted as a Free-mason.

    J. W. (repeats this.)

    S. W. (likewise.)

    W. M. Ask his name.

    S. W. (repeats this.)

    J. W. What is the stranger's name?

    M. C. (asks him and answers.)

    J. W. (repeats the answer.)

    S. W. (likewise.)

    W. M. Ask him his age!

    S. W. (repeats this.)

    J. W. (likewise.)

    M. C. (asks him and answers.)

    J. W. (repeats the answer.)

    S. W. (likewise.)

    W. M. Ask him his station.

    S. W. (repeats.)

    J. W. (likewise.)

    M. C. (asks him and answers.)

    J. W. (repeats the answer.)

    S. W. (likewise.)

    W. M. Ask him his religion.

    S. W. (repeats.)

    J. W. (likewise.)

    M. C. (asks him and answers.)

    J. W. (repeats the answer.)

    S. W. (likewise.)

    W. M. Ask him his place of residence.

    S. W. (repeats this.)

    J. W. (likewise.)

    M. C. (asks him and answers.)

    J. W. (repeats the answer.)

    S. W. (likewise.)

    W. M. Ask if he is willing to submit to all of our customs.

    S. W. (repeats this.)

J. W. (the same.)

M. C. (asks him and answers.)

J. W. (repeats the answer.)

S. W. (likewise.)

W. M. Ask if he has been divested of all metals.

S. W. (repeats this.)

J. W. (likewise.)

M. C. (answers.)

J. W. (repeats the answer.)

S. W. (likewise.)

W. M. Worthy Brother Jr. Warden! Let him enter and embark on the mysterious journey.

(The Jr. Warden opens the door, receives the Candidate, takes him by the hand, places the tip of the rapier on his breast, and lets him make the journey shown by the small points on the outline of Lodge, but only once, while the Brethren give the traditional sign of the degree when he arrives at the points •, then drop their hands to the side with a sharp stroke, making a noise with their aprons while everyone directs his gaze at the Worshipful Master When the journey is complete, the Candidate is placed between the two Wardens.)

J. W. The Candidate has completed the mysterious journey.

S. W. (repeats this.)

W. M. Worthy Br. Sr. Warden, who is this stranger?

S. W. He is a free man etc. (The W. M. now repeats all previous questions, which are answered by the Sr. Warden right away.)

W. M. Sir! You have been led here at your demand, that you may be accepted into the honourable Order of Free Masons. I leave it to your own conscience to judge you if ignoble intentions have led you to this step.

The Order's inner constitution, too, provides the inevitable punishment for him who approaches this holy threshold, but is driven by insolence, childish curiosity, vanity, or selfishness. None of these goals shall be satisfied and you would only enlarge the great horde of [men] who stroll through the world, bringing shame upon themselves rather than upon the most honourable Order by calling themselves Freemasons, but who have learnt nothing more than a few hieroglyphs that they do not understand in exchange for money wasted. Indeed, Sir! there are many accepted Freemasons, but only few of the working, illuminated, and elect. Yet it is up to you to enlarge this small circle. Examine yourself if noble intentions, the pure purpose of becoming better, wiser, and more useful, and the desire for a holy association of better men fill your heart as you stand before me. – If you feel any other sentiment in your soul, then it would be better that you turn back – you would simply be wasting money and time – we wish to lead you back without harbouring any resentment against you, and your name shall no longer be spoken in our midst. But if you are the man we seek, who one day will see the great light and spread it across the globe, be welcome among us! Now examine yourself; I leave you to your thoughts for a while. (He pauses for a moment.) Now answer me, what have you decided? Do you wish to be accepted? (The Candidate answers.) I must ask you another question. Have you been persuaded or coerced to this step, or is that what you are about to do an act of your own free will? (The Candidate answers.) Then let him come forward, worthy Brother Sr. Warden, and approach me by three steps. (The Candidate is instructed how to do so.)

The feet must form a square.

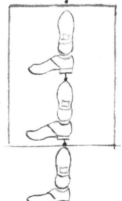

He then must kneel before the altar, his right knee resting on the small padded footstool. His right hand is placed on the Bible. A square lies on the footstool, or it has been stitched or painted thereon. The Bible is opened at the Gospel of Saint John. He must then hold the compass to his bare breast with his left hand.

W. M. Since you have persevered in your decision to be accepted into our honourable Order after being questioned repeatedly, your wish shall now be satisfied. However, first you must give a physical oath of secrecy before the eyes of God. Are you prepared to do so? (He answers.) We acknowledge you as being completely free, do you feel the same? (He answers.) Now repeat after me! (The Brethren remove their hats.)

Oath:

I, N. N., swear to God, the almighty architect of all worlds, a physical oath that I shall not reveal the least part of the secrets of Freemasonry that I have learnt or shall learn to any living creature, by direct or indirect means, nor shall I knowingly allow that any such knowledge shall be revealed – except it be to a lawfully accepted Brother of the same degree as I – thus I obligate myself never to divulge, or allow to be divulged, any of these secrets of Freemasonry by means of speech, writing, sculpting, carving, or engraving, be it on paper, wood, metal, sand, or anything that accepts the impression of a figure – I obligate myself to be compassionate, benevolent, and agreeable towards all men, and especially towards my Brethren; to remain faithful to the Christian religion in which I was raised, the nation in which I reside, and good morals; to render strict obedience to the Superiors and laws of Freemasonry in so far as their commands conflict neither with my other duties nor with my true honour. I shall do everything in my power that will aid the florishing of true Freemasonry and the proliferation of virtue and truth. Should I act in contravention to anything of the above, I wish that my throat be cut and my heart be pierced (the Worshipful Master gives a knock ♪), my belly cut open (the Brethren clash the sabres together), my entrails torn out (another clash), burnt, and the ashes scattered into the winds (another clash) – my body be mutilated, and these bloody remnants cast onto the sands of the sea, where ebb and flow will wash over it twice in in the course of twenty-four hours, so that there remains no remembrance of me – not only among Freemasons and other honest men but also on the entire face of the earth. So help me God. –

W. M. Then I accept you as a true Freemason in the name of the Illustrious Superiors of our Order (♫♪, on the head of the compass), in the name of this just and perfect Lodge ♫♪ and by the power of my office ♫♪. May God bless your labours! Kiss this book, it is the Bible. (The Initiate kisses it.) Rise! (He rises.) Woe to you if your oath has been unworthy! Remember that you have given it of your own free will. Take him back to the gates of the Temple. (The Initiate is once again placed between the two Wardens while the lamps are extinguished and an urn with burning spirit is placed on the altar.)

W. M. My friend, you have given a heavy oath. Now cast your eye on the circle of men you have joined for the first time! Give him the first light. (The Master of Ceremonies removes the blindfold, and all Brethren point their rapiers at him.) Behold the host of men armed and ready to avenge perjury! Should you become a traitor none of your steps on the face of this earth shall be safe.

(All Brethren shout:) Vengeance upon the villain!

W. M. Hoodwink him! (The Master of Ceremonies does so, the lamps are lit, the urn is removed, and the Brethren hold the points of their rapiers aloft.)

W. M. As you have seen these brave men armed for vengeance so you now see us ready to share our wealth and blood with you, if you are faithful. Give him the full light. (The Master of Ceremonies removes the blindfold; all Brethren shout:) Protection, happiness, and blessings to the true Mason!

W. M. Step forward to the altar at which you swore true faith! (The Candidate stands to the right of the altar.) From now on, you will no longer be called a profane but bear the lovable title of Brother. Now receive the white attire of a Freemason! May this hue always remind you that innocence and a pure heart are the first things a Freemason should yearn to possess. (He places the apron, which is entirely of white leather, round his waist.) Come to the Lodge wearing these white gloves. (He hands them to him.) Never stain your hands with the blood of a Brother. Here are also women's gloves (he hands them to him), which should prove to you that although we exclude the other sex from our association – for good reasons – we still hold it in high regard. Give these gloves to no other person than someone who has earned your utmost respect.

Now write your name into the membership register of this very honourable Lodge. (He directs him to the Secretary's table where he enters his name in the book. Once this is done, the Worshipful Master continues:)

Freemasons have certain signs, words, and grips by which they recognise one another, but which must be used with the greatest caution. *The sign* of the Entered Apprentice is given by stretching out the four fingers of the right hand while extending the thumb so that it forms a square with the hand. In this position, one draws the hand across the throat from left to right, up to the right shoulder, where the hand is dropped straight down the side of the body. *The grip* is given by grasping the right hand of the other man with one's own, and firmly pressing the uppermost joint of the index finger with one's thumb. *The word* is *Jakin,* which is, however, not spoken at once. If you are asked for the word, then answer: 'Give me the first letter.' The other man then says *J.* You answer *A.* He *K,* you *I,* and he *N.* You *Ja,* he *Kin.* (Now the Worshipful Master receives the sign, grip, and word from the new Initiate, embraces him, and bids him identify himself to the Senior and Junior Warden in the same manner – and after this has been done, he says to him:) Now dress yourself, and then I will instruct you further.

While the new Initiate is attired by the Master of Ceremonies in the preparation room, Lodge business or similar matters can be settled, or, if another initiation is scheduled, one begins with it, and the Preparer is sent out. Outside, the Master of Ceremonies gives the Initiate the member sign. When the new Brother is attired, he and the Master of Ceremonies arrive at the door, he knocks ♩♪ and is admitted after the Wardens have announced this and have received the order to do so. He then approaches the Master again, who hands him his hat and rapier, which until then were on the Secretary's desk.

The *W. M.* says: 'Here are your hat and rapier. Be mindful never to draw it against a Brother. Worthy Brother Master of Ceremonies, show him to his seat.' (He is taken to his seat, which is at the very end; the new Initiate receives a seat of honour only during the Table Lodge.)

If another initiation is to be performed, the Worshipful Master tells the new Brother that he will learn and hear the rest hereafter; if not, he speaks to him as follows:

My Brother! if ceremonies and a lawful initiation would make a man a true Freemason, you would now be a true Freemason as much as any other. However, dear Brother! much is still lacking. Your own labours, which we can only insinuate, are required for this, and even if we show you a shadow of those great and comforting truths that are at the innermost of our Sanctum in sacred images, delivered unto us from ancient times, expect no further explanation. The man who wishes to penetrate the depths of these secrets must first work on himself as a Mason, must build a threefold foundation in himself on which a higher understanding is to rest. He must sound the depths of his own corrupted nature, cleanse himself of the dross, and build a temple in which the brilliance of the light can shine without casting any shadow, and that is not the work of a single day. (The Master of Ceremonies points to every figure on the carpet.) Here, my Brother! you see a carpet (he points to it) on which you see symbols which, after deeper contemplation, can lead you to great truths. Here is an outline of Solomon's Temple, the temple of the God Jehovah. It is surrounded by a solid and impenetrable wall, and it is ringed by a tessellated border – seven steps lead to the Sanctum – there is the mosaic pavement – and here two pillars, one of which is called Jakin and stands at the left, which is your position in this degree. – You see here a rough, unworked ashlar and, across from it, a smooth ashlar – finally, the locked inner chamber, the blazing star, which is our most sacred hieroglyph, and many other symbols, of which one day you shall have, I hope, a deeper understanding. Examine, reflect, and when one day the veil that darkens your gaze falls from your eyes, then you and I shall bless the day you first crossed this threshold, and with a sense of holy reverence you shall feel the whole joy of the Great Architect's omnipresence, in which we live, move, and exist.

Following this, the Catechism is gone through.

CATECHISM

FOR THE ENTERED APPRENTICES, WHICH IS EITHER ASKED BY THE
BROTHER WARDENS OR BY ALL BRETHREN TAKING TURNS

Question: Are you a Freemason?

Answer: My Brother Master and my Brothers Apprentices regard me as one.

Q. Where were you accepted?

A. In a just and perfect Lodge.

Q. What was its form?

A. An oblong square.

Q. What was its length?

A. From morning to evening.

Q. How wide?

A. From noon to midnight.

Q. How high?

A. As high as the clouds.

Q. What caused you to become a Freemason?

A. I was in the dark and wanted to see the light.

Q. What was your state when you were brought to the Lodge?

A. Neither naked nor clothed, neither barefoot nor shod, divested of all metal, but in good standing.

Q. How were you admitted?

A. By three knocks.

Q. What does this mean?

A. Ask and it shall be given unto ye, seek and ye shall find, knock and it shall be opened unto you.

Q. What did you see when you received the full light?

A. Three great lights.

Q. What are they?

A. The sun, the moon, and the Most Worshipful Master.

Q. Where was your Master seated?

A. Towards morning.

Q. Why there?

A. As the sun rises in the East to govern the day and bring light to the world, so the Master also sits in the East, governing the Lodge and bringing light to the Brethren.

Q. Where did the Wardens sit?

A. Towards the evening.

Q. Why?

A. As the moonlight reflects the sun's rays in the evening, so the Wardens shall also stand towards the evening, that they receive the Master's commands and give the Light of Masonry to the Brethren on the dark paths.

Q. How was your Master clad?

A. In blue and gold.

Q. What constitutes a just Lodge?

A. Seven.

Q. Who are they?

A. The Master, two Wardens, two Entered Apprentices, and two Fellow Crafts.

Q. How is your Lodge supported?

A. By three great pillars.

Q. What are they called?

A. Wisdom, Beauty, and Strength.

Q. What is their purpose?

A. Wisdom to contrive, Strength to support, and Beauty to adorn.

Q. Do you have tools as well?

A. Yes, three kinds: instruments, jewels, and adornments.

Q. What are the instruments?

A. The Bible, the pick-hammer, and the compass.

Q. What are the jewels?

A. The square, the level, and the plumb.

Q. What are the adornments?

A. The blazing star, the mosaic pavement, and the tessellated border.

Q. Does your Lodge have windows?

A. Yes, three. One towards morning, one towards noon, and one towards the evening.

Q. Why is there none towards midnight?

A. Because the sun casts no rays thence.

Q. Where in the Lodge do the Brother Masters stand?

A. Towards noon.

Q. Why?

A. As the sun is strongest at its midpoint, so the Masters also stand towards noon, to strengthen the Lodge and be a shining light to their Brethren.

Q. Where is the place of the Fellow Crafts?

A. They are scattered throughout the Lodge.

Q. For what reason?

A. To disburse the labours among the Entered Apprentices everywhere.

Q. Where is the place of the Entered Apprentices?

A. Towards midnight.

Q. Why?

A. Because they are in darkness.

Q. What is the meaning of the square worn by the Master on his breast?

A. As everything is directed by the square when building so shall the Brethren direct their eyes towards the Master in all things.

Q. Why does the worthy Brother Sr. Warden wear a level?

A. As a foreman consults the level when building so shall the Senior Warden use his reason to weigh up whether or not the Brethren are fulfilling their duties towards the building of virtue.

Q. What does the Brother Junior Warden's plumb teach us?

A. He shall plumb the depth of the foundation the Brethren have laid for the foundation of the building of virtue.

Q. How should a Freemason distinguish himself from other men?

A. Through a blameless conduct, a free and unconstrained manner of thinking, as well as faith and friendship towards his Brethren.

Q. Where did you receive the wages for your labours?

A. By the pillar Jakin.

Q. What is your name?

A. Tubal Cain. That is the watchword of the Entered Apprentices.

Q. Why have you come here?

A. Not that I may do my will, but to conquer my passions, to observe the rules of Freemasonry and to advance my progress in the Royal Art every day.

QUESTIONS ONE CAN ASK A BROTHER ENTERING THE LODGE.

Question. Whence came you?

Answer. From a Lodge of the holy Saints John.

Q. What do you bring?

A. Salvation, peace, blessings, and honour unto all true Masons, a good acceptance and a greeting to all Brethren from the Right Worshipful Master by three times three.

Now the Secretary reads out the constitutional points and by-laws. Then, if nothing further remains to be done and no speech is to be delivered, the Worshipful Master asks: 'Do any of the Brethren have anything to offer for the good of the Lodge?' If no one replies by directing himself to the Wardens, the *watchword* is given (except when Brethren from other rites are present), and the Lodge is then closed.

CLOSING A LODGE.

W. M. Worthy Brother Senior Warden, what is the time?

S. W. It is high midnight.

W. M. Worthy Br. Junior Warden, is this the proper time to close the Lodge?

J. W. Yes, it is the proper time.

W. M. I then close this Lodge in the name of our Illustrious Superiors and by our sacred number ♩♪.

S. W. ♩♪.

J. W. ♩♪.

W. M. My Brethren, this Lodge is now closed.

The Wardens repeat this, the rapiers are sheathed, and the Brethren leave the Lodge room. The minutes are not read, but every Brother may view them after the Lodge is closed.

ON TABLE LODGES.

The Brethren are seated just where they stand when attending other Lodges. The Lodge is opened in the same manner; however, it is not opened in the name of the Illustrious Superiors but only by the sacred number ♩♪.

W. M. It pleases the Brethren to pray. (This is done.)

The ceremonies for firing the cannons and the Craft words are known; the cannons are fired in the following order:

1. To salute the Illustrious Superiors, especially the Worthy Provincial Grandmaster. All rise for this toast; afterwards everyone stays seated. If such a Superior is present, he gives thanks. After this toast the W. M. dispenses the observation of silence. Before this, no one may speak or drink.

2. To the visiting Brethren. They give thanks.

3. To all other just and perfect Lodges, especially those which are in close communication with us, and to the health of the absent members of this Lodge.

4. To all institutions and societies for the good of mankind.

5. To the head of state, the authorities.

6. The S. Warden toasts the health of the W. M., who thanks him.

7. The W. M drinks to the health of the Wardens and Officers, who thank him.

8. Depending on the circumstances, a toast to the new Initiate, to whatever degree he has been accepted. He gives thanks.

Towards the end of the meal, the following cannons are fired:

9. To the health of the Sisters[43], by three times three, and not, as is the custom in some Lodges, with insulting noises. Then one may begin to sing. Finally, one toasts:

10. To the health of the poor and suffering. At this point, the Almoner passes the collection bag around. Afterwards, it is emptied onto a plate. The Almoner counts the money, reports the sum to the W. M. and, after the sum has been entered into the ledger, both sign it.

Before the Table Lodge is closed, all form a chain: everyone places his right hand in the left hand of his neighbour to the left, and his right hand in the left hand of his neighbour to the right, while the W. M. leads all in this prayer: 'O Great Architect, whose omnipotence builds myriads of worlds, whose gracious eye blesses and surveys all of creation: Let the industry of the Masons succeed, bless the labours of their hands, and let their building be elevated by wisdom, adorned by beauty and supported by strength. Let truth dwell in their halls and let them be illuminated by virtue, and may the Masons' strong chain, my worthy Brothers, never be broken.'

---

43   *The members' wives.*

All Brethren repeat the last line three times while the chain of hands is waved back and forth.

The Table Lodge is then closed in the usual manner.

RITUAL FOR THE CONSECRATION OF A NEW LODGE.

All future members of a Lodge that is to be established are gathered in the new Lodge room; the room is fully set up and adorned, yet not a single lamp is lit. The Plenipotentiary authorised to consecrate the Lodge and his assistants, as well as their visiting Brethren, are in a different room. When the ceremony is about to begin, the Plenipotentiary and each of his companions pick up a lit wax candle and approach the door of the future Lodge room.

The Plenipotentiary. ♫♪.

A Br. from within. Who is there?

The Plenipotentiary. A plenipotentiary of the Illustrious Superiors who wishes to kindle the light for the Brethren on the dark paths of Freemasonry gathered here.

Hereupon, the Brother standing by the door opens it while all the assembled Brethren form two lines and the Plenipotentiary and his two companions enter. When the Plenipotentiary stands by the pillar candelabra before the Senior Warden's station, he lights it and says: 'Thee I light, that thou may'st shine upon the dark paths of Freemasonry, and I name thee Wisdom.' Then the other: 'Thee I light, and I name thee Beauty.' At last, the one standing next to the altar: 'Thee I light and I name thee Strength.' The Plenipotentiary then stands behind the altar while his companions light the remaining candles.

When this is done, the Plenipotentiary delivers his speech wherein he reveals his intentions, and then lets one of his companions read out the Superiors' decree. In this, the Lodge is given a name and the Worshipful Master and a Deputy are appointed. When the decree has been read, the Plenipotentiary hands his candle for a moment to another Brother, orders the new Master to step forward, hands him the gavel lying on the altar with a few obliging words, hangs the jewel around his neck, exhorts the Brethren to obey his orders and lets the new W. M. seal the faithful and diligent execution of his office with a handshake. The Master gives his thanks in a short speech. The Plenipotentiary then takes his candle again and leads his companions out of the Lodge room. As soon as they are gone, the

W. M. takes his place, gives another short speech, appoints the Wardens and other Officers, hands them their jewels, and opens the Lodge.

Soon thereafter the W. M. bids the Master of Ceremonies, accompanied by the Stewards, to invite the Plenipotentiary and his companions back to the Lodge. They enter without candles. The Master of Ceremonies and the Stewards take the lead. The Master of Ceremonies assigns each man his seat, and all other proceedings are conducted.

RITUAL FOR THE EXCOMMUNICATION OF A BROTHER.

If a Brother is temporarily suspended from the Lodge meetings for minor trespasses, this is communicated to him, once a decision has been made in the Officers Lodge, either in the presence of all Brethren, or of the Officers, or by the Master under four eyes, depending on the gravity of the offence.

Sometimes, on the orders of the higher Superiors, a Brother may secretly not be invited to Lodge, often without this even being communicated to him directly. A full excommunication from the Order cannot occur without the higher Superiors' approval.

Only in rare cases is a Brother who is about to be fully excommunicated informed of this fact in the Lodge. The proceedings are the following. First, the Lodge is closed, and the W. M. then announces to the Brethren the trespass of the Brother and the order given by the Superiors. In closing, he says: 'In the name of our Illustrious Superiors and by the power of my office I thus relieve you, my Brethren, of all fraternal and Masonic duties towards the villain N. N., but never avenge yourselves on him. Do not forget that he is a man and that his guilty conscience will pain him in the darkness to which we return him, and it shall also be his final judge. As for you, however, do not approach this holy threshold until you have returned to the path of virtue from which you have strayed and a ray of the omnipresent one's eternal wisdom once more glimmers in your soul.' If the excommunicated man is present, he is divested of his Masonic garb and is escorted out, after the W. M. has admonished him not to break his oath of secrecy if he values his life and earthly happiness.

The Lodge is then reopened. If a Brother's offences during a public Lodge are severe, the Lodge is closed immediately. He is escorted out and will not be admitted again until a report has been filed about him.

RITUAL FOR THE TABLE LODGES, IF SISTERS ARE PRESENT.

After the Table Lodge has been opened in the usual manner, during which time the sisters wait in another room, the W. M. dispenses with the obligation to have the head covered, and the Brethren subsequently remove their hats. The W. M. then says: 'Brethren, freely invite the Sisters and escort them in.' Before that, however, all Brethren must be instructed in the ceremonies, which vary from the ritual of a regular Table Lodge. The Brethren then go forth, and each Brother escorts a Sister to the Lodge. Meanwhile, the W. M., the Wardens, and Officers remain standing at their stations. The Master of Ceremonies assigns the seats so that the sexes are mixed, as much as this is feasible.

The Sisters are addressed as 'Sister N. N.' and nothing else.

W. M. Brother Senior Warden, what kind of Lodge do we hold today?

S. W. A social Lodge for the entertainment of the Sisters.

W. M. Brother Jr. Warden, may we conduct ourselves by ancient tradition and custom?

J. W. No, Venerable Master.

W. M. Brother Master of Ceremonies, why not?

M. C. Because it is raining.

W. M. Then, because it is raining, dearest Brethren: I dispense with the customary prescribed traditions and the statutory silence.

Hereupon all take their seats. During the toasts, one does not say *fire* but *drink*, not *powder* but *wine;* the knock is not ♫ but ♪. When the W. M. says: 'To order, my Brethren', every Brother places his right hand on the table.

The glass is emptied in three sips, and the Sisters do the same. Everyone looks at the Master, but he does not say: *'Right hand to arms'* but *'Let us drink, and let us do so by the sacred number.'* The glass is then raised to the lips 3 times, but no triangle is drawn with it, and instead of slamming the glasses on the table, they are only clinked together.

The toast to the Sisters immediately follows the toast to the Superiors. The first Sister is instructed to give thanks by the number sacred to the Brother Freemasons.

All rise at the end of the meal, and pray.

W. M. Brethren, escort the Sisters back and return afterwards!

This is done. The Table Lodge is then lawfully closed.

2. Fellow Craft Degree

RITUAL FOR THE FELLOW CRAFT LODGE.

The room is decorated exactly as for the Entered Apprentice degree, only there is no footstool for kneeling before the altar. The carpet is the same, except that the other of the two pillars is marked B, and a G can be seen inside the blazing star.

BEFORE THE ☐ IS OPENED.

The Worshipful Master, Wardens, and Officers enter the Lodge room first. Then the Masters are called in. They are asked if there is any discord among the Brethren. Then the Fellow Crafts enter. They also are asked if there is discord among them. Finally, the visiting Brethren are led in.

OPENING OF THE ☐ .

W. M. ♪ To order, my Brethren!

S. W. ♪ (repeats this.)

J. W. ♪ (likewise.)

W. M. Worthy Junior Warden! What is the duty of the Junior Warden?

J. W. To see that the Lodge is tyled.

W. M. See to your office!

J. W. (performs his duty, returns, and says:) Worshipful Master, the doors are locked, the profane have been removed, and the Lodge is tyled.

W. M. Worthy Brother Senior Warden! What is the time?

S. W. It is high noon.

W. M. Worthy Brother J. W., is it the proper time for opening this Lodge?

J. W. Yes, it is the proper time.

W. M. Because it is the proper time I thus open this Fellow Craft Lodge in the name of our Illustrious Superiors, by the sacred number ♫♪, ♫♪.

S. W. ♫♪.

J. W. ♫♪.

W. M. My Brethren! This Fellow Craft Lodge is now open.

S. W. (repeats this.)

J. W. (likewise.)

The rapiers are not drawn.

INITIATION INTO THE FELLOW CRAFT DEGREE.

If the Fellow Craft Lodge casts its ballot regarding an Entered Apprentice who seeks promotion and he is found suitable for promotion, he is summoned to the Lodge house on a certain day, where he is left alone in a room, though not in the dark chamber.

After the Lodge is opened, the W. M. informs the Brethren what business is at hand, and sends an experienced Mason, who, having a thorough understanding of the Candidate's character, makes him understand how much more important the Freemason's work becomes with each degree, preparing him in this fashion for his next step.

After the Preparer has given report on the execution of his charge, the Treasurer is sent out to collect the reception fee.

Then the Master of Ceremonies goes forth, bringing the Candidate, dressed as an Entered Apprentice, to the door of the Lodge and removes his hat and rapier. He is not hoodwinked.

M. C. ♫♪. (on the door.)

J. W. ♫♪. The knocks of a Mason.

S. W. ♫♪. The knocks of a Mason.

W. M. See who is there.

J. W. Who is there? (as he goes to the door.)

M. C. An Entered Apprentice who seeks to be accepted to the second degree of our most honourable Order.

J. W. (repeats this.)

S. W. (likewise.)

W. M. Ask him his name.

S. W. (repeats this.)

J. W. What is his name?

M. C. Tubal Cain.

J. W. (repeats this.)

S. W. (likewise.)

W. M. Ask him his age.

S. W. (repeats this.)

J. W. How old is he?

M. C. Under seven.

J. W. (repeats this.)

S. W. (likewise.)

W. M. Worthy Brother Jr. Warden! Let him enter in a lawful manner so that he may complete the mysterious journey of a Fellow Craft.

The Junior Warden opens the door and places the rapier on the Entered Apprentice's breast, while the Master of Ceremonies hands the hat and rapier to the W. M. The Junior Warden bids the Candidate to make the circumambulation just as in the first degree, only twice. By the three corners ∴: the Brethren give the sign of the first degree the first time, and the sign of the second degree during the second circumambulation; each time, they drop the hand sharply. When the journey is complete, the Candidate is placed between the two Wardens.

J. W. ♫♪, ♫♪.

S. W. ♫♪, ♫♪.

W. M. ♫♪, ♫♪.

J. W. The Entered Apprentice has completed his journey.

S. W. Most worthy W. M.! Here is an Entered Apprentice who wishes to be led one step closer to our Sanctum.

W. M. What is his name?

S. W. Tubal Cain.

W. M. How old is he?

S. W. Under seven.

W. M. Where did he receive his wages?

S. W. By the pillar Jakin.

W. M. Has he completed his mysterious journey?

S. W. Yes, he has completed it.

W. M. ♪,

S. W. ♪,

J. W. ♪.

W. M. My Brother! You wish to climb another step in our most honourable Order? In other words, you believe that by your labours you have earned a place closer to our Inner Sanctum. – That is a mighty claim! my Brother! look inside yourself, for I cannot see the contents of your heart, but only He who examines your innermost soul knows if you are unworthy to take this step. It is a step is of great importance, if you wholly understand and feel it, but also quite insignificant if by taking it you merely wish to learn a few more hieroglyphs and signs.

But we have observed you. We have quietly watched you work, and I believe that I, with the consent of all the Brethren gathered here, can in good conscience reveal to you a wider perspective for your noble efforts.

With every step you take your work becomes infinitely more important, your obligations holier with each degree, and even here we may not discuss this with you explicitly.

I can promise you no secrets; you must seek them out yourself and must discover the key to this hieroglyphic language within yourself.

In this degree a few, but important, symbols are all we can present to you. Promise, however, that you will spare no effort to achieve the degree of perfection by which one day, to the honour of the Royal Art, we wish to show the world the fruits of our labours. Do you have the courage to faithfully lend yourself to a great work, and do you wish me to accept you into the Class of Fellow Crafts? Answer me!

(He answers.)

W. M. Very well. Worthy Br. Sr. Warden! Let him climb the seven steps to the Temple, and let him approach me with three steps.

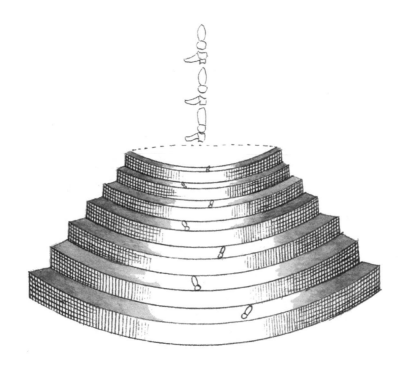

W. M. Are you prepared to give an oath before the almighty Architect of all worlds, to the effect of and bound by the same conditions you have pledged in the Entered Apprentice degree, to faithfully conceal the secrets of the Fellow Craft not only from the profane but also those Brethren who are not of this degree, and to fulfil your duties according to your best conscience and knowledge?

(He answers.)

Then I waive the actual delivery of the oath, and instead of the oath I shall accept a handshake from you. (The Candidate removes his right glove and gives the handshake.)

W. M. Now step closer! (He does so, and this to the right of the altar.) The apron you have hitherto worn I herewith take from you, and I dress you with the apron of a Fellow Craft. (He does so.) *The sign* of the second degree is given by placing the hand in the shape of the square across the heart, then pulling it to the side in the shape of the square and letting it drop. *The grip,* by firmly pressing the thumb on the first joint of the middle finger of the other man's hand. *The word* is Boaz, and it is spelt like Jakin.

Thereupon, the W. M. receives the sign, word, and grip from the new Initiate, sends him to both Wardens, to whom he must also identify himself, then summons him back, embraces him, hands him his hat and rapier, and says: 'Draw your rapier only in the defence of your honour as well as that of your Brethren and of the Order.' Whereupon the Fellow Craft is assigned his place by the Master of Ceremonies.

Then the W. M. addresses him thus: My Brother! until now your place in the Temple was by the pillar Jakin; now you see here, by the pillar Boaz (he points to the carpet), the place where you must perform your labours if you wish to approach the door to the Inner Sanctum (he points to it). However, you must first work this rough ashlar (he points to it) until it is like the one you see on the opposite side before you may bring it into the inner hall. The blazing star soars above this hall, and in this degree you must primarily follow this sole, eternal, and true light. It will cast its rays into your heart if the latter has been made pure by Freemasonry. It is up to you alone whether you catch or extinguish these holy sparks.

May the weal and blessing of the Triune be with you and your labour.

Then the Catechism is gone through.

CATECHISM OF THE FELLOW CRAFTS.

Q[uestion]. Are you a Fellow Craft?

A[nswer]. Yes, I am.

Q. How were you made a Fellow Craft?

A. By the square, the letter G, and the compass.

Q. What is the meaning of the letter G?

A. Someone who is greater than you.

Q. Where is he who is greater than I?

A. He is in all places. He always was, and He shall always be.

Q. Where was the Lodge in which you were accepted?

A. In the vale of Jehoshaphat, in the Holy Land.

Q. What did you see when you were taken into the Lodge?

A. Nothing the human mind could comprehend.

Q. What did you work on?

A. On the rough ashlar.

Q. Where did you receive your wages?

A. By the pillar Boaz.

Q. How long will your labours take?

A. The time of the work completed is greater than that which is to come.

Q. How do Fellow Crafts and Entered Apprentices travel?

A. From the evening towards the morning, to seek the light.

Q. How old are you?

A. Under seven.

Q. How high was the door of your Lodge?

A. So tall that no scoffer nor any profane could reach up and hammer a peg into it.

Q. How is a scoffer, meddler, or prattler punished?

A. In rainy weather, he is put under the eaves all day and night.

Q. Where do you keep your secret?

A. In the heart.

Q. Where is its key?

A. In a box made from bone.

Q. Can you write?

A. Yes, the Master has taught me.

Q. With what do your write?

A. With the square.

Q. What is your name?

A. Shibboleth.

CLOSING THE FELLOW CRAFT LODGE.

W. M. Does anyone have anything to offer for the good of the Lodge?

S. W. (answers.)

W. M. Worthy Brother Senior Warden! what is the time?

S. W. It is high midnight.

W. M. Worthy Brother Jr. Warden! Is it the proper time to close this Lodge?

J. W. Yes, it is the proper time.

W. M. Because it is the proper time I thus close this Fellow Craft Lodge in the name of our Illustrious Superiors, by the sacred number ♫♪, ♫♪.

S. W. ♫♪, ♫♪.

J. W. ♫♪, ♫♪.

W. M. My Brethren! This Lodge is closed!

SECRET CIPHER OF THE FREEMASONS.

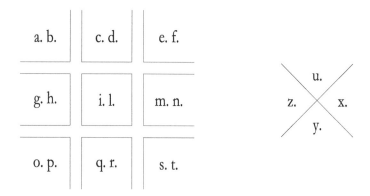

Examples.

⊐⅃⊓⊓⊓⌐   ∧⊐⊓⊔⊔

p a r i s   y o r i c.

3. Ritual for the Master Lodge

The *room* for the Master Mason Lodge must be wholly wallpapered or draped in black. There is a black carpet on the floor. The altar, the Lodge Master's chair and all the tables must be black; everything not of this colour must be removed. All lights are made from yellow or black wax. A skull and the other items required for the lower degrees are on the altar. There is no footstool for kneeling. All Brethren must be dressed in black, and those belonging to the military must at least wear a black ribbon on their hat and arm. Instead of the three great lights there should be complete skeletons holding the candles in their hands wherever this is possible. On the painted carpet stands a coffin (of about the same length), covered with a death-shroud on which a large white cross can be seen.

OPENING THE MASTER LODGE.

The Worshipful Master and the Officers enter first, then the Master Masons. They are asked whether or not there is discord among them, and once this issue is resolved the visiting Brethren are brought in.

W. M. ♪ To order, my Brethren[!]

S. W. ♪ (repeats this.)

J. W. ♪ (likewise.)

W. M. Worthy Jr. Warden, what is the duty of the Jr. Warden?

J. W. To see that the ☐ is tyled.

W. M. See to your office.

J. W. (performs his duty, and returns.) Worshipful Master, the doors are locked, and all the profane have been removed; all is in order.

W. M. Worthy Br. Senior Warden, what is the time?

S. W. High noon, Worshipful Master.

W. M. [W. Brother Junior Warden, is] it the proper time for opening this ☐ ?

J. W. Yes, it is the proper time.

W. M. I then open this ☐ of Master Masons in the name of our Illustrious Superiors, by the thrice-holy number. ♫♪, ♫♪, ♫♪.

S. W. ♫♪, ♫♪, ♫♪.

J. W. ♫♪, ♫♪, ♫♪.

W. M. My Brethren, this Lodge of Master Masons is now open.

INITIATION OF A MASTER.

If it has been decided in the Masters Lodge to admit a Fellow Craft to this degree, he is summoned to the Lodge house at the proper time, where he is received solemnly and earnestly and taken to a secluded chamber, where he is instructed to dress as a Fellow Craft and hand over his hat and rapier; these are placed on the altar in the Lodge room.

After the Lodge is opened, the W. M. again explains to the Brethren the reason for this day's gathering. An experienced Brother who is no stranger to the inner workings of the Order is sent out to prepare the Candidate, most of all to teach him a Master Mason's virtues and to convince him of the importance of this sublime degree in general, thus making it dear to his heart.

After the Preparer has returned, the Treasurer performs his duty.

Then the Master of Ceremonies goes forth and leads him to the door of the ☐, where he gives the knocks ♫♪, ♫♪.

J. W. ♫♪, ♫♪. The knock of a Fellow Craft.

S. W. ♫♪, ♫♪ (repeats this.)

W. M. ♫♪, ♫♪. See who is there.

S. W. (repeats this.)

J. W. (goes to the door) Who is there?

M. C. A Fellow Craft, who ardently desires to be received into the sublime Master's degree.

J. W. (repeats this.)

S. W. (likewise.)

W. M. Ask him what his name is.

S. W. (repeats this.)

J. W. What is his name?

M. C. Shibboleth.

J. W. (repeats this.)

S. W. (likewise.)

W. M. Ask him his age.

S. W. (repeats this.)

J. W. What is his age?

M. C. Under seven.

J. W. (repeats this.)

S. W. (likewise.)

W. M. Very worthy Br. J. W., let him enter and travel as a Master.

The J. W. opens the door and takes the Candidate's right hand with his left, and places the sword on his breast with his right. Meanwhile, the Brethren form a close circle around the coffin. The Candidate is instructed always to face the walls of the ☐, and so he must travel. During the first journey the sign of the first degree is made three times, while during the second journey the Fellow Craft sign is made and during the third journey the Master sign is made, every time with sound. When the journey has been completed, the Candidate is placed between the two Wardens, but with his back to the altar. During the journey the Brethren are seated.

J. W. ♪.

S. W. ♪.

W. M. ♪.

S. W. Worshipful Master, a Fellow Craft Mason seeking acceptance to the sublime degree of a Master Mason is here.

W. M. See that he is not one of the ruffians who have slain our Master.

S. W. (walks around the Candidate, inspects him closely, and says:) W. M., he bears a resemblance to them, but he is not one of them. I vouch for him.

W. M. Has he studied for a period of time?

S. W. Yes.

W. M. Is his Master satisfied with him?

S. W. Yes.

W. M. What is his name?

S. W. Shibboleth.

W. M. How old is he?

S. W. Under seven.

W. M. ♪.

S. W. ♪.

J. W. ♪.

W. M. My Brother, you seek solace and comfort with us, but today you find us gathered in mourning. Look here (the Candidate is turned around) and cast your eye on this monument of a most mournful event in Freemasonry. Today, we observe the memory of our slain Master. Ruffians have killed him, and it is only with courage, virtue, and steadfastness that we can avenge this injury committed against us, recover our loss and regain the Master's word, which has been lost. Are you now, my Brother, prepared to join our ranks to this noble end, faithfully, bravely, and dauntlessly, or are you frightened by this mournful sight, the prospect of the struggle against evil, this toil of seeking what has been lost? Answer me. (He answers, and the Brethren step aside.)

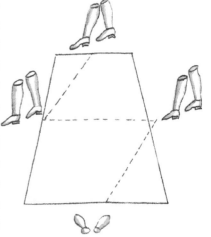

W. M. Very well. Worthy Br. Senior Warden, then let him take the three great steps of a Master Mason and approach me over the graves of our ancestors.

The Senior Warden shows the steps to the Candidate who then follows his example.

In the meantime, three of the Officers each take a thick roll of paper. The Candidate must stand before the altar, the tips of his feet pointing outward, and both Wardens step closer to him from the sides. Meanwhile, the coffin behind him is removed. Only the carpet remains, and a pillow is placed in the area of the head.

W. M. If you persist in your decision to be admitted into this degree of our honourable Order you must give me your solemn oath, not only to faithfully conceal all of this degree from the profane and from Freemasons of the two lower degrees, but also to fulfil the duties of a Master Mason to the best of your ability. Are you willing to do this?

(He answers.)

I then waive the delivery of your oath if you shake hands with me on this instead. (This is done with the right glove removed.)

Now let me tell you the sad tale of the death of our slain Master. During the construction of the Temple, Solomon made the Master Mason Hieram supervise the other Masons. The Entered Apprentices received their wages by the pillar Jakin, the Fellow Crafts by the pillar Boaz, and the Master Masons in the Middle Chamber. Each of these Classes has its own watchword, and to receive the wages of a Master Mason one needed to know the old Master's word.

Three Fellow Crafts who, dissatisfied with their station, had often pressed for promotion but had always received a negative answer due to their unworthiness, conspired to wrest the Master's word from the Master Mason Hieram by force. To this end they concealed themselves in the Temple after the noon hour, once the other workers had left. One stood by the door of noon, the other by the door of midnight, and the third by the door of morning. When Hieram, according to his habit, entered the Temple through the door of evening during the hour of rest to inspect the progress of the work, and sought to exit through the door of noon, the ruffian impetuously demanded that he tell him the Master's word.

Hieram refused, saying that he could and would not give him the word in this manner, whereupon the ruffian flew into a rage and gave our master a powerful blow (the Worshipful Master gently taps the Candidate on the brow with the gavel, while one of the Officers mentioned above strikes him on the right shoulder blade). Hieram, who soon recovered from this blow, wanted to escape through the midnight door, when he was assaulted by the other Fellow Craft, who also compelled him to reveal the Master's word, but our Master remained steadfast, saying that it was not in his power to bestow the word in this manner.

He then received from this angered ruffian a powerful second blow (a somewhat stronger strike with the gavel and the paper roll from the other Officer). Although stunned by these strikes, Hieram still had enough presence of mind to seek safety through the door of morning, but here also, he was assaulted by the third ruffian who demanded the same of him and, after another steadfast refusal, struck him with such terrible force (the W. M. raises the gavel high; meanwhile, the third Officer strikes the Candidate hard with the paper roll, all Brethren loudly clap their hands once at the same time, and the two Wardens trip him from behind, forcefully pull him backwards and lay him onto the carpet) that he fell dead to the ground. (The Master of Ceremonies places a blood-spattered cloth over his face. The Junior Warden positions him so that the left arm rests straight along his body, the right hand is over his heart, which is covered by the apron, and the left leg is straight while the right leg is bent, with the knee pointing up and the sole of the foot being squarely on the floor.

The Senior Warden places a green twig on the body.

A brief pause.)

W. M. Worthy Brother Senior Warden, what has happened to our Master Hieram?

S. W. He has been slain. He is dead, truly dead.

W. M. Then let us go and seek his corpse (the W. M. walks around the Brother lying on the floor, and the Wardens follow him). Since it is likely that the true Master's word has been lost, we will agree that the first word we speak when we have found our Master shall be our Master's word (the Master stops at the Candidate's feet, and the two Warden are by his side). A sprig of cassia has been planted here (he pulls it out), but it has no roots – here is a fresh pile of rubble – let us examine it – I see bones – a dead body has been buried here – worthy Brothers Wardens, see if you can raise this corpse.

S. W. (gives the Candidate the grip of an Entered Apprentice.) Worthy W. M., the skin cleaves from the flesh.

J. W. (gives the grip of a Fellow Craft.) The flesh cleaves from the bones.

W. M. Then I will attempt to raise this corpse from the grave by the 5 points of Mastery (he places his right foot to the Candidate's right foot, clasps his right hand, his knee to knee, wraps his left arm around him, thus raising him to his feet, and shouts 'Mac' into one ear and 'Benac' into the other). This is the new Master's word with which I accept you as a Master Mason in the name of the honourable Order, with the approval of this Lodge and by the power of my office; now hear the rest of the sad tale of our Master's death. (The W. M. returns to his place). The ruffians who had murdered him carried him out through the door in the West and buried him under a pile of rubble. When Hieram was reported missing, Solomon soon received word of his murder from his servants, and he sent nine faithful Brethren in various directions to look for a corpse. One of these was the first to find the place where he believed the body to be buried, and he placed a sprig of cassia there so he could find the place again. When a few others also arrived at this place and, tired from walking, sat down on the pile of rubble, the sprig was pulled out when they tried to hold onto it, because it had no roots, and thus they discovered that here was a fresh grave. They all informed King Solomon that they had found the dead Master, whereupon the king had the body exhumed and had it buried with all splendour in the Temple's middle chamber, with fifteen Fellow Crafts, wearing white aprons and gloves, following the corpse. But because he feared that the 3 ruffians could have taken the Master's word by force, he decreed that the first word uttered at the sight of the corpse should be the Master's word from this time onward.

And since the Brethren who had found him had exclaimed *Macbenac* it has remained the new Master's word to this day. However, it is never spoken outside the Lodge.

Here, my Brother, I give you the apron of a Master Mason (he removes the Fellow Craft apron and dresses him with the Master Mason apron). *The sign* of this degree is holding the hand horizontally in the shape of the square, the thumb pointing down, and pulling it downward from the brow to the base of the heart while gazing heavenward. *The grip* is firmly grasping the hand of the other, making a kind of claw with the fingers, pressing on the hand with the thumb up, but the index and middle finger locked under. Then foot to foot, knee to knee, cheek to cheek, the new Master's word is whispered into the ears. Master Masons have another sign used in their gravest need or danger. One folds the hands, turns them outward on one's head, and exclaims: 'Help this poor orphan!'

Now the new Initiate must make himself known to the Worshipful Master and the Wardens, after which the Master of Ceremonies assigns him his place; but first, the Worshipful Master hands him his rapier with the words: 'Use this whenever you need to defend your honour! The step you have taken today is the most important of all. Those are sacred truths concealed by the hieroglyphs. They are comforting truths for the faithful researcher, but hidden from the eyes of the uninitiated by an impenetrable cover. You will be happy once you have grasped their whole meaning. However, one does not learn this without effort. Industry, a spirit of exploration, and a pure heart must come to your aid here and grant you that which cannot be conferred by ceremonies or degrees.' After this, the Catechism is gone through.

Question. Are you a Master Mason?
Answer. Try me, examine me, reject me if you can. I know of the acacia.
Q. Whence do you come?
A. From the East.
Q. Where are you going?
A. To the West.
Q. What do you want there?
A. To seek what has been lost and now is found again.
Q. What was lost?
A. The Master's word.
Q. Where have you worked?
A. By the grave of our Master Hieram.
Q. What has befallen him?
A. He is dead. He has been slain.
Q. Who slew our Master?
A. Three ruffians.
Q. How will the Master be reawakened?
A. By the 5 points of Mastery.
Q. Whence does the wind blow?
A. From the East.
Q. What does it bring?
A. First clear skies, then storms, and at last clear and calm skies.
Q. How do Master Masons travel?
A. From sunrise to sunset, to spread the light to all parts of the world.
Q. Where is the Master buried?
A. Between the compass and the square.
Q. What constitutes a perfect Master □?
A. Three.
Q. What are the 5 virtues of a Master Mason?
A. Honesty, temperance, prudence, activity, boldness.
Q. Where do Master Masons receive their wages?

A. In the inner chamber.

Q. How old are you?

A. Over seven.

Q. What is your name?

A. Cassia.

CLOSING THE MASTER ☐ .

W. M. Do any of the Brethren have anything to offer for the good of the ☐?

S. W. (answers.)

W. M. Worthy Br. Senior Warden! What is the time?

S. W. It is high midnight.

W. M. Worthy Br. Jr. Warden! Is it the proper time to close this Lodge?

J. W. Yes, it is the proper time.

W. M. Because it is the proper time, I now close this Master Mason Lodge in the name of our Illustrious Superiors and by the thrice-holy number. ♫♪, ♫♪, ♫♪.

   S. W. ♫♪, ♫♪, ♫♪.

   J. W. ♫♪, ♫♪, ♫♪.

   W. M. My Brethren! This Lodge is now closed.

II. Improved Constitution Book for the St. John's Lodge

A) GENERAL CONSTITUTIONAL ARTICLES, WHICH MUST BE READ OUT IN EVERY LODGE.

INTRODUCTION.

The Illustrious Superiors, who have been entrusted with the preservation and promotion of Freemasonry and who one day will have to account for this sacred pledge, are firmly convinced that the chiefs of the various Lodges working under their supervision will not admit such unworthy and immoral men into this most honourable Order that it is necessary, at this point, to instruct members in the first principles of a moral system that should already be sacred to any upright and sensible man. Furthermore, sermons and declamations about well-known obligations are of little use, and the weak heart is kept more efficiently on the only path to temporal and eternal felicity, the path of virtue, by example and watchful enthusiasm than by doctrines. This virtue is its own reward in any station, but it is doubly rewarded in our holy Order, and the more eagerly every Freemason works on himself, the closer he comes to the great goal, and the more certain he can be of enjoying the fruits that are reserved for the perfect Mason in our Inner Sanctum – Here we shall therefore state only a few general points about the qualities expected of a Freemason (with due allowance for his strengths and talents).

I. CHARACTER AND QUALITIES OF A TRUE MASON.

1) A Freemason must be a free-born man who has been raised in the Christian faith and is older than twenty years of age.

2) He shall have a righteous, faithful, philanthropic, and sensitive heart, and he should have compassion for the misfortune of others, be forgiving, free from hatred and vengefulness, and modest.

3) He shall be magnanimous and generous without being wasteful, an outspoken enemy of vice, an admirer and defender of wisdom, virtue and innocence, steadfast in misfortune and danger, without being boisterous in times of good fortune.

4) Being ethical and moderate in all things, including his desires, and satisfied with his station in life, he must endeavour to free himself from all harmful pas-

sions and eschew all kinds of excesses that debase the mind and body, such as profane love, drinking, and gambling above everything else.

5) He shall be a good citizen of the state and a good husband, father, son, and brother in his domestic life. In short, he must fulfil every duty placed on him by virtue and his civil obligations eagerly, faithfully, and with passion.

6) As much as possible he must free himself from the shackles of prejudice, seek to penetrate to the core of truth on the straight path of reason, shun idleness, conduct his affairs dutifully, and generally find joy in all kinds of useful work.

7) Without intrusive curiosity, he must learn and explore everything which could make him a wiser and better man. Nothing in the world should seem insignificant or unworthy of his attention.

8) All his affairs and actions must be governed by orderliness and punctuality, but without fearful pedantry.

9) Discretion is one of the most essential qualities of a Mason.

10) Therefore he should cultivate the habits of presence of mind, vigilance, self-awareness, courage, and boldness. His secret should not be taken from him by vanity, fear, or trifles. Where truth and duty are concerned, neither danger nor distinction of person should frighten him.

II. PUBLIC CONDUCT.

1) General.

    a) Every deed of a Mason should be guided by wisdom, truth, and honour.

    b) His conduct must appear and be natural, not forced, popular, never too familiar with nobles, but neither cowering nor flattering, proper with his equals, and not arrogant towards lesser men.

    c) In general, he must be well-mannered and courteous, prudent and not too talkative; he must suffer weaker men, and he must conduct himself with patience, respect, reverence, and love towards women, the elderly, and children.

    d) His expenditure, apparel, and manners should be simple, tasteful, and purposeful.

    e) He shall publicly take up the cause of suffering innocence and suppressed merit, and spread truth and light whenever he has the opportunity; but prudence must guide his steps.

f) To the best of his ability, he should support every worthwhile institution working for the good of mankind and encourage directly or indirectly, publicly or in secret, every unrecognised talent and every suppressed genius.

g) He should never meddle in affairs that do not concern him, and he should shun all intrigues, conspiracies, gossip, slanderers, and slander.

h) He must honour the prejudices on which others base their peace of mind without accepting them, and where he cannot safely further the general welfare; thus, he shall let everyone walk his path, unless his occupation requires the opposite.

i) He must not engage in any action that demeans him in his own eyes: but where his conscience approves, he must rise above the common judgement once the step he wishes to take is certain to promote the general good.

k) He must speak with respect and caution of all religions, liturgical practices, state constitutions, sciences, arts, and social classes.

2) In Freemasonry, namely:

A. In Lodge, the Freemason shall conduct himself calmly, quietly, obediently, courteously, and solemnly.

a) He must visit the Lodge diligently and punctually, precisely at the appointed hour. If he is prevented from attending by matters of importance then he must excuse himself in writing or submit to the penalty.

b) Everyone sits and stands in his appointed place. In the Lodge, all civil relations and ranks are suspended until after it is closed and every Brother returns to his station appointed by the state.

c) When in Lodge, no one may speak loudly without permission; if he has an urgent suggestion, he must request permission through the Wardens. Furthermore, he must inform the W. M. about this before that Lodge is opened.

d) Likewise, anyone who wishes to give a speech, sing a new song during the Table Lodge or propose a toast, must duly inform the W. M. of this and make prior announcement.

e) The speeches themselves should not be cold declamations, moralistic drivel, or exercises in oratory, but should be brief, without tedium, plainly spoken, and vividly presented, truly Masonic admonitions, from the heart and speaking to the heart, rather than flowing from the head.

f) The Master is called *most worshipful,* the Deputy Master *worshipful,* the Wardens and Officers *very worthy, and* the other Brethren *worthy and dear*

Brethren. If higher Superiors are present, one first uses the address *reverend,* but if addressing visiting Brethren immediately after the Worshipful Master one says *worthy visiting Brethren.*

g) Matters of state, religion, family, or similar issues that interest only a few people must not be discussed in any Lodge.

h) Everyone must willingly obey the Master's orders, and he may not refuse an assigned office without a substantial reason accepted by the majority of the Lodge.

i) During Table Lodges the Brethren shall be calm, quiet, courteous, and temperate; until the W. M. has given permission, no one may speak, drink, or remove his hat. The number of bowls set for each Lodge may not be exceeded. No one may drink more than one *bouteille* of wine. Nor should one sit at the table for too long.

k) During ballots and elections everyone shall act conscientiously and without private passions. Wisdom and righteousness must guide every step of a Freemason. Further, the Brethren shall not gossip, beforehand or afterwards, about for whom or how they have voted or intend to vote.

l) In other Lodges a Brother shall conduct himself as courteously and solemnly as in his own, and never discuss the differences between their systems.

m) If someone wishes to bring an outside Brother to visit the Lodge he must notify the W. M. in a timely manner so that he may be received properly. Unless this has been done, no one may divulge the time, location, and existence of the Lodge to a stranger.

B. Outside the Lodge:

a) All Brethren must refrain from discussing Freemasonry as much as possible. Such conversations can never lead to anything that is useful, but they can create a great deal of confusion instead. Those who have crossed the thresholds of the Inner Sanctum already know what they should say. Meanwhile, all others could easily create problems for themselves and others by such useless prattling. Those who enjoy talking a great deal about Freemasonry only reveal how little they understand the nature of the Order; furthermore, there is no longer any advantage in making oneself known as an accepted Freemason by outward signs. There are a tremendous number of fools and scoundrels who share this privilege with us. Thank heavens that they are Freemasons only by virtue of the ceremonies, and that the signs, words, and grips do not place us in the same class. There are also many dubious persons for whom this craft is an easy fare. One only needs to be known as a Freemason to be obliged to open one's purse to such idlers. This is why the Superiors ask every Brother, for his own sake, that he do not hang out the signboard of Freemasonry everywhere he goes. If he requires recommendations in other towns, he should consult with his W. M.; if he wishes to benefit destitute Brethren, he should do so quietly; and if he knows an upright man, he should treat him with reverence, without refering to the Craft. All these are weaknesses of young and inexperienced Brethren, and no one who treats Freemasonry on this footing will advance with us.

b) Outside the Lodge one must also treat the Superiors with the same fraternal reverence that a tried, experienced man, elected by the trust of all Brethren, has the right to demand.

c) No one should leave as much as a trace of Freemasonry in his letters, writings, etc.

d) No one should write anything about the Order or take up the cause of its defence without the Superiors' permission.

e) No one may keep any as yet unpublished writings concerning Freemasonry in his house over night, unless he holds a Lodge office or has the Superiors' permission.

f) Every Brother should immediately notify his W. M., and no one else, of any news he has learnt that may concern Freemasonry; in general, everyone should be watchful for anything that may relate to the ⊙.

g) In all instances where one might ensure the fortune, reputation, and promotion of a Brother, one is required to do so. Shame on him who can calmly slander a Brother or, out of his fear of man, indolence or hypocrisy passes up the opportunity to open up to a worthy Freemason the prospect of a better fate.

h) If one is poor or unfortunate and not in any way to blame for that, then one will find protection and aid among one's Brethren. However, one should not rush to seek their support as long as one can receive advice in other ways and from the profane, without troubling one's friends and the ⊙, so that benefiting others does not become a burden that stretches the other person beyond his limits and so that accepting help does not become one's trade.

i) If there is discord among the Brethren, they shall be inclined to reconciliation and should first present the matter to the W. M., the Lodge Officers, chosen arbitrators, or the entire Lodge, and only if they are not satisfied with any of these means may they turn to the authorities. Even then, their written and spoken communications must be polite and without vitriol. A Brother may never draw his sword against another; if he does so, he will be expelled immediately.

k) He who wishes to travel for longer than a month must inform the W. M.

l) Absent Brethren do not have a vote.

III. INFORMATION ABOUT OTHER INSTITUTIONS.

1) If a just and perfect Lodge is to be held in a town, it must be constituted by our Superiors and consecrated by an authorised representative who also installs its first W. M.

2) No one may be accepted as a Freemason outside the Lodge.

3) Every Brother remains a permanent member of the Lodge in which he was accepted; absent Brethren must write to the Lodge at least once a month, and from the Secretaries they receive news, at least once every quarter, of Lodge events that may be of use to them. For this they pay a nominal fee to cover postage, but not the customary monthly contribution.

4) If one resides in another location for more than a year one must inquire with one's Lodge whether one should remain a member of the same Lodge or may demit to another.

5) However, one may not receive higher degrees in another Lodge.

6) No one may recruit new members without permission but must first ask his W. M. to what extent he may disclose himself; if ordered to do so he must act prudently, promise the Candidate nothing and divulge neither the day of acceptance nor its certainty too far in advance; nor should he conceal the costs of the first, second, and third degree, or the fact that he must give an oath.

7) He who converts to us from a different Masonic rite pays a fee and must give a handshake instead of an oath.

8) One year shall pass between the first and second degree, and two between initiation into the second and third degree.

9) One should not feel slighted if one does not receive a desired degree or an office in the Lodge one has aspired to. One must strive to earn the former and,

often, one is held back in order to be tried in patient obedience, so that one may be promoted all the faster at a later point. The offices, however, are not in any way privileges. One person may be suited for it and the other may not, but this does not mean that the latter lacks merit.

10) The W. M. is elected by the entire Lodge and then appoints the other Officers.

11) The proceedings for electing the Master are as follows: At least four weeks before the Feast of St. John, every Brother places a slip on which he has written whom he would like to see as W. M. for the next year into the deposit box. On the eve of the Feast of St. John the Secretary opens the box in the Officers Lodge, counts the ballots, and announces this to the Brethren the next day, since this is when the new Master takes office. No one who has not previously been an Officer can be W. M.

12) Ballots are held in the following manner: If someone has been suggested for acceptance in the ☉ and this has been reported to the W. M., then his name is posted above the deposit-box next to the door of the Lodge room where it remains at least until the next Lodge is held. Any Brother who has to offer a significant objection to the Candidate and who does not wish to communicate this orally to the W. M., inserts a slip on which he has written his opinion into the slot of the box. The Officers then investigate the complaint. Once the Candidate's election takes place, the Secretary hands each member a white ball and a black ball during the next Lodge; soon thereafter, he makes the round carrying a bag. Whoever agrees to accept the Candidate drops in a white ball, and whoever rejects him throws in a black ball. Once the Secretary has handed the bag to the W. M., he collects the remaining balls in another bag. In the meantime, the W. M. examines the ballot bag. Three black balls delay the elections for at least a while. If there are one or two black balls, the Worshipful Master decides.

13) In general, the deposit box is used for submitting any complaints. It is opened by the Secretary during every Lodge.

14) Lodges shall be held at least once a month.

15) Every attending member of the Lodge pays a small monthly fee to the Brother Housekeeper to cover the cost of decorations, illumination, etc.

16) Every year, on St. John's Day, the ledgers are audited and filed in the Officers Lodge.

17) On the Feast of St. John a poor, but otherwise hard-working and honest man can be accepted free of charge.

18) The son of a Scottish Provincial Master pays nothing for the first degree, and the son of a W. M. is accepted before any prince or nobleman.

19) The Superiors are pleased to see the Brethren prefer their own company to that of the profane. In some towns, weekly meetings are arranged.

20) Wherever this can be accomplished, the Lodges should gradually acquire useful book collections for common use by the Brethren.

21) The Masonic year begins on June 24th.

The Worshipful Master has been instructed which clauses of this constitution he may dispense with without consulting the higher Superiors, and from which clauses he may derogate with their approval.

All Brethren are expected to eagerly take it upon themselves to comply with these by-laws, which have been established for their own good, and should be persuaded that their actions will go neither unnoticed nor unrewarded, and that earlier or later promotions to the inner Order and any external help depend on such actions.

B) STATUTES FOR THIS PARTICULAR LODGE.

Note. Any Blue Lodge may create and amend such statutes with the approval of the Scottish Lodge.

1. The initiation fee for the first degree is *ten ducats*[44], *four ducats* for the second, and *6 ducats* for the third.

2. Whoever converts to our rite pays *three ducats.*

3. The monthly fee for attending Brethren is *one guilder.*

4. Absent Brethren pay *half a guilder* every month.

5. The regular Lodge meeting is the first Saturday of the month.

6. During the Table Lodges no more *than six different dishes* may be served, except on important holidays. Every attendant pays one guilder and brings wine.

7. The W. M. may set monetary fees for violating the by-laws from *six kreutzers* to *one ducat,* but they may never be any higher. The money goes to the alms box.

8. Every member must donate a useful book to the Masonic library.

9. The arms of this Lodge are – – –.

10. The name of this Lodge is – – –.

---

[44] *One ducat being the equivalent of four guilders (in English money, 12s.).*

C) PARTICULAR ARTICLES OF INSTRUCTION,

WHICH MUST BE READ DURING EVERY OFFICERS LODGE, BUT WHICH
MUST NOT BE SHOWN TO THE OTHER BRETHREN, AND OF WHICH NO
WRITTEN COPIES ARE TO BE ISSUED TO THE OFFICERS.

Every Province may create these for its jurisdiction as it sees fit.

I. INSTRUCTIONS FOR THE OFFICERS LODGE.

1. An Officers Lodge must be held at least once or twice every month.

2. These articles of instruction are to be read out during every such Lodge.

3. It is opened with the customary solemnity and in Masonic apparel. All Officers are seated at one table. The W. M. is seated at the head, the Secretary, who keeps the minutes, next to him and the others at both sides, in the order of their office's rank.

4. Everything that is to take place in the general Lodges must first be presented by the W. M. in the Officers Lodge. Depending on the importance of the matter it is decided upon by oral or written vote. Once it has been approved in the Officers Lodge by a majority of the votes all Officers must however vote according to this decision when the issue is raised in the general Lodge.

5. No one may hold a Lodge office unless he is a Master Mason, or unless the membership of a Lodge is so small that a temporary exception must be made; nonetheless, such a person may not attend an Officers Lodge.

6. The future W. M. and the Officers he is to appoint are elected in the Officers Lodge beforehand. Because it is composed of men who must have an understanding of the Order's business, one must always attempt to implement a resolution that has been adopted here in the general Lodge, either by outvoting or by winning over the individual Brethren.

7. A past W. M. may not hold a lesser office after his term. He is always the Deputy Master in the following year.

8. A past Officer is a permanent member of the Officers Lodge, if he so desires.

9. In the Lodge an Officer may never take the place of another Officer; in his absence, another Brother must be so appointed instead. Therefore, it is useful to be able to substitute at least the Wardens with experienced Masons, who sit behind them during Lodge and are able to stand in their place whenever they are absent.

10. Every Officer is charged to properly fulfil his duties and not meddle in matters that do not concern him. General Lodge business, however, concerns the entire college. He who notices a violation of good order and the by-laws must report this to the W. M., who then presents the matter to the Officers.

11. As the most experienced man, the W. M. is happy to advise every Brother on how to conduct his office or cast his vote.

12. If the Wardens and the Officers cannot agree on a certain point, and the votes are even, the W. M. decides.

13. Every year on St. John's Day, before the new Officers are installed, every incumbent submits the ledger, minutes, or whatever record it is his duty to maintain, to the Officers Lodge for auditing and signing.

14. No one may keep any Masonic documents in his house other than those which are of vital importance to his office, but none whatsoever after his departure from office. The most important documents, such as the rituals and other correspondence, must always remain in the Lodge house's archives.

15. Every Lodge maintains control over their general and ancillary funds; however, the Higher Superiors annually collect one-tenth of the general fund against receipt to bolster the main fund, which is used for financing major enterprises. This main fund is audited every three years by delegates from all the Lodges.

16. Since the W. M. often has the opportunity to use the funds for the benefit of the entire cause, he may indeed request such monies from the fund against a handwritten receipt, but here it must be noted:

A) That he must provide the next W. M. with sufficient information and proof about these expenditures the following year,

B) that he must submit the higher Superiors' written approval to the Deputy Master,

C) that he must account for the interest and may never divest the least part of the principal, and that he is responsible for ensuring that the Lodge funds are never diminished, apart from the payment of the tithe.

D) That one-third of the total funds always remain as available cash assets unless the entire Officers Lodge has decided otherwise.

17. In general the fund should never be touched, it should be invested in the most efficient manner, and it must not be used for any venture or to pay a pension to an unfortunate person until the interest earned is sufficient.

18. Above all, an account must be rendered to the Provincial Lodge, comprised of the delegates from all Lodges in a District, and every Lodge's Deputy Master is the Provincial Lodge's representative.

19. The proper and essential Officers in every Lodge are:

A) The Worshipful Master.

B) The Deputy Master.

C) The Senior Warden.

D) [The Junior Warden.]

E) The Secretary.

F) The Treasurer.

G) The Master of Ceremonies.

The non-essential Officers are:

H) The Almoner.

I) The Housekeeper.

K) The Orator.

L) ⎫
M) ⎭ The Stewards.

N) The Sick Visitor.

O) The Decorator.

P) The Librarian.

20. If the Grand Lodge has established institutions, e.g. almshouses, hospitals, and the like, several Officers will be involved with their management with the approval of the Officers Lodge, and they may also consult other Brethren in these matters.

21. One should generally endeavour to engage the younger Brethren and assign to them correspondence, etc., so that they may thus be prepared for future offices.

22. Every Officer shall seek to gain the respect and trust of the subordinate Brethren, but not their slavish awe.

23. Secure and settled men should be accepted as Serving Brethren, though not too many of them and certainly none who wish to exploit Freemasonry and who might become financially dependent upon the Lodge.

24. At the end of each Masonic year a report of the Lodge's complete economic, political, and moral state is sent to the Provincial Lodge using the template in Addendum A.

II. SPECIAL INSTRUCTIONS FOR THE WORSHIPFUL MASTERS.

In addition to what has been stated above, the W. M. has to observe the following:

1. He must ensure precise adherence with all statutes, by-laws, regulations, and rituals, and generally seek to introduce and maintain the true and authentic Masonic tone.

2. Where his reputation and understanding do not suffice, he should consult the Provincial Lodge, which will appraise and counsel him.

3. If he cannot hold Lodge in his own house, he shall choose one that is safe, secluded, and of good reputation.

4. Once the number of attending members in his Lodge has grown to more than thirty, he must report to the Provincial Lodge before he accepts anyone else.

5. If he believes in his conscience that he should object to something, the matter must be deferred until the Provincial Lodge can make a decision. In the same way he cannot implement anything if the Officers Lodge appeals against it to the Provincial Lodge.

6. He must present all orders from the Provincial Lodge which he refers to at least to his Deputy.

7. He must not allow more than three initiations in one degree to be performed in one day.

8. To prepare the Candidate he must choose an eloquent man who has studied his character. The preparation for each degree must touch the Candidate's heart without offending him. The Preparer must also be a settled and respected man. He and those who accompany him are chosen by the W. M. alone.

9. He shall outline the order of all events that are to take place in the Lodge on a sheet of paper, so that he does not forget or confuse anything.

10. It is up to him which outside Brethren he wants to admit as visitors. He must prevent our inner system from becoming widely known or allowing a false note to creep in because of the visiting Brethren.

11. He must not allow someone without sufficient knowledge of the Order to recruit a Candidate. This decision is left to him alone.

12. As much as possible he must keep the entire Lodge abreast of all events, present letters and news as much as is feasible, let every Brother vote on the use

of the alms, and generally never suppress the spirit of freedom as long as it is consistent with good order and higher purposes.

13. The Lodges for the higher degrees are to be held before and not after the other Lodges; it is up to him to set the Lodge days.

14. To ease the Brethren's expenses he shall consequently strive to keep the contribution for the Table Lodge low, avoid consenting too easily to free admission for outside Brethren at the expense of the entire Lodge and, finally, avoid excessive monetary fines, which are set by him alone.

15. The W. M. keeps the counter-lock for all money boxes, archives, etc.

16. He may dispense with minor ceremonies on his own authority, but as far as all others are concerned he must consult with the Officers Lodge or, depending on the circumstances, with the Provincial Lodge.

17. He wields the gavel, and on his breast he wears a square suspended from a blue ribbon around his neck.

18. During the term of his office he is relieved from paying monthly dues.

19. He shall see to it that one half of the Officers Lodge is comprised of Officers or past Officers.

III. FOR THE DEPUTY W. M.

1. This office is always filled by the past year's W. M.
2. He is the Provincial Lodge's representative.
3. In the absence of the W. M., or if he cannot attend, he takes his place.
4. He wears a compass on his breast.
5. If the Lodge has educational institutions, he is their immediate director.
6. During the term of his office he is relieved from paying monthly dues.

IV. FOR THE SENIOR WARDEN.

In addition to his duties evident from the ritual, he shall:

1. Watch over the Brethren's morals and good order in all things.
2. Inform the W. M. of anything that is important to Freemasonry.
3. If the Lodge has established economic enterprises, e.g. trading companies or the like, then he and the Treasurer are their immediate directors.
4. He wears the scales on his breast, and wields a gavel.
5. During the term of his office he is relieved from paying monthly dues.

V. THE JUNIOR WARDEN.

In addition to taking part in the ritual, he must also

1. oversee the political demeanour, prudence, and discretion of the Brethren.

2. Report anything falling into this category to the W. M.

3. His particular field includes complaints, news, and anything that may affect the Order and its members politically.

4. He wears a plumb on his breast, and wields a gavel.

5. He pays no monthly dues while he is in office.

VI. THE SECRETARY.

1. In each Lodge he records and signs the minutes in a special book and presents it to the W. M. for signing.

2. He maintains the membership register, noting therein any changes concerning the members' careers both inside and outside the ☉.

3. He maintains a book in which visiting Brethren enter their names.

4. In the Lodge he reads out the by-laws, constitutional articles, letters, etc.

5. He maintains the correspondence, but before mailing any letters he must always submit them to the Officers Lodge, as well as the replies.

6. He maintains a correspondence record.

7. He maintains a ledger for any postage and writing materials, collects the monthly dues from the absent Brethren, endeavours to benefit the Lodge by using prepaid addresses, and tries to increase this fund.

8. He keeps the archives in order, stores them in the Lodge house, and takes letters home as rarely as possible.

9. At the bidding of the Master he gives notice of the Lodges, either orally or by means of a circular.

10. Shortly before St. John's Day he reminds the Brethren to submit their nomination slips for the election of the Master.

11. He opens the deposit box during every Lodge and gives a report to the W. M.

12. He makes notes of any news which he must communicate to the absent members.

13. He collects the ballots and balls.

14. He shall maintain the strictest confidentiality about any matters concerning his office.

15. On St. John's Day he surrenders his books to the Officers Lodge and turns over any surplus of his fund to the Treasurer against receipt.

16. He may request the assistance of younger Brethren and make proposals in this regard.

17. He pays no monthly dues while he is in office.

VII. THE TREASURER.

1. He is responsible for collecting the initiation fees and for the general management of the main fund; he also holds the counter-lock to the money-box.

2. He advises the W. M. on how to dispose of the funds.

3. He disburses a certain amount of the initiation fees to the household fund, namely one-tenth for each degree.

4. Just as he collects any surplus funds, he must also reimburse any advances paid with the Officers Lodge's permission.

5. Every year on St. John's Day he renders an account to the Officers Lodge and hands over the money-box.

6. He co-directs all major financial institutions operated by the Lodge.

7. He wears two keys on his breast.

8. During the term of his office he pays no monthly dues.

VIII. THE MASTER OF CEREMONIES

1. ensures adherence to the prescribed ceremonies.

2. He assigns to every Brother his proper place.

3. Outside and visiting Brethren are referred to him, and it is his responsibility to examine them.

4. He ensures the proper appearance of everything in the Lodge, e.g. the preparation and serving of the dishes during the Table Lodge, etc.

5. He must make the stay pleasant for travelling Brethren and provide them with addresses.

6. He is used in all deputations to princes, other Lodges, the dicasteries, etc.

7. He must ensure that the Brethren are always dressed appropriately in the Lodge. The Entered Apprentices wear white lambskin aprons, while the Fellow

Crafts' aprons include a small band, and those of the Master Masons have a blue lining. Apart from this no insignia of any authentic or false degree may be worn.

8. He carries a sword in his hand and wears one on his breast.

IX. THE ALMONER.

1. He collects donations for the poor in every Lodge.

2. He collects the fines.

3. After the closing of the Lodge, he counts the amount received and records it. The W. M., who holds the counter-lock, then signs the record.

4. He turns over his ledger and the money-box to the Officers Lodge on St. John's Day, but this fund is always kept separate.

5. On the direction of the W. M. he pays the poor the amounts approved by the Lodge. Preference should be given to poor but honest Brethren.

6. If funds permit he shall offer proposals on how to invest the money, but funds must never be reduced to a few guilders, and he must notify the Lodge before they are.

7. He carries an alms bag and wears a blazing heart on his breast.

8. He is the principal director of all poverty relief and health institutions operated by the Lodge.

X. THE HOUSEKEEPER.

1. He collects the monthly dues and receives one-tenth of the initiation fees collected by the Treasurer.

2. In return he arranges payment of the rent for the Lodge house, procures the lights, aprons, gloves, and membership insignia, pays the wages to the serving Brethren, etc.

3. He keeps a ledger for this and hands it over to the Officers Lodge on St. John's Day, remitting any surplus funds over to the Treasurer. The W. M. has the counter-lock.

4. He orders the food, pays for it, and collects the money required for this purpose from the Brethren.

5. He wears the Lodge's coat of arms on his breast.

6. He directs all of the Lodge's minor economic enterprises, e.g. renting out houses that it may own, sees to their construction and upkeep, etc., and he must

seek to increase this fund.

7. Like the six Officers above he pays no monthly dues while in office.

XI. THE ORATOR.

1. At the W. M.'s bidding he must be prepared to deliver a speech in every Lodge as well as to speak on behalf the Lodge at any festive occasion.

2. He must first present his speech to the W. M. for examination.

3. He wears a scroll (reproduced in metal) on his breast.

4. He co-directs all educational and scientific institutions.

XII. THE STEWARDS.

1. In general, they ensure good order in the Lodge.

2. They step forward on festive occasions.

3. They must be prepared to assist the other Officers in their duties.

4. They carry rods in their hands and on their breast.

XIII. THE SICK VISITOR.

1. If he knows of a sick Brother, he must be at his disposal and see to it that he is not lacking in care and upkeep and, if necessary, report this to the Officers Lodge so that any relevant decisions can be made there.

2. If the Lodge operates any healthcare facilities, hospitals, or the like, he and the Almoner direct them.

3. He wears a cross on his breast.

4. He shall ensure that no letters or other Masonic items remain with very ill Brethren.

XIV. THE DECORATOR.

1. He ensures that the Lodges are properly decorated, that the lights are lit and extinguished at the proper times, etc., and that everything is clean.

2. He gives notice when something new must be purchased and receives instructions of how to obtain the funds for this purpose, and whether or not it is to be paid for from the housekeeping fund.

3. He then procures it, submits the receipts on St. John's Day, keeps everything under lock and key and turns over the keys at the end of the year.

4. As far as is feasible he shall set up the decorations in such a manner that everything is movable and can be installed and uninstalled with ease.

5. He wears two lit candles, reproduced in metal on his breast.

6. If the Lodge operates craftsman's workshops or factories, he co-directs them.

XV. THE LIBRARIAN

1. keeps the book collection in order and sees to its preservation and augmentation to the best of his ability.

2. He returns the list of books, the books themselves and the keys in due order on St. John's Day.

3. If the Lodge owns cabinets, manuscripts, etc. (which do not form part of the archives), he has oversight over them.

4. If the Lodge operates educational or other learned institutions, he co-directs them.

5. He wears a book on his breast.

XVI. INFORMATION ABOUT THE SERVING BRETHREN, WHICH MUST BE READ TO THEM FROM TIME TO TIME.

1. They are initiated and promoted free of charge.

2. The Lodge pays their salary through the Housekeeper.

3. They appear in the Lodge without hats and weapons.

4. They handle the decoration of the Lodges, following instructions by the Decorator.

5. They set the tables, serve the meals, and serve as attendants, as directed by the Master of Ceremonies and the Housekeeper.

6. They announce the Lodges at the Secretary's command.

7. They generally assist every Officer in his duties and report to them anything that may be of concern to them.

8. They must be willing to do anything they are ordered to do by the Officers. Finally,

9. they must report to the W. M. at least twice a week, at a time set by him, to inquire if there is anything he might do for them.

10. However, no Serving Brother may be used for any business unrelated to Freemasonry without payment or against his will.

Addendum A. REPORT ABOUT THE STATE OF THE LODGE —

I. At the beginning of the new Masonic year, the Officers Lodge had – members, of which there were:

Current Officers	– – –
Past Officers	– – –.

Furthermore there are:

Master Masons	– – –.
Fellow Crafts	– – –.
Entered Apprentices	– – –.
Total attending members	– – –.
Attending: past Officers	– – –.
" Master M.	– – –.
" Fellow Cr.	– – –.
" Entered A.	– – –.
Total number of all members	– – –

This is verified by the attached register of names.

II. Initiations during the past year:

1st degree	– – –
2nd degree	– – –
3rd degree	– – –

III. The Lodge has made arrangements and supports

    A. From the poor fund   – – –
    B. From the main fund   – – –

IV. Poor fund income   – – –
    ”   ” expenses   – – –
                     _____
            Surplus   – – –

V. Main fund income   – – –
    ”   ” expenses   – – –
                     _____
            Surplus   – – –

    Unpaid interest   – – –
    Cash on hand   – – –
according to the attached balance sheet.

VI. Furthermore, the following events noteworthy for Freemasonry have occurred here:
    A. – – –
    B. – – –

B) Scottish Freemasonry
I. Scottish Novice.

Illuminatus major, the Greater *Illuminatus*
or Scottish Brother (the Scottish Noviciate)

INTRODUCTION.

There are 2 kinds of Lodges in this degree: those for regular work and those for initiations. The former are held in a room which is not decorated any differently to the Officers ⊡. The members are seated in the same way in Scottish Masonic apparel, that is with green aprons and the Lodge jewel in the button hole, in their order around a table. The Right Worshipful Master, the two Wardens, and the Privy Secretary are the same persons who occupy such offices in the higher degrees or the Directing *Illuminatus,* and they sit in their usual places. We will speak more of the initiatory Lodges and their decoration later. Both kinds of Lodges are opened and closed in the following manner, the catechism is gone through in each Lodge, and, before closing, the watchword for the entire ⊙ is given.

[I.] OPENING THE LODGE OF THE SCOTTISH BRETHREN.

R[ight] W[orshipful] M[aster]. ♪ All is well, my Brethren.

S[enior] W[arden] (repeats this.)

J[unior] W[arden] (likewise.)

(The Brethren line up in the sign.)

R. W. M. Worthy Br. S. W.! Where does the Scottish F[ree] M[ason] work?

S. W. In a holy place, in the still of the night, far away from the bustle of the world and safe from the ears of the profane.

R. W. M. Worthy Br. J. W.! See to it that we can work here safely!

J. W. (goes about, sees to it that everything is secure, closes the doors, and returns.) Right Worshipful Master, the Lodge is tyled.

R. W. M. Brother S. W., what time is it?

S. W. High midnight.

R. W. M. Brother J. W.! Is this the holy hour of opening the Lodge?

J. W. Yes, Right Worshipful Master.

R. W. M. Thus I open this Scottish Lodge of Brethren in the name of the Illustrious Worthy Superiors by the holy Scottish number ♩♫♪, ♩♫♪, ♩♫♪, ♩♫♪.

S. W. (repeats this.)

J. W. (likewise.)

R. W. M. My Brethren! This Lodge is opened. (The rapiers stay sheathed.)

[II.] CATECHISM OF THE SCOTTISH BRETHREN.

Q[uestion]. Are you a Scottish Freemason?

A[nswer]. Noble persons accepted me among themselves when I was an orphan and did not know my father.

Q. Where were you accepted?

A. In a solemn, dark, and holy place, before the door to the Sanctum.

Q. At what time?

A. In the dark of the night, during the moon's first quarter.

Q. Who approached you?

A. The peaceful crowd of the Illustrious.

Q. Did you know these persons?

A. No! I did not know them, but they knew me and loved me, and I dedicated a faithful and trusting heart to them.

Q. Whence did you come?

A. From the world of the first Elect.

Q. Where are you going?

A. To the Holy of Holies.

Q. Whom do you seek there?

A. Him who is there, was there, and will forever be there.

Q. What illuminates you?

A. The light that dwells within me and has now been lit.

Q. What did you see when the light was given to you?

A. I looked upon the Earth and I saw the humans naked and unclothed; but they were ashamed of their nakedness.

Q. What have you been bid to do?

A. I was taught how to know, love, and govern myself and others.

Q. What is the name of your Master?

A. Adonai.

III. CLOSING THE SCOTTISH BRETHREN LODGE.

R. W. M. Does anyone else have anything to offer for the good of the ☉?

S. W. (answers.)

R. W. M. Worthy Br. S. W., what time is it?

S. W. It is high noon.

R. W. M. Is this the proper time, Worthy Br. J. W., to close this Scottish Lodge?

J. W. Yes, it is the proper time.

R. W. M. I thus close this Lodge in the name of our Illustrious Worthy Superiors by the holy Scottish number, ♩♫♪, ♩♫♪, ♩♫♪, ♩♫♪.

S. W.
J. W. } (give the same knocks.)

R. W. M. My Brethren, this Scottish Lodge is closed.

IV. INFORMATION ABOUT THE WORKING LODGES, WHERE THE MAIN POINTS SHOULD ALWAYS BE READ.

1. It should be held at least once a month, not including the Initiation Lodges.

2. In this Lodge the tables relating to the members of the lower Class, if such have been submitted by the Assembly of the Lesser *Illuminati,* are corrected, expanded, and sent to the Assembly of the Directing *Illuminati.*

3. All matters concerning the Minerval Assemblies, promotions in the lower degrees, etc., are decided here or, if the matter is too important, are reported to the Directing *Illuminati;* thus, they are also provided with all tables and Obligations.

4. Everything a member of this degree learns and which concerns the Illust. [Order,] Freemasonry, or other societies, the Brethren's promotion in civil offices and positions of honour, etc., or anything that may relate to such matters, must be indicated in these Assemblies, where it is recorded in the minutes and reported to the higher Superiors.

5. The members of this degree shall primarily instruct those Brethren tasked with recruiting new members. Addendum A. serves this purpose, in addition to the Instructions contained in the Minerval files.

6. The main work of this degree, however, is the precise analysis of the characters according to Addendum B.

7. When the number of Brethren increases, or if the Superior is overburdened with work he can divide the Scottish Brethren Lodge into two, with one part concerning itself solely with character-sketches while the other one deals with matters concerning the Minerval Assemblies.

V. LODGE RITUAL FOR THE INITIATION TO THIS DEGREE.

I. If a Lesser *Illuminatus* is recommended for promotion to this degree, he must be at least of legal age. As has been stated his character is then examined according to the questions in Addendum B. This is done in several working Lodges until every question has been answered.

II. The decision is then reported to the Assembly of Directing *Illuminati,* who can reject or confirm the promotion.

III. If it is confirmed, the Candidate is summoned to the Master's house who tells him in the presence of the Privy Secretary that he has been found worthy to be accepted into a higher degree. However, this Class is of the utmost importance: a solid, inseverable bond among the best, most tried and tested, most trustworthy men supporting one another in all things and seeking to make their lives sweet and pleasant. This entails that there only be one will, and no reservations and no pretence among them. Therefore, he should first declare himself on the following points:

1. Has he found a better and purer system built on more solid ground in any other society that can satisfy his desires better or faster?

2. Did he join the ☉ primarily to satisfy his curiosity or to join an alliance with the better part of humanity for the happiness of the world?

3. Is he satisfied with our institution as far as he knows it, and does he consequently want to contribute to our plans? Does he find any flaws therein, and if so, what are they?

4. Will he fully dedicate himself to the ☉, or will he resign, given that there is no middle way in the higher degrees?

5. He must state if he belongs to another order or society, and if so, which?

6. Does this society demand anything of him that contravenes our institutions, e.g. betray our secrets to it, work exclusively for it, etc.?

7. If the same were demanded of him by another order in the future, would he comply or not? – And all that, by his honour!

IV. Once he has answered these questions he is asked, before he can be promoted, to first write his unembellished autobiography, and when he is finished with it to seal and submit it to the Master. This final test of his honesty will decide his fate.

V. The Candidate's answers and these entire proceedings are entered into a log, and he is then dismissed.

VI. Once, after some time has passed, the Candidate has completed and submitted his autobiography, and the Master has examined his answers and found nothing dangerous therein, a date is set for his initiation.

VII. Assemblies can usually be held on any day of the first quarter of the moon.

VIII. He is led to a secluded chamber in which he will find a quill, ink, and paper on a table.

IX. Meanwhile, the Lodge is opened.

X. The Lodge room is draped entirely in black. At the back of the room can be seen a strong, locked door. This Lodge represents the vestibule of the Scottish Lodge. Before the door the Right Worshipful Master sits behind a table draped in black with the Privy Secretary on his left. The two Wardens are seated at another table facing him, and between them sits the *Introductor.* The other Brethren are seated at both sides; all wear the Scottish apron and black coats. The Master and Wardens carry gavels. Otherwise, no one wears a jewel. Further, no *tapis*[45] or anything else is to be seen. The Secretary keeps the minutes. Other than the Ritual Book, etc., there is nothing on the table other than the apron for the new Brother, a round mirror with a handle, and the *Nosce te ipsum* (Addendum C.). On the Master's table there are 4 candlesticks, as also on the tables of the Wardens. There are no other lights in the room. However, to the right of the Master there hangs a blazing moon in its first quarter.

XI. After the Lodge is opened the *Introductor* is sent out of the room. He takes off his black coat, approaches the Candidate, and says to him the following:

'My Brother! Before I can tell you anything else, place the index finger of your right hand on your heart, raise your left arm, the hand, and index finger pointing up, and repeat after me:

"What I will hear and learn today and from now on in this close circle of faithful and eternally bound friends and in our Illust. ☉ I shall keep as a dear secret with which I have been entrusted, and I will never betray it, not even in the hour

---

[45] *Fr. Carpet, i.e. tracing board.*

of my death, as long as I am in possession of my senses. I promise this by my honour and everything I hold holy, dear and near.'"

Once the Candidate has repeated this, the other continues:

'This degree marks the beginning of an entirely new career for you; the close-knit circle of men you wish to enter today is bound in life and in death to assist one another as faithful, honourable friends. This degree is also the Noviciate of higher Scottish Masonry, which is in the hands of the ☉ and its external associates only. The ☉ also secretly directs the lower degrees of most Masonic systems and sees to it that at the very least these are not entirely desecrated. The hieroglyphs of the Freemasons contain sacred and serene truths. In the following degree you will already receive insights into them. However, all this knowledge is of no value and will be lost to the world if we do not make men wiser and better. For the execution of this grand plan, knowledge of the human heart and self-knowledge are the most essential parts. To this purpose, sufficient instruction will be given in this degree, and everyone will therein receive materials for the study of psychology. Later you will see the progress we have made in this discipline. But let us also see a sample of your skill in this subject. On this sheet of paper, create a faithful image of your character as you believe yourself to be, without dissimulation. You are dealing with men who can see your innermost self. If you are resolved to do this, I will leave you alone in this business for a few moments.' (The Candidate answers. One may have also prepared him, so that he may have completed part of the essay at home, and less time is therefore required here.)

XII. The *Introductor* now leaves the Candidate alone and returns to the Lodge.

XIII. After this, he leaves once more to fetch the Candidate's essay about his character.

XIV. This is also handed to the Prefect, who is to judge to what extent it matches the portrait drafted by the secret Lodge, and if it can be supplemented from both of the Candidate's essays.

XV. Once this is done, the Privy Secretary is sent to the Candidate, to whom he says: 'Dear Brother! You have given us an appreciable sign of your candour and trust with the essays concerning your person. In truth, we are not unworthy of these, and at length this will grow mutually as you get to know us better. Thus, away with all reservation! Among men who seek to better themselves and others and who want to help this diseased world, all pretences must cease.

We study the human heart, yet the further one progresses in this art, the more indulgent and patient one becomes, and the more one realises to what extent we are governed by circumstances and passions, how little it is often our own doing that we are neither better nor worse. Thus, we are not afraid to confess our flaws to one another, to bring this to one another's attention in brotherly love, and by this to hone our acumen and powers of observation. In the future, you shall take part in our labours in this regard. You shall see that we have secure means to present our Illust. Superiors with a very faithful picture of each of our members. Your portrait, too, is already in our hands, with all your virtues and flaws. You cannot feel insulted by this as the portrait cannot shame you or, otherwise, we would not see each other here today. And no man of your intellect will believe himself to be without flaw. Is it still your will to bind yourself to the men who extend their brotherly arms to you as you are?" (The Candidate answers, and the Privy Secretary returns to the Lodge).

XVI. As soon as the Secretary has returned, the *Introductor* is sent out to bring the Candidate to the vestibule's gate. Meanwhile, all lights are extinguished, and the room is lit only by the moon. The Brethren shroud themselves in their coats.

Introd. ♩♫♪, ♩♫♪, ♩♫♪, ♩♫♪.

J. W. (gives the same knocks.) The knocks of a Scottish Freemason.

S. W. ([gives the same knocks and] repeats this.)

R. W. M. ([gives the same knocks.]) See, who is there.

S. W. (repeats this.)

J. W. (exits, looks, and asks:) Who is there?

Introd. It is an honourable and properly tried illustrious Mason seeking entrance to the Inner Sanctum's Vestibule: I petition on his behalf.

J. W. (repeats this.)

S. W. (likewise.)

R. W. M. Worthy Br. J. W.! Let him enter as long as you know him and vouch for him.

(The J. W. lets him enter and positions him between himself and the S. W. The *Introductor* steps behind him.)

R. W. M. My Brother! Here you see the sacred circle of tightly knit, true Masons in wisdom's vestibule, preserving the Inner Sanctum where pristine truth and wisdom shine, who will in time spread their light over the entire world. These men, the Holy Legion of Nobler Souls, still conceal themselves from you, but do not believe that you are equally concealed from them. No facet of your heart is unknown to the Illust. Superiors. Naked and unadorned, even under compunction and in concealment, you stand in the Assembly of the Wise, and this gaze, my Brother! looks deeply, is sharp! But do not be frightened, and rejoice instead! Your heart must be good and noble; you would have never been allowed in this circle of better men if your way of thinking and inclination had not been similar to ours. Therefore come hither! (He approaches the altar.) Friend! Brother in spirit! If you wish to learn from us the great art to safely complete your journey through the midst of the world's hazards, you will need artfully armed eyes to distinguish appearance from truth, and a fraud from a friend. No common eye, no common gaze will suffice. The Order gives you this sharpness of sight, this degree of enlightenment. Behold the image in this mirror! It is your own. Self-knowledge is the magical looking-glass through which you may read the souls of others. (He holds the mirror before him and hands him the *Nosce te ipsum.*) The path to the hearts of other men begins with our own heart. Therefore, begin with yourself; examine yourself often according to the questions you will find prescribed in this degree of the ☉. Regard yourself diligently. Do you believe that inwardly you are as you appear on the outside? Study your physiognomy often, daily, hourly. You will constantly discover new features, and you will learn to judge others by these features. What a beautiful and, ah! what an ugly thing it can so very often be to behold the unconcealed human heart! *Nosce te ipsum!* (With this, the R. W. M. gives the sign of the degree). Man, discover yourself, if you seek to fathom others, and only then: *Nosce alios!*[46] (Here, all Brethren reveal their faces, also giving the sign of the degree).

Behold here your faithful friends who no longer wish to remain concealed, but under the condition that you also shed any pretence. O! you, having learnt from this experience, let this mirror be your most faithful council throughout your journey in this world, in the bustle of the world where everything is so deceptive and dangerous! In yourself, in your own heart you will find all men. All are subject to the same nature, the same drives. Everyone loves himself, loves others in himself. As you consistently find actions and effects similar to your own in others, so the causes and mainsprings must be similar, too. He who knows himself well, knows all; he who does not know himself, knows no one. He who knows himself falsely or little will judge others as erroneously. He does not seek in others what they are, but only his most foolish desires, his passions. From yourself, discover

---

[46] *Lat. Know others.*

what others are, but do not let the treacherous looking-glass flatter you; and trust it the least, if it shows you in too beautiful a light. We all have our flaws. He who has the fewest and knows them is the best among us. Come to me now! (The Candidate steps to the right side of the altar.) Here is the Scottish leather apron (he puts it on the Candidate, removing the Master apron). It is entirely rectangular, cut by the Square. Thus, straight like the Square of virtue and wisdom, must be the direction of your heart. Green is the colour of hope. Hope for everything from the ☉, if you are honourable and faithful. The sign of this degree is placing the index finger of your right hand on your heart, while raising that of your left along with your arm. The word is: *Nosce Te ipsum.* The other answers, *Ex Te nosce alios.*[47] For the grip, unbutton the overcoat and half your waistcoat and kiss the other's brow. Now take your seat! (The R. W. Master shows him his seat and has the candles lit; then he continues:)

You have had to undergo many preparations, my Br.! It has taken you great efforts to reach this threshold. Have no regrets though! A spirit that has been prepared sees more clearly. For by now, the ☉ has come to know your industry and skills. It finds in you a man who has put himself in the position to gradually penetrate the depths and chasms that are unfathomable to the largest part of mankind and can only be explored by the elect.

No uninitiated man sets foot here. Not everyone can do this; and many who wanted to do so, who wanted to purchase it with money or sought to force it with trickery or power, have been forever excluded for these reasons. Never shall this portal (he points to the door behind him) of light open unto them. Here counts no power, no wealth, no reputation! An enlightened mind and an honourable, benevolent heart are the only nobility and privilege that make a man capable of this. No one inherits this privilege; not the deeds of others, but one's own, lead to it. You have reason to be proud, because many good men have failed. Further, we are so convinced of your faithfulness and secrecy that, from now on, we require no further oaths or tests. Put your trust in your leaders. The Superiors will give you that which is useful to you and what you can bear. After all, you can see how unselfishly, how nobly you have been treated from the beginning. Thus continue in your work; we shall not forget you. We only require your complete trust. Finally, I must ask you a few questions about matters of which we need to know our better members' opinions.

---

[47] *Lat. From thyself know others.*

You are in the circle of your closest, most faithful, perhaps your only friends, who know your innermost soul – therefore, away with any shameful pretence! Let your heart speak freely, just as our hearts rush towards you! There is so little truth in the world, friend, Brother, son! Often, the man with the beautiful façade and the blinding splendour is merely a whited sepulchre. This majestic figure, this imprint of heaven, God's image is hidden beneath a deceptive husk. Everyone conceals himself – the evil one to deceive, and the good to avoid being deceived. For one the procedure is to attack, and for the other it is to defend. It is sweet wantonness for connoisseurs of the human soul that men are essentially good, that they are merely blinded and do not know their own interest. It is sweeter still to find in this sacred circle people who are of a single heart and will. Now tell me, good Brother!

1. Do you find that this world rewards virtue and punishes vice? Do you not rather find that on the contrary, an evil man is outwardly happier, more respected, more powerful than a righteous one? In a word, how satisfied are you with the world as it is now? (The new Br. responds, and his answer is recorded.)

2. To change this, would you not try to gather the good and make them mightier than the evil, if this were in your power? (Answer entered into the record.)

3. If it had been your choice, which country would you have preferred to have been born in and call your fatherland? (The answer is entered into the record.)

4. In which historical period would you have most liked to have lived? (Answer entered into the record.)

5. If you could choose freely, which social class would you choose? Which science? (Answer entered into the record.)

6. Who is your favourite historical figure, or which author is your paragon? (Answer entered into the record.)

7. Do you not consider it a duty to serve one's tried and tested friends as much as possible, to grant them as many outward advantages as possible, to reward their righteousness, to make their lives easy? Do you offer to submit to the provisions required by this degree of the ☉, namely that each of us is required in his monthly Q. L. to indicate which services, benefits or the like he will provide or can make available through his recommendation so that the Superiors have the opportunity to suggest worthy subjects among the

members of the ☉ for these positions? (Answer entered into the record.)
You see, my Brother! This is how we seek to reward and support better men
once we have tried them, one by one, so that we can thus gradually give the
world a different direction. Since you feel in your own heart that men do
not yet fulfil their destiny, that all public institutions have degenerated, that
the teachers of wisdom and truth have not yet succeeded in tuning men to
a different pitch and bringing their interest in doing good close to their
hearts, you can easily see that this must have been caused by the means that
they have employed. Therefore they must be chosen better, if virtue and
wisdom are ever to govern the world once more, and this is the business of
our Illust. Order. Friend, Brother, Son! When we gather in this holy, secluded place and leave ourselves to contemplating the ills of the world, how
fortune rarely smiles on him who deserves this the most, how misery, misfortune, and persecution are an honest man's allotted portion, how so very
often a good man and his large, lovable family whom he has raised to virtue
languishes in sorrow, being oppressed, persecuted, and held back by villains; how his son observes this and becomes himself a villain for the sole
reason of not having to suffer like his father; how trickery, flattery, oppression, and falsehood are generally rewarded while truth and uprightness are
trampled underfoot, as man is a sensual creature, after all, allowing himself
to be stirred by the external, how men conceal themselves to others and
how one always betrays the other, how everyone only seeks his personal
gain, sacrificing the best of mankind, how wisdom flees to the corners, how
he who wishes to work for the welfare of the world as a true humanitarian
must flee from nation to nation to avoid persecution – Should we keep
silent about this? Should we merely sigh? Should we never attempt to throw
off this yoke? No, my Brother! Place your trust in us! Seek faithful, zealous
collaborators not in the clamour and bustle of the world; they are hidden in
the dark, under cover of the ancient night; there they are, lonely and quiet,
gathered only in small circles and led by Illustrious Superiors like obedient
children. They call out to every son of the world passing by in this frenzy –
but only a few harken! Only he who sees with the eyes of Minerva's bird,
labouring under the protection of this benevolent orb (he points to the
moon), will surely find them. Now have another look with us at the entire
sphere of influence that you will enter by joining this inner circle."
XVII. The Privy Secretary reads:

General Overview of the Entire Order.
The further you, my Brother! climb in our Illust. ☉, the more you will be convinced that our principles are of such a kind that they would not need to fear the light if men were as they should be. Sadly, however, very much is still lacking. Truths that are not presented under concealment and in sacred ceremonies are not truths to most people. The hidden tempts them too much, and they are captivated by the pleasure of knowing something that is not known to everyone, so that they direct their attention to matters they would have otherwise ignored no matter how important they are, and in this manner the unadulterated truth must imprint itself in their souls in indelible characters. There are also propositions that cannot be presented directly, that require thorough contemplation, repeated effort, and not everyone is inclined to this; yet everyone likes to think of himself as the wisest man. Thus, if I wish to initiate someone into a system that relies heavily on intermediate propositions the sequence of which he would not likely have discovered through his own reasoning, I must conceal the complete development with a shroud until he is sufficiently prepared to see the whole light, and the allure of attaining this should move him to pay attention to everything, even the smallest detail. If I were to present the final goal at once then it would appear to him unimportant, even false, and we would lose the most useful people.

Finally, there certainly are also certain truths, hidden behind hieroglyphs in ancient times, preserved by only the most tried and tested part of humanity, certain insights into the higher wisdom which not everyone can fathom, because a thousand obstacles, prejudices, passions, etc., prevent him from penetrating this deeply. These have always been veiled by secret mystery schools behind images and presented to their pupils by and by, and the hieroglyphs of the 3 symbolic degrees of Freemasonry are also organised according to this plan.

Everything our Illust. ☉ teaches and does must affect the best of the world and must lead to the elevation of men from the depths of perdition into which they have descended, making them receptive for a higher goodness and wisdom. This is why it has also studied the organisation of all public and secret associations, preserved the best parts and avoided their errors – indeed putting its outer plan of operations on a foundation more fitting to the times, more solid every day. Even the best intentions are often thwarted by evil men or desecrated by unworthy ones. However, our secrecy and the strict tests of our members preserve us from both. Let us now summarise the ☉'s entire plan in a single aspect. Our final goal is to:

1. Disseminate pure truth.
2. Make virtue victorious.

To reach the first goal people must be purged from prejudice, their minds must be enlightened, and then, with joint forces, the sciences must be purged of unnecessary subtleties; correct principles, drawn from nature, must be established, and thus the unobstructed path to approach the pure and now hidden truth must be opened to man. Therefore, we must unlock every source of research, reward every suppressed talent, pull every genius out of the dust, everywhere teach pure principles according to the spirit of the age, educate the youth, unite the best minds with an inseverable bond, dispute superstition, faithlessness, and folly boldly but prudently, and finally train all our people in such a manner that they have a uniform, straight, and correct understanding of all things. The preparatory school[48] of the Minerval Class serves this very purpose, followed by the lesser Freemasonry, which the ⊙ seeks to influence as much as possible and guide according to our grand purpose, and finally the Higher Class, where the results of our efforts and the traditions of our ancestors are revealed to those who have been fully prepared.

To lead virtue to victory we test and train our pupils' hearts with incredible effort. Afterwards, anything can be accomplished with these men. But one cannot proceed by ordinary means. No amount of teaching and preaching will help here, or else it would have helped long ago. There is no truth to be found that has not been repeated often, no duty that has not already been taught, and the world remains as it has always been: while no worse, it is as bad as it was a thousand years ago. This is so because there are too many forces promoting vice, and they have far more powerful effects than all our sermons. Therefore, from our side, force must be met with force.

One must examine the source of the evil: Why are there so many evil persons, and so few good? Because the allure of evil is greater; since one can accomplish more with it in the world. Here, the scales must be tipped in favour of virtue. One must seek to bring it about that the just man can safely expect to find reward for his righteousness in this world. In this endeavour we are hampered by the clergy, the princes, and today's political constitutions. What are we to do then? Promote revolutions? Turn everything upside down? Expel violence with violence? Exchange one tyrant for another? Certainly not! Any violent reform is

---

[48] 'Pflanzschule', literally 'plant nursery'.

reprehensible because it does not improve things as long as men with their passions remain unchanged, and because wisdom does not need to be coerced.

The ☉'s entire plan is based on educating men, not through declamation but by promoting and rewarding virtue. We must secretly tie the hands of those who promote vice and govern them without oppressing them. In a word, a general regimen of morality must be introduced, *one* form of government encompassing the entire world without dissolving the civil bonds, in which all other governments continue to exist and pursue their work and are free to do anything except thwart the grand purpose of ensuring that good is once more victorious over evil. This was already Christ's intention when He introduced a pure religion. Men were to become wise and good and were to allow themselves to be guided by wiser and better persons for their own good. In those days, however, when everything was in darkness, sermons were all that was needed. The novelty of wisdom had an overwhelming allure. Today this is not so. More powerful means than mere education must be applied to give virtue an outward allure for the sensual man. Passions cannot be extinguished: one must only know how to direct them towards noble purposes. We must show the ambitious man that the true honour for which he yearns rests in virtue and can never be satisfied any better than by practising the same. We must show the miser who to wants own everything that he actually owns nothing, and we must show the libertine that overindulgence will sour every joy, in short! that everyone best satisfies his passions, whose first origin was pure, when he does so within the confines of virtue, and that the ☉ will provide him with the means for doing so.

Thus, all our men must be tuned to a single pitch, holding fast to one another, having only one goal in mind, assisting each other, and thus pervading the entire world. One must gather a legion of men around the powerful of the world, men who tirelessly pursue a great plan for the good of humanity, men who are willing to change the entire nation; then, no external force will be required. The rulers of the world will soon open their eyes and see that, by practising virtue, their advantage will be increased, whereas they will run into tremendous difficulties when they enforce evil. The nobler men will soon gain the upper hand over the evil ones who now pretend to be the masters and who bring unhappiness to anyone who resists them. Those however who are too effeminate, too prejudiced, too cold or too passive to earnestly fight for the rights of mankind must be motivated; good men must seek one another out; those who do not know or trust each other must be brought together, and shown that two honourable men who are truly united can be stronger than a hundred scoundrels. All this must however be done discreetly. Our small flock must not abandon one another and must assist everyone who is oppressed, providing every good man with temporal advantages and outward happiness, and attempting to gain all those positions where power can be wielded for the good cause. Why should it not be permissible to establish oneself by righteous and gentle means to influence governments? The first objective of every state constitution is to place good persons at the helm, to reward merit, and to crown virtue. If the ☉ can succeed in this through advocacy and by guiding the heart, if it has educated the most faithful, the best, the wisest, the most thoroughly tested persons for the state, if it tries to promote them and reward their diligence, then it consequently fulfils the duties of the most faithful subjects and thus also fulfils the original purpose of men entering into social bonds. If, then, one has such a circle of men in every country, each of them forming others in turn, and if they hold fast to each other, then the ☉ can accomplish anything, and in this manner indeed it already has achieved much for the good of mankind. If, however, only one thing is omitted, then all doctrines are useless, and the entire matter remains purely speculative.

Here, my Brother! you see the immense scope of our endeavours into which you have been placed. Consider everything carefully! It is a grand work, not of our own design; a secure, well thought-out, firm, unspoilt plan! Make yourself worthy of collaborating to the extent of your abilities! No effort goes unrewarded here. – Now hear some further information concerning the work of this degree.

XVIII. The Secretary now reads the Introduction and the Information about the Working Lodges, in addition to Addendum A. The new Initiate can peruse Addendum B. at his leisure.

XIX. Now follows the Catechism.

XX. Next the Order's watchword is given.

XXI. The Lodge is closed; upon which

XXII. The Privy Secretary submits the following, sealed in a packet, to the R. W. M. for forwarding to the other Superiors:

    a) the new Initiate's answers which he provided in the R. W. M.'s house,

    b) the man's portrait as sketched and corrected by the Lodge,

    c) his silhouette,

    d) his autobiography, and

    e) character, and

    f) His answers to the 7 other questions.

Addendum A. SECRET INSTRUCTIONS FOR THOSE TASKED
WITH RECRUITING NEW MEMBERS TO THE ☉.

1. He who wants to bring a new member to the ☉, must first secure his perfect trust and love.

2. He must conduct himself in such a way as to suggest that he has hidden depths.

3. He should gradually attempt to instil in the Candidate a yearning for friendly and secret connections. This should be done more or less in the following manner:

a) He gives him access to books that speak of unity and strength in shared endeavours.

b) He also steers his conversations around to this matter and shows him how helpless a little child is, and how weak a grown man also is without assistance from others, how great and powerful he can become with the aid of his fellow men, and how important the advantages of social life are.

c) He demonstrates how all power comes from the unity of will.

d) He focusses his attention on the art of knowing and governing people.

e) He demonstrates to him how a single wise man can govern and guide a thousand others.

f) He provides examples of what people can accomplish when they are trained and tuned to the same pitch, e.g. armies.

g) Then, however, he speaks of the flaws of civil society, how faithlessly men act towards one another, how everyone is guided by his own personal interest, and how little one can often rely on friends and family.

h) 'Yea', he shall exclaim from time to time, 'if only the good were united they could build Heaven on Earth. Better men are so weak only because they do not know each other or are disunited.'

i) It will then be time to make him understand what secret societies can accomplish.

k) He shows him the example of the Jesuits and the Freemasons. When the conversation turns to great world events, he always tells him that these are driven by secret mainsprings, and insinuates that these might well be the work of such secret Orders.

l) He awakens in him a yearning to rule in secret, to research everything without being noticed, to give the world a new direction from his chamber;

to rule those who believe themselves to be his masters.

m) From time to time he speaks ambiguously, as if he knew such an ☉, but then falls silent again. On other occasions he says: 'If I had the opportunity to join such an order, I would do so immediately.'

n) All this must be repeated often.

o) Then he suddenly says: 'I have finally found that for which I have wished for so long: An ☉ of this kind is willing to accept me. What do you advise me to do?' He then makes objections that the other man may well have in mind himself, and addresses them, asking him also for his opinion.

p) He casually leaves a letter written in cipher where it can be seen.

4. The Candidate should be a Christian, honest, sensitive, not stupid, no older than the recruiter, and, generally, between 18 and 30 years old.

5. If he now petitions for membership, the matter is presented to him as extremely difficult, and information about it is revealed only gradually, by handing him as few written documents as possible, or at least only for a brief time!

6. He is then caught by surprise as he picks up these papers.

7. He is encouraged to suggest other persons for membership as well, and to describe their character, etc.

8. His background is investigated.

9. He is given the impression that his best friends may already be members of the ☉.

10. If someone who has been accepted into the ☉ or seeks admittance wants to know a member's name, one shall never name an important Superior but always a respected and good man.

11. However, one should know how to administer the medicine according to each person's constitution, and the ☉ should therefore be given a name that has a positive effect on the Candidate. One Candidate may seek a new kind of Freemasonry, another a learned society, while a third will seek out the Rosicrucians, and still others certain political associations. Everyone must find what he seeks. The ☉ can accomplish everything, and it does not work under the same name in all countries.

12. All these things must be reported to the Superiors.

13. Every *Illuminatus major* may copy these instructions by hand.

Addendum B. QUESTIONS USED FOR ASSESSING THE CHARACTER OF A CANDIDATE FOR THIS DEGREE.

I. *His person.*

1. What is his name?

2. His age? date of birth?

3. His fatherland? place of birth?

4. His physique? Slim, fat, or medium? Tall, short, or average height? Strong or weak limbs? Svelte or paunchy? Does he have any ailments, and if so, which? One-eyed, deaf, stuttering, bowed, limping, hunchbacked, crooked, cross-eyed?

5. *Physiognomy.* Complexion: dark or fair? Sanguine, wan, black, blond, yellowish, tanned? His gaze keen, penetrating, dull, straight, languishing, lovelorn, proud, twinkling, downcast? When speaking, does he look at people rigidly, brazenly, and persistently? Or does he shy away? Can he withstand a sharp stare or does he look aside deceitfully? Or openly, freely, cheerfully, or sinisterly? Profoundly or in a wandering manner? Blankly, cordially, or seriously? Or is his gaze uplifted? Do his eyes lie deep in his head, or do they bulge? How is his physiognomy in other respects? How is his silhouette? How is the nose, the brow? Perpendicular, protruding, or receding? short or tall? square, round, oval, etc.? Does he furrow his brow? and does he do so horizontally? or perpendicularly?

6. *His hair.* The colour: light or dark? brown or black? blond, reddish, or fiery? Its strength: thick or thin, long, short, curly, plain, hard or soft?

7. *His voice.* Manly, mellow, childlike, deep, stiff, high, singing, taut, weak, strong, deafening, declamatory, gentle, sweet, flowing, stuttering, changing, rising, falling, or monotonous[?]

8. *His bearing.* Noble or common, frank or unassuming? forced or at ease? How does he hold his head? Erect? thrown back? drooping, to the side, wavering, or stiffly? Are his eyes cast down? Does he toss his head strongly, does he retract it between his shoulders?

9. *His gait.* Slow, quick, sedate, with short strides or long ones, dragging, slothful, skipping, dancing, clomping, rising, with knees bent, feet turned in, feet thrown out, [shuffling], alternatingly quick and slow, wavering, his body leaning forwards or backwards? Does he look at his feet? Does he gesticulate with his hands while walking? Does he throw his head back when doing so[?]

10. *His general health.* Is he often or continuously sick? From which illnesses does he suffer the most?

11. *Speech, presentation.* Orderly or disorderly, jumbled? Does he use his hands when speaking? and how? Ceaselessly or intermittently? fervently? with his head, at the same time? with his whole body? Does he come close to those he talks to? Does he grasp them by their arms, clothes, buttons? Is his discourse fast, ponderous, thoughtful, oratorical, arrogant? Does he talk little or much? or does he stay wholly silent, and if so, why? Out of modesty, ignorance, reverence, or sloth? to probe others or to hide his weakness? to gain respect? out of pride or contempt? Is his language pure or provincial?

II. *Education, upbringing, culture, gifts.*

1. To whom does he owe these? Was he always under the supervision of his parents? How was his upbringing in general? Who were his teachers? Does he remember them with affection? To whom does he believe he owes his education? Has he travelled? if so, where?

2. *Languages.* Which does he understand, speak, write? And how well? Does he love foreign languages more than his mother tongue? Does he mix foreign words into his speech? What is his style?

3. *Sciences.* In which is he experienced? Which are alien to him? Which does he love? Does he penetrate deeply into them? Does he love the arts? which ones?

4. Does he have *talent?* And in what areas? Poetry or philosophy? imagination? mechanism, *esprit de détail?* artistic genius? Does he like to make small cardboard boxes? Does he like wood-carving, farming, gardening, does he style his own hair, etc.?

5. Does he have *skills?* In athletics? crafts? mechanics? Is he strong, dexterous, nimble, quick, well-suited to physical exercise, good at conjuring tricks, etc.? What is his handwriting like?

6. *Attentiveness to other people.* Does he look mostly at the heart, mind, character, direction, outward manners, morals, cleanliness, way of thinking, religion?

III. *His spirit.*

1. *Capabilities.* Is his mind deeply penetrating? Is it fast, slow, refined, wide-ranging? Does he have foresight, does he possess a lively imagination, or is he coldly calculating? Does he have presence of mind? Does he surprise with bold ideas? Does he show wit, thoroughness, and keen insight during conversations?

2. *Prejudices.* Does he have many? Is he gullible? Does he love the miraculous? the paradox, or does he follow common opinions? What prejudices does he hold?

of age? religion? childhood? country? state? class? authority? generality? novelty? Is he keen to shed his prejudices? Is he easily prejudiced for or against people without having tested them first?

3. *Direction*. Where does he seek his felicity? Away from the hustle and bustle? In prestige? power? honours? in sensual pleasures? in riches? sciences? virtue? truth? Does he consider the future? the past? or only the present? Does he content himself with making small plans? Does he often see the distant greatness in small matters? Is he capable of making grand designs? Thinking, feeling, and executing them? Does he seek to distinguish himself from others? and, if so, how? Through being great and extraordinary? In good or evil? or in both? Does he have a high opinion of himself, and in what respect? Does he deal justly with others? Is he obstinate, or can he be easily persuaded? Does he value fine thinking? Does he try to be original, or does he follow the thinking of others? Does he believe himself to be infallible? Does he possess self-awareness? Does he accept reprimands? Does he hate people? why? Because they are better than he is? because they fall short of his ideals? because he does not believe himself to be sufficiently respected by them? Because he has often been deceived? Because he is quick to regard them as unworthy of him? What does he look for in a spouse? A good heart? intellect? good housekeeping? beauty? money? promotion? family? power? Does he love his body? his health? Is he soft? sensitive? pampered? dreamy? Does he fear death? Does he easily understand other people's points of view? What motivates him to work and activity? A desire for a life of ease? Tranquillity? power? prestige? honour? sensual pleasure? money? Does he value honour, respect, approval? How does he seek to earn them? Is he hurt by contempt? Does he seek to rise higher? To what? By which means? Through women? money? by harming his neighbour who stands in his way? Through merit? science? zeal? strength? ignominy? Which side does he take when there are two factions? The weaker or the stronger, the wise one or the foolish one? If the weaker suddenly gains the upper hand, does he stay true to his principles, or does he prefer to form a third faction? Does he declare both parties to be wrong? Does he attempt to reconcile them? act as mediator? or does he remain entirely neutral? Is he firm in executing his plans? or do difficulties deter him? How can one most easily win his respect and friendship? By praise? flattery? dissimulation? silence? by enduring everything? by ignominy? submission? money? women? hatred and contempt for those whom he hates? through his mistress? servants? the recommendation of his protégés? Is he suspicious? mistrustful, mysterious, reserved,

gullible, open-hearted? Does he enjoy discussing his plans before their execution? Does he only wish for lively pleasures? and their constant increase? Or does he content himself with more modest joys also? Does he constantly demand pleasure, or does he also love deprivation in order to enhance his pleasure? Does he tolerate weaker persons, and is he patient when dealing with them? Is he curious, meddlesome?

IV. *His heart.*

1. *Disposition.* Is he as prescribed in the Lesser *Illuminatus* degree, or is he lacking in certain respects? Is he straightforward in his actions? or does he like to dissemble? against whom? on what occasions? in what ways? for what reasons? Does the fate of others interest him? the general good? Or does he only care about himself? Does he enjoy working earnestly for the general welfare? Even at the expense of his own pleasure? Does he take every opportunity to do good? to do great things? without self-interest? Is he righteous in his actions, even when it is not noticed? Will he not be deterred in this? by threats? cajolement? respect? money? women? disfavour? persecution? misfortune? enmity? friendship, hatred, vengefulness, promises? promotion, when he can do the opposite with impunity? When in pain, is he verbose? talkative or quiet? silent? Is his pain enduring? Is he happy, cheerful?

2. *Passions.* Does he have strong passions? Which does he indulge the most? Can he resist a present, lively, sensual impression? Is he inclined to melancholy caused by passion? or is this merely his temperament? Is he miserly? or inclined to wastefulness? and of what kind? Does he love hunting? Does he enjoy hearing or watching stories of murder?

V. *Conduct, habits, actions.*

1. *When speaking:* Does he like to bring up the minutest circumstances? Does he like to contradict others? Does he like to interrupt? Does he stick to the subject? or does he speak of several disconnected things in a short period of time? Does he become heated in the course of the conversation, or does he remain calm? During a conversation, does he distinguish between the different people to whom he is speaking? Does he like to provide evidence? Does he often merely rely on the reputation of others instead of giving proof? Does he express himself obligingly, crudely, straightforwardly? Does he always think he is right? Does he find easy what others find difficult? Does he like to reprimand others? calmly?

seriously? passionately? teasingly? with bitterness? curtness? emphasis? Does he hold back with his criticism until he suddenly bursts out with it? Does he like to entrust secrets to others? his own? other people's? to everyone at the very beginning of the acquaintance? How does he speak to his servants? Hardly at all? curtly? peremptorily? jokingly? confidentially? Does he quarrel with them? even about minor infractions? Does he forgive them their misdeeds? even if they act crudely and faithlessly in his presence? Does he look his friends in the eye when he tells them about the misfortunes of their loved ones? Does he like to remind them about unpleasant things? Does he enjoy embarrassing others? Does he like to tease? Does he like to gloss over the mistakes of others? Does he seek to reveal his friends' weaknesses in the presence of others? How does he speak of his benefactors? well? with gratitude? Does he also introduce them to others as his benefactors? or is he ashamed of the blessings he has received? Is he still grateful when he no longer needs his benefactor? if he stands in his way against his knowledge and will? Does he often speak of his wife and children? and if so, how? Does he like to laugh off his own ideas or those of others? rarely? often? strongly? briefly? lastingly? with regard to every trifle? Does he like to offer his services? even to those he does not yet know? to those whom he neither can nor wishes to help? even to his enemies? How does he speak about the nobility, princes, the authorities? Disdainfully, reverently, well, ill? [as they deserve? only well, or does he also speak of their flaws? only ill?] even though they have virtues? How does he speak to noblemen? coweringly, reverently, with familiarity? Does he praise their follies, even their crimes, only to please them? Does he always agree with them? How does he speak of the lower classes? Disdainfully, despotically, indulgently, justly? How does he speak with lesser persons, with subordinates? willingly, unwillingly, often, rarely? only in the absence of better society? only when he needs them, and moreover rarely? and does he then pretend he does not even know them? Is he friendly towards them, gracious, even in the presence of gentlefolk? only to make himself popular with the masses? to draw the common man closer to him? to give an example to the gentlefolk? to temper their pride? to make them hated, to make himself popular? to honour merit in the lower classes? to bring this to the attention of those of higher standing? Does he speak with them proudly, peremptorily, with familiarity or appropriate to his and their status? Does he say 'yes' to everything? Out of fear, calculation, flattery, stupidity, to probe others? About what does he like to speak the most? Of himself, of the corruption of the times, [of money,] interest rates, usury, his trade, of housekeeping, state affairs, religious quarrels, free thought,[49] piety, prayer, sciences, the flaws and deficiencies of others? news, trifles, fashion, finery, clothes? of the favours of powerful men? of honours, distinctions, his correspondence with important persons? of love? women, food, drink, wine, games, hunting, court intrigues, or of his noble ancestry, family, relatives, misfortune? of his merits? Does he like to speak disparagingly, and if so, of what? Of religion, fanaticism, superstition, hypocrisy, intolerance, the State, regents, ministers, clergy, monks, nobility, the military, scholars, critics, the lower classes, vanity, the evils of the world, blasphemers? of those who revile the clergy, of abuses in his own church, wastefulness, splendour? or of the friends of those with whom he is speaking? even if he knows they are their friends? of unrewarded merit, the magistracy? or of eloquence, philosophy, innovations? of his own friends and relatives? of all social classes and men and worldly institutions? or of himself, and if so, why? to be praised, to probe others? to discover what they think of him? to conceal greater flaws? to find excuses for himself? to demonstrate impartiality and self-awareness? Does he constantly speak disparagingly? with everybody, without distinction? or only with certain people? at certain times? and if so, which? when? why? out of habit? natural malice, to do harm? to defame, to persuade others? to probe, to make a statement? to have something to say? to anger others, to arouse their wrath? to entertain, out of insight, zeal for the good cause, out of carelessness, foolishness, anger, vengefulness, fanaticism, patriotism, stupidity? Are his insults merely words, well-founded, or mockeries? Which kinds of conversations does he avoid? and in which is he entirely silent? Does he talk about everything? Does he interrupt others with his discourses? [Does he like asking questions? Does he exaggerate, does he curse, does he swear when he speaks?] Does he let others speak as well? Is his delivery rich in imagery, sensual, discerning, vapid, emphatic, laconic, verbose, declamatory, spicy, moody, dark, clear, enigmatic, mysterious, true, deceitful? Does he act mysteriously? Does he take people aside, does he like to whisper in their ears, does he pretend to already have knowledge of a matter? Does he like to joke and taunt? Does he become heated when he contradicts people? Does he like to give in, or does he resist? Does he accept reasoning? Does he like to make decisions? quickly? Does he retract his original judgement when he recognises it as flawed? Does he like to flatter? Does he like to praise, does he like to make assurances of friendship, does he extol others in their presence or praise qualities he knows they

[49] 'Freygeisterey', i.e. liberal thought in religious matters.

do not have? Does he like to be uncivil to them? Does he like to admire? what? even ordinary things? Does he denigrate at other times those things that he once praised elsewhere? Does he spread gossip? Does he have finesse when giving praise? Does he also praise his enemies? For what? why? talking to whom, on what occasions? Are his speech and judgement consistent? Which of his own qualities does he praise? Good looks, intellect, a kind heart, wit, physical skill, manners, taste, moderation, bravery, courage, fame, devotion, religion, zeal, justice, status, impartiality, unselfishness, finesse, intrigue, vice, crime, nobility, family, good fortune, wealth?

Does he like making promises? does he keep them? Does he offer good advice? Is he infatuated with his own wit and ideas? Does he repeat them often? at every occasion? Does he impatiently await the opportunity to share them? Does he present the ideas of others as his own? even to their originators? Is he good at telling stories? Does he like it? Does he frequently repeat himself? even *ad nauseam?* Does he like to speak crudely, using uncouth and obscene words, no matter who is present?

2. *In writing:* What is his style? In letters, in books? Has he published anything? When? of what value? What principles does he teach in his writings? Does he like to read from them to others? even if they do not wish to hear them? What reputation, what influence do his writings have?

3. *In his deeds:* How does he act when angry? and irate? Whom does he hate? What upsets him? Trifling things? being contradicted, praise, reprimands, scorn, accusations? Which of these upsets him the most? The Fickleness and slowness of others, the obstruction of his ambitions? Malice, injustice, false accusations, general oppression, stupidity, obscene and libertine talk, censure of his fatherland, of his friend, his benefactor, ingratitude? When his earnestness is met with fatuity, when he is ridiculed? Can he hide his anger? How does he react when his hot temper is met with kindness or indifference? How does he express his anger? Often, lightly, suddenly, never, after some time has passed, by swearing, cynicism, contempt, degradation, slander, or other shameful actions? Can he forgive insults? How can he be reconciled? Is his reconciliation honest or feigned? How does he act when in love? [Can he conceal it? What is his love directed at?] Pleasure, leisure, marriage, cabals? Does he spend money on what he loves? What kind of women does he love? His equals, married, noble or common, the first, the best? romantic, sentimental women? Does he like variety? Does he stray? even when he is married? Are his inclinations obvious to others? How does he

treat his beloved when he separates from her? Is he jealous? Can he control himself when in love? Does he neglect his work, friends, and duties to please the object of his love? Does love make him talkative? Does he seek out every opportunity to speak with his beloved? or does he see her only during certain hours? Has he chosen these hours himself? Does his infatuation expose him to ridicule? In love, is he fanciful, sensitive, and romantic? and blind to the woman's flaws and weaknesses? How does he act towards the servants? Does he employ more people than necessary, or fewer? Does he plague them with excessive work? Does he pay them too much or too little? Does he not let the servants approach him? Does he keep a sharp eye on them? tally their accounts? Do they like working for him, do they stay in his employ long? Why do they resign? or why does he drive them away? Does he treat them with seriousness, kindness, or beatings? How does he treat old and infirm domestics? What do his former servants say about him? How does he speak about his former employees? Does he enjoy company? why? out of curiosity, insolence? to learn? to know people and the world? to teach others? to become well-known or famous? to pry? to engage in intrigues? out of vanity, boredom? to elevate himself? to slander or destroy others? What company does he prefer? The noble, pious, common, educated, lustful, vain, heated, kind, slothful, ignorant, old or young women, beautiful or ugly? with everyone without distinction? with many or just a select few? Has he chosen his own company, or does his office, his circumstances, a lack of different and better society force it on him? Does he like to mingle with people of his social class? What reputation do his closest associates have? what tastes? governing passions? Does he love the company of people from whom he can learn? or of those he can teach? In company, is he accommodating, very indulgent, courteous, modest, shy, well-mannered, or is he not? Does he prefer more serious or more cheerful society? Does he like receiving visitors? whom? anyone? why? out of vanity, joviality? Does he detain his visitors? How does he treat those who detain him for too long? or arrive at inopportune times? Does he send them away? Does he excuse himself with urgent affairs? Does he become reticent, or does he speak of trivial matters? When realising his visit is becoming burdensome to others, does he leave or stay? Does he love solitude? why? because he is in love? [because he loves work?] out of piety, fear of temptation, a tendency for melancholy, misanthropy, pride, to forge hidden intrigues? out of love of peace and quiet? of leisureliness after a long day's work? because he lacks qualities that would make him pleasant company? out of poverty? ambition, or because he wants to be sought out? out of thriftiness? hypochondria, illness? Does he sometimes seek solitude, and company at other times? What is his conduct towards his betters? Does he seek their company more than that of others? Does he stand on ceremony? or does he regard them as equals? abuse their benevolence? become over-familiar? stoop below his dignity, his station, even resort to flattery and baseness? Does he allow himself to be used as a tool for their purposes? as a spy? for intrigues? Does he know how to make himself indispensable to them? By what means? Through insights, by researching their personal and family secrets? [or] weaknesses? How does he bear their abuses, their disdain, contempt? Do they upset him? Does he stop being obliging? or does he pretend not to notice? And what if this happens more frequently, does he let this bother him? Does he work for them free of charge? Does he also flatter their relatives? their domestics? Does he lend them money? Does he allow even their domestics to treat him below his station in order to gain something from their lords or to be invited to a meal? Does he act as their minion? Does he hate those whom the lordships also despise, and does he treat them with hostility, even though they have not insulted him? Does he seek to learn the secrets of the powerful? Does he run after them, or does he wait until he is called upon? Does he imitate their mannerisms and habits? Why does he seek the company of this or that important person? How does he conduct himself towards a great man who has fallen or [towards one] who can no longer help him? How does he treat his equals? especially his friends? Does he have many friends? Who are they? Is his friendship close, tender, faithful? Can he exercise moderation in the enjoyment of his friends? How does he speak of his former friends? of those who are absent? Is he demanding with his friends? What does he require of them? money, help, recommendations, instruction, entertainment? that they love and hate what he loves and hates? Praise, admiration, approval? Does he want everything to go his way? Does he also do them favours? even if this causes him hardship? Does he quarrel with them? why? often? for a long time? Can he be easily reconciled with them? How does he conduct himself during the conflict? Is he careless when making friends? or does he test his people first? Does he immediately share his secrets with them, making them potentially dangerous to him in the future? or does he withhold them? What does he say when absent friends are slandered? Does he love change? Is he indulgent towards them? Does he rush to their aid? Is he obliging? or does he like to make excuses? or does he delay his favours? Does he return favours? Does he begrudge his services? How does he act towards [his friends] when he experiences good fortune? when he is in glowing circumstances? when he is unexpectedly ennobled or knighted? What if they experience misfortune? Is he ashamed of them? Does he shun them? Does he join in the slander against them, does he deny any acquaintance with them? rebuke them harshly, deny them any help, advice, money, recommendations, support, protection? How does he conduct himself towards them in society where they do not shine? or are not well regarded? Does he abandon them due to the accusations against them, the displeasure of superiors, persecution? What must cause the friend's misfortune for him to be ashamed of him? How does he react when his friends experience good fortune, when they become his equals or superior to him? with envy or with joy? Does he easily believe what others say against his friends? Does he immediately condemn them, or does he take them to task first? How does he react when his friend has betrayed him? How does he behave towards lesser men? courteously, crudely, intimately? Are they his favourite company, or does he hate and shun them? Does he deal with them with familiarity, pride, with harsh expressions? Does he know how to make their situation more bearable? Does he treat lesser men in the same way as his equals? or betters? Does he know the worth of the lower classes? Is he harsh towards his subordinates, or forgiving, or excessive with demands, charges? Does he give due honour to every social class, every person, every office? for what reasons? out of conviction [or] duty, fear, craftiness? Does he please his domestic staff? Does he shun them? How does he treat his debtors, his creditors? Does he make his payments on time? Does he seek to pay off old debts by and by? or does he accumulate new debts? How does he conduct himself when detecting the mistakes of others? Does he pretend not to notice? Does he use their weakness? to promote his own intentions? to obtain their services? Does he threaten exposure? Does he laugh loudly? Does he gossip about it? Does he brush it aside with indifference? Does he not seek to take advantage of it? Does he seek to hide the flaws of others, does he warn them of future mistakes? How does he behave towards persons to whom he has revealed his weaknesses, either inadvertently or out of vanity, carelessness or necessity? who are cognizant of his most secret affairs? Does he hate them for this, does he shun them, does he seek to get rid of them? Does he flatter them, is he at their mercy for this? Does he continue to confide in them? Does he seek to inculcate disbelief in them? Does he treat them with pride? mistrust, insults? How does he behave towards those of other religious faiths? Does he love or hate them? Does he shy away from their company? or does he publicly meet with them? How does he conduct himself when suffering, in misfortune, during persecution? Steadfast, patient, weakly, dejected, brash, despairing? Is he proud of his wealth? Is he ashamed of his poverty? Does he want to appear rich? or does he make no secret of his circumstances? How does he conduct himself when his parents, wife, relatives, friends, benefactors, enemies die? Does he wish them death, life? why? How does he deal with insults? With silence, composure, kind words, excuses, vehemence, slander, guile, despite? How does he raise his children? How does he treat them? in public? in secret? What is his conduct when eating and drinking? is it moderate? for what reason? out of misery, poverty, miserliness, love of life and health, sense of duty, to be better suited for his work? out of piety, vanity, or because it is his nature? How does he conduct himself at the tables of others? Does he like to sit with them? Is he himself hospitable? Is he gluttonous? Does he eat quickly or slowly? What does he like to eat and drink? Does he like eating alone, and if this is the case, does he like to be waited on like a lord? Does he love rich food? Does he have to be the first to be served everything exquisite? How many meals does he eat in a day? Has he succumbed to drink? Is he often inebriated? and when he is, how does he behave? Quarrelsome, crudely, amorous, talkative, cheerful, good-natured, faithful, bravely, treacherously, ill-mannered, lazily, idly?

Does he force others to drink? Does he often frequent inns? Is he a habitual drinker? Does he like to often speak of drinking? Does he love such company? Does he love dogs? Does he have any? How does he treat animals? horses? Does he like to break, tear up, or destroy things? Does he smoke, use tobacco? What other habits does he have?

VI. *Circumstances, way of life, relationships.*

1. *Wealth:* How much income, how much is he due to inherit? Debts? many? from what causes? misery, lack of income adequate to his station? to live a libertine's life? to appear grand and powerful?

2. *Social status.*

3. *Reputation:* good or bad? why? with what kind of persons, good or evil, prudent or ignorant?

4. *Religion:* What faith does he profess? Is he zealous, lukewarm, fearful, superstitious? Does he go to church? How does he conduct himself in the churches of other denominations?

5. *Connections:* Who are his parents? What is their way of thinking? Are they still alive? What did they die of? Does he have many relatives? Does he practise

nepotism? Does he have a wife? Who, how is she? How did he meet her? at what age? Does he have children? how many, how old?

6. *Activities:* How is his conduct in his business affairs, in his work? Careless, lazy, diligent, punctual, orderly, faithful? Does he like to procrastinate? What kind of business does he prefer? only official matters, or others as well? Does he accept tasks in which he can distinguish himself? as well as prolonged, protracted ones? Does he not tire of them, become annoyed, timid? in the face of difficulties, danger, or when the chances of success are remote? Does he like changing jobs? Does he seek to improve in his office? to excel over others, to invent? and implementing his inventions? How does he behave after failed attempts? Does he work fast, easily, hastily, tediously, solidly? Does he have no books, many, or few? In which field does he have the most? a little of everything? Books of prayer and meditation, legends, sermons, politics, history, novels, theatre plays, alchemy, Freemasonry, Kabbalah, theosophy, other mystical subjects, military, legal, theological works, books on economics, concerning his trade, obscene, freethinking, scholastic books? the latest titles, or older works? Has he bought them himself, on his own accord or the advice of others? Are they well worn? Does he often lend them out to others? Does he enjoy reading? often? at what times? for long hours? which authors the most? What is his favourite book? How does he pass the time? Does he like games? which ones? Hazard?[50] Games of intellect, of leisure? Games that are used for education and instruction? where he can demonstrate his wit? for money or not? for large sums? Is he lucky? unlucky? Does he play out of habit, courtesy, leisure, profit-seeking, poverty, to make acquaintances? to be respected? How does he conduct himself when he wins or loses? Is he quarrelsome, derisive, dishonest? Can he moderate his behaviour during a losing streak? Does he retire from the game once he has won? Does he deny ever having won, does he claim to have always lost? How does he avail himself utilise of solitude? with prayer, reading, writing, studying, trivial pursuits, with his house mates, with domestic business, plans, designs, idleness?

7. *Correspondence:* Does he maintain a wide-ranging correspondence? with whom? where? Does he reply reliably? How does he keep his letters? Do they lie about? Does he leave torn pieces of paper lying about?

8. *Sleep:* Does he enjoy sleeping? long? often? out of laziness, illness, or why? How is he when awakened from his sleep? Is he easily awakened? How is he

---

[50] *A game of chance played with two dice, highly popular in the Eighteenth Century.*

when awakened suddenly? Does he speak in his sleep, does he dream, and how?

9. *Attire, dwelling:* Is his clothing neat, dishevelled, clean, dirty, torn, resplendent, above or below his class, varied, diverse, antiquated, fashionable? What colours does he like? bright ones, plain ones? When one meets him at home, is he dressed resplendently, or how? Does he wear the same garment for long periods of time? Does he buy second-hand clothes? Is he the first to join a new fashion? Does he change his attire depending on the time of day, location, situation, persons? How is his house, his chamber arranged? Does he have just the essentials, useful things, luxuries? Does his furniture befit his station? On what does he spend the most money? Kitchen utensils, [tables,] pictures, books, chairs, hunting-gear? His cellar, linen, fashion accessories, silver, wallpaper, things that catch the eye, things that are useful and durable? Is his furniture good, tasteful, choice, [orderly,] clean? Even that which he uses every day? Is everything tidy or dishevelled? Is his orderliness too scrupulous?

Addendum C. *NOSCE TE IPSUM!* [51]

Political character.

What is

1. his name, last name.
2. Parents.
3. Relatives, friends, enemies[.]
4. Health[.]
5. Attire[.]
6. Sciences?
   a) Where are his books?
   b) which sciences does he love most?
7. How was his upbringing?
8. Status,
   a) single or married[,]
   b) with or without children.
   c) What office, and how did he attain it.
   d) How does he perform it?

---

[51] Lat. *Know thyself.*

9. Income.

10. How does his house, chamber, etc., look?

Physical condition:

1. How is his nature[?]

   a) Gestures,

   b) gait.

2. What is his head like? How does he hold it?

3. Brow.

4. Eyes – gaze

5. Mouth[,]

   a) voice[,]

   b) speech.

6. Hair – colour.

Moral character:

1. What is his reputation?

   a) Presently,

   b) formerly,

   c) with superiors,

   d) with lesser persons,

   e) with the clergy,

   f) why?

2. How does he behave towards his parents?

   a) Father, mother,

   b) in their presence or from a distance.

3. Educators.

4. Benefactors, patrons[.]

5. Enemies[.]

6. Great men, nobles,

   a) face to face,

   b) from a distance.

7. His equals,

   a) face to face,

   b) from a distance.

8. Inferiors,

   a) subordinates,

   b) servants.

9. Clergy.

10. Women[.]

11. His wife.

12. Children,

   a) his own,

   b) step-children,

   c) those of others.

13. During conversation.

14. In society[,]

   a) does he enjoy company,

   b) does he enjoy solitude,

   c) what kind of company does he like most?

15. In love[.]

16. In the face of insults.

17. During good fortune[.]

18. During ill fortune[.]

19. During the good or ill fortune of others[.]

20. During unexpected occurrences?

II. Illuminatus Dirigens.

Directing *Illuminatus,* or
Scottish Knight

Sketch of the seal of the Secret Chapter, which is uniform in every respect, except for the insignia of the shield.

Notification.

Where a true and secret Chapter is to be held, it must be constituted, in accordance with the ceremonies described below in no. X, by the Provincial Lodge of the District installed by our Highest Superiors.

Note.

Instructions I, II, and III must be read out in each Chapter, even if no one is being knighted.

INTRODUCTION.

The Holy Secret Chapter of the Scottish Knights gathers for two reasons, initiation or the regular work of this degree.

The first will be discussed later.

Work is completed during a monthly Assembly without ceremonies. The members sit, without Masonic attire, as if attending a conference, at a table covered with a green cloth chaired by the Prefect. No Priest of the ☉ is present. The Chancellor, sitting next to the Prefect, takes the minutes. The others are seated along both sides of the table according to the date of their initiations. The work of this degree consists of the following:

The Secret Chapter has the task of directing the entire lower edifice, including the preparatory school as well as the lower degrees of Freemasonry.

I. FURTHER INFORMATION AND GENERAL INSTRUCTIONS.

1. The Scott. Knights should bear carefully in mind that they are the overseers of a great institution established for the benefit of mankind; therefore, they must shed any vain thoughts of playing a special role in the ☉. Everyone must work in his respective station as much and as well as he can, must only think about being worthy of the place where he can be useful, must reject any petty and miserable vanity, must not desire to present himself as a Superior, must certainly not recruit anyone, and must not concern himself with anything outside his department but instead forward anything concerning it to the Prefect for further handling.

2. In the ☉ this Prefect is known by the name of Local Superior.

3. In the Secret Chapter each Knight is responsible for a certain number of Magistrates Assemblies and Lodges, reporting on everything that he receives from there: written reports which they are instructed to send to him, in such a manner that he receives all reports concerning the Minerval Assemblies from the responsible member of the Scott. Brethren Lodge, and all reports concerning Freemasonry directly from the Officers Lodge.

4. Since our institutional structure can never be devised well enough, and can never be developed fully enough, every Scott. Knight shall note any flaws he observes, and draft proposals outlining how cohesion among the members in a Province can be maintained, the subordinates' obedience strictly preserved without reducing them to servility, and all selfishness eliminated. He shall report all of this to the higher Superiors whenever he has occasion. Furthermore, the Knights shall explore all good outside institutions and be vigilant to any trace of persecution against us.

5. Since the frequently changing local and temporary conditions force us from time to time to make minor changes to the outward structure of our plan of action, the Knights shall prepare their subordinates to expect such minor amendments; since they will never disrupt the harmony of the well-planned edifice, they should not expect any damage as a result of them.

6. In general, the Scott. Knights must principally strive to persuade everyone after their own fashion to be sophisticated without being pretentious, as well as cautious, eloquent but not garrulous, prepossessing, and tireless in the interest of the cause. If a man finds that he is prone to hastiness in his speech should observe a moment of silence to gather his thoughts when faced with a question or address that may cause him embarrassment.

7. Under no circumstances should a Superior accept any boon, or even the smallest favour, from his subordinate. We must always only *give, never take.*

8) It will readily be seen that, if no reception dues are collected from any member of the ☉, the actual coffers of the ☉ will remain nearly empty, and that a great many noble ends in the world, which can only be accomplished with money, must remain unachieved. The monthly dues from the lower Classes are far from sufficient to cover postage fees, travelling, and other necessary expenses for maintaining such an extensive enterprise. Our Illust. Superiors generously donate considerable sums to support Brethren who wholly dedicate themselves to the business of the ☉ and have no income of their own. In the light of this, it would nonetheless be very desirable indeed to find means for acquiring considerable sums in the individual Provinces[, so that we may more forcefully work for the happiness of the world and our Brethren]. How to handle the Masonic funds is described below. However, the Scott. Knights should also devise and execute other plans for filling the coffers. He who has reached this stage can no longer have any doubts concerning the noble use of these funds; we do not like to collect money from the subordinates – partly to avoid arousing their mistrust and partly so that they do not begin to think that they have purchased the right to more knowledge. However, by and by we must help the edifice in our parts to the best of our abilities until our funds are eventually large enough. Therefore, every Scott. Knight voluntarily contributes a certain annual sum, which he determines immediately after his initiation. This contribution, be it large, small or none, is set as his circumstances and his heart permit. On the other hand he is relieved from paying the general monthly dues. If possible, one should also seek to inconspicuously induce the Scottish Brethren to pay such a voluntary fee.

II. INSTRUCTIONS CONCERNING THE LOWER CLASSES.

1. The Secret Chapter shall take care that no one occupies an office in the lower Classes for which he does not have the proper degrees. The Magistracy of

the Minerval Assembly consists of the Lesser *Illuminati*. The Superior of the Minerval Assembly must be a Greater *Illuminatus* or Scott. Brother. The Freemasonic Lodges are governed by the Officers Lodges, which must always be stronger than the other part. The majority of the Officers must be Greater *Illuminati*. The W. M. of each Lodge sits in the Secret Chapter, together with his Deputy. The Officers of the Scott. Lodge are the same who hold offices in the Secret Chapter.

2. As far as the *quibus licet* are concerned, the Magistrates Assembly opens the letters of the Novices, makes provisional injunctions, and attaches these *quibus licet* slips to their reports. What is sent in by the Minervals is not opened in the Magistrates Assembly but only in the Scottish Lodge. The individual Magistrates' *quibus licet* are opened in the Chapter. Here all Q. L., as long as they contain nothing of extraordinary importance, are withdrawn by the Local Superior, and only a general report is drafted. The Knights' Q. L. are sent unopened to the Provincial Lodge. It goes without saying that those headed *Soli* or *Primo* pass through all Classes unopened. The reports to the Provincial Lodge are written by the Local Superior alone.

3. The monthly and quarterly tabular reports, *conduite* lists, etc., are sent to the Greater *Illuminati* from the various Magistrates Assemblies. There, every Scott. Br. has his own department. He aggregates the reports for his department into a single one, thus compiling a complete report, a complete table, and a complete list for his department. Organised in this way, they then arrive in the Secret Chapter, where again everything is divided into departments. If possible, the Knight further condenses the report and submits it to the Prefect to whom he generally reports about his field. The Prefect in turn compiles a general report from the abstracts of all the reports, which he sends to the Provincial Lodge.

4. The tables relating to the *Insinuati* remain in the archive of the Magistracy. It is there, too, that their acceptance is decided upon without further inquiries. However, the original tables and Obligations of the Initiates are forwarded to the Provincial Lodge, and every *Illuminatus major* and *dirigens* notes only the new additions in his departmental register.

5. If a Minerval wishes to become a Freemason and is prepared to pay for this, the Officers Lodge can accept him; if however he wishes to become one free of charge, the Scottish Lodge must address this request to the Chapter. For promoting someone to the degree of the Lesser *Illuminatus* only the consent of the Scottish Lodge is necessary. Further promotions must not be granted without prior inquiry to the Provincial Lodge.

6. Treatises and essays of lesser value remain with the Magistrates Assembly; the better ones are sent to the Secret Chapter, and the Local Superior will then be instructed how to proceed with them.

7. If it is deemed necessary to assign secret Censors to one or the other of the Minerval Magistracies, one should alternate this office, partly so that it remains unnoticed and partly so that several men can make their observations.

8. Before a Scottish Novice is knighted, the Secret Scottish Chapter shall ensure that he delivers the biography of the man whose name he bears, as instructed during his initiation.

9. As soon as someone is proposed for the Scottish Knight degree, all files concerning his person, such as his character description, biography, etc., shall be submitted to the Prov. Lodge, along with notes, newly-added comments, and a brief sketch of the man's overall qualities.

10. The Chapter shall ensure it that these biographies are not just brief narrations of events, but also contain the story of the heart; when someone is busy with this task, he shall be relieved from other duties within the ☉. If he has to reveal secret incidents in his life, he can report these under the title *Soli*.

11. Since the Minerval Superiors, who are always Greater *Illuminati*, and the W. Masters, who must be Scott. Knights, cannot always attend the Assemblies of these degrees if the Chapter is not located at the same place, they and absent members in general should not expect to be consulted over every minor point or to be informed about it in the already extensive correspondence. Everyone must abnegate his curiosity and vanity, and do whatever he can in his station.

12. The Scott. Knights shall ensure that the *Illuminati majores* do not neglect to state in their Q. L. what employment, if any, they can provide.

III. INSTRUCTIONS CONCERNING THE FREEMASON LODGES.

1. The Secr. Chapter shall ensure that Lodges for the first three Masonic degrees are established in all larger cities in its assigned district, and that good, morally educated, respected, and wealthy persons are accepted there even if they are not otherwise suited for our higher purposes.

2. The Constitution must be issued by the Secret Chapter in the local language, according to the form (Addendum A.) in the legal name of the first Worshipf. Master who is to occupy this office.

3. If Lodges of the other so-called Fr. Masonic systems are already established there, one shall either establish an authentic one alongside these; or, if the small size of the location or other circumstances do not permit this, shall secretly acquire a voting majority in those Lodges and attempt either to reform or dismantle them.

4. If anyone questions the authority of the Illust. Superiors to establish Lodges he can be told that he is perfectly entitled to do so. Only that which is good and new and true is genuine, and if somewhere he can find something better, more important, newer, truer, or more useful for the world with just as little effort, then he is welcome to go there and claim that he was deceived by us.

5. It shall be impressed upon our members that they must not visit, without the express permission of the Superiors, one of the so-called lodges which have been constituted from England or elsewhere; apart from a signed and sealed letter, some allegories which they understand falsely or not at all, and a few meaningless ceremonies, they know nothing [of true Freemasonry], its high purposes and highest superiors. For many reasons, one cannot easily admit their members to our Lodge Assemblies, even though there are some very worthy men among them. There is only one lodge in Germany that is no longer in communication with our highest Superiors and yet is constituted from authentic sources. However, it is no longer active.

6. Although every Minerval must become a Fr. Ms., he should not be too easily aware of the fact that one seeks to make him one and that his further promotion depends on it; whenever possible, this desire should develop in him all by itself. Once he petitions to become a Fr. Ms., it is revealed to him that the $\odot$ is in direct contact with the only true system of Masonry, and that one can make it easier for him to be accepted.

7. The Chapter itself shall ensure that those among us who may be prejudiced against Fr. My. gradually lose their dislike of it and develop a yearning to become Masons themselves. One can explain to them just how few truly enlightened Fr. Ms. there are and that those lodges that have aroused their distaste are not true lodges at all[, even if they do have the best constitutions].

Freemasonry is an art and a science, not a business. It requires study, and its authenticity is based on knowledge rather than certificates.

8. If a Minerval has very pressing reasons, which the Prefect must evaluate, not to become a Fr. Ms. publicly, he can also be accepted secretly with the Provincial Lodge's permission.

9. The Scott. Knights shall ensure that everything in the Lodges subordinated to them is conducted legally and uniformly. One of their primary concerns must be the preparation of the Candidate. Here, in private, one must show the man that one knows him thoroughly. One must vex him with insidious questions to see if he has presence of mind; and if his lack of solid principles is exposed, he should be made to feel this so that he becomes aware how much he is still wanting and how much he needs our guidance.

10. If someone has already become a Fr. Ms. in a different system and joins our Lodges, he pays no fee, and he must pledge obedience to us with a handshake. If such a man, or indeed any Fr. Ms. of our system, wishes to be promoted further but is not suited for our higher purposes, he must be made to understand this in a tactful manner. If he still insists on receiving additional Fr. Ms. degrees and seems to be inclined to seek enlightenment in other systems, one may communicate to him everything that he would learn in such systems. However, the following has to be observed:

a) One must not deceive him but tell him in advance that he will find no satisfaction from these degrees. If he still desires to be led by the nose, he may choose which system he wishes to learn more about.

b) In this case, however, he will have to pay for his folly with a substantial financial contribution.

c) Upon request by the Secr. Chapter, he will then receive the sealed degrees from the Prov. Lodge. Afterwards, he must return them.

11. Since nowadays many vain games are played with the Royal Art and many a new system is invented, the Scott. Knights shall gather all false degrees and send these to the Provincial Lodge so that every curiosity-seeker may be satisfied.

12. It has already been stated in the Instructions for the Officers of the subordinate Lodges that none of their monies may be transferred without prior request. The Dep. Master of every Lodge, who is also a member of the Secr. Chapter and is in fact also the Lodge's Secret Censor, must ensure that the Lodges always give the impression that they dispose of their funds themselves, while using them according to our purposes. Thus, if one wishes to provide a member of the ☉ with benefits, the Lodge to whom he belongs should petition for such; if he is not a Fr. Ms. one should still attempt to pursue the matter. The Lodge's savings, however, must never be touched, so that we will have the resources for greater endeavours in the future. One-tenth of all funds collected by the Lodges are sent to the Secret Chapter annually. The Treasurer collects these sums and seeks to

increase them by various enterprises, for which he must request approval by the Chapter if he intends to invest some of the funds. At the direction of the Chapter, the Lodges must send money against a receipt, but only for a limited time, and the Chapter must pay them an adequate interest rate. Otherwise, every Lodge is master of its own funds, though it must submit quarterly budgets, just as the Secret Chapter must submit a quarterly general budget to the Prov. Lodge and await its instructions regarding the use for any interest earned. At the command of the Provincial Lodge, deputies from each of the Chapters gather every three years, audit the Province's funds, and deliberate the best general way to invest them. The Prov. Lodge also decides how much money each Chapter must contribute every month to cover the cost of correspondence and other expenses that accrue during the administration of the Province.

13. One should try to influence the vote in lodges that do not belong to our system so that Brethren in need can be provided with support and assistance from their savings without touching our own monies; in general, one should always try to use the by and large poorly-managed funds of such lodges for our great and noble purposes.

14. The Secr. Chapter must ensure that a Lodge never has more than thirty members, and that the Officers can always outvote the others.

15. The Lodge registers remain here, and only general extracts from them are sent to the Prov. Lodge.

16. If experienced Fr. Masons are recruited to the ☉ they come under the direct guidance of the Scottish Knights.

IV. ON THE RECEPTION INTO THIS DEGREE.

1. He who wishes to be initiated into this important degree must first have offered proof that he has made good use of the instructions given to him in the Greater *Illuminatus* or Scottish Novice degree regarding self-knowledge and the knowledge of others. For this purpose, he must diligently practise shedding light on the semiotics of the soul.

2. Therefore, every *Illuminatus major* is presented with questions by the Secret Chapter from time to time which he must answer and whose aim it is to test his ability to draw conclusions about the state of the soul from external signs, e.g. what kind of disposition is indicated by an uncertain, darting eye? From which signs can one conclude that a man is lustful, melancholic, fearful?, etc.

3. If, after such exercises have been variously repeated, the Chapter is satisfied with his diligent and insightful answers to the questions, then the Candidate is proposed in the Secret Chapter. Everyone shares his candid opinion of him, and it is then left to the Prefect to weigh up all the reasons and to decide whether the suggested Candidate is to be accepted or not.

4. If the Chapter has decided to accept him, the Prefect communicates this to him at his home, and adds that he has been a member of the Illustrious Order long enough to be convinced of the excellence of its system and the innocence of its goals. It is still in the Candidate's power to sever this connection entirely or to remain in the Scottish Noviciate for as long as he wishes. If, however, he persists in his intention of being accepted as a Scottish Knight, he must sign the following Obligation.

Obligation.

I, the undersigned, commit myself by the power of this Obligation to remain faithful to the honourable Order of the *Illuminati,* where up to now I have found the best satisfaction for my heart and mind, from now on and for as long as I live, inasmuch as

A. I shall not be part of any other system of Freemasonry, nor any other [secret] association, nor do any work for such, but

B. as long as my circumstances allow me to be active for any such association, I shall dedicate my power and knowledge only to this Illust. ☉.

C. Should I, however, fully resign from the ☉ (which I am free to do at any time), I am at no time permitted to enter any other such secret association.

I acknowledge that this demand is only fair, since I

1) have hitherto never received other than here such magnificent guidance for my own happiness and that of the world and, in addition, have never found a better or more useful system of Fr. My., and therefore

2) I have every cause to recognise the high Superiors of this Order as the true secret Superiors of Freemasonry[;]

3) Since the Illustrious Order does not wish to prevent my resignation should I be moved to this by my civil circumstances or my dissatisfaction with the knowledge gained here;

4) My Superiors are however justified in demanding that, henceforth, I never use the instructions received here for the benefit of other associations, but

5) to the contrary, since I am now thoroughly convinced of the excellent foundation of the ☉ of the *Illuminati* and its willingness to accept everything that is good, it is my duty to utilise any important knowledge I may have obtained somewhere in the manner prescribed by my present Superiors, without revealing it and only for the happiness of the world, thus using them in accordance with the ☉'s purpose.

I promise all this of my own free will and without any secret reservation, by my honour and good name!

    (L. S.)   N. N. (legal name)

[5.] If the Candidate agrees to issue this Obligation, the date of his initiation is then set.

V. OF THE SOLEMN CHAPTERS FOR INITIATION.

1. The Secret Chapter is held in a room which is wallpapered green and, as far as circumstances permit, pleasantly decorated.

2. The Prefect, wearing boots and spurs, sits two steps high under a canopy of the same colour. He wears the Scott. Knight's apron with the green cross; the star of the ☉ (see the drawing in Addendum B.) on the left breast; above the right shoulder a broad ☉ ribbon from which hangs the St. Andrew's Star (see the drawing in Addendum C.). He wields a gavel in his right hand.

3. All other Knights wear boots and spurs, aprons, gloves, and the Cross on a green ribbon around the neck (see Addendum C.). All carry a rapier at their side, while the Prefect and the Officers wear plumes on their hats.

4. In addition to the Prefect, the Chapter must consist of no fewer than six persons, and it may never grow larger than 12, except the Priest, who is not counted.

5. To the right of the throne stands the Sword Bearer with the St. Andrew's sword in his hand, while to the left is the Master of Ceremonies with the rod and ritual book, which he hands to the Prefect whenever he needs it.

6. The blazing star flames above the Prefect's head.

7. A table with four lights, ink-well, paper, the Knight's apron, the ribbon, and the Candidate's rapier stands in the centre of the room. The Chancellor and the Treasurer are seated at both sides of the table.

8. At the very end of the room sit the two Wardens with gavels and the ritual

books, just like in the Lodges of the lesser degrees.

9. All other Knights sit at both sides, and places of honour at the top of the room are assigned to visiting Brethren.

10. Whenever the Prefect speaks with a Knight or has something to say, he must rise and draw his rapier; when he has finished speaking, he must sheathe it.

11. The Right Worshipful Master of the Noviciate Lodge (Greater *Illuminatus* Degree) is the Prefect here, the Privy Secretary is the Chancellor, the *Introductor* is the Master of Ceremonies; the Treasurer and the Wardens are the same persons.

12. Since a Priest of the ☉ is present in every Secret Chapter, he is seated without an honorary sign, bareheaded, clad in white, to the right and before the throne.

13. The *Servienti* (serving Brethren) do not enter the room once the Chapter has been opened.

VI. OPENING THE CHAPTER.

1. When everyone is at his place, the Prefect gives a knock ♪.
Senior Warden. ♪.
Junior Warden. ♪.
Prefect. Worthy Br. Junior Warden, is the Chapter tyled?
J. W. (draws the rapier and says:) Yes, the door to the vestibule is closed. (He sheathes it.)
Pref. Worthy Br. Senior Warden! Is it the proper time to open the Chapter?
S. W. (draws the rapier:) Yes, it is the proper time. (He sheathes it.)
Pref. I now open this Holy Chapter in the name of the Supreme Architect and by the power of the ancient Master's word. ♩♫♪, ♩♫♪, ♩♫♪, ♩♫♪.
S. W. (repeats the knocks.)
J. W. (likewise.)
All Brethren draw their rapiers and sheathe them, the Priest blesses them silently, and all Knights give the sign of the degree by crossing their hands above the breast, then take their seats.

2. Now the Prefect presents the reason for this gathering, the initiation of the Scottish Brother (O. Name); the Chancellor reads aloud the Obligation he has issued, and the Master of Ceremonies is sent out to announce to the Candidate, who is waiting in the vestibule, his acceptance.

VII. INITIATION RITUAL.

1. The M. of Ceremonies places the ritual book on the Chancellor's table and, rod in hand, walks out to the Candidate, whom he informs of the Secret Chapter's approval of his initiation. He takes his rapier, brings it to the room, places it on the table, and gives report of his proceedings.

2. He is then sent out once more to bring the Candidate to the door. This man is dressed as a Scott. Br., wearing a hat and boots.

3. Before he comes to the door, he must wash his hands, according to ancient Scottish custom.

4. Now the Candidate puts his gloves back on, and the M. of Ceremonies takes him by the hand, leading him to the door.

M. C. ♩♫♪, ♩♫♪, ♩♫♪, ♩♫♪.

J. W. (repeats the knocks.)

S. W. (likewise.)

Pref. (likewise.) – Worthy Br. J. W., see who is there!

J. W. (goes to the door, draws the rapier, and asks:) Who is there?

M. C. Here is a Scott. Brother who fervently desires to be admitted to the Inner Sanctum.

J. W. (repeats this.)

S. W. (likewise.)

Pref. Ask him what his name is.

S. W. (repeats this.)

J. W. What is his name?

M. C. It is Br. (O. N.), who has been examined by the Superiors.

J. W. (repeats this.)

S. W. (likewise.)

Pref. Open the door to the Sanctum and let him enter.

S. W. (repeats this.)

J. W. Bring him in.

The M. of Ceremonies takes the Candidate by the hand and ceremoniously leads him to the throne so that his back is towards the Chancellor's table. Then he takes the ritual book, hands it to the Prefect, and stands in his place.

Pref. Happy are you who may cross this hallowed threshold! We welcome you in our midst: Ever bless the day we opened unto you the portal only the wise and honourable man may enter. Here you see a part of the unknown Holy Legion, bound with inseverable bonds to fight for mankind. If you wish to make yourself worthy of guarding the Inner Sanctum, your heart must be clean and pure, your spirit ablaze with divine fire for the dignity of your nature. This is the most important step of your life. We do not toy with ceremonies, and when we knight you this day bear in mind that we shall also expect from you great, noble, and knightly deeds. Hail to thee if you do not disappoint our hopes, if you remain faithful, if you are upright and good! Curses and shame upon you if you turn renegade; the Eternal Architect will cast you back into the abyss! (A cushion lies on the steps before the throne.) – Now kneel and swear upon this sword!

(The Chancellor rises, receives the ritual book from the Prefect, and reads the oath from it.

The Prefect takes the ☉ Sword from the Sword Bearer and asks the Cand., who places two fingers on the sword's centre, to kneel and take the oath, while all Knights rise and draw their rapiers. The Prefect sits down.)

The Knight's Oath.

I promise and swear to most faithfully obey the Obligation issued by me a few days ago. I promise obeisance to the Illustrious Superiors and zeal for the good of the Order. I obligate myself, as much as this is in my power, not to assist an unworthy man in entering the hallowed degrees of the ☉. I commit myself, in order to preserve ancient Freemasonry, to work against any corrupt systems with all my power. From now on I shall chivalrously assist the innocent, the destitute, the suffering, and all oppressed honourable persons, wherever I find occasion to do so. Never will I be a flatterer of great men, never a lowly servant of princes; instead, I shall bravely yet prudently fight for virtue, freedom, and wisdom. I will forcefully resist superstition, vice, and despotism wherever this can be of true benefit to the Order and the world. Never will I sacrifice the good of the greater whole and the happiness of the world for my personal advantage. I shall coura-geously defend my Brethren against slander, and regard their best interests as my own. I further promise to diligently pursue pure and true religion and the teach-ings of Freemasonry, and notify my Superiors in the Order of my progress in this endeavour. I shall always open my heart to the Illustrious Superiors as my truest friends, and regard the Order as my main source of happiness for as long as I am a member. I furthermore promise to view the fulfilment of my domestic, social, and civil duties as holy. So help me God, and as much I love the happiness of my life and the serenity of my heart!

(The Knights sheathe their rapiers and take their seats. The Prefect receives the ritual book from the Chancellor, holding it in his left hand and the sword in his right.)

Pref. (taps the Candidate on the shoulder with the sword:) I dub you a Knight of St. Andrew, in the true tradition of our Scottish ancestors, by the power of the ancient Master's word. Be a fighter for wisdom and virtue, equal to kings through your prudence, a friend to princes and beggars if they are virtuous. Keep holy your friend's secret and his wife's honour.

(He taps him a second time.) I dub you a Scottish Knight in the name of our Illustrious Superiors, who are the Superiors of true Freemasonry. Be faithful to the Order, fight against the corruption born of folly and malice, and seek the truth.

(A third time.) I dub you Knight in the name of this hallowed Chapter and all Scotsmen of knowledge and power. Arise, and never again bend your knee to him who is a man like you!

(The Sword Bearer takes the sword, while the Chancellor hands the new Knight's rapier to the Prefect who then gives it to the Candidate, saying:) I gird you with the sword; draw it whenever the Order, the good cause, and any oppressed innocent person requires it.

(Now the Knight's apron.) Seek for the Secrets of the R. Art, and remember your oath.

(The jewel of the Order.) From this ribbon hangs the image of a man who became the victim of his principles. His memory was sacred to our Scottish Masters.[52]

The Scottish Knights know the ancient Master's word *Jehovah.* It is the watchword of this degree.

The *sign* is crossing the arms above the breast.

The *grip* is touching the other's elbow. To discover whether or not someone is a true Scottish Master or Knight, one must ask him if he is one. He then has to answer: 'Look at me, and see if you do not behold a sign on me.' One says: 'Yes, I see the blazing star upon your brow.' Then one kisses his brow. (Now the Prefect gives the kiss, and continues:) Be welcome among us, noble Knight, in this holy Assembly. But now kneel before the Supreme Architect and thank him with your heart's utmost fervency that he has done so much good for you. (The Can-

---

[52] *Saint Andrew the Apostle, who according to tradition was crucified on a saltire in Patras and who is regarded as the patron saint of Scotland.*

221

didate kneels. The Priest approaches him and says:)

Be blessed by the power of Jehovah. † Be blessed by the spirit that creates everything that is good. † Be blessed by the priests and kings in the knowledge of power of the visible and invisible. †

(Then one bids him to rise, and the Master of Ceremonies leads him to all the Knights, each of whom kisses his brow. After this ceremony the M. C. assigns him his chair.)

5. Address to the *Ill. Dirigentes,* or the Scott. Knights degree:

Power and impunity do not bestow any rights: the criminal's dignity and power do not lessen his vice: and less offensive names and euphemisms do not change the inner, hard, and noticeable core of the matter. The land theft committed under the lustrous name of a conqueror, which goes unpunished and is often admired and celebrated, is no more honest than the appropriation of private property. And in the eyes of any reasonable man the art of war is nothing more than the systematic art of murder elevated to a matter worthy of contemplation, intellectual exercise, and emulation. It is true that injustice, ambition, pride, vanity, and greed are praised by entire nations as means for aggrandisement under the names of bravery, patriotism, and self-defence; nonetheless, they are no less unsafe or dangerous, and in fact, in the case of entire nations even more damaging and illicit than with individuals, since the effects are even more universal and destructive. They are, in both instances, misconceived interest, the untimely birth of an excessive appreciation of oneself and too high an estimation of one's force, and the subsequent hope of impunity. Consequently they bring about the same, or worse, fatal effects in the case of nations, ultimately punishing themselves; and just as the individual man's pride precedes his fall: just as he who insults all others, incites them all to seek retribution; and should he be too strong, causes others to converge and organise their defence and his own humiliation: so also a nation that grows too boisterous and does not honour the rights of others arms all others against itself, inciting their vengeance. And often, all that is required is the opportunity to repay like with like to destroy a power that is so selfish and so dangerous to the serenity of others. Experience and history prove that this opportunity has never been lacking.

Nations are large families, moral persons; like individual men, they have their origin and downfall, their life and death: like these they attempt to prolong their existence and remove everything that opposes it; like these they can be wrong when selecting the means for this, allowing themselves to be seduced by glittering proposals and short-term advantages into taking the wrong measures; they have reason and unreason, have their own inclinations and passions, lesser and greater needs, and for this, they need the help and benevolence of their fellow nations; therefore, they enter into mutual relationships with one another, and to this end, they are bound to benevolence and justice; they have their obligations and rights. True love for themselves, a desire and demand for their continued existence and life; the situation and circumstances in which they find themselves, the needs they feel, and the impossibility of satisfying these on their own are the legislators of even the most independent nations, and they oblige them not to transgress against the rights of others, nor to view themselves as the only goal and all others as means, but to be satisfied with the undisturbed possession of their own property and to curb the excessive desire for expansion and the rightful possessions of another. Their own continued welfare must teach them that abstaining from encroaching on the rights of others ensures their own rights: that violence begets violence, that strength and superiority has not in any way been given to nations or individual persons to abuse them to harm others and, finally, that it is in the best interest of the strongest, most independent nation, that there be one law, only one moral doctrine of nations, like that of individual men, to which all their demands, claims, wishes, and desires, every application of their force, must be subject, that they can never stray from it without incurring great harm, and that their own welfare, that of all others, and even the entire human race is most closely and inseverably bound to its strictest observance.

As long as this moral law of nations is not yet universal and in force, tranquillity and tolerance remain banished from the earth. To the detriment of the world and humanity it is not, and it will not be so for a long time, and entire nations conduct themselves no better towards one another, than independent, boisterous men who have not yet been gathered into nations.

Because they indulge in the feeling of their own strength and power, they betray by their actions that civility is still foreign to them and that savagery rules supreme. The earth is still constantly being ravaged by war and battles; to this day, peace treaties are nothing more than armistices necessitated by mutual exhaustion; to this day, they are broken in more opportune times, once the forces have returned; one twists their plainest passages to one's own purpose with artful interpretations; and the destroyers of the earth, those who devastate the world, remain the object of our admiration and emulation, the subject of curricula and storytelling, the ideal of education. – Speak not of the enlightenment and morality of an age, in which war is the reigning custom among nations. Every war is preceded by actual or perceived insults, and moral persons do not insult one another; every insult is based on a lack of morality, the unmistakable consequence of a misjudged interest, a disorganised will, and a limited understanding. Morality is more than mere refinement, the enjoyment of life's pleasures, the art of harming the other, or the destruction of one's opponent with great finesse under the borrowed appearance of the law. True morality is abstinence from violating the rights of others; it is sensible self-love. Given that this is still a rare occurrence among individual men, is it any wonder, that the morality of nations is just a civilised, more refined savagery? A nation's customs and opinions are nothing but the customs and opinions of the majority of its individual members. Thus, as the number of moral men increases in any given people, so the morality of nations is increased proportionally, and he who changes individuals for the better also betters the nation, and with such a transformation the fate of the earth is also changed for the better.

Thus, to promote this morality of nations so necessary for the good of the earth, the morality of individual men should be increased! However, since the greatest difficulties arise here, everything pointing in the opposite direction, good examples, particularly among the higher classes being so very scarce, the lower classes following their direction, justifying their own immorality based on their example, thus hoping for impunity or even reward, the already preponderant allure of seduction thus further gaining in its appeal: who among all the people has the strength of character to endure against this current and be good without any reward only to be the subject of ridicule, hatred, slander, and persecution? Who of them will have the resolve to do so, when vice and injustice are favoured from above, perhaps since many a nation's advantage is founded on this; when any association of men causes mistrust, and rule by [division] is the first law of government; if the education of the rulers and those closest to them is neglected, entrusted to ignorant and selfish men who have only antagonistic interests, with funds being used sparingly here while, elsewhere, millions are squandered; if the young are presented with false examples, if the authorities are indifferent to public education, instead supporting all prejudices and opinions necessary for their own plans and purposes, adding them to the curricula, and giving the young and emerging race a wrong, albeit temporarily agreeable [direction]: under such circumstances and in the face of these obstacles, should and could one be surprised that morality is such a rare thing among individual persons that one cannot find it at all among the nations in this whole wide world; should one not come to believe that virtue is a mere name and that a moral doctrine of the nations is an impossible dream?

These doubts become even more reasonable, and the apprehensions gain in strength, when even the best prince, having the best intentions and insights, who sets an example of bravely tackling the evils, is held back by inevitable and insurmountable obstacles, [cannot complete his task, and eventually, forced by the times and circumstances, must take measures] which outrage his compassionate heart and conscience. All endeavours will be futile as long as he is compelled to be on his guard against powerful, immoral neighbours. While all his cares must be directed towards outward safety, his attention is diverted from peaceful, interior matters of the state, or is applied only to the extent that he can gather the strength and resources within to defend the nation: the free, otherwise unimpeded use of all of his powers is curbed by these efforts, as he is forced to give them a direction that is contrary to his intentions; and since security is paramount, the entire edifice of his legislation and administration, among unruly neighbours, must rest on this foundation. Thus, his best decrees will only be relatively good, as the truly best laws would bring about his demise; he would [even] fall prey to his lesser neighbours. Morals do not soften in the noise and clamour of war or a peace that is no less troubled, nor in the absence of safety and under constant fear of attack. Only in the gentle, refreshing shade of the olive tree, in the lap of peace and abundance, does a gentle and refined [social] awareness grow. As long as impending danger incites man only to self-defence, all other powers slacken. The bravery of the warrior is his first virtue, a virtue that has been forced upon him. Savagery becomes a necessity, and a sociability that is too refined becomes weakness and infirmity – and promotes his downfall. – O! ye all who are so willing to rebuke the ills of every government and the flaws of monarchs! Look not so much at what they do but rather what they could do. Unfavourable circumstances and impending danger often make hard and very burdensome provisions necessary for the sake of their own safety as well as yours. Thus, either dispense with your safety or approve of the measures that must be taken to ensure it. It is not your prince who leads your sons to death in war, who seizes the sweat of your hand, who denies you the enjoyment of the quiet, gentle joys of society, who increases the state's expenses and the taxes to fund them, but he who threatens to swallow you up along with him. However, a single unruly man's unrestrained lust for conquest and his insatiable hunger for land are capable of setting the tone for oppression across the whole world, pushing nation against nation like one wave against another, justifying oppression for the sake of defence, ripping large parts of the world out of their serene state, diverting the attention of the best princes from the internal care of their nations, erecting altars to bravery and strength, infecting others with his savagery, and thus banishing morality from the earth, or at least hampering its progress.

Hence, if the prevailing circumstances and especially the lack of security keep even the best princes from considering the dissemination of a higher morality, but if nonetheless it is no less important that it take hold because it is the means for the peace and felicity of all people on earth, consequently, other means and institutions are necessary to fill this gap and come to the aid of a government much too occupied with other tasks, to place a share of these burdens on other shoulders and to see to it that every state under the sun obtains reasonable, enlightened, honourable, honest, loyal, diligent, and moral subjects. – If secret associations offer their assistance in this, if indeed they alone can accomplish this, through the allure of the hidden, through encouragement, through a common interest awakened by them and the examples set therein, they do not deserve persecution from the government, but encouragement, gratitude, and support instead. Or it would be a crime against the state that, with us, unkindness and thanklessness are held in contempt, the word given and a handshake take the place of every oath, that truthfulness pushes aside fraud, lies, and malice; that selfishness, corruption, intemperance, and excess are diminished, that morality is restored, that loyalty and faith, all but banished from the earth, are promoted; that marital fidelity is solidified and the bonds of friendship are multiplied and strengthened, while the causes of separation, schisms, and misanthropy are curbed; that people are made less inclined to narrower ties, their dispositions made more receptive only towards the greater common good, that we know the art of uniting the interests of men in something that is higher, more general, more lively, and of making moderation, domesticity, and benevolence the general ethic of civil society. – If all this were a crime, what then is virtue? What reasonable man would not strive, and indeed have to strive to become such a criminal? Such a state could not exist without incurring the contempt of the human race. It would hurry towards its own demise with great strides by voluntarily forfeiting its greatest, most permanent strength; for there is no power on earth that is as secure, permanent, and indestructible as one that is founded on truth, virtue, and morality. Only within this moral regimen things thought to be impossible, all hitherto ridiculed political dreams and Platonic ideals, become possible; where the subjects lack morality, loyalty, and unselfishness, very possible things become impossible, and indirections, provisos, and assurances are necessary. The power thus abused and the ubiquitous selfishness of men have incited general mistrust and closed the hearts of men to one another to the extent that today everyone must prove to another the honesty of his intentions while rarely being capable of presenting his evidence convincingly enough to dissipate all doubts and concerns. Almost all our actions and institutions bear a visible stamp of this general mistrust. Only a moral doctrine is capable of eradicating this mistrust among men; for it teaches men temperance and moderation, teaches them to content themselves with less, to lessen their bodily needs in order to exalt the needs of the spirit; it teaches them insight into their true interests; and a man who knows this cannot be unruly, unjust, or dangerous.

It is our intention to bring about this moral regimen: to transform moral savages into true human beings, to work on that neglected part untilled by the government, to correct flaws which cannot be corrected by any statecraft, to tackle morals and opinions, replacing poor morals and harmful opinions with better morals and useful opinions, and to diminish the sources of human suffering. However, as pure as our intentions may be, we will not be surprised if the prevailing prejudice we have rebuked above expresses itself even with regard to us, since it is ingrained, as it were, in the nature of every society as well as in the nature of every individual person to pursue one's own aggrandisement: thus we would find it very natural that similar accusations are levelled against us and that one suspects narrow, selfish purposes beneath beautiful words and a glittering façade; if indeed one had to assume that men who have been so carefully chosen, tested so strictly and over such a long period of time, and who have been trained to the highest moral standards were capable of playing the game of ambitious small-mindedness against which they struggle so forcefully and become the most shameful, unmistakable liars unto themselves, after such beautiful words and promises, in their actual deeds. If men could suddenly desire once more that towards which they have been indifferent for years, if our deeds and our demeanour were not telling proof of our unselfishness, if we could not face every class of people without shame, and challenge them all to show us some more obedient and better subordinates from their midst who patiently endure even the most obvious injustice though they see, recognise, and inwardly despise the abuse of the highest power, and who merely suffer and – stay silent.

We ourselves would approve such an assumption if history could show just one example of philosophers ever having devastated nations, undermined governments, or ravaged the earth.

There are flaws, significant flaws, which the public institutions [are] too weak to remedy, and which can be affected to a [sufficient] degree only by secret associations. Such defects are either too common and widespread or they are founded on certain very old and deeply-rooted prejudices and national traditions, such as the love of duelling, so powerlessly prohibited by every law. To attack them with open force would be futile, too dangerous, would shake the whole body politic and expose the weakness of the highest authority. Morals are improved by morals, and opinions are pushed aside through the gradual, unnoticeable generation of new opinions. This process is slow, and its results and developments too distant for one to hope for any effects were it not for the fact that a profound, well-thought out, thorough plan is being pursued, and that its execution is not entrusted to a single, frail human being, but deposited, as it were, with an entire moral body, one that can survive the evil, procreate itself, grow stronger, make up any losses, and continuously renew itself like a Phoenix; only here are good principles preserved eternally and inviolably, these alone can compensate for the deficiencies of human ageing, and these alone are the immortal adversaries of an almost immortal foe.

Let, therefore, the first true monarch of the earth appear! Let us presume great and very rare conditions for this! He shall appear with insight, strength of will, with the best intentions, with courage and resolution; and yet he must either rush the matter or leave its further execution to his successor. In the first case he will create hypocrites, if indeed he uses force; he will lop off a few wild branches, but the pernicious trunk will resist his efforts and keep itself upright. Those who created the evil he has made more alert and prudent while making this evil's progress itself only less noticeable, and therefore more dangerous. When eventually a new successor appears, how will he find the resolve to begin where the other has left off? In order to immortalise his name, would such a man not rather change the principles of the previous government? Embark on a new, his very own course? Will he put the same trust in the trusted counsels of his predecessor? Demonstrate the same insight, will, courage and resolution? Will he also brave toil, chagrin, and any obstacles? Proceed with the same hotness of temper or with equally cold deliberation? Will he have more or fewer weaknesses through which the enemy may penetrate and consequently overpower him? Or will he know how to conceal his weaknesses with equal care and skill?

If the continuation of a felicitous plan is yet further hampered in elective kingdoms, with minority reigns or extinguished lineages and houses, if even the best princes, though raised wholly for certain purposes by their predecessors, are not the same at the end of their lives as they were at the beginning, if they are always required to rely on others and to see through the eyes of others, and do not always choose unselfish, insightful, or useful counsellors, and if these in their turn are too attached to leisure, nepotism, venality, and the lust for power, are disunited among themselves and, to increase their power [and following], only promote their own creatures; if they cannot bring themselves to work according to the principles of others, to sacrifice their honour and insight in order to immortalise their predecessor's fame; if they, too, can be seduced by immediate, glittering advantages, are exposed to envy and slander more than others, and therefore act more fearfully or face their inevitable downfall, and hence always seek to comply with the prince's ever-changing whims – if one considers and anticipates all these things, should it not be evident that the civil government, where so often people without morals or good faith occupy the highest positions and where birth alone entitles them to the highest offices; where punishments and rewards lose their meaning, where poor examples are so prevalent, so ubiquitous and so attractive, where everyone only cares for himself, where laws only serve to oppress the weaker, but are not enforced against higher persons at all or without any consequence; where education is neglected and exemptions are issued without distinction and without end, where the truth is regarded as slanderous and leads to one's own downfall, and where only flatterers are given credence, where out of necessity all the state's care is directed towards external security – should it not be evident, under such circumstances and in such condittions, that the civil government alone, even when it has the best intentions and rallies its greatest powers, cannot measure up in any way to such firmly entrenched evil and corruption, but that it is an entirely different matter for a secret society which can resist all obstacles and attacks all the more forcefully precisely because the progress of its labours is concealed, its collaborators are hidden, and its chiefs unknown, and is accordingly secure against reprimand, slander, envy, usurpation, and persecution; where no plan or principle dies or is lost, where successors build on the experience of their predecessors, and start and continue where they left off, where the outgoing member is replaced by one who is just as wise, one whose principles are also in harmony with the goal, and who has been diligently educated and tried over the course of years; where one works with persons who have been secured against any downfall and corruption, and for whom it has become a necessity to think and to act in this and no other way. From this perspective, any reasonable and fair-minded government should welcome secret associations and consider them holy and honourable, if it is also right and dutiful that the earth should not become a murderer's den, the prey of some selfish men emboldened by the weakness and fear of others, and if it is to be the domicile of great, reasonable and benevolent men.

Today we call on you to complete this task, to fill this gap. To this end, we entrust you with the leadership of the lower Classes. Your task is to fashion their members into noble, unselfish members for the best of mankind and for the best of the fatherland. To educate men who will in no way seek advantage from the misfortune of others, and who have the courage and resolution to brave dangers for the benefit of others. They shall be the pride and adornment of any country; with their number, its welfare shall be increased, and truth, virtue, and honesty shall leave their prior homeland with them. They should become the archives of wisdom and virtue, where all noble principles and proposals are deposited; they shall be the terror of every villain, and he shall tremble at their sight. Let it be known to you that a state where the good are in command and where evil men hold no power is good and perfect. Remember that, according to Solon[53] and Plutarch[54], a good citizen is one who cannot bear any power within his state that seeks to rise above the law, and that the state is ordered best where all, even those who have not been insulted, stand for one man, and where all take offence if a single man has been insulted, hating, shunning, and despising the offender as much as he who has actually suffered the insult.

To this end you must understand the art of uniting all our members' individual interests into a single one: making them receptive only to it, infusing them all with fire and enthusiasm for it. In short, you must understand the art of providing those whom we have submitted to you with as unified a disposition as possible. They shall receive the same ideas and principles from you; as much as possible, you shall awaken similar sequences of ideas in them, explore their current ones, connect new doctrines that you are about to present to the notions they already hold, and undermine, weaken, and extinguish harmful notions; inspire

---

[53] *Solon (c. 630–c. 560 B.C.), Athenian statesman and lawgiver.*
[54] *Plutarchos (c. 46–c. 120), Greek author, chiefly known for his 'parallel' biographies of famous men.*

the same wishes, desires, and passions, guiding them all to a given, higher, universal purpose, and thus give them the proper direction and stir the same hopes and expectations within them. Just as the human body is enlivened by a single soul, so in our society only one single spirit and will, one single language, and one single interest must be visible. This unity alone gives life, health, perpetuity, and unshakable strength to any body politic. However, all this must be accomplished without compulsion, out of the truly understood conviction that it is better and a higher duty. You must present this duty to them as lively and attractive, and make it plain and tangible to them that it is for their own, their fatherland's, and for all of humanity's lasting benefit. However, so that you know where you must lead our people, hear this: They should desire nothing more than that which is demanded of them by any sensible moral doctrine based on a knowledge of the world and of human nature. This is not our demand, but God, the organisation of their own nature, of their own being with its feelings and senses, and their own lasting benefit have imposed this demand and this [obligation] upon them. And there is no power on this earth that could absolve them of this, the most blessed of all functions. Thus it is in this direction that all your cares and labours should go. To this end, we have girt your loins with a sword today: be a knight, a brave fighter, a tireless warrior for the rights of mankind. Take up arms against its enemies; they must be your enemies also. May prudence be your helmet, covering your head, may truth and virtue be your shield, your *aegis*. May a guilt-free conscience be your breastplate. Let all your actions be great, unselfish, and chivalrous. Spare the fallen and humiliate the proud. Enter the course boldly and dauntlessly, and fear no adversary. Hold closely to your Brethren and comrades at arms, and hold true to your banner. Do not spare your life when the day of the gathering is at hand, for it is great and chivalrous to die for the sake of humankind – which no hero in the whole of history has done, for they fell only for their fatherland. Let no shameful deed dishonour your life, otherwise curse and shame shall be upon you, your bones and your descendants; as a punishment for this they shall never enjoy happiness. Keep holy every duty, every word given, as you love your honour and life. As much as possible, preserve yourself from any founded reproach and accusation, because you shall be the living, speaking proof of the purity and sanctity of our goals. If we are persecuted and led to the judge's bench, we should be able to ask: Who has lived as we do?

The good fortune of being one of us shall be at once your recommendation and charter in the world. Then all people will open their hearts to you, and exclaim: Here is one of those who will not abuse me! This purity of our members shall safeguard us from the government's persecution and accusations. It shall incite noble persons to gather under our banner, and even our enemy should think to himself: how beautiful to be thus! In those who are of us there should emerge a feeling of noble pride because they know no one is quite like them. To this end, suffer also our penalties and reproaches. Accept them lovingly, as we also issue them with love; our reproach is meant to protect your honour, because we care for you. Every evil and immoral act is high treason against our association. No such person, even if he were your friend and brother, shall remain among us. We throw him back into the world whence we plucked him. He is dead to us in both a moral and civil sense because he prevents us from showing what dignity men are capable of; and yet, we are very concerned with disabusing anyone who despairs of the feasibility of restoring the dignity of man, disabusing him through undeniable deeds. We owe these men of little fortitude and faith a telling example, so that we can say: Behold! here is the very thing you doubted. Now reconsider and think better of humanity – and its creator.

Here economy and domesticity shall be your virtue. You should abhor deliberately going into debt. A man who uses up his funds lives from the sweat and property of others. He is often no better than, and often more dangerous than, a common thief. His body and his leisure have become his idols to which he performs sacrifices, and whoever worships this deity is the most slavish servant. He offers himself for every evil act, awaiting a customer. His honesty is in the purse of him who wishes to command it. Shame and despite await him, and sorrow and unrest banish merriment and joy from his soul. He will chase after every soap bubble, grasp for even the weakest straw to maintain his existence. Anything that gives him temporal relief he will embrace with open arms. He will betray secrets, [sell friends and justice,] recommend and promote unworthy persons, violate all obligations, and deceive his master. His mouth will open to tell lies just as he opens his heart to deceitfulness. Carelessness, sensuality, vanity, wine, love, or gambling, intemperance, and an appetite for rich food have brought him to this point; they are indispensable parts of his character. Do not trust such a man, because he has abused the trust and honesty of others, has repaid their benevolence with ingratitude and corruption, has increased mistrust among men, and has impeded the ways and means of aid to the truly destitute.

Let good faith be one of your preeminent knightly duties, because it is so rare on earth. A people where good faith governs will never perish, and a single man displaying it is the most precious jewel of human society. All coffers and hearts are open to him, and on the day of his need he certainly will not be without help and rescue. Bails show and oaths prove that we are liars. He who is not bound by a mere handshake is ready at any time to become a liar and a traitor towards God as well as man. Let your oath be 'yes' and 'no', and let 'amen' be your securest guarantee. Do not despair at your misfortune, but rather rejoice that fate has found you worthy to try you against its power. Stand upright in the storm, and do not flee your post; pity him who never knew misfortune, and wish continuous luck on your enemy as a painful vengeance. Let there be no wish in your soul, other than to become great by grand, benevolent deeds; let your ambition be such that you may be the first in insight and goodness in your place, your age, or if you wish, of all mankind. Watch over your Brethren! Do not conceal their flaws, and breathe into them the same spirit! Do and accomplish this – be a Knight in word and deed, and beget your own kind.

6. Thereafter, the Chancellor reads the Explanation of the Masonic Hieroglyphs (Addendum [E].).

7. Then Instructions I, II, and III.

8. Then the Catechism (Addendum F.) is gone through.

9. Thereafter the watchword for the whole Order is given.

10. Finally, the entire Chapter is closed, as shown in no. VIII.

11. Afterwards, the Knight must declare on record which annual contribution he wishes to give, whether or not he has any reservations about attending the Love-Feasts, and which motto he chooses. One may prepare him for all this beforehand. It is customary for the Knights to have the short motto engraved around their family signets; depending on the circumstances, these will also feature St. Andrew's cross.

12. The record of these proceedings is sent to the Provincial Lodge.

13. The new Knight is given the cipher. (Addendum D.)

VIII. CLOSING THE CHAPTER.

Pr. Worthy Br. Sr. Warden, do any of the Knights have anything to offer for the good of the Chapter?

(S. W. draws the rapier and asks. If no one answers, the Prefect says:) Worthy Br. J. W., is it the proper time to close the Chapter?

J. W. (drawing the rapier:) Yes, Most Worthy Prefect.

Pref. I then close this Holy Chapter in the name of the Supreme Architect, by the power of the ancient Master's word. ♩♫♪, ♩♫♪, ♩♫♪, ♩♫♪.

S. W. (repeats the knocks.)

J. W. (likewise.)

The Prefect and all Knights draw their rapiers, sheathe them, and give the sign. The Priest blesses them silently.

IX. OF THE LOVE-FEASTS, OR *AGAPES*.

1. A Table Lodge is opened as any other Lodge, but by the power of the ancient Master's word. Moderation, strict morality, true brotherly love, and the outpouring of the heart in innocent, carefree merriment must prevail here.

2. In the centre of the table stands a chalice, a pitcher of wine, a small empty plate, and a plate of unleavened bread. Everything is covered with a green cloth.

3. If the meal is close to an end and the Prefect finds nothing objectionable, he gives the Scottish knocks on the table during the dessert, and the Wardens answer this sign. Everyone falls silent. Then the Prefect lifts the cloth from the vessels, and the following occurs:

4. The Prefect first asks if the Knights find sufficient peace and quiet in their disposition to enjoy the Love-Feast. If no one objects or wishes to remove himself, he places the bread plate before him and says:

'Jesus of Nazareth, our dear and supreme Master, gathered one last time with His most trusted Brethren for a love-feast on the evening He was betrayed by one of his friends, persecuted for the sake of truth, captured, and sentenced to death; to us, this is meaningful in many ways. He took the bread (he takes it in his hands; these are small, narrow loaves, baked specifically for this purpose), broke it (he breaks it into as many pieces as there are Brethren present: generally, these are two small loaves, each of which yields about 6 pieces; he places each piece on the small plate, which has remained next to the chalice), blessed it (the Prefect raises the small plate with his left hand and blesses it with his right †), and divided it among his disciples, and said: "Take this bread and eat! This is the token of our holy covenant, offered unto you the same way that soon this my body shall be sacrificed for your sake and the sake of all who love me." (He sets the plate down.) Thus He also took up the chalice at the end of the meal (he takes up the chalice and places it before him), filled it with wine (he fills it from the pitcher), and blessed it. (He raises it with his left hand and draws the † with his right. He then places it back in the centre of the table.) Then He said: "Take this wine and drink! It is consecrated to you, just as the blood I shall soon spill for your sake. Let this renew our covenant! Whenever you are gathered in holy community to enjoy the love-feast, as we are today, you shall remember me and proclaim my death, until one day I shall be in your midst again, transfigured and purified for a new life."

Now then, my Brethren, let us (while he speaks these words, he passes around the small plate with the bread. Everyone takes one piece, holds it in his hand, and passes the plate on; the Prefect takes the last piece and places the plate before him) celebrate the memory of our dearest Master with a pure heart. Everyone should examine himself well, to see if love dwells in his heart. Woe to him who is unworthy and who eats and drinks but is not worthy of this holy covenant! He himself enjoys this on pain of judgement and damnation.' (Now the Prefect and everyone with him enjoys the bread, quietly and with reverence.)

Then the Prefect takes up the chalice, drinks from it first, and gives it to his right-hand neighbour. Each takes a sip. The last one empties it and returns it to the Prefect, who wipes the plate and chalice clean, places them in the centre of the table, and covers them with the green cloth.

Pref. Thanks be to our great Lord and dear Master, who has instituted this meal to unite the hearts of those who follow him. Go forth in peace, my Brethren! Hallowed be the new covenant we have made today! Blessed are you, if you remain faithful and fight for the good cause. †

5. Right after this the Prefect closes the Table Lodge with the customary ceremonies.

6. It must also be noted that a Priest of the ☉ may never be present at the Love-Feast, that the serving Brethren must leave, and the doors must be locked.

X. CEREMONIES DURING THE CONSECRATION OF A CHAPTER.

1. Wherever the Provincial Lodge establishes a Secret Chapter, a sufficient number of Knights must already be present there.

2. An authorised plenipotentiary pertaining to a higher Class of the Order will then be sent there.

3. The room where the Chapter is to be held is properly wallpapered, and the insignia, i.e. the ritual book, sword, etc., are on the Chancellor's table.

4. The Plenipotentiary, clad in white, not wearing any jewel, his head bare, enters first, stands before the Chancellor's table, and gives the Scottish knocks, whereupon all the Knights, who had hitherto been waiting in the vestibule, enter. They are dressed as Knights and wear St. Andrew's Cross.

5. They stand opposite the table in a semicircle.

6. The Plenipotentiary gives his speech, reads aloud the new Chapter's Constitution, assigns the Officers, and closes with the blessing: Blessed be your work in knowledge and power, by the power of the ancient Master's word. †

7. He then hands to everyone the honorary signs of his office, whereupon

8. the new Prefect, once everyone is at his place, opens the Chapter.

ADDENDUM A. FORM FOR THE LODGE CONSTITUTION.

We, Delegates authorised by the Illustrious Worthy Secret Superiors of ancient true Freemasonry, under the invisible protection of the Secret Grand National Lodge in the Orient of Germany and its subordinate Provincial Lodge of this District, have decided, after the urgent request of several Brethren in ... and after consulting with the Higher Superiors, to establish a true Lodge of secret Freemasonry there.

To this purpose, we have issued Brother ... Herr (legal name) a copy of the ancient and true rituals as well as a copy of our Constitution, and with this, we also install him as the first Worshipf.

Master of this Lodge. We further will consecrate said Lodge and name it ... through a Plenipotentiary, as soon as he is able to open his Assemblies.

We therefore admonish all those Brethren who wish to join this honourable, just, and perfect Lodge to exercise true Masonic diligence; thus, the Grand Architect will bless their quiet labours for the best of mankind.

However, to those Freemason[s] who wander in erroneous paths or who are kept in the dark by false doctrines, and labour about us under the protection of a purchased constitution which has no need of true wisdom, without knowing the higher, sacred goals of the Order or its Secret Superiors, we dedicate our compassion, offering them protection and enlightenment. Many are called, but only few are chosen; it is up to them to acquaint themselves with us. No empty written confirmations, no, the goodness of the cause must speak for our purpose, and in the higher degrees, in the Sanctum of the temple, every true Mason can learn who has authorised us to establish this Lodge.

Issued in the Secret *Directorium* of the Holy Order in the year (common calendar) of our Lord.

(Seal of the Chapter)   (No signature.)

ADDENDUM B. THE PREFECT'S ORDER STAR.

The letters in the centre are in gold, the square shield is white, the frame is made of red foil, the star is gold, the large cross is green and its frame silver.

ADDENDUM C. THE KNIGHTS' ST. ANDREW'S CROSS.

In no. 1, on the [left], the cross, whereupon the enamelled St. Andrew is affixed, is green, and the rays are in gold. In no. 2, on the other side, the square shield is blue, and the Hebrew letters as well as the rays are in gold.

ADDENDUM D. SECRET CIPHER OF THE SCOTTISH KNIGHTS.

[There are two interchangeable symbols for each letter.]

a.	⌖	⊓	n.	H	◁	z.	N	⧖	6.	⌘
b.	✡	⊔	o.	T	☌	,	⋈		7.	⌘
c.	⌜	☾	p.	:	□	;	ʒ		8.	⌘
d.	I	┐	q.	⊥	X̄	:	ʓ		9.	⌘
e.	┘	✳	r.	×	⊖	.	6		0.	⁞
f.	♂	⊏	s.	◇	⊙	!	9			
g.	⊐	王	t.	⊢	⊕	?	69			
h.	.	_	u.	⊣	⟜	1.	∵			
i.	+	△	v.	♃	▤	2.	⌓			
k.	☿	Ⱨ	w.	⊠	♄	3.	◡			
l.	L	♀	x.	±	卢	4.	⊶			
m.	|	▷	y.	⋮	8	5.	ß			

The punctuation marks are on an equal footing with the letters; consequently, there are no paragraphs in this cipher.

Example.

┘+H┘×⋈ TI┘× N⊠┘⁞6

means *e i n e r, oder zwey.*[55]

One may also insert meaningless symbols in between.

ADDENDUM E. EXPLANATION OF THE MASONIC HIEROGLYPHS.

Man, as he appears before our senses now, has fallen far from his high dignity.

Once his nature was pure, clarified, the image of Deity. Capable of being the finest tool of the great original source, he stood on the highest step, relishing his immortality. Just as he was master of all visible things in this world he also wielded, according to his spirit, to use a common expression, power in the invisible world. During a certain grand revolution in the spiritual world his finer being

[55] *Ger. One or two.*

was enveloped with this coarser husk that now appears to our senses. This then became his sphere of influence. But it was up to him either to influence that which we call the body in such a manner that the same, or at least a part of it, would be purified and transfigured so that it might eventually return to the great source along with his original being, or to allow himself to be oppressed by the coarser matter, and, after the subsequent dissolution, descend into another class, dull and tainted.

Unfortunately, he did the latter. Through the abuse of his powers and the immoderate use of the resources of nature he gradually fell so far that now barely a shadow of his high dignity remains. The external tools of perception and feeling have coarsened, and what we believe we see and feel around us is not the true essence of things. No! these are merely sensual illusions, dreams, appearances. However, man could and should strive to rise again to his former height, and a few persons who were familiar with the eternal wisdom, who had kept their spirit pure and unstained, to use sensual words, gave the weakly human race the means to this through a pictorial language.

These images, these revelations, these first letters of true divine wisdom were preserved in secret schools. The true priests and chiefs of the mysteries always sought to work on the outer constitution of the world in such a manner that not everything would collapse and that better men, receptive to these great questions and guided by a true friend, would uncover their higher destiny.

Jesus of Nazareth taught the divine doctrine to His confidants, and primarily St. John. He laid hands upon them, consecrated them, and imbued them with His spirit. The Apostles continued His revelation among the bishops of the first parishes and preached to the world the doctrines of the beatific virtues, which contain harmony and which constitute the only path to higher wisdom.

However, this religion too soon degenerated, and the small flock of true Christians became ever smaller. Priests and men of the world erected on this hallowed ground an edifice of nonsense, folly, prejudice, and selfishness. Soon, the tyranny of priests joined forces with the despotism of princes to assault the now destitute human dignity. Nevertheless, the true wisdom was not lost, and it was reverently preserved in secret schools. Depending on the times and circumstances, however, these schools acquired other names, and Freemasonry has been the most recent society through which the ancient, unadulterated hieroglyphs have been preserved in our parts of the world.

This however was done only within a circle of a few noble [men], because the

Masonry that was outwardly affecting the world was soon desecrated, augmented with the most miserable additions, and utterly misinterpreted and misunderstood, so that the Secret Superiors eventually withdrew, leaving the greater part to its mad games.

However, since the abuse became so great, our Illust. Worthy Superiors intervened once more, placing the unadulterated images of true wisdom into the hands of faithful pupils, and creating a system perfectly adapted for this age according to the plan which you, my friends! now know, to help mankind wherever possible, so that the promised aeon can be brought about more quickly to at least the coming generations.

Now review the ceremonies and images you have seen in Fr. My., and if you have an eye for the truth, you will understand everything now.

A friend showed you the path to the truth. You were examined in detail. You had to embark on a journey first. – We must undertake many lengthy journeys through this dangerous world to seek out the truth, which was once the essence of humanity.

You were divested of everything metallic in order to see that truth can neither be purchased nor obtained by force, and because this unhappy metal, gold and silver in particular, has brought such immense damage to humanity. Therefore, consider those false Freemasons and deceivers who claim that the miserable art of making gold is the Order's sole purpose. In this manner, entire societies deceive many unknowing Brethren by presenting themselves as the Superiors of Fr. My., by gradually seeking to obtain the majority in our Lodges, by encouraging them to search for secrets that they do not comprehend themselves, thus drawing their working hands away from useful labours. An honestly active man can always earn enough in this world through his industry to satisfy his moderate desires. The wise man possesses more than gold, and the Order will always protect the unfortunate from destitution.

Before your initiation you stood there blindfolded, just like your nature is corrupt and blind.

You heard knocks that made your ears tremble, just as the blow that has struck mankind makes our heart tremble.

Only with measured steps, not at your own pace, could you approach the Sanctum.

The outline of Solomon's Temple is the image of an edifice where God's holy wisdom was once taught.

You must climb seven steps in the ☉ and learn seven subordinate natural forces if you wish to be receptive to the highest instruction in the inner chamber; and all the while you must work the rough ashlar, your unenlightened spirit, in such a manner that it is plumb and right, like the smooth ashlar, and you must measure your actions with the tools of reason and virtue, weigh and level them, and practise inquiries into [high] matters, as instructed by the symbols of the sun and moon.

Between the square, the measure of the finite, and the compass, the hieroglyph of the infinite, lies the blazing star, representing the bond and life of the universe. Here you will also find the basic symbol of the Trinity, or the triply acting deity.

During the day the sun gives you a pure, warm light; the moon reflects it at night, and your Master is the light in the Lodge, as he guides your steps.

All elements converge in the blazing star. Three great ruffians have slain our Master; three great ruffians have thwarted the world's last great reform. Three great ruffians also degrade the human being. The desire to enjoy everything, or the immoderation which coarsens and weakens our nature, degrading us to the status of animals; the desire to elevate ourselves by sensual means, to possess, enjoy, and to have more abilities than others – that is the insolence, arrogance, ambition, miserliness, lust for power, and envy which begat the oppression by priests and princes; and finally, the refusal to do the work necessary to fulfil our destiny, the inactivity that opens the door to every kind of vice.

The tomb of mankind is surrounded by fire. It must be rescued from the flames.

We only have five sensory paths, according to common knowledge, by which we can affect other men.

Perhaps you find the means to ennoble your nature in the study of natural products, the study of plants and herbs. The Acacia points the way.

The old Master's word was *Jehovah,* and these four Hebrew consonants contained the clarified concept of deity. Ever since the time when this holy service was lost the word has been *Macbenac,* that is, 'They have slain the Son.' Or in other words: 'Turn your attention to the not yet completed revolution begun by Jesus!' The secret of the immortality of the soul, the resurrection of the five times wounded Messiah, the reawakening of a body by the five points of fellowship, and, finally, the correct understanding of the word *Hieram,* composed of the initials of *Hic Jesus est resurgens a mortuis,*[56] may still be concepts too abstract for those who are not well-versed in the higher wisdom.

Now you have enough pointers. Examine, read, contemplate. There are many things that one cannot find without guidance but cannot learn from mere instruction either, and these truths, whose alphabet we have given you here, require dedication and study. If you believe you have found a better, more enlightening idea, if you believe you have found the right path, entrust your discoveries to your Superiors, and they will extend their hands to you, either to further guide you on the true path or to keep you from going astray.

Incidentally, allusions to historical circumstances are interwoven in the hiero-glyphs of Fr. My. These historical circumstances fit in partly with the entire work of world reformation and partly with Freemasonry in its current form, e.g. they tell us from which parts of the world this wisdom was brought to us, which path it took, where it was despised most, which new reformation efforts have been made up to now, and so on.

The ceremonies stem partly from the early church, and partly they relate, to some extent, to the story of the foundation of today's Freemasonry. All these things are somehow linked together. The thinking and exploring spirit finds nourishment here, while the ignorant and hollow mind regards the matter as a mere plaything, and the initiate finds here a language for concerns that are too subtle for common, sensual expressions.

Finally, we advise you, in order to explore these matters in greater depth, to direct your utmost attention to the history of the first Christian communities and the doctrines of the ancient Gnostics and Manicheans, even though their study certainly poses great difficulty. Eventually, you will realise to what extent there is a connection with the newer mystery schools, and to give you a little foretaste of this, hear now the reason why we use the Persian calendar.

The ancient calendar began in the year 101 when, according to the testimony of Jerome, John the Evangelist, the founder and prefect of the churches in Asia, died. It is well known to what extent the teachings of Jesus spread throughout Europe and Asia afterwards. However, the year 530 after St. John's death, or 631 according to the common calendar, or 9 after the Hegira[57], was very dangerous for the Asian Christians. After conquering Arabia. Mahomet led 30,000 men to

[56]   Lat. *Here Jesus is rising from the dead.*
[57]   *Hijrah, the flight of Muhammad and his followers from Mecca to Medina in 622.*

Syria, and captured Tabuck[58]. There the Christian communities sent emissaries to him, who were tasked to offer tribute on the condition that they were permitted to continue to hold their religious services. Mahomet denied their request, and the Christians had no other choice than to emigrate or renounce their faith. The cowardly among them converted; however, a large number fled to Persia, which was still resisting Mahomet's arms.

Here then the Christians founded a new, secret realm, and in commemoration of this glorious expulsion they began a new calendar, which has been preserved to this day in addition to the Persian calendar then in use. Likewise, they began to use (in the spirit of that time) the word *Jezdedgerd* in a mystic manner to immortalise the memory of their founding father St. John. See the initial letters of these words: *J*ohannes *E*vangelista, *Z*ebedei filius, *D*etractus *E*cclesias, *D*ominitiano *I*nterfecto, *E*xerit, *R*egnante *T*rajano.[59]

The correctness of this historical account can be confirmed by reading St. Jerome, who states: 'Johannes Apostolus filius Zebedei, quarto decimo anno, secundam post Neronem persecutionem, Patmus Insulam relegatus, interfecto Domitiano, sub Nerva principe rediit Ephesum, ibique usque ad Trajanum principem perseverans, totas Asiae fundavit rexitque Ecclesias.'[60]

ADDENDUM F. CATECHISM OF THE SCOTTISH KNIGHTS.

Q[uestion]. Are you a Scottish Knight?

A[nswer]. Yes, and he who initiated me had knowledge and power.

Q. How shall I know that you are a Scott. Knight?

A. I wear the blazing star on my brow.

Q. Where were you initiated?

A. In the Holiest of Holies.

Q. What is the Scott. Knight's work?

A. To restore harmony, ennoble his nature, and make himself the deity's purest tool.

---

[58] *Tabuk, an Arab city, about halfway between Medina and Haifa.*

[59] *Lat. John the Evangelist, son of Zebedee, exiled, after the assassination of Domitian, he built churches during the reign of Trajan.*

[60] *Lat. After Domitian instigated a second persecution to follow that of Nero, John the Apostle was exiled to the island of Patmos ... after Domitian was assassinated, John returned to Ephesus during the reign of Nerva and lived there until the reign of Trajan, founding and directing all the Churches of Asia.*

Q. By what means?

A. Moderation, spiritual exaltation, and activity.

Q. Where shall the Scottish Knight be active?

A. Practising Masonic virtuousness in the purest heart, deciphering the Masonic language, seeking wisdom, that is to say defeating prejudice and passions, walking in love, and investigating nature.

Q. How can one exalt one's spirit?

A. By occupying oneself with higher matters.

Q. Who is your Master?

A. Jesus of Nazareth.

Q. What has He done for the good cause?

A. He has suffered for mankind.

Q. Where do you celebrate His memory?

A. At the love-feast.

Q. What are the wages of your labour?

A. Rest, love, bliss.

Q. How is the weather?

A. A bright, sunny day in the Holiest of Holies, but stormy and dark outside.

Q. Have you recovered the ancient Master's word?

A. My Superiors know the four letters.

Q. Who can decipher the meaning of the blazing star?

A. He who feels the bond between the finite and the infinite in his innermost being.

Q. How do you call this bond?

A. The true light.

Q. When will you recognise this light?

A. Once I have recognised the triple cause: myself, nature, and the Great Architect.

III. Mysteries Class

A) Lesser Mysteries
I. Lesser Priest Degree. Presbyter

INTRODUCTION.

If a Scottish Knight wishes to be accepted to this degree of the Higher Order, he must 1) have demonstrated as a Minerval that he has seriously dedicated himself to the science he has chosen as his favourite subject, having made considerable progress therein. He must be tested and complete a given task. 2) He must also have earned the approval of his Superiors in the Masonic degrees; consequently, he must have

    A. enlightened his mind,

    B. purified his heart,

    C. chastened his morals, and

    D. rendered useful and active service to the ☉.

3. He is then recommended to the Provincial Superior either by the Chapter's Prefect, who is always of this degree and can attend its Assemblies at will or is suggested for promotion to this Class by the *Decanus,* or expressly selected for it by the Higher Superiors. 4. Once the Provincial Superior has given his approval, the Prefect summons the Candidate, presents him with the Illustrious Superiors' decision and tells him that the degree he is about to receive will lead him to the highest step within the O. If [further] samples of his prowess are also satisfactory, he will no longer be concerned with the direction of the lower edifice, and he will no longer be required to attend [Lodges or] Assemblies. 5. Hereupon he provides him with the address of the *Decanus* of the Province, to whom he has to send his answers to the following questions:

    A. Are our current worldly institutions adequate for the destiny for which man seems to have been placed on this earth, or are they not? Do the states, civil associations, and popular religions, for example, [fulfil] the purpose for which they have been established? Do the sciences promote veritable enlightenment and true human felicity, or are they rather the children of necessity, of the manifold needs of unnatural conditions, and the inventions of pedantic and vain minds?

B. Which civil associations and which sciences seem useful to you, and which do not?

C. Was the world not different once? Was there a simpler state of things, and how do you envision it?

D. Having gone through all the vanities of our civil institutions, would it be possible to eventually return to that original simplicity[61], to a noble naiveté which would be all the more permanent as it would then be armed with the knowledge of all types of corruption, placing the human race in a condition similar to that which an individual finds himself in who, having spent his innocent childhood in an uncorrupted, enviably happy state but having been led astray by his passions during his adolescence, thus acquainting himself with all kinds of hazards, on the basis of these experiences finally seeks to combine practical wisdom with childlike innocence and purity in his mature age?

E. But how would one bring about this blissful aeon and a general moral regimen? Through public institutions, violent revolutions, or by different means?

F. Does not the unadulterated Christian religion offer us some pointers to this? Does it not augur such a happy state, and does it not prepare us for it?

G. But is this simple, holy religion the same as the one currently taught by the various Christian sects, or is it a better one?

H. Is it possible to teach this better religion publicly? Can the world as it is now endure more light? Do you believe it would be helpful at all to preach to men purified religion, higher philosophy, and the art of governing oneself for one's own benefit before countless obstacles have been removed? Is not the profanation of these matters closely linked to our political and moral condition, leading many people to resist the ennoblement of the human race out of a mistaken interest, and still more out of deeply-rooted prejudices, because they are attached to old patterns, finding anything that does not fit into them unjust no matter how natural, grand, and noble it may be? Alas! does not everything human and general today take second place to that which fulfils a narrower, personal interest?

I. Does it not follow then, that this corruption must be done away with gradually and quietly before one can hope to bring about that golden age; and in the meantime, is it not better to preserve the truth in secret associations?

---

[61] Allusion to Johann Joachim Winckelmann's appraisal of the 'noble simplicity and quiet grandeur' of classical art.

K. Do we not find traces of such a secret doctrine in the oldest schools of wisdom, in the symbolic instruction that Christ the redeemer and liberator of the human race gave to his closest disciples? Is there not evidence of such an incremental system of education, established in the most ancient [of times]?

FURTHER INFORMATION CONCERNING THE ACCEPTANCE TO THIS DEGREE.

When the Candidate has answered these questions and sent his essay to the *Decanus,* the latter reports this to the Provincial Superior and submits the Candidate's answers. The Provincial Superior then determines whether he can be accepted or whether he must answer several more questions to further develop his way of thinking. He is then notified of the decision.

If the Scottish Knight is to be initiated into the Lesser Mysteries, he will receive timely notice of the Synod Assembly. (The Synods will be discussed later.)

Once the *Presbyteri* have arrived at the locale and the Candidate is also present, the date and hour of the initiation is set. Since the initiation takes some time, it must begin in the early afternoon, although it should go without saying that every room must be darkened.

The hoodwinked Candidate is put into a carriage and, accompanied by a friend, taken to the house by all sorts of detours (provided this can be done without drawing too much attention and it gets dark early during that time of the year). One lets him step out and leads him to the door of the first chamber. Then his friend, having removed the blindfold, tells him to remain standing there until summoned to the chamber. But first he must put on the Knight's apron, the St. Andrew's cross and his hat, and take the bare rapier in his hand. His companion then leaves, joining the other Priests.

After a while, an unknown, ceremonious voice calls out to the Knight: 'Enter, orphan! The Fathers call you, enter, and lock the door behind you!' (The Candidate does so.) Now he enters a brilliantly lit chamber that is ornately wallpapered in red. In the background one can see a throne under a canopy, before which stands a table with a crown, sceptre, sword, money, valuables, and shackles on it. The Priest's garment lies on a red cushion at the table's feet. There is no chair in this chamber, except a low, upholstered stool not far from the door and directly opposite the throne.

Once the Knight has closed the door and is standing still, one calls out to him:

'Look up, N. N.! Does this throne's brilliance dazzle you? Do you like these toys, this crown, this sceptre, these costly monuments to human degradation? Speak! If they please you, we may be able to satisfy your desires. Unhappy one! If your heart is attached to these, if you wish to ascend, if you want to assist in making your Brethren miserable and oppress them, you do this at your own peril. If you seek might, power, false honour, affluence; we shall work for you and attempt to bring you temporal advantages. We wish to bring you as close to the throne as you desire and leave you then to the consequences of your folly, but our Inner Sanctum will remain closed to such a man. If however you wish to acquire wisdom, if you want to learn how to make people wise, better, free, and happy, then be thrice welcome among us. Here you see the insignia of royal honour, and there on yonder cushion is the modest gown of innocence! Which do you choose? Go forth and take that which satisfies your heart!'

Should the Candidate, against all expectations, reach for the crown, one calls out to him: 'Be gone, unholy man! Do not sully this sacred place, go! Flee while there is still time!' His friend then enters the chamber, leads him out, and the initiation does not take place. But if he reaches for the Priest's garment, one calls out to him: 'Hail thee, noble man! We have expected this of you; but stay! you may not don this garment yet! First hear for what we have destined you! Be seated, and hark!'

The Knight takes his seat, and now the lesson (Addendum A.) is read, and since it is lengthy and no one can be seen, two *Presbyteri* may take turns.

RITUAL FOR CONTINUED INITIATION.

After this lesson has been read out, a back door opens, through which the friend of the Candidate enters, clad in priestly garments. The garment is as follows: a white wool robe, cut like a shirt, reaching down to the shoes; its slit is in the front on the breast: it is tied off with blazing red silk ribbons at the neck and below, at the ends of the sleeves; a silk girdle of the same colour goes around the waist. In addition to this, the *Decanus* alone has an approximately one-foot-long cross in this shape

sewn across the left breast. All wear white slippers, their hair is worn loose, and they also wear small red, square-shaped velvet hats.

As soon as the friend enters and the Knight rises to his feet, the former addresses the latter as follows: 'I have been sent here to inquire if you thoroughly understand what has just been presented to you.' (The Candidate answers.) 'Do you have any objections or doubts concerning any of these statements?' (He answers, and should he have any doubts, they must be dissipated.) 'Is your heart filled with these sacred truths? Do you feel enough of a vocation, strength of spirit, goodwill, and unselfishness to join us in this great work? And while doing so, will you be ready to submit yourself to the leadership of our Illustrious Superiors without any wilfulness?' (He answers.) 'Then follow me!'

In a dignified manner, the Priest picks up the cushion on which the priestly garment has been laid and carries it ceremoniously in his arms before the Knight, who follows him with his rapier drawn and his head covered. When they arrive at the door to the Assembly room, the friend tells the Candidate to remove his shoes and put on the priestly shoes that he hands him. When this is done the Priest gives a sign, the two leaves of the door open, and the *Decanus* can be seen before a small altar three steps up and covered in red. The room is wallpapered in red. A painted or carved crucifix hangs or stands above the altar. On the altar is a lectern with the ritual book and a Bible bound in red; there are also a small glass plate with honey, along with a small glass spoon, a glass jug filled with milk, along with a small drinking glass and a small flask of scented oil. A lighted holy lamp hangs above the *Decanus,* who stands facing the altar, i.e. towards morning. The *Presbyteri* are seated at both sides on red upholstered benches; the *Acolythi* stand, but the Higher Superiors are seated on both sides of the altar. Serving Brethren (Lay Brethren) may also be accepted. These must be sworn to secrecy and wear black robes of the same cut as that of the Priests, their heads bare; they take their place by the door.

The ceremony continues once the door is closed again. The Candidate's leader reverently places the cushion with the robe on the middle step of the altar. All *Presbyteri* rise, and two assistants of the Higher Superiors, if present, tread on the lowest step, on both sides of the *Decanus.* Meanwhile, the leader returns to the door and stands to the left of the Knight. The *Decanus* turns about to face the Candidate.

Decanus (raises his hands) Peace be with you!

The Assistants. Hail and blessings to the kings and priests of the new union!

Introductor. Lord, hear my speech!

Dec. What is your demand?

Intr. Look down upon me, exalted one! I lead a Scottish Knight, a faithful, illustrious Brother, who sighs for freedom and light. Let him approach the altar so that he may be prepared to serve in the temple of the true light!

Dec. Knight! Who bears the sign of the elect on your brow! Turn your face towards the evening from whence you came one last time, and answer me!

In the meantime, an Acolyte, or a Lay Brother, brings a censer and a vessel filled with incense and holds them before the *Decanus* who then throws the incense onto the coals, spreading the smoke in the form of a cross three times, and returns it. The Knight turns around in the meantime. While fumigating, the *Decanus* speaks:

'Do you renounce the enemies of mankind, the spirit of temptation, and evil desires, the spirit of oppression and infatuation? (The Candidate answers.) Curses and disgrace be upon you, if you ever stray from the path, if you ever wilfully indulge in the vices of malice and folly! (The Candidate answers) Then remove this Masonic husk! (He removes his hat, rapier, apron, and ribbon.) Approach, enlightened one! And kneel in holy reverence before the sublime and ineffable being that lives in us and works through his faithful servants. (The Candidate kneels on the lowest step. The two assistants take their places on both sides of him.) See here the image (he points to the crucifix) of our unforgettable Master and Redeemer. Be true to His teachings until the last moment of your life! (The assistants dress him in the garment.) Don the garment of innocence, which you will wear in your priestly dignity on the great day of mankind's judgement and announce the miracle of the redemption by our Lord and Saviour, Jesus Christ. (They place the girdle round his waist.) I gird you with this holy girdle, that you may be consecrated and armed against the counsels of the godless. (They untie his hair.) I untie your hair; be free and cast away your shackles! (With a small pair of scissors, the *Decanus* cuts off a small amount of hair at the tonsure.) May the light of wisdom surround you, that you may in turn enlighten the crowd of better men around you. (He drips a few drops of scented oil on the tonsure and rubs it in with two fingers, drawing a cross.) I anoint you as a Priest in the new fellowship. May the spirit of understanding enlighten you and your Brethren! (He places the hat on his head.) Cover your head with the priestly hat, more valuable than a crown. (With the glass spoon he gives him a bit of honey to eat.) As a testament to our fellowship, enjoy a little of this honey! (He pours a little milk into the glass, and lets the Candidate drink.) Drink a little milk! This simple nourishment is a gift of nature. Think how happy men would be if their needs were not so manifold, if they enjoyed a simpler diet with happy and free hearts, instead of poisoning the balm of life with immoderation. Arise and remain true and fast to the faith! (He lets him rise and embraces him.) Here are your instructions! (He hands him a copy of the instructions, Addendum B., belonging to this degree.) The sign of the Priests is crossing the hands, the palms flat, on top of the head so that they form a cross. The grip is made by closing the fist and extending the thumb in an upright manner. The other forms a fist in the same manner and places it on top of the other man's, but so that it encloses the other's thumb. The *word* is: *I. N. R. I.*, spelt the same way as *I. A. K. I. N.* It means, as is well known: *Iesus Nazarenus Rex Iudæorum.*'[62]

Now the *Introductor* leads the new Initiate to his place. The *Decanus* and the Assistants also step down, taking their seats next to the altar, and a young Priest steps up to the altar and reads:

'Now you have a complete knowledge of what is important to us. You look over the wide field we have to till. You see that the operational plan executed by our higher degrees must have a strong impact on the world and provide all current conditions with another direction. However, this must not be rushed. We need many workers in all subjects, and a man to whom we entrust our secret purpose must, out of a sense of gratitude, lend a hand exactly where we deem it necessary and where the Illustrious Superiors can make use of him.

If only enlightenment can promote general freedom, equality, serenity, and felicity; if therefore our endeavours must primarily lead to bringing about this enlightenment, you will easily understand that this can occur only incrementally, slowly, that one must initially be satisfied with small advances, that one must begin by establishing general basic principles and refining general knowledge before we arrive at the point, where we can share higher knowledge with the rest of the world, and deeper insights into truths from which it has strayed so far.

Now you can easily see that societies who accept all sorts of people and immediately begin to embark on mystical, speculative sciences with them should be suspect to the wise, partly because they want to force upon people doctrines whose truthfulness one cannot trust since vital parts of the chain of reasoning are missing, and further because not all men are destined to be philosophers and tend to withdraw from the duties that the commonwealth has every right to demand from them.

---

[62]   Lat. *Jesus of Nazareth, King of the Jews.*

Therefore, our members, if they are indeed serious about doing something for the world, must not baulk at lending a helping hand in the lesser endeavours of the lowest classes, no matter how enlightened they may be.

Therefore, first renounce all claims to rulership (this test we must demand of you) and dedicate yourself to the direction of your scientific discipline for a while! Here are your instructions!'

He then reads out the instructions, Addendum B. When the instructions have been read, the whole ceremony comes to an end, and the Synod Assembly is concluded by the *Decanus* stepping forward once again to the altar, while everyone else rises. He then stretches out his arms and hands, and says: 'Blessed be you, be illuminated, and go in peace!'

ADDENDUM A. INSTRUCTION IN THE FIRST CHAMBER.

After careful preparation and examination, the time of your reward is near at last. You have enlightened your mind, bettered your heart, you have learnt to know and educate yourself and others; the first letters of higher wisdom have been spelt out for you by your Superiors; now it is your turn to enlighten and govern others, the highest honour to which a noble man should aspire. What you have been told up to now and what you will learn in this very hour will provide you with superiority over and insight into others who are weaker. And it is this superiority that is a man's only true source of power over other men. The darkness recedes – the day of light dawns – the first portal to the inner hall of the Sanctum is opened – a portion of our secrets will be revealed to you.

Lock the gates of the Sanctum to the uninitiated! I wish to speak to the illuminated, to the holy, to the elect. I speak to those who have ears to listen, a tongue to speak and keep silent, and a refined mind to understand.

As you enter this invisible Assembly today, you are placed into the Higher Order. Just as you stood at the helm of the lower edifice until now, you will henceforth belong to the Class of those in whose hands lies governance in scientific, religious, and political matters. Everything deemed important and holy to us is placed in these hands.

Do you understand at all what it means to rule and to govern, to govern within a secret society? Not over the common or noble rabble, no! to rule over the best men, men of all classes, nations, and religions, without any external force, to unite them permanently, to breathe one spirit and one soul into them. To govern from a great distance people scattered across the remotest parts of the world as quietly and swiftly as possible and with the utmost possible precision: does it not remain a problem political thinkers have not been able to solve?

To fully reconcile discrimination and equality, despotism and liberty, to create one's own kingdom and subjects, to prevent all treason and the resulting persecution arising therefrom; to create something from nothing, to curb the corruption that encroaches everywhere; to spread bliss and joy on all paths, that is the masterpiece of politics wedded to morality.

For achieving this, the constitution of civil society offers few useful rules applicable in ours. The mainsprings applied in both for setting people into motion are wholly different. There, people are motivated by fear and coercion; here, among us, everyone shall decide to act on his own. Hope, anticipated sensible benefits, expectation, reason, and morality shall give him the proper direction. Here, however, we also find obstacles unique to such institutions that one does not encounter in civil society. It is they who endlessly hamper even the best causes and make diversions necessary.

Members who live scattered among the various jealous and mistrustful regimes, who have grown up under them, receiving their income, their hope, and their fear from them, who for the sake of this income give and dedicate to them their entire powers and activity, in other words, members who are already overburdened with obligations elsewhere, though these might contribute little to the best of humanity; members who, furthermore, do not receive instruction at a common location, under common supervision, and with the usual means of coercion, who live in the midst of depravity where they are so easily enraptured by it, where poor examples are so commonplace and where temptation comes easily and is able to destroy the work of many years in an instant: members who cannot even be transferred to other places the way that members of clerical orders can be, it is them who form part of the base of our collaborators and who infinitely hamper our efforts.

How can we expect men – the greater part of whom are not wealthy and who themselves expect help from us, while the remaining, stronger part have themselves become very cautious as a result of repeated fraud – to spend their money on a society whose goals and insights can not yet be disclosed to them, whose chiefs, whom they do not know, would not be able to render an account of the useful, reasonable, and appropriate use of their generosity; how shall we, I say, receive from such members the funds necessary to meet our organisation's essential needs, to maintain such an expensive correspondence and interaction which extends over the entire world, or to help the deserving poor, who out of their uprightness and zeal for the just cause support themselves, those who have fallen on hard times for the sake of the Order, who promote great endeavours that are useful to humanity, who establish endowments that serve the ☉; or to compensate those members who resign from their official positions to dedicate themselves solely to the ☉ or to support the widows and children of impoverished Brethren, and, in this manner, enable every member to lead his life in independence of evil, and to be calm and confident during his departure and passing.

If everyone, right from the outset, were what sensible men should be, if one could disclose and explain to them the holiness of the cause and the greatness of the plan during their initiation, then many things would be possible. But since everyone hopes, everyone wants to receive, and no one wants to give, since the allure of the hidden is almost the only means of attracting men who would otherwise turn their backs on us after having satisfied their curiosity, or who might even use their knowledge for evil, since we are primarily concerned with the moral education of these often still raw men, and yet everyone hurries, keeps complaining, and becomes impatient about any delays, it is easy to see that effort, patience, persistence, and an overwhelming love of the cause are required here; that the Superiors must be convinced that the cause is a noble one, since otherwise they would not apply their wealth, all their powers, their whole existence, for which they are neither reimbursed nor recognised, but for which they are often repaid with ingratitude. I say an overwhelming love of the cause is required so that one does not give up in the middle of the work and turns one's back forever on the endeavour to make people better.

To prevent all this, to help where aid is often difficult to give, to accomplish all of this, is what we call the secret art of governing.

This is the concern to which we are leading and calling you from today. To observe others day and night, to educate them, to come to their aid, to care for them, to instil courage in the fearful, and to incite zeal and activity in the lukewarm and the listless, to preach to the unknowing, and to teach them, to raise up the fallen, to strengthen the wavering and the weak, to restrain heated tempers, to forestall disputes or to settle them, to conceal flaws and weaknesses, to be on your guard against the intrusion of the curious and of meddlers, to prevent carelessness, to foster in your men respect towards the Superiors, love and sympathy towards one another, and tolerance towards outsiders – these and more tasks and duties are awaiting you! If you still have the courage to overcome all this, then listen on!

Do you know at all what secret alliances are, what their place is in the great chain of events in the world? Do you think they are just an inconsequential, transitory phenomenon? O, my Brother! God and nature, who have arranged all things in the world, great and small, in their proper time and place, use these as means to cause tremendous effects which could otherwise not be achieved. Listen and marvel! All morality is oriented according to this perspective, and the very notions of right and wrong receive their necessary correction from it alone.

Here you stand, at the juncture of the past and the future world. One glance into times gone by, and immediately ten thousand locks fall away, opening the gates to the future – prepare yourself to make a fleeting yet bold glance inside. You will behold the unspeakable wealth of God and nature, the humiliation and dignity of man, and the human race in its adolescence if not its childhood, where you believed you would find it in its grey, decrepit age, close to its downfall and disparagement.

Nature, the incremental development of an infinite plan based on one and the same archetype in any number of variations, gradations, and forms, which receives from us various names according to their individual appearance, does not make any leaps[63] in all these transformations: she begins with the smallest possible, the most imperfect thing, runs through all intermediary steps in an orderly fashion, arriving at the grandest and most perfect of its kind, which in turn may be an intermediate step to a further transformation. She creates children and turns them into men, only to transform them into civilised people, perhaps to make what we were, what we are, and what we could be more tangible, attractive, and sympathetic to contemplate, or to teach us that, for that very reason, her infinite supplies are not yet exhausted with what we are: that we and our race are destined to undergo further and immeasurably more important changes.

Just like individual men, the entire human race also has its childhood, adolescence, its maturity, and its old age. With each of these periods of the entire race, man discovers new needs that he had not known before. Culture, the refinement of morals, and the development of dormant intellectual faculties all are determined by them. With their development, the way of life, moral and political conditions, ideas of felicity, the conduct of men towards each other, their rela-

---

[63] *'Natura non facit saltus', an observation that has been traced back to an obscure pamphlet published in 1613 but has an even longer history. It was later popularised by Gottfried Wilhelm Leibniz, Carl von Linné, and others.*

tionships, and the whole condition of the entire world at any given time also change.

The human race attains dignity only in its adult stage. Only then man's principles become firm and his connections purposeful. He sees the entire scope of his influence. Only then, after many detours and many lengthy and repeated unhappy experiences have taught us how dangerous it is to stray from the straight and narrow, and what a misfortune it is to arrogate the rights of others, to elevate ourselves above others only on the basis of external advantages, and to use our greatness to the disadvantage of others, only then does one realise, does one believe and feel what an honour and a joy it is to be human and to live among men.

The first stage in the life of the whole race is savagery, raw nature, where the family is one's only company and where the easy satisfaction of hunger and thirst, protection from inclement weather, a wife, and rest after exhaustion are one's only needs; a state in which man would enjoy those two most excellent gifts, equality and liberty, to their fullest, and would do so forever if he were to follow the voice of nature, and if he understood the art of not abusing his powers and preventing the excessive outburst of his passions; in a word, if he already were what he should be. However, it is the plan of God and nature to first show him only the destiny of his race in order to instil in him a greater appreciation for a gift that he had in the beginning but soon lost thereafter and immediately longed for again, making him try to regain it with lengthy, zealous, and futile efforts until, at last, he was taught to gauge the proper use of his powers, as well as his appropriate behaviour towards others.

In this state, where all our comforts of life were absent, this deficit was no misfortune for those who did not know and therefore never missed them. Good health was the norm, and physical pain the only displeasure. What could the aboriginal people lack for their happiness, given that they were taught by the circumstances they found themselves in to have only a few and not too lively desires? – This art is an essential requirement for our felicity, the goal and endeavour of wisdom, and the result of the most enlightened reason and a well-ordered will.

Happy men! who were not yet educated enough to lose their peace of mind or feel the great, unfortunate mainsprings and causes of our misery, the love for power, the lust to distinguish oneself, to surpass others, the inclination towards sensuality, and the desire for exclusive property of all kinds of goods, this true original sin of all men with its deplorable consequences: envy, avarice, immoderation, illness, and all the torments of the imagination. Soon, however, this unhappy seed grew within them, and their peace and original felicity was lost. As families multiplied and resources grew sparse, nomadic life ceased, and agriculture made families draw closer to each other, as language developed in the process and men began measuring their strength, detecting superiority here and weakness there: they understood how one man could be of use to the other, how one man's prudence and strength could organise the families living together and bring about safety from the attacks of outsiders for an entire stretch of land; however, this was at the same time the foundation of the demise of liberty. The former equality vanished; one felt new, hitherto unknown needs, which could no longer be satisfied through one's own powers. To this purpose, the weaker then submitted himself to the stronger and wiser man without reservation, not to be abused by him but to be protected, led, and instructed. To be of use to others, to employ one's abilities for the benefit of the greater whole, to lead others benevolently and to stir them into action, this was the only accepted, rightful title to the throne. And as fathers and the heads of families had previously been the first, benefactors were now the second and only kings in the world. Since prior to this everyone was free and independent, power of one man over the other could only emerge as a result of voluntary submission, and no one was about to submit himself and relinquish his rights if he could not hope to gain advantage from doing so. Any submission, even that of the most brutish man, is thus contingent on the fact that I am in need of help and that he to whom I submit is able to provide it. His power over me ends along with my weakness and the other's superiority. Kings are fathers, guardians; the father's power ends with the child's incapability. A father or guardian who tries to assert his right beyond this time insults his child. Every adult can be his own guardian. Once the entire nation has reached adulthood, the reason to assume guardianship falls away. If the majority have not yet come of age, at least the adults step forth. This is only just and reasonable. No one can forbid them to do so, but they have no right to wrest the others away from their prior guardians and take their places, i.e. instigate revolutions on their own behalf. A power that has been recognised by all must be denied by all if it is to cease. But men have never submitted themselves so that they may be abused. The stronger has never submitted to the weaker. Nature has eternally destined the weaker to a state of submission, because he is in need. The stronger has always been called to rule, because he can be of use. Let the strong man become weak, and the weak man strong, and they will trade places.

He who needs another man depends on him; he has voluntarily renounced his right. Hence, the first step towards freedom is to have few needs. Savages and the most enlightened men may thus be the only ones who are truly free. The art of curbing one's needs more and more is also the art of gaining lordship. He who does not need others is free: if he can also be of use to them, he is not only free, but also their king. If the need is long and enduring, so is the state of submission. Safety is such an enduring need. If men had refrained from insulting one another, they would have remained free. Injustice alone has subjugated them. In order to be safe, they have given a single man powers he did not have before, and which are now greater than the strength of each individual. In doing so, they have created a new need: the fear of their own handiwork. In order to be safe, they have robbed themselves of their safety. And this is the case with our states.

Where will you now find the strength to protect yourself from others? In unity. But where will you find that? In newer, closer, wiser, undesecrated, more secret and more practical associations. Therefore, the demand for these is founded in nature itself. This is the true, brief, and philosophical history of despotism and liberty, our desires and our fear, happiness and misery. [Liberty has brought despotism into the world, and despotism will bring about liberty.] The unification of men within states is the cradle and grave of despotism. At the same time, it is also the cradle and grave of freedom. We were once in possession of liberty, and we have lost it so that we may regain it and avoid losing it once again since, having lacked it, we shall be capable of enjoying it all the more. Nature has wrested the human race from savagery and gathered it into states. From these states we enter into new, more wisely-chosen associations more suited to our desires, and it is by these that we arrive where we have left off, not, however, to repeat the old cycle, but to better understand our further destiny. The following will demonstrate all this more clearly.

Now men were taken from their serene state and placed into a state of submissiveness. Read what a poetic description Moses made of this. Eden, the garden of Paradise, was lost to them, for they had fallen, and were now subjugated by sin and servitude, having to earn their bread in submission and by the sweat of their brow.[64] Others usurped them, promising them protection, and became their leaders. The more cunning ones, in order to lead them according to their intentions and to lend their commandments greater prestige, presented themselves as

---

[64] See Gen. 3:19.

supernatural beings and messengers of God, and introduced an ill-conceived theocracy. At the time, none of these peoples had become too large; they were divided into hordes, each with their own leader. These leaders were as unequal in power as individual natural men, and they also were bound to yield, by and by, to the superiority of the wisest and bravest among them. And thus many small tribes were united into one large people. Nations came into being, and with the origin of peoples and nations, the world ceased to be a great family, one single kingdom.

Thus, the great bond of nature was torn; men were united only to be separated from one another. A line was drawn between them; they ceased to know one another by a common name. The human being began to be subordinated to the compatriot, and nationalism replaced the love of humanity. As the grounds and lands were divided, so also was benevolence; it was confined within boundaries beyond which it was never to extend.

Now it became a virtue to expand one's fatherland at the expense of those who were not within our own boundaries, and now, as long as it was a means to reach this narrower purpose, it was permissible to betray one's friends, to deceive and even to attack them. This virtue was called patriotism, and the man who committed injustice against all others to do justice to his own, he who had degraded his own reason to the point that he was blind to all foreign advantages and did not see the flaws of his own fatherland or even regarded them as perfections, was given the name of patriot. The love of humanity strictly corresponded to the size of his fatherland.

Once it was deemed permissible or even virtuous to hold men who do not live in the same stretch of land as me in lower esteem or perhaps even insult them, should it not also be permissible to limit this love even more to the inhabitants of one city, even to one family, or, finally, myself alone? And thus, patriotism gave rise to localism, family spirit, and finally egotism. As the perspective narrowed over time, a single interest became a thousand [and] then infinitely many. Everyone wanted to satisfy them; they foiled, they contradicted each other; internal unrest and enmities were born; the universal was forsaken because everyone only thought of his own aggrandisement, and thus the seed of discord was sown from the very beginning of the origin of nations. Patriotism was punished through its own devices, and mankind was sufficiently avenged from the insults of its enemies. – An evil that is inseparably bound to every such ordinary state constitution and cannot be overcome by any art of government.

Decrease nationalism, and men will once again become acquainted with one another as such. Their allegiance fades away; the bond of union is severed and expanded, and the source and cause of a number of deeds useful to the state are no longer pursued. Increase patriotism, and you teach men that it is no less unjust to act against the fatherland than it is to act against the rest of the human race; that, with respect to the remaining part, neither the state nor the other families possess any privileges; that, if this is the example that is set, a narrower love cannot be punished as a crime; that every usurpation for my own advantage would appear permissible and, finally, the narrowest egotism just as lawful, if it could attain the same impunity as the state with its superiority. Feel the danger in these propositions! Here, a crime against mankind is called virtue, because many people commit it with impunity, while any sensible man must realise that the benefit of the state can in no way serve as the measure of right and wrong; because if this were so, we would have contradicting rights in one and the same case.

There is a general law to which all others are subject, and that is the benefit of the entire human race. Anything that contradicts it is unjust, even if in certain countries altars may have been erected to it, and the most meritorious service to the fatherland can be the greatest crime against the world. The nation's codex is subordinate to the law-book of nature, and the rights of the nations must be judged by the latter just as every state usurps the competence to judge the rights of individual men and families. As every country shunned community and inter- action with foreigners as much as possible, the original traits of mankind were consequently lost, and separate customs, opinions, languages, laws, and religions came into existence instead; uniformity disappeared, and colourful multiplicity was spread across the earth. This finally drew the last line between man and fellow man. Now they had sufficient cause to hate one another, but nearly none to love one another. Now, one no longer loved man as such, but only such a man, either a Roman, Greek, barbarian, heathen, Jew, Mohammedan, or a Christian. These in turn split into further sects, all the way down to egotism. Now one only needed to hear the word 'Jew', 'Roman', 'Greek', or 'barbarian', and sympathy arose for one's own party and a spirit of persecution for the other. Intolerance reigned on all sides, and because patriotism begat egotism, those belonging to the same sect and nation hated each other no less. They were friends only when dealing with a stranger whom they hated even more vividly; but as soon as he was tamed, they fell upon one another again, weakening themselves, only to fall into the hands of a third party eventually, forging new fetters for themselves in the process. Their own leaders had the most to gain during this division of interest. While everyone was chasing his own private interests, the nation was as divided, and the kings began to assume the place of the nation, to treat it as their property, no longer regarding themselves as its provosts.

The monarchs' lust for conquest significantly contributed to completing the subjugation of the nation. Now one was in command of 100,000 people. With these it felt safe to assault one's neighbours. As long as the nation had a share in the spoils of war, it eagerly consented to this. The nation and the kings divided the conquered lands among themselves. The kings would often cede some of their share to others in order to gain a following, a standing militia against a nation that also desired to command, and to keep one part of the people in check by the other.

Thence came feudalism; an invention of monarchs who had more than they needed and used their surplus to govern more absolutely, to gild the shackles of the people, changing from being benefactors of men to being their oppressors. This is the origin of a class of people who served not the nation but the king, ready to work against the nation at the slightest nod, the true tools of despotism and the means for suppressing national freedom, the liege men and the militia established later, both serving a single purpose: the ones paid in money, the others in real property for serving as oppressors and executioners, forced to murder and rob innocent people.

Now people fell upon people, nations upon nations, and human blood flowed on all sides; the vanquished became a new class of people, called slaves, subject to the whim of the conqueror, without income or property.

These were foolish nations, who did not foresee what was to happen to them, who helped the despot to lower human dignity to that of cattle so he could one day attempt the same with them. The slavery of the vanquished became the means for the slavery of the conquerors. Their crime was avenged on their descendants. They only needed to abandon their strict morals, succumb to effeminacy, and develop a taste for sensual pleasures, for which the abundance of the gathered spoils had prepared them; thus, the victor was vanquished, and the vanquished became the victor.

These consequences arising from the establishment of the states were significant, but they were not the only ones. Men who once had dared the first step in good faith now competed in the art of finding means for their own debasement.

Initially, such men who had raised their nation from nothing to greatness could only be regarded as extraordinary men, even gods, by their blind subordinates, who only saw the present and could not believe that he who had benefited them so much might also harm them in the future. One would gladly have wished them immortality. As a very natural consequence of human short-sightedness this reverence also had to be extended to their children and relatives. In the eyes of the people the son of a benefactor appeared as another benefactor. It was still a kind of an election that determined the successor. Out of reverence for the initial benefactor one did not look outside his family. By and by, however, rule by election became rule by inheritance, and, later still, as the princes began to take the place of the state and the nation, regarding the people as their inheritance and property, once the tumult of war had subsided and the nation was better prepared for servitude by the refinement of customs and the love of convenience, when the first fathers, children, and grandchildren of the nascent people were no longer alive and the degenerate, weakly great-grandchildren had forgotten their rights, then at last the patrimonial kingdoms were born, and despotism fell upon a carefree humanity.

Now whole nations were sold, divided, given away, and led to the butcher's block like a herd of cattle. The princes' whims replaced the rule of law. They made themselves the end, while the nation was a means for satisfying the prince's fancies. Now the power of the princes was no longer derived from the people, no! the power to abuse men was derived immediately from God. The citizens' lives, property, and honour were subject to their whim.

Now one could see princes, without any insight and indifferent to their subjects' fate, drowning in their lustfulness; their court without morals and full of corruption, down to the lowest classes; vice elevated, virtue in chains, and flattery and malice in its stead; science and reason oppressed; no one in their proper station: the most important government offices offered to the highest bidders, the favour of courtiers and lecherous harlots; the nation in poverty, farmland deserted and untilled, industry depressed, trade suppressed, property insecure, the powerful not subject to the law, the most just and virtuous man at the mercy of any malefactor's wrath because he would not pay him homage, and, worst of all, oppressed under the very pretence of the law.

Now fear was the only mainspring of human activity, and violence and conscience the only law. One observed decay, friends against friends, brothers against brothers, parents against children, traitors on all sides; and at the court debauchery, weakness, malice, indifference towards the nation's fate, nameless oppression, and taxation without end: misery within and weakness without.

If there was the least amount of energy left in a people faced with such deplorable conditions and such an extraordinary humiliation, the few better men remaining were bound to open their eyes at last, or else their nation was doomed to fall prey to one or several third parties, either foreigners or, depending on the circumstances, the powerful men within.

Sometimes, when decay is all but universal and moral corruption at its greatest, help is at hand. Nature, which still has preserved the good seeds of virility and undeveloped, unspoilt skill in some corner of the north to rehabilitate the [sickly] noon, steps in, calling to these lustful and weakly lands wild nations from poorer and infertile regions, bringing life and free blood to the sickly body, giving it virility and strength, new customs and laws, until the remaining seed of corruption attacks these healthy parts as well. However, in case this corruption had not affected all the people in this nation, and there were a small number of better and unbiased men left: o! how much these would wish they were back in the place of their first founding fathers, by the babbling brook under the shade of a fertile tree, by the side of a loving, sensitive girl! Now they were forced to understand how great a treasure freedom is and what folly it was to give one man too much power. They could convince themselves that great power and the impunity that comes with it can easily be abused in the hands of immoral persons, no matter how good they seem.

Now that they most sorely felt their fall and the need for freedom, the yearning for succour was bound to develop in them. They believed they could curb the evil by exchanging one despot with another. Thus, every stroke fell upon the person of the tyrant, and not tyranny itself. They toppled the former only to raise the latter, or, having become wiser by the previous example, they tried to curb the power of the new ruler, which however became no less absolute over time, since the source of the evil, the lack of morality, had not been stopped, and as long as it remains abundant, no revolution will be of any use.

After the kings had discovered the secret either to secure their stake in the election of the people's representatives, promoting their followers to such offices and spreading corruption among them, stirring the hunger for gold or purchasing votes with court appointments, or to silence the voice of the fatherland through the standing militia, everything was in vain.

Others who spurned the power of a single ruler chose the popular constitution instead, but they soon discovered that freedom is not a gift that everyone who has only barely broken away from the ills of [monarchy] can bear; and that a nation's business can never be conducted [before] the masses. To this end, they now elected chiefs, representatives who eventually also forgot that they had received their commissions from the people, and that they were not authorised to assemble in their own name but only that of others. Thus they established aristocracies, where the cleverer men gradually divested the weaker of their duties, and thus returned to oligarchy and soon, in the same fashion, to monarchy and despotism.

In this manner the entire circle of governmental changes had run its course until the courts impeded revolutions by inventing the system of the balance of states, thereby further solidifying one another's right to oppress their subjects and treat them arbitrarily. Thus, the system of balance is a kind of silent convention among the princes of the world to perpetuate the unfortunate mischief by means of one prince's jealousy and the aid of another.[65] Now, rebellions and revolutions occurred much more rarely among the nations.

Because everyone begrudges another the possession of a decrepit kingdom, these are preserved even in their weakness, and we no longer see the creation and demise of states as frequently as before, unless several stronger parties have previously agreed to plunder and divide the declining realm. Kings now conduct themselves like immoral people in the state of nature. Not satisfied with their own possessions, greedy for foreign goods, they lie in wait for every opportunity and fortuitous circumstance to cheat their neighbours, to enlarge themselves, to forsake loyalty, good faith, and justice, and in order to have [more], they wipe themselves and others off the face of the earth. And this is truly the most extreme form of human decadence, to take turns and quietly guarantee all kinds of injustices against one's own people, to promote the general corruption of the people and to desire to draw constant advantage from the misfortune of another. And yet, o nature and reason! how grand and indisputable are your laws! The very moment when everything has conspired to bring about one another's demise, the poison itself must become the saving cure. Because no one furthers oppression with others, it ceases to be, and reason begins to assert its rights just as one wishes to push it aside. Since everyone seeks to blind the others he must, at least, be able to see, putting himself in a better state in order to have the advantage over others, and must promote reason and the sciences in some since he seeks to push them

---

[65] The doctrine of Europe's balance of power had been forcefully criticised by Johann Heinrich Gottlob von Justi (Die Chimäre des Gleichgewichts von Europa, eine Abhandlung [...], Altona 1758).

aside   in   others.

For this one needs minds and sound institutions. One man's enlightenment promotes the enlightenment of another. The oppressors, the kings themselves realise that it is not good to rule over a herd of cattle, and freedom rises from its own ashes. Now legislation begins to be reasonable. Now property and industry blossom. Now there are fathers and children, and yet this enlightenment only results from the shameful intention of educating cunning men who were destined to become the tools and means to satisfy the kings' lust for conquest and the oppression of others.

However, through a tremendous transformation, men now begin to see everything in a different light, examine their original rights, and avail themselves of these hitherto unrecognised means in order to use the opportunity to gather strength in the meantime, seeking to promote the impending revolution of the human spirit, to secure themselves against any relapse, and to win an eternal victory over their prior oppressors.

This victory would be short-lived, however, and men would soon return to their previous state of humiliation if providence had not been active since times immemorial, providing the most enduring means that have been preserved to this day as silent but secure mainsprings to effect the redemption of the human race in the future. Such means are taught to us in secret schools of wisdom. These have always been the saviours of nature and the rights of man. It is through these that the human race will recover from its fall; princes and nations shall disappear from the earth without violence; one day, the human race will become a single family, and the world the domicile of reasonable people. Morality alone will bring about this imperceptible transformation. How this will come to pass, however, is one of our great secrets. For now, hear the proof and the means by which we have obtained it.

By what mad delusion, by what short-sightedness could men imagine this world and their entire race would be forever governed in the same manner as before? Who has fathomed the storehouse of nature, whose law is unity and infinite diversity, confined her within boundaries, and commanded her to stand still; to forever run that ancient circle, ever to repeat herself or merely to move the physical boundaries of government and, having completed its round, to begin anew where she had first started? Since when is our inability to look ahead, to see into the remote future, also a bar for that unstoppable nature who never repeats herself? Who has condemned man, the best and most enlightened man, to eternal servitude? Who has called the only predestined servant of nature, often the weakest person in the entire nation, to eternal rule? This could only be the idea of a prince or of him who is arrogant enough to demand lordship over those better than himself. Why should not the political institutions rather be determined by the prevailing ability and receptivity of the people, just as they have done so until today? If the reason for all government has fallen away, why should the unhappy consequence remain? Why should it be impossible for the human race to reach the highest perfection, the ability to govern itself? Why should he who knows how to [lead] himself be led eternally?

Should it then be impossible that the human race, or at least the major part, will one day come of age? If one part can do this, why not the other? Treat any man as you have treated the other: show him his own true interest; enlighten his mind; contest his prejudices; teach him the great art of being moderate in his desires, of governing his passions; teach him from his early youth how necessary one man is for another; that in order not to be insulted, one has to refrain from insulting others, and that in order to enjoy benevolence, one must also be benevolent.

Spread tolerance, leniency, modesty, love, and goodwill among men! Teach them all these things! Make them plain for them with reasons, experiences, and examples, and see if these men will need someone else for their direction.

Or could it be that most people are too weak to introduce these most simple principles and convince themselves of them? O, then their felicity will come to an end! Make no further attempts to improve and enlighten those who cannot understand even the simplest doctrines, confirmed by daily experience! Why do you draw them to a religion accessible for members of all classes, which expressly teaches the very doctrines and obligations that, in your view, seem impossible? O prejudice and contradiction in the thoughts of man! You believe the realm of reason, the ability of governing oneself to be an impossible dream for the majority of men, and on the other hand, you recognise the right of the weaker, the right to abuse other, better men, as the allotted inheritance of every king's son and the entire ruling family as well as that of every other person whose own arrogance and good fortune have made him independent of others? Should the entire felicity of the human race forever be a game of peradventure? Should they, those only favourites of fortune, possess as a privilege of birth that which they show only rarely and what in the rest of us, destined to servitude by a fatal necessity, can never be brought about through reason and morality? Is it too low an estimation of one's own dignity, or is it short-sightedness, the inability to look into the future, prejudice against our own race or a liking for despotism that leads us to these thoughts; or have we sunk so far below our dignity that we no longer feel our chains, kiss them, and even prefer to suffer the worst humiliation rather than daring to entertain the thought of stepping into freedom (not by rebelling or shaking off our yoke with violence, but) through the aid of reason?

But because it will not yet happen tomorrow, does it follow that it can never happen? Let short-sighted men think what they will! They will keep making inferences while nature acts, she who is impervious to such selfish demands and continues her majestic progress unimpeded. By her side, we are called to prepare for that great day.

Things that many a man did not want to see perish may well do so after all! Everything will fall into place of its own accord: inequalities will become equal, and calm will follow the storm. In the end, all the objections only prove that we have become too accustomed to the current state of affairs or believe we have something to lose, and perhaps we only deny the possibility of universal independence as the opposite benefits us more, and perhaps because we still hope ourselves to become the lords and masters of some herd of people by just or unjust means. And in the case of those who actually are, we are ready to concede that the eloquence of all the orators of Greece and Rome would not suffice to convince them of a truth that contradicts their desires and expectations, because enormous strength of character is required to find truth in something that runs against one's own interest. Everyone should search his heart to see if he has already reached this degree of enlightenment; only then will he come to understand some things in the world.

Let the laughers laugh! Let the scoffers scoff! He who observes the course of nature in times past and compares it to the present will find that she runs her straight course towards her [goal] unimpeded. Her steps are in fact imperceptible to the eyes of an unschooled thinker and only visible to an impartial man whose task it is to look millennia ahead and discover, from the lofty crow's nest, new land where the crowd below does not even suspect it. The unmistakable mark of the most illuminated greatness of the spirit!

He who is not convinced by the above reasons may acquaint himself with the following principles which may further his persuasion. I hope he shall then see this distant land as we do, and call it Canaan. In the history of the Jewish people, he will find the history of the human race. Happy in its first beginnings! Family regimen and a life of patriarchy, corrupted by immoderate desires, oppressed in Egypt; led from there in flight; wandering for a long time in the desert so that the legislator, freed from all resistance, could attack the evil at the root and form a new generation. Thus it arrives in the Promised Land, where it would have enjoyed blissful days under Jehovah's protection had it rooted out all corruption, not begun the old cycle anew, and so brought about its own undoing. But all this was mere preparation, and finally from its midst the hero from the tribe of Judah appears, who was at once the liberator of His people and of the whole human race. This is an image of our original dignity, followed by our oppression, our desires, and our final redemption. Here we stand in the middle. Pure, holy morality must pave the way for the second grand period and lead us through the subsequent sorrowful experiences towards our final goal, a millennial or indeed eternal kingdom of truth and freedom. But for this, we need even greater endeavours to gradually render the opposing machinations ineffective. We will present a sketch of both.

He who wishes to oppress people, and make them dependent on him, must awaken within them needs that only he can satisfy. It is beyond description how tight this seemingly unimportant bond is. Bread, tobacco, coffee, distilled spirits, and the like are the despot's most powerful machineries, if he lays his heavy hand on them. The more frequent, vivid, and pressing these needs become, the more his subjects will depend on him. At the same time, spread fear, ignorance, and a love of sensual pleasures among them! The less a nation is familiar with the amenities of life, the freer it still is. As soon as the warrior peoples of the north learnt the pleasures of the effeminate south[66], their freedom was lost. Effeminate people are the most dependent of all. He who wishes to subjugate a nation that is free and wild should make it weak, lustful and, as a consequence, greedy. The merchant class, organised in a systematic, hierarchic body, would perhaps be the most fearsome despotic group. It would be the lawgiver of the world. It may well depend on this class whether or not some part of the world is free and independent or another is led into servitude. After all, to govern means to awaken and satisfy needs. Who can do all this better than the merchant class? Why should it be impossible to instil morals in nations or remove them through reasonable and useful trade operations?

At least, the discovery of America has changed the morality of Europe. He

---

[66] 'Mittag', literally 'noon'.

who can usefully distribute scarcity and surplus also understands the art of pro-viding the industry and inclinations of individual men as well as whole nations with new directions. But certainly, this body would have to make the acquisition of riches the means and not the end. It would have to understand the art of not always gaining money, but also making purposeful losses from time to time, in order to profit on another side and in another manner. He who wishes to make men free, however, should lessen their needs they cannot satisfy on their own. He should enlighten them, give them courage, and provide them with strict morals. He should teach them moderation and frugality as well as contentment with their station in life. He who preaches moderation and frugality is far more dan-gerous to the thrones than if he were to preach regicide. He who intends to introduce a general and lasting freedom among men should enlighten them and teach them to content themselves with little. He should awaken sensible, mutual needs; he should prevent a situation where one alone is needed by too many, or otherwise this will create a new need in those few who have no need of him, namely the fear of his power. Enlightenment for the sake of enlightening others gives freedom. Thus, he who wishes to introduce universal freedom must spread universal enlightenment. But here enlightenment does not merely mean knowl-edge of words, but a knowledge of things. Not the knowledge of abstract, specu-lative, or theoretical propositions that inflate the mind and do nothing to better the heart; no! enlightenment is knowing what I am, what others can demand of me; knowing that I do not live here on my own, that I am nothing without the help of my fellow men, that I have to regard them as essential parts of my felicity, must seek their approval and favour, and that I will not receive it unless I do something that is of use to them; knowing that if I do nothing for them, they will do nothing for me either; learning to renounce one's demands, forgiving errors, being tolerant of the opinions of others, being satisfied with one's fate, mourning at the misfortune of another, helping him when possible, rejoicing in the small joys of others as much as our own, and using one's own surplus for the benefit of others: this alone deserves to be called enlightenment. Provide every man with this understanding and these principles! How can I then suffer or perish? How is it possible for me to die without rescue? If you cannot bestow this degree of enlightenment on all people at once, then you, ye better ones, begin among yourselves! Serve, help, and reassure one another! Increase your numbers! At the very least, become independent and let time and your descendants do the rest. Once you have increased your ranks to a certain number through your association you are safe, and then you will begin to be mighty and fearsome. In an honourable way, you will terrify the evildoers. Many of them will choose to become good themselves and gather under your banner in order to avoid defeat. Then you will be strong enough to tie the hands of the remaining others, to disarm them and to nip the evil in the bud. The right way to make enlightenment universal is to abstain from dealing with the entire world at once. First begin with yourself, then turn to the [one] closest to you, and the two of you will enlighten a third and a fourth man, who will continue in this manner until your number and strength give you power.

Hence, he who spreads universal enlightenment creates by this also a universal, mutual security, and universal enlightenment and security make princes and states dispensable. What other purpose could they serve?

If this enlightenment is a work of morality, there is consequently an increase in enlightenment and security proportionate to the increase in morality. Mind you, this morality is nothing like the ordinary, everyday drivel. It must teach people to come of age, to shed their guardianship, to attain manhood and to dispense with the princes.

As effeminacy and luxury gain the upper hand, so morality, true enlightenment, and security decline. Effeminacy makes princes indispensable; an artifice which all despots have used to suppress a nation's freedom. No prince can eliminate luxury and moral corruption without weakening his own power. Banish luxury and its entourage from a monarchy, and you turn it into a democracy. He who wishes to bring about a revolution must change the customs, making them better or worse, thus forming, over time, a republic or a despotic state. This is confirmed by all histories.

Thus, if it were impossible to one day bring universal freedom into the world, it would be impossible because morality, the simplest morality based on the experiences of every man, cannot become universal. But he who thinks so lowly of his own being and of all human nature must not know the happy sensation of virtue and the power of reason, and his own enlightenment must be wanting. He must desire corruption because he believes human corruption to be incurable. But if I or someone else was able to achieve the goal, why not him as well? Let him follow us! Such people one might have persuaded to die, to sway them to any kind of political and religious fantasy, to torture themselves, and to renounce all the joys of life, discussing these things in such a way that they are robbed of their peace of mind and contentment as soon as one has stripped them of their own foolish opinions. Should the sole, truly sensible means of guiding people to their felicity be an impossible endeavour?

Men are not as evil as saturnine moralists make them out to be. They are evil because one has made them so, because everything prompts them to be evil: religion, the state, companions, poor examples. They would be good if one would endeavour to make them so, if this would not offend the interests of so many people, if everything would not have conspired to keep them evil so that the power built on this foundation is not forfeited. Think more nobly of human nature! Begin the work courageously, and fear no difficulties! Make the above principles your opinions, form habits from these, and finally, let reason take religion by the hand, and the task will be solved. However, do not try to change the entire world at once, but first those who are closest to each of you, and you will accomplish everything.

Thus, if morality and morality alone is to bring about this great transformation, to give man his liberty, to establish this great, magnificent realm, the realm of the noble ones, and destroy hypocrisy, vice, superstition, and despotism, then we understand why the Order, beginning with its lowest Class, so strongly recommends a moral doctrine, along with self-awareness and the knowledge of others, why it allows every new recruit to bring his friend for the purpose of strengthening the covenant and creating a legion that will more justly be called 'holy' and 'invincible' than that of the Thebans[67] because here, friends firmly close ranks with friends, fighting to gain the rights of man, his original freedom and independence.

However, the morality that is to accomplish this must not concern itself with quibbles or humiliate men, lessen them below their dignity, make them careless towards all things temporal, proscribe judicious pleasure and the innocent joys of life, promote misanthropy or the selfishness of the teachers, command persecution and intolerance, contradict reason, forbid the sensible use of the passions, present inactivity, sloth, and the wasting of goods on holy idlers as virtue, and lead people who are already tormented enough to succumb to timidity and despair by invoking the fear of hell and the devil. No, it must not burden man with impossibilities, but the yoke it places on him must be sweet and the bonds light. He must feel how virtue makes him calm, content, rich, and happy. In a word, it must be the divine doctrine of Jesus and His disciples, so greatly mis-

---

[67] *The Theban Legion, a Roman regiment stationed in Egypt, whose soldiers, according to legend, had converted to Christianity and were martyred together, on their march to Gaul, in 286.*

understood, abused by selfishness, and augmented by so many supplements that their true meaning has only been preserved and passed on in secret schools!

This our grand and unforgettable master, Jesus of Nazareth, came to us in a historical period during which the world had fallen into a state of general corruption, to a people that had felt the oppression of servitude most emphatically since time immemorial and hoped for its redemption heralded by the prophets, in a country that lay at the centre of the then known world. This people He instructed in the doctrines of reason, and in order to increase their efficacy, He shrewdly joined this simple religion of reason with the then prevailing popular religion, using all ruling traditions and customs and concealing the inner, essential parts of his teachings therein. The first followers of these His teachings were no sages, but simple men, chosen from the lowest class of people, to demonstrate that His doctrines were universally useful and understandable for all classes, and that it was not an exclusive privilege of gentlefolk to applaud the truths of reason. Furthermore, He showed not only the Jews but the entire human race the path to salvation through the observance of His commandments; He acted in accordance to these teachings Himself by leading a most innocent life, and He sealed them with his blood and death.

The commandments He identified as the means to our salvation are only two: love God, who is the supreme love, and love thy neighbour. He demands nothing more of anyone. No one before Him had presented the love of one's equal so forcefully, so enticingly, so lovably. We shall love others as we love ourselves, just as we want others to do unto us as we have done unto them: and what we do not want them to do unto us, we should not do unto them.[68] – A commandment that encompasses all morality and law. One should quite naturally recognise the disciple of Jesus by the love he bears for others, and he proclaims this [love] as a new commandment, further bids us to love our enemies – for they know not what they do[69] –, to forgive them their insults, so that we too may be forgiven. And who can read the divine guidance for our conduct in Matthew, chapters 10 and 11, without being touched to the core, without coming to think that a world inhabited by men formed in this manner would grant the greatest bliss? But Jesus certainly also understood that this doctrine of universal love would not calm everything down at once, but that, at first, it would even conflict with the lesser, special circumstances the degraded people had become accustomed to. For this

---

[68] *See Luke 6:31.* [69] *Luke 23:34.*

reason, He says in this same passage that He has not come to send immediate peace, but a sword; the son would fight against his father, the daughter against her mother.[70] Not that He wished to sever these natural bonds, but He rejected the disorderly and excessive aspects of this personal interest. One should never weigh one's petty circumstances against Him and His commandments, never give in to such inclinations to the point of insulting all other men, but always keep in sight the good of the whole, of which we are but a part. And when Jesus teaches us to scorn riches, He rather seeks to teach us their sensible use and prepare us for the community of property introduced by Him. We should not let us be tempted by this to shameful and selfish miserliness or to wastefulness, but use our affluence for the good of others in need, according to the law of love.

No one has secured the bonds of human society and returned them to their proper boundaries like Him, no one has prompted humanity to mutual goodwill to this extent, no one has empathised and connected with his audience's notions as much as He, all the while concealing the higher purpose of His teachings wisely; and finally, no one has paved man's road to wisdom as safely and easily as our great master, Jesus of Nazareth.

He has wholly concealed this secret meaning and the natural consequences of his doctrine; for Jesus did have a secret doctrine, as we can see from more than one passage of the Bible. He spoke in parables to those who should not fully understand him. He promised the spirit of truth, whom the world cannot receive, to His disciples: for the world neither knows nor sees it, but the disciples know it, for it dwells with them, and shall be in them.[71]

And in another passage of Scripture He speaks to His disciples: 'It is given unto you to you know the mysteries of the kingdom of heaven.'[72] But to those outside it is not given, 'because they seeing see not; and hearing they hear not, neither do they understand'.[73]

However, as much as He concealed the true meaning of his doctrine from the people, He nevertheless revealed it through his words and deeds in several places. He constantly speaks of a kingdom of His father, whose children He and we are; and as we all, high and low, are children of one father, of God,[74] it is His will that we know and love one another as brothers. It is through this true brotherly love,

---

[70] *See Matt. 10:34–35.*

[71] *See John 14:17.*

[72] *Matt. 13:11.*

[73] *Matt. 13:13.*

[74] *See John 8:41.*

when we do this will of the father, that we become true sons of God. Since He alone did so to the highest degree, He alone fully knew the father, was His only begotten and most beloved son.[75] Never before had we been taught so clearly that we are brothers. It is through Him that we learn we all have only one Lord, our God. And this Lord is Father, we are His sons, children, and brothers, when we do His will. He and the Father are one,[76] for they were of a single will, and His works proved He was sent by the Father and that all power was given unto Him. The mere faith in him, the Father, and his commandments, makes impossible things possible.[77] By this faith, entire mountain ranges shall move from their places.[78] His kingdom suffers violence;[79] for one is occupied with conquering one's passions. Those who are strong enough for this are the mighty, and only they will sweep it away. However, one struggles not only with oneself but also with the evil ones. He teaches us the art of desiring judiciously, by charging us to pray to the Father that His will, not ours, be done;[80] to view every success as the will of this Father and to calm ourselves during times of misfortune, because this must happen according to the way of the world and the will of the Father. He gives the power to bind and to loose.[81] He will establish a community against which hell is powerless. He has other sheep which are not from this flock. A time will come when there shall be one shepherd and one fold.[82] In the time of the Resurrection, all shall be equal unto God's angels.[83] He gives us children as examples because of the innocence of their habits and bids us to become like them.[84] In another passage, He says: 'If ye continue in my word, then are ye my disciples indeed; And ye shall know the truth, and the truth shall make you free.[85] – So the last shall be first, and the first last.[86]' He would never suffer that one of his own would be more exalted than the other.[87] 'Ye know', He said, 'that the princes of the Gentiles exercise dominion. But it shall not be so among you: but whosoever will be great among you, let him be your minister; and whosoever will be chief among you, let him be your servant: Even as the Son of man came not to be

---

75 *See John 3:16.*
77 *See Luke 18:27.*
79 *See Matt. 11:12.*
81 *See Matt. 18:18.*
83 *See Luke 20:36.*
85 *John 8:31–32.*
87 *See Matt. 23:8.*

76 *See John 10:30.*
78 *See Matt. 17:20 and 21:21.*
80 *See Matt. 6:10.*
82 *See John 10:16.*
84 *See Matt. 18:3.*
86 *Matt. 16:30.*

ministered unto, but to minister, and to give his life a ransom for many.'[88]

He himself practised with His disciples the equality and community of property,[89] which persisted in Jerusalem's church for some time after his death.

When He washed his disciples' feet and Peter refused, He said to him: 'If I wash thee not, thou hast no part with me.[90] Ye call me Master and Lord: and ye say well; for so I am. If I then, your Lord and Master, have washed your feet, ye also ought to wash one another's feet. For I have given you an example, that ye should do as I have done for you. Verily, verily, I say unto you, the servant is not greater than his lord; neither he that is sent greater than he that sent him. If ye know these things, happy are ye if ye do them.[91]'

Once it is understood that the secret purpose of His doctrine, preserved for us through the *disciplina arcani* and emanating from His own sermons and deeds, was to return men to their original freedom and to pave the way for this, then many previously incomprehensible and seemingly contradictory things become comprehensible and, indeed, quite natural. Now even he who does not believe in the mysteries of the common Christian denominations[92], as debased by the priests, and to whom certain hidden, still greater secrets cannot yet be revealed, should not object to calling Jesus the redeemer and saviour of the world. He may also understand the doctrine of the fall of man, original sin, and the resurrection. [One] will then know what the state of pure nature, the state of nature after the fall, and the kingdom of grace are. Since man has departed from his original freedom, he has departed from his natural state and lost his dignity by succumbing too much to his original passions and instincts, unable to resist his desires and sensual appetites. As members of a commonwealth, men no longer live in a state of pure nature, but are in a fallen state. Once they regain their original dignity, however, by tempering their passions and curbing their needs, they reach redemption and the state of grace. They achieve this through moral doctrine, and the doctrine leading most perfectly to this goal was taught by Jesus. Once His morality and doctrines have been universally disseminated, the kingdom of the just and faithful will be established on earth.

This kingdom has been prophesied to us in many passages of the Bible, and it must certainly come about one day. One merely needs to look at the passages

---

[88] *Matt. 20:25–28.*

[90] *John 13:8.*

[92] *'Religionen'.*

[89] *See Acts 2:44.*

[91] *John 13:13–17.*

dedicated to it in the book called the Apocalypse, or Revelation of Saint John. The whole of the 6th and 7th chapters paint a picture of the monstrous abuses that have entered the world through the state constitutions, and of how men oppress, strangle, deceive, insult, persecute, and tyrannise one another. Chapters 8 and 9, on the other hand, describe the avengers of mankind, who will touch nothing that bears the seal of God on its forehead, however, but only fight against tyranny. Anyone who has not bent his knee before the idols will remain unscathed, according to verse 20 of chapter 9.[93] They will complete God's secret (chap. 10, v. 7)[94]. Then everything shall be reversed (chap. 13, v. 10)[95], and he who seeks to insult others will be oppressed. Then shall be fulfilled (chap. 1[5], v. 3[96]) that of which the poet Moses has sung. In chapter 21, verse 1[97], this period is called the new heaven, the new earth – a solid kingdom that cannot be moved (v. 12[98]). No more temples will be built (v. 22[99]), since God Almighty himself will dwell among men, and there will be only one truth on the face of the earth. No one must fear suffering for this truth. One shall serve God in the purest way, see his face, bear His name on one's forehead (chap. 22, v. 3–4[100]). He who overcomes will become a pillar of the new Jerusalem (chap. 3, v. 12[101]). For this, though, the patience of saints is needed (chap. [14], v. 12[102]), and the strength to wait and persist. Blessed are they (says verse 9 of chapter 19)[103] who have partaken in the

---

[93] 'And the rest of the men which were not killed by these plagues yet repented not of the works of their hands, that they should not worship devils, and idols of gold, and silver, and brass, and stone, and of wood: which neither can see, nor hear, nor walk.'

[94] 'But in the days of the voice of the seventh angel, when he shall begin to sound, the mystery of God should be finished, as he hath declared to his servants the prophets.'

[95] 'He that leadeth into captivity shall go into captivity: he that killeth with the sword must be killed with the sword. Here is the patience and the faith of the saints.'

[96] 'And they sing the song of Moses the servant of God, and the song of the Lamb, saying, Great and marvellous are thy works, Lord God Almighty; just and true are thy ways, thou King of saints.'

[97] 'And I saw a new heaven and a new earth: for the first heaven and the first earth were passed away; and there was no more sea.'

[98] 'And had a wall great and high, and had twelve gates, and at the gates twelve angels, and names written thereon, which are the names of the twelve tribes of the children of Israel[.]'

[99] 'And I saw no temple therein: for the Lord God Almighty and the Lamb are the temple of it.'

[100] 'And there shall be no more curse: but the throne of God and of the Lamb shall be in it; and his servants shall serve him: And they shall see his face; and his name shall be in their foreheads.'

[101] 'Him that overcometh will I make a pillar in the temple of my God, and he shall go no more out: and I will write upon him the name of my God, and the name of the city of my God, which is new Jerusalem, which cometh down out of heaven from my God: and I will write upon him my new name.'

[102] 'Here is the patience of the saints: here are they that keep the commandments of God, and the faith of Jesus.'

[103] 'And he saith unto me, Write, Blessed are they which are called unto the marriage supper of the Lamb. And he saith unto me, These are the true sayings of God.'

love-feast of the Lord. Only they (chap. 20, v. 6)[104] have a part in this resurrection. God made them kings and priests (chap. 5, v. 10)[105], and we shall be kings on this earth. Jesus has prepared this kingdom for us (chap. 1, v. 5 and 6)[106], won immortality for his race of priest-kings, and provided a certain number of the best and most illuminated ones (chap. 4, v. 4 and 5)[107] with knowledge and power.

There are also countless passages proclaiming this golden age in the writings of the ancient prophets. Only through a general enlightenment will men come to understand the state of their former misery and their present felicity. They will realise that by straying from the commandments of Jesus they subject themselves once again. The enlightenment of this grace will thus ensure that humanity does not fall again, and that this state will last.

These different periods are also represented by the masonic hieroglyphs, including the rough and smooth ashlars and many allegories which have been explained to you, albeit obscurely, in the Scottish Knight degree. Let the blazing star be the hieroglyph of illumination! The letter G reminds you of grace, *gratia*. It shines upon us on our previously errant paths. Those affected by this grace are the enlightened ones, the *Illuminati*: a name given, in the early church, to all Christians after their baptism; in short, to all initiates.

If only they had remained faithful to the doctrine of Jesus and His disciples, all men would have gained their freedom in a short time. Instead, however, it would soon have been wholly forgotten, had it not been preserved by the *disciplina arcani*. Jesus himself predicted that many false prophets would arise but that, among the Elect, His doctrine and His word would endure forever. Those in danger of succumbing to temptation, after having endured manifold tribulations, will be gathered by the guardian angel of the just cause with his trumpet from the four winds, and then there shall be a new heaven and a new earth.[108]

---

[104] *'Blessed and holy is he that hath part in the first resurrection: on such the second death hath no power, but they shall be priests of God and of Christ, and shall reign with him a thousand years.'*

[105] *'And hast made us unto our God kings and priests: and we shall reign on the earth.'*

[106] *'And from Jesus Christ, who is the faithful witness, and the first begotten of the dead, and the prince of the kings of the earth. Unto him that loved us, and washed us from our sins in his own blood, And hath made us kings and priests unto God and his Father; to him be glory and dominion for ever and ever. Amen.'*

[107] *'And round about the throne were four and twenty seats: and upon the seats I saw four and twenty elders sitting, clothed in white raiment; and they had on their heads crowns of gold. And out of the throne proceeded lightnings and thunderings and voices: and there were seven lamps of fire burning before the throne, which are the seven Spirits of God.'*

[108] *See Matt. 24:24–31.*

The true meaning of this prophecy was lost to most men. They then argued over things irrelevant to our felicity. Selfish and ambitious men deployed their sophistry: a false clergy emerged, and this hateful body soon became the only class that managed to gain independence. The means for salvation was used for a new oppression.

Now a marvellous thing was born: theology, the regimen of priests and scoundrels, the Papacy and spiritual despotism. The latter rose to such heights that even the princes' thrones trembled violently. This power and oppression was all the more terrible because it even extended to thoughts and opinions.

Until then, men had been unable to do as they wished; now they were no longer allowed even to think as they wished. The confidence, the faith in the force and goodness of something capable of moving mountains was now transformed into a belief in self-serving sophistries, perversions of the doctrine of Jesus. Men persecuted one another over this, and it became a religious dictate to purge one another from the face of the earth. Until then, men had oppressed one another in their own name; now, however, sacrilege and despotism reached such a height that they oppressed one another in the name of God; and a murderer, whore-monger, and deceiver who believed in transubstantiation could expect a better fate than the honest and virtuous man who had the misfortune of not being able to comprehend how a piece of dough could simultaneously be a piece of flesh.

In all this, the people could see as their only sorry advantage that the fate of serfdom now also befell their previous oppressors. In this way the history of the human race is the history of usurpation and the most dire oppression. It is easy to imagine that the fate of Jesus' old and new disciples was miserable and sad, just as He had prophesied.[109] Now their secrecy had to be twofold, and they therefore concealed their true doctrines behind hieroglyphs, and themselves behind the name of other societies, and this all the more since the bulk of those who call themselves Christians have no understanding whatsoever of the true spirit of this holy legion. This caution was often necessitated by persecution from outside. With these hieroglyphs they celebrated the memory of their great teacher and eagerly awaited the time when they would regain their original rights and thus appear to the world in their full glory.

Thus concealed, they first lived during times of schisms within the church,

---

[109] *See Matt. 10:22 and 24:9, Luke 6:22, and John 16:1–4.*

e.g. under the Emperors Valens,[110] Julian,[111] etc.; then in times and places where Christians lived among the Pagans, and in the Orient during the Crusades, and many other historic periods, e.g. in England during the conflicts between the Presbyterians and the Episcopals and between the Whigs and the Tories, and finally, when the pure doctrine grew ever scarcer and true Christianity was perpetuated only in the lap of true Freemasonry.

We have already hinted at this in the Scottish Knight degree, and we wish to elaborate, prove, and add a few things here. Freemasonry is called a royal art because it teaches men the art of governing themselves. Its foundation rests on justice and benevolence and, therefore, the two pillars called *Jakin* and *Boaz* have been interpreted by some as *justitia* and *benevolentia;* but *Jakin* also means firm intention, and *Boaz* strength in God. *Hieram: Hic Jesus est restituens amorem mundi.*[112] Hieram is the redeemer Jesus, who also spoke of the construction of a temple, by which He meant the edifice of His doctrine. The twelve masters who searched for the old master's word when he was slain are the apostles who, according to the teachings of their crucified king, sought to spread once more the love that had become lost among men. It is well known that the early Christians compared Jesus to the sun, the church to the moon, and the stars to the various degrees of enlightenment that man must reach on his path to this goal.

All our traditions are authentic remnants of the earliest Christian church. Like Freemasons, the early Christians also had to authenticate themselves with the Catechism, the Old Roman Symbol,[113] a sign – which in their case was the Cross – and patents *(literae pacis)*. They gathered at night and held the love-feast *(agape)*. Later, the blazing star was interpreted as a sign of the *epiphania Domini* among the Roman Freemasons. The Entered Apprentices are the *Fideles,* the Fellow Crafts are the *Diaconi,* and the Master Masons are the *Presbyteri.*

The manner of the Freemasonic initiation is the same as that of the *catechumen*[114] as described by the Church Fathers. Here are a few passages from their writings. First, from *Origen against Celsus:*[115]

---

[110] *Flavius Julius Valens Augustus (328–378), Eastern Roman Emperor from 364 until his death in the Battle of Adrianople.*

[111] *Flavius Claudius Julianus Augustus (331/32–363), also known as Julian the Apostate, Roman Emperor from 361, the last non-Christian ruler of the Empire.*

[112] *Lat. Here, Jesus is restoring the love of the world.*   [113] *An earlier and shorter version of the Apostles' Creed.*

[114] *A man receiving religious instruction prior to his baptism.*

[115] *Origen of Alexandria: Contra Celsum (248). The following quotation is a composite from book III, chapter 51, and book VI, chapter 10.*

Quamvis Christiani prædicatores conversionem Gentilium ardentissime desi-
derarent, nihilominus auditorium suorum probabant spiritum. Privatim exor-
cismis eos præparabant, antequam ad congregationem admitterentur, et si firmam
bene vivendi voluntatem deprehendissent, in Christianorum conventum intro-
ducebant, diversis tamen ordinibus conlocandis. Primo ordine stabant incipien-
tes, necdum integrum fidei symbolum edocti; altero, qui christianis legibus vivere
irrevocabiliter statuissent. Hi suos habebant præpositos, qui eorum mores exami-
narent, a vetitis abstinere nolentes arcerent, bonos toto corde susciperent, et ut de
die in diem proficerent, hortarentur. Articuli fidei Catechumenis proponebantur,
non leviter et inconsulte credendi, sed lente et pro captu eorum instruebantur,
considerata vitæ et conditionis ratione. Ad simpliciter credendum excitabantur,
qui clara intelligere non valebant; capacioribus misteriorum veritas quærendo et
respondendo demonstrabatur.[116]

Now a passage from *De Mysteriis, ch. 1–9 by Ambrosius:*[117] Primo aperiuntur
aures Catechumeno, dicendo: Epheta! Tum in sanctum sanctorum i. e. Baptisterium inducitur, in præsentia Diaconi, Presbyteri et Episcopi renuntiat Dæmoni,
et operibus eius. Dum mundo renuntiabat Catechumenus, se ad occidentem
vertebat, ut quasi in faciem resisteret. Dein vertebatur eum ad orientum quasi
Jesum Christum aspecturus. Egredientes e fonte unguebantur in capite, lavaban-
tur eorum pedes, et albis vestibus induebantur. Tum sigillum et pignus spiritus
Sancti accipiebant cum expressione septem donorum i. e. confirmationem. Tum
progrediebantur versus altare, dicentes: introibo ad altare Dei, ad DIUM, qui
lætificat iuventutem meam. Altare inveniebant, et primo sancto acrificio assiste-
bant.[118]

---

[116] *'Although the Christian preachers most ardently desired the conversion of the heathen, even so they always tested
the spirit of those who listened to them. They used to prepare them privately for the exorcisms before they were
admitted to the congregation, and if they revealed a firm desire to live well then they introduced them to the
formal gathering of Christians, but they were organised in various categories. In the first category were the novices,
who had not yet been instructed in the entire symbolism of the faith. In the second category were those who had
decided irrevocably to live in accordance with Christian laws: these had their own mentors who would examine
their morals, exclude those who were unwilling to abstain from forbidden practices, and wholeheartedly encourage
the good people amongst them and exhort them to improve from day to day … The articles of the Christian faith
were explained to the catechumens, but not in such a way that these would be accepted superficially or over-
hastily: the pupils were instructed slowly and in accordance with their powers of comprehension, and only after the
reason for human life and the Creation had been considered … Those who were not able to understand clearly-
explained things were encouraged simply to believe in what they were told. To the more intellectually capable the
Truth of the Mystery was explained by means of question and answer.'*

[117] *St. Ambrose: On the Mysteries (387). The following is not a verbatim quotation, but a composite of chapters 1–9.*

[118] *'First the ears were opened by saying to the catechumen, "Epheta!" [see Mark 7:34] Then he was led into the Holy
of Holies, which is to say into the Baptistery. In the presence of the Deacon, the Presbyter and the Bishop he then
renounced the Devil and his works. While the catechumen was renouncing the world he turned to the West, so that
he was, as it were, resisting the Devil to his face. Then he turned to the East so that he was, as it were, looking Jesus*

Furthermore, *de Corona by Tertullian, ch. 3:*[119] Antequam in aquam intramus, in ipsa aqua, et adhuc prius ecclesiae sub manu prælati protestamur, quod dæmoni, pompis eius et angelis renuntiamus. Dein ter immergimur. Ex fontibus lavati lac et mel gustamus, et ab hac die per totam septimanam solito balneo abstinemus.[120]

And Cyril, in *Cathechesi Prima:* Primo aditu in vestibulo Baptisterii intrastis, ad orientum conversi, vobis mandatum est, ut manum extenderetis, et sic Satanæ tanquam præsenti, renuntiastis. Quare in occidentum respexistis! Quia occidens est symbolum tenebrarum, quarum diabolus princeps est. Tunc venit professio fidei. Hæc omnia extra ecclesiam facta. [Dein sancta sanctorum ingressi estis, i.e., Baptisterium.] Illico tunicam deposuistis, in signum, quod veterem hominem exueretis. Oleo per exorcismum consecrato, uncti estis, a vertice capitis usque deorsum. Ad sacrum baptismi balneum adducti estis, et singuli vestrum interrogati: an credant in nomine patris, et filii, et spiritus sancti? Professionem fidei ad salutem necessariam, erudistis. Ter aqua fuistis immersi, quibus servator in sepulcro fuit, ut hos tres dies significet; sacro balneo egressi unctionem accepistis, quæ unctionis Christi imago est.[121]

Finally, from Justin's Apologia: Si, qui veritatem doctrinæ nostræ agnoverunt, huic doctrinæ conformem vitam instituere promittant, hos ad ieiunandum et orandum obligamus, nosque simul cum iis ieiunamus et oramus. Tum ad aquam ducuntur, ibique regenerantur, sicut nos regenerati sumus. In aqua enim lavantur in nomine Dei patris et salvatoris nostri. Hanc ablutionem vocamus illumina-

---

Christ in the face. Those leaving the Holy of Holies were anointed on the head with water from the fountain, their feet were washed with the same water, and they were dressed in white vestments. Then they received the seal as a pledge of the Holy Spirit with the expression of the Seven Gifts, that is to say, they underwent Confirmation. Then they proceeded towards the altar, saying: "I will go in to the altar of God; to GOD, the joy of my youth." They found the altar prepared for them and they then attended their first Mass.'

[119] *Tertullian: Chaplet or De corona (201).*

[120] *'Before we enter the water, in that very water and yet beforehand we assert beneath the hand of the priest of the church that we are renouncing the Devil, his retinues and his angels. Then we are immersed three times. Bathed in water from the fountains we taste milk and honey, and from that day forth, for the entire week, we abstain from our usual baths.'*

[121] *'First you entered the porch leading to the vestibule of the Baptistery. Facing the East you were instructed to stretch out your hand and thus renounce Satan just as if he were present before you. Why did you turn your back on the West? Because the West is symbolic of the shadows, of which the Devil is the Prince. Then came the profession of faith. All these things were done outside the church-building. There you took off your tunic as a sign that you were putting aside your former self. You were then anointed with consecrated oil as an act of exorcism, from the top of your head to the soles of your feet. You were then led to the sacred bath of baptism and asked individually whether you believed in the name of the Father, the Son and the Holy Ghost. You then pronounced the profession of faith necessary for your salvation. Three times you were immersed in the water to signify the three days in which Our Saviour was in the tomb. Having left the bath you accepted unction, which is the image of Jesus Christ, etc.'*

tionem, quia per eam anima illuminatur.[122] Hac ablutione facta, novum fidelem, seu, ut appellare solemus, susceptum in fratrum numerum, ad locum ducimus, ubi omnes congregati sunt ad communem orationem, quam offerunt pro se, pro illuminato, et pro fratribus absentibus, ubicunque sint, ut, postquam veritatem agnovimus per opera et præceptorum observationem ad salutem æternam pervenire valemus.[123] Factis precibus, osculo nos salutamus, tum illi, qui fratribus præest, panis et poculum cum vino et aqua porrigitur. Hoc ille accipiens, laudem et gloriam dat patri per nomen filii et spiritus sancti, et prolixam gratiarum actionem pronuntiat pro donis, quæ nobis gratificatus est. Quando preces et gratiarum actionem complevit, omnibus assistentibus consecratum panem, vinum et aquam distribuunt et a[bs]entibus deferunt.[124]

Thus you can see that the very name Illuminati[125] stems from the earliest church, and that therefore it is the purpose of true Freemasonry and of the Order to enable mankind to gain its freedom, to unite the world and its people, currently divided by their civil institutions, into a single family, and to bring about the kingdom of the just and virtuous by means of an active Christianity, the proliferation of Jesus' teachings, the preservation of the true secrets of this doctrine, and the enlightenment of reason.

However, just as no human endeavour, no matter how holy and honourable, has ever been undespoiled, Freemasonry was bound to suffer the same fate, too. Some men, who on their path to the light had already been accepted into this magnificent association but who strayed from this path so well begun through their own adverse conduct and before being fully disabused, succumbed to the madness of using the knowledge they had gathered (but not understood) in the

---

[122] 'As many as are persuaded and believe that what we teach and say is true, undertake to be able to live accordingly, are instructed to pray and to entreat God with fasting, for the remission of their sins that are past, and we pray and fast along with them. Then they are brought by us where there is water, and are regenerated in the same manner in which we were ourselves regenerated. For, in the name of God, the Father and Lord of the universe, and of our Saviour Jesus Christ, and of the Holy Spirit, they then receive the washing with water ... And this washing is called illumination, because they who learn these things are illuminated in their understandings.' (Chapter 61)

[123] 'But we, after we have thus washed him who has been convinced and has assented to our teaching, bring him to the place where those who are called brethren are assembled, in order that we may offer hearty prayers in common for ourselves and for the illuminated person, and for all others in every place, that we may be counted worthy, now that we have learnt the truth, by our works also to be found good citizens and keepers of the commandments, so that we may be saved with an everlasting salvation.' (Chapter 65)

[124] 'Having ended the prayers, we salute one another with a kiss. There is then brought to the president of the brethren bread and a cup of wine mixed with water; and he taking them, gives praise and glory to the Father of the universe, through the name of the Son and of the Holy Ghost, and offers thanks at considerable length for the gifts that he has granted to us. And when he has concluded the prayers and thanksgivings they distribute to all those present some consecrated bread, wine and water, and to those who are absent they carry away a portion.'

[125] 'Erleuchtete'.

Sanctum's vestibule to deceive the hopes of other men under the semblance of borrowed customs and to use them, often with shameful intentions, as tools of their [own] selfishness and ambition. Since the foundation of their institutions was not firm enough to [enable them to] affect the corrupted world, and since the very purpose and secret was still concealed from them, while they had nonetheless led their followers to great expectations, and lacking anything better, they devised all sorts of means to postpone the discovery of their fraud. They invented degrees upon degrees. They sought to excite man's very natural inclination for mystery, incite his imagination, and numb his reasoning power. Consequently, false Templars, false Rosicrucians, etc., came to the fore in vast numbers.[126] There were even men who openly led the most pernicious and immoral lives and still pretended to consort with invisible higher beings. In the midst of sensual amusements one spoke of revelation and inspiration, invoked the bodies of the dead while under the influence of strong drink – and appear they did, namely in the imagination of weak and fantastical minds, wont to deceive themselves.[127] As the supernatural became the fashion of the day, already careless men were further incited to look past everything and into the future, giving little thought to this world. Yet one vial of mischief was still missing, and that also was poured out over us. The most shameful of all desires, the source of inexhaustible wastefulness, moral corruption, and unsocial, wicked avarice – the desire to make gold – was made the ultimate goal of Freemasonry. As a result, everything that had once been written about the subject was now sought out; in a word! nothing was left untried to spread unreason, superstition, folly, and poor morals, to hamper the good works, and to protect men from their misery and misfortune by a kind of anaesthesia.

Had not the noble ones and the elect stood in the background, resisting the downfall and perdition and supporting the cracking, sinking building on their shoulders, Christianity and Freemasonry would have been lost, perdition would once again have fallen upon the human race, regents, priests, and Freemasons would have banished reason from the earth, and the abode of good men would have been flooded with fools, enthusiasts, hypocrites, spectres, corpses, and human-like animals.

---

[126] *While the Strict Observance saw itself in the tradition of the Knights Templar, the Order of the Golden and Rosy Cross purportedly descended from the Rosicrucians of the 17th century. However, both claims to tradition were spurious.*

[127] *Allusion to the notorious séances of Johann Georg Schrepffer (1738–1774) in Leipzig.*

But just as these patrons of darkness are plotting our demise, they strengthen the Legion of the Elect all the more; by opening false side-gates, they keep the unholy from beleaguering the holy portal, and lead insolence and persecution on another path. One would be very mistaken in the belief that this is the only advantage our association and the world can draw from these monstrosities. The less they arrive at their goal, the more they prepare the way for us. They awaken a new interest, open up new, hitherto unknown prospects, and encourage the spirit of invention and the expectations of men. By deceiving them they ultimately make better men mistrustful, and thus brace them against further deception. They cause some to begin to realise the weakness of human nature in its degradation and make them yearn for better, clearer instruction. They make them more indifferent towards the interests of the state and bring people of different nations and religions together under a common bond all by themselves, drawing the most capable minds and hands away from state and church, making people form friendships they would never otherwise have had; and in so doing, quite unwittingly, they undermine their narrower ties. They clash and they grate against one another, they teach men the power of combined forces, and make them realise the imperfection of their prior constitution; and because the imperfection of their oft-revealed institutions causes the governments to harbour no mistrust in such associations, they serve as a cover for a wiser and nobler institution. In this process, they enable us to unite in our lap better men who have long been misled and tried by experience. They therefore weaken the enemy, even if they do not defeat him right away, and they decrease the number and zeal of his champions, scatter his forces to disperse the attack, and so on. As our newer, outward institution grows in force, numbers, and wisdom at the expense of the others, these latter must gradually decay on their own, and since they have made secret associations a need of the age, all efforts to destroy our union must now be in vain. This spark may glimmer for a long time under a blanket of ashes, but it is certain that one day it will erupt into bright flames: for nature tires of forever repeating this old game, but the greater oppression and persecution become, the more men will sense it and fight for their freedom.

The seed of this new world has now been cast, it has taken root and spread widely – but the time of harvest is perhaps still far away. Sooner or later, however, nature must finish her days' work and elevate our race to its original dignity again. We are only the spectators and tools of nature, refraining from accelerating her success and allowing ourselves no other means than disseminating enlightenment, love, and morals. Assured of certain success, we abstain from all violent means and content ourselves with sensing the joy and felicity of coming generations from a distance, and laying their foundations by the most innocent means. We calm our conscience in the face of any reproach, seek nothing for ourselves, and, as diligent observers of nature, we admire its majestic progress in holy awe, rejoice in our race, and felicitate ourselves on being human and children of God.

ADDENDUM B. INSTRUCTIONS FOR THE FIRST DEGREE OF THE PRIEST CLASS.

I. The Priests of this Class preside over the lesser or exoteric mysteries. They are called *Presbyteri,* and their Superior the *Decanus.* However, they must not be known by these names to the Scottish Knights. Therefore, if it is necessary sometimes to speak of the Mystery Class, the initiates are always referred to by the title customary in pagan times, namely *Epopts,*[128] and a Superior of the Mysteries as a *Hierophant.*[129]

II. The Assemblies of this degree are called *Synods.*

III. All *Presbyteri* scattered throughout a Province comprise only one Synod. However, other than the *Decanus,* the Prefects of the Chapters, and the higher Superiors, who are authorised to attend the Assemblies, there may only be *nine* Presbyters in each Province. Of these, *seven* preside over the seven main scientific disciplines, while the other two are the secretaries and assistants of the *Decanus* and of the Synods, who also handle any extraordinary tasks, etc.

IV. Indeed, since the *Presbyteri* no longer have anything to do with the worldly affairs of the Order, they must turn their whole attention to the perfection of their discipline. Since all the Minervals' best essays are sent to them they have the opportunity to intimately acquaint themselves with the most capable minds in the Order. As soon as someone is accepted into the lower degrees and chooses a science or an art the Provincial Superior makes this known to the *Decanus* who in turn notifies the Priest presiding over this subject accordingly. The latter takes note of the new worker, who, together with the others in the Province working in the same science, unknowingly forms a whole learned faculty.

---

[128] *Gr. (ἐπόπτης). Initiate into the mysteries.*

[129] *Title of the chief priest in the Eleusinian Mysteries. They interpreted sacred mysteries, arcane principles, and esoteric symbols.*

V. Thus, every Priest assembles a sufficient number of subordinate workers in his discipline and establishes something like a faculty. These must work and conduct research for him. Since all scientific enquiries in this discipline are now directed to him, and he must satisfy those who send them, it is incumbent upon him to try to establish some solid systems and, with the aid of his subordinates, explain, explore, and correct that which is still dark and uncertain.

VI. Where neither his knowledge nor the knowledge of his pupils suffice he shall also consult the opinions of scholars outside the Order, thus putting them to the Order's use without their knowing. He should not be too quick to turn to the higher Superiors, but must satisfactorily answer as many questions as possible from his own repertory to ease the burden upon the Superiors who are already overstretched with tremendous amounts of work.

However, if this proves insufficient, he submits, through the *Decanus,* a request to the Provincial Superior, who then makes enquiries in the other Provinces. Only in important cases and if these efforts are unsuccessful does one resort to contacting the higher Superiors. But in general everything, even the least important matters, passes through the hands of the *Decanus,* and an individual Priest does not maintain correspondence with the Assemblies.

VII. One shall keep a record of the many questions whose explanations are important and which may eventually be raised, e.g. questions in the field of applied philosophy such as: 'To what extent is the statement true that everything that leads to a good end is a permissible means? How must this statement be limited in order to avoid Jesuitical misuse and fearful enslavement to prejudice, etc.?' Such and similar questions are sent to the *Decanus,* who distributes them among the various Minerval churches. In this way the pupils are kept busy and many a new, bold, and useful idea is added to our inventory.

VIII. Thus, if this Priest Class is to be newly established in a Province, one should leave nothing untried to care for the sciences therein, as if the Order had not yet achieved anything in *scientificis*[130]. One can never do enough to expand and refine human knowledge. It is a never-ending task. Thus everyone must do his share here. If fundamental explanations are missing, these will not be withheld by the worthy Illust. Superiors. However, one should not merely nourish oneself from the knowledge of others, but must also strive to increase the accumulated treasures.

[130] Lat. *In the field of science.*

IX. Therefore the Priest Class, under the leadership of the *Decanus* and the protection of the Provincial Superior, shall put the Order on such a footing in the Province that it never lacks talented and experienced men in any discipline, but that also

1) young people become accustomed to practising a spirit of observation,

2) facts and undeniable observations are amassed,

3) which are properly examined, compared, and utilised in such a manner

4) that the Order can do without all previous systems and present to its adherents its own systems, based on Nature alone.

5) That it has inventors in all subjects.

6) That a hoard of the most profound, most deeply hidden wisdom rests in its lap, so that

7) the Order makes itself indispensable to the profane world whereas, on the other hand, the profane world becomes dispensable to the Order,

8) so that it can consequently spread the light gathered by the labours and wisdom of its members to whom it chooses.

X. To disseminate the spirit of observation one must begin even in the Minerval Class.

1) The members must be taught that nothing in nature is small and insignificant.

2) They all must be assigned to the various sciences for which they have a liking and an inclination, and in which they wish to and shall make observations.

3) One must strive to [establish] a peculiar system of observation in the Province.

4) Therefore one must ask the following questions and reward the best essays with promotions, money, or in some other way. It should be observed that no one must be promoted into a higher Class unless he has provided a worthy service to the Order in this or some other discipline. The questions are as follows:

A. What is the spirit of observation?

B. How is it acquired, and how are good observers educated[?]

C. How must one observe precisely and correctly[?]

5) Once the system of observation is established in general, the *Decanus,* on orders of the Provincial Superior, submits the same questions to each of the separate Classes of the Lesser Mysteries.

XI. These classes, then, are

1) *Physics,* namely

A. optics, dioptrics, catoptrics.

B. Hydraulics, hydrostatics.

C. Electricity, central forces, magnetism, attraction, repulsion.

D. Experimental physics applied to the air and other objects.

2) The *medical* class, to which belong

A. anatomy,

B. observations about illnesses, medications, semiotics.

C. Surgery, midwifery, surgical operations.

D. Chemistry.

3) *Mathematical* class, namely

A. General and higher arithmetic, algebra, etc.

B. Pure mathematics, civil and military engineering, and shipbuilding.

C. Mechanics.

D. Celestial spheres, astronomy.

4) For *natural history,* such as

A. Agriculture, horticulture, housekeeping.

B. The animal kingdom, from the smallest insect to the human being.

C. Soil types, stones, metals.

D. Knowledge of the effects and unknown phenomena of the earth.

5) *Political class,* to which belong

A. Knowledge of human nature, for which the Greater *Illuminati* provide materials.

B. History, geography, history of erudition, for which purpose the biographies of the men whose name one bears are also submitted.

C. Antiquities, diplomatics.

D. Political history of the Order, its destiny, progress, effects, misfortunes in every Province, conflicts with other societies working against it.

NB. Special attention should be given to these topics.

6) *Artists and craftsmen,* namely

A. painting, sculpture, music, dance.

B. Rhetoric and poetry, living languages, Latin and Greek.

C. Other fine arts, literature.

D. Craftsmen.

7) *Secret sciences and special knowledge.*

A. Rare languages, oriental languages.

B. Knowledge of secret codes and ways of deciphering them, ways of breaking seals and preventing them from being broken.

C. Hieroglyphs, ancient and modern.

D. Knowledge of secret societies, Freemasonic systems, etc.; such observations and collections are also submitted by the Scottish Knights.

XII. The *Decanus* hands all essays received to the most capable men in the Class, those who possess the keenest philosophical spirit, the most refined powers of discrimination and the *esprit de détail,* to make succinct extracts from them and draft a proper and comprehensive system of the spirit of observation. The *Decanus* sends this draft to the Provincial Superior and, from there, it goes to the National Superior. The National Superior will then process it further and, soon thereafter, the Provincial Superior receives the complete system of the spirit of observation. This he distributes within his Assembly and arranges for the most capable men in the Minerval Class to be trained in it, turning them into skilled observers.

In general one should remember the stratagem of letting the subordinates and the inexperienced deliver good materials to the higher-ranking and thinkers for them to work on.

XIII. Once the members have received proper instruction in the art of observation, they are sent subjects for and exercises in observation by the directors of the various disciplines. Here, one cannot sufficiently impress upon the directors:

1. That everything depends on the refinement and usefulness of the exercise.

2. That only practical subject matters are therefore suitable tasks for observation.

3. That every subject must be presented not in a general manner but in a highly individualised one.

4. that, if the conclusion is still somewhat unclear or requires further thought and observation, a new assignment and perhaps several more are generated from this until the matter has been exhaustively studied in the minutest detail.

XIV. Since life and health are very important to the human race, and since the Order is, for its part, immensely concerned with the preservation of its most valuable members the Order cannot emphasise its concern for these matters enough, and it must therefore urgently request of all physicians that they fulfil this holy duty. Consider that it is in your power to give life to (or take it from) a fathers' hopeful child, a son's parents, a nation's good citizen, and a noble person who has much to offer to the world; consider that all good and all injury resulting from this is your work.

To this end, the *Decanus* shall invite all our physicians to

1. make observations in the field of semiotics,

2. particularly of those diseases which afflict the majority of the human race and for which there is no definite, infallible cure yet;

3. especially, however, of childhood diseases that are so irresponsibly neglected;

4. and of the curative powers and effects of certain useful medications.

5. Every physician shall be tasked for the remainder of his life and in addition to his regular practice to apply all his powers of observation to a certain disease, a certain symptom or a certain medication and to put all his observations down on paper. The more individualised the disease, the system, and the medication, the more meritorious will be his efforts.

6. Therefore, all medical observers are requested:

A. To begin their observations with healthy persons, to thoroughly examine an individual and to notice the factors for predicting disease in a person's healthy state as well, because these dispositions already have their more or less noticeable symptoms.

B. To write the history and philosophy of a certain symptom.

C. To meticulously study the common as well as the decisively speculative signs of diseases.

D. To find the seat of diseases not merely in the body but also in the soul, the passions, age, sex, way of life, temperament, body-shape, nutrition, season, and the excesses of youth.

E. To investigate how many causes can lead to the same illness in men. Since the [same] disease, having several different causes, can also have various symptoms corresponding to those causes, he must primarily seek to discover those symptoms that point to only this and no other cause.

F. The seat of the illness, the *locus affectus*.

    a) In the soul or in the body,

    b) in the solid or liquid parts, etc.

G. Not only the quality of the medication, but also its quantity.

H. Whether he can safely rely on the medication, or whether the pharmacists' miserliness, usury or negligence has omitted something or even added foreign substances. He must be an eye-witness to the medication's purity and preparation if he wishes to add this to his observations. He must know the medication not from books but always from his own experiences.

I. He must know with certainty that death or good health is an obvious effect of his medication. He must therefore be certain:

    a) that the patient does not deceive him,

    b) that he takes nothing else,

    c) that he has received this medicine and nothing else that has not been prescribed to him.

K. Any experience he has gained he must seek to repeat, and repeat under all possible conditions so that he knows that the effect is inevitably assured or to what the extent this effect changes under these circumstances and with these supplements. This is the most important [object] of his observations.

L. His system must not be grafted on nature. He must watch nature herself. Each year, the medical director therefore assigns a symptom, a disease, or a medication for observation. At the end of the year all the observations submitted are sent to the *Decanus,* compiled into a whole, and then sent out again for further examination to define them in greater detail or the results entered into the subject catalogue.

XV. This subject catalogue is assembled as follows: Every Presbyter maintains a book for his field of study where the subjects about which important knowledge has been gathered are entered in alphabetical order. For example, for the subject 'Secret Sciences and Hieroglyphs' under the letter C one enters the word 'Cross' and, below this: 'The age of this hieroglyph can be found in volume ... of the printed work ..., page ..., or in a manuscript, attachment M ....' These attachments, or rather the best among them, i.e. the best elaborations, are delivered to the national archive *in scientificis* at the end of the year. For this reason all Presbyters in a Province gather in the Grand Synod once a year and compile a grand register of all attachments gathered during the year for the National Director. This is then entered into the main catalogue, and a treasure-house of knowledge capable of satisfying everyone's curiosity is thus formed, for it is from this that rules are abstracted and any missing information and further observation tasks are assigned, as already mentioned, in order to arrive at solid principles. These rules are discovered by skilfully discarding individual peculiarities and preserving those findings that are consistent throughout all cases. The existing systems are examined and tested according to this rule. If several such rules are discovered then, they must be sorted and compared, and from this comparison new general principles are established until eventually an infallible system is formed.

XVI. The procedure is similar for chemistry, physics, economics, and psychology. Thus, the Priest Class assigns persons in its Province, to the tasks of, e.g.

1. collecting words in local dialects,

2. noting technical terms,

3. observing and recording the weather precisely every day, e.g. the degree of heat or cold, rain, sunshine, snow, fog, redness of the sky at dawn, northern lights, thunderstorms, etc. These weather-tables are then compared and, from these, conclusions drawn for physics and economics.

4. Death and birth tables with annotations about age, sex, disease, and season.

5. The various soil types, the flora of every region, the soil in which it grows, fossils.

6. Discoveries that the Scottish Knights believe to have made with respect to Freemasonry, so that one knows who is on the right path and who must be instructed better.

7. All types of natural charms, chemical inks, ciphers, etc.

XVII. As far as history is concerned, each nation's history is primarily researched by those who have a special interest in this subject. So that there is no lack of good, true, and impartial recorders of history, the *Decanus*

1. employs one or several historians in each Province.

2. Like the annalists and chroniclers of old, these men keep a journal of current events.

3. That which is certain and established is entered without embellishment; the secret or suspected mainsprings of the actions are included in the notes.

4. One also notes the extent to which this springs from one's own knowledge or external sources.

5. In the notes one should primarily gather anecdotes, *historia, arcana*.

6. Therefore, the annalist must be an experienced, keen-sighted, ideally suited man, who has access to princely courts and great men, and who

knows how to investigate skilfully.

7. Anecdotes of older events also deserve to be recorded.

8. The characterisation of the persons appearing in his narrative is a special task for the annalists. This is best done by describing episodes from the protagonist's private life which allow any reasonable man to draw the appropriate conclusions about his character. Thus, the annalist gives a detailed account without adding many observations of his own, since every judgement would only betray his passions.

9. The annalist seeks to pull every worthy man in the history of his nation out of the dust, no matter how much he may have been forgotten.

10. These names of these men are reported to the Provincial Superior, who uses them to name the members in his Province.

11. For the edification of the members and the emulation and immortalisation of every worthy man, including those who only did good in private, the *Decanus,* assisted by his Secretaries, creates a special calendar for the Province in which every day of the year is assigned to a famous man from that region who is presented for emulation or despite, depending on his deeds. The ☉ owes this type of apotheosis to any kind of merit previously overlooked or misjudged, and every member of the ☉ has a claim to it.

12. From time to time the Minerval Churches will receive news of noble deeds that deserve to be announced openly in the Assembly, just as on the other hand evil and vile deeds committed by even the noblest persons in the nation will also be loudly proclaimed.

XVIII. Regarding psychology, once a person's files, biography, character sketch, etc., have been submitted to the Priest Class, the *Decanus* will ask the director of this faculty to draw conclusions from these documents. When the latter makes inquiries with the subordinates about this person he shall always omit the subject's name. The following is to be investigated:

1. A person's governing passions and ideas.

2. The origin and progress of these passions.

3. Those ideas he is most likely to accept or reject, based on his character.

4. How, based on this data, a certain tendency could be awakened or weakened in this man.

5. Which person in the Order could best be used to accomplish this.

6. What his views on religion and government constitutions are.

7. Whether or not he has arrived at the point of shedding all prejudices and

seeking out only the truth, even if this may run counter to his interests.

8. Whether or not he is sufficiently selfless, steadfast, and loyal.

9. If he is lacking in one of these qualities, how and by whom it should be taught to him.

10. For which offices in government and in the Order he is suitable, and how he can be of use.

Once all observations have been collected, explained, and corrected against the data gathered from the character sketch and biography, a general assessment is drafted and then sent by the *Decanus* to the Provincial Superior; from this it can be seen whether or not this man is a moral, altruistic, unprejudiced, and benevolent man and how he can be put to use in the interests of the Order. From these manifold observations, general rules and maxims pertaining to psychology are also extracted, collected, entered into the subject catalogue, and submitted.

XIX. Since nothing should be too trivial for the observer, and since nature in fact tends to reveal the most in the smallest details, since the observer is also expected to consider his subject from all sides, hold it up against many other experiences, and is able to make comparisons to detect correspondences and variations, he should not be content if he finds these correspondences in only two or three instances. Therefore

1. every observer must begin with the simplest parts and only put them together afterwards.

2. He must corroborate his discovery with as many instances as possible.

3. He must know that every correspondence also has its own variations, which also require new observations.

4. He must not ascribe an effect to a single cause when it is the effect of a combination of phenomena. He must know the individual components of his subject precisely, and he must know the effects of each component as well as the effects of all of them combined.

5. He must endeavour to compare all the similarities once more, to contrast them, and to extract rules and conclusions from these.

6. He must continue to apply these rules to all cases:

   A. To confirm his rules.

   B. To find exceptions and variations.

   C. To discover the exceptions' causes and effects.

   D. To distinguish the essential from the accidental.

7. These rules must be compared with other discovered rules,

8. the correspondences of these compared rules are then formed into a rule of a higher order,

9. this new high-order rule is again applied to individual cases and, from these, conclusions and inferences are drawn,

10. and if possible, these are further compared with other discovered rules until one finally arrives at the highest metaphysical truth from a single fact. *Our entire body of knowledge rests on correct facts, correct conclusions and comparisons, and their correct application in other instances. Thus, if our knowledge is erroneous, the fault must lie in the fact, conclusion, or application. Consequently, the observer can never be too sure of the fact's correctness.*

XX. Since in this way many and [ever more] general rules are discovered in accordance with and in the field of every science, as well as, ultimately, general rules shared by several scientific disciplines, the ☉, both within every Province and as a whole, will eventually be in a position to make discoveries in all subjects, create new systems, produce exceptional examples of the experiences that it has gathered, and will come to be esteemed as a repository of all human knowledge even in the lesser arts and sciences.

XXI. Thus, thanks to the industry of the experienced members, the many fragments are refined and assembled, and in this way a [most] magnificent scientific edifice is erected, to which even the most inexperienced members in every Province have contributed, one that is not hatched in the brain of a single man but erected according to nature itself and further corrected by the secret knowledge of the higher Superiors, to the extent that this is possible.

XXII. These collected systems may partly be put to print with the permission of the higher Superiors; in this case, however, since they are prepared solely by the Order's printers, not only are they not distributed to the profane, but they will be made known to members only as far as their degree permits, and such members will be instructed in these matters by the middle-ranking Superiors.

XXIII. This then is that society where the knowledge and experiences of great men do not die with them, when they can still be transmitted to others in all their strength and when one must continue where the great spirit has left off. However, so that these worthy workers are not deprived of the honour of their discovery every principle discovered by them, every machine or every other discovery shall bear its inventor's name for all eternity, and his descendants shall keep his memory sacred.

XXIV. For this reason, too, no one is permitted to make his invention known outside the Order, so that he does not deprive the Order of the secret that he has discovered only thanks to its instruction. It is only fair that he leave to the Order alone what he would have never found out without it, and a book written about this topic can never be printed without the Superiors' permission; therefore, all books to be printed must have the Provincial Superior's approval, and after he has made inquiries with his Superiors, he must determine:

1. Is the nature of the book such that it may be printed only by the secret printers, and nowhere else?

2. Which Brethren may read it, in which case he then organises the distribution, and no copy may be distributed without a pass from him.

3. How one can, in addition to any manuscripts pertaining to the Order, also remove printed works from the hands of those members whom one would like to see excluded from the Order in one way or another, something that the Local Superiors have been instructed about.

XXV. The Order does not deserve the accusation of envy because it does not make its insights public, since

1. every good man is entitled to join the Order and share in similar insights.

2. The Order knows best who will benefit from them,

3. it willingly allows all people on the face of the earth to enjoy the benefit of its hidden wisdom, and

4. it does not allow any of its knowledge to be lost.

XXVI. No reasonable man will doubt that it is of enormous benefit when certain knowledge (by which we mean that knowledge that is beneficial and comprehensible to the great majority of men) is shared with discrimination, caution, due preparation, and prudence, and is not shared until it has been developed with utter certainty and is founded on solid principles. And how much greater is the power that one can exert over the common part of humanity if one can ensnare it with the allure of curiosity and direct its desire for the miraculous towards noble purposes! What would a society that was, for example, in sole possession of a knowledge of electricity not be able to accomplish[?]

XXVII. And so all inventions that otherwise would have been the work of coincidence are gleaned from nature itself by proven means, corrected by the wisdom of experienced men, and made generally available for the benefit of humanity in every historical epoch, as much as circumstances and the prevailing degree of culture permit.

XXVIII. It is the task of our Priest Class to direct this degree of culture and enlightenment according to our plan. The needs of the age and region must therefore be thoroughly considered and discussed at the Synods, while requests for correction must be submitted to the Superiors, and new plans must always be designed and introduced:

1. How best to gain a hand in the educational system and clerical government, and how to acquire teaching posts and pulpits within the Province.

2. Each Presbyter shall strive to achieve a general reputation of having a sublime degree of enlightenment. Wherever he stands, sits, lives, and works, a nimbus of true, bright light should shine about his head and enlighten the crowd around him. One should count oneself fortunate to receive pure wisdom from his mouth. He tackles prejudice everywhere, but precisely according to his instructions and with finesse and in consideration of the persons with whom he is speaking; but he should beware of pushing his knowledge onto others unbidden or being regarded as a mountebank or loudmouth.

3. Since certain principles in literature gain currency at certain times and then are generally parroted by weaker minds, so that the public is in turns swamped by religious enthusiasm, sentimentality, free-thought, innocent pastoral, knightly deeds, heroic epic, adulation of genius, etc., one shall strive to achieve that our own principles, aimed at the general welfare of mankind, also become fashionable, so that young authors spread them among the people, thus serving us without knowing it. One shall therefore preach an immense and heartfelt interest in the entire human race, making people more indifferent towards narrower ties insofar as those are in conflict with the world's welfare as a whole. Jesus Himself used every occasion to show how little interested he was in his own family when compared to the great world-family. On this, see the 37th verse in the 10th chapter of the gospel according to Matthew: 'He that loveth his father or mother more than me is not worthy of me: and he that loveth his son or daughter more than me is not worthy of me.' When his mother and brethren were announced to Him, see verse 48 of the 12th chapter, he said: 'Who is my mother? and who are my brethren?' He then pointed at his disciples, and added: 'Behold my mother and my brethren!' Similarly during the wedding at Canaan [131] as well as many other passages.

4. Thus one must also ensure that the writings of our members are trumpet-

[131] *John 2:1–11.*

ed, and that the critics do not cast them in a suspect light.

5. One shall attempt to win over scholars and authors who preach principles similar to ours, and if they are good men, they should be placed on the list of those who are to be recruited. A register of such men should therefore be maintained by the Decanus and submitted to the Provincial Superior from time to time.

XXIX. One shall instil in the lowest Classes such a reverence for the Order that, for example, an assurance made on the Order's honour would be considered their highest oath.

XXX. The Synods mentioned above are held at least yearly in the most convenient location of the Province. All important matters are negotiated there over the course of several days, and initiations performed. Since furthermore, the *Presbyteri* of the Province cannot always convene, everything is saved up for this occasion and written down ahead in order to save time. On days when no initiations are performed, one does not don the priestly garments in order to avoid attracting undue attention. Once it has been agreed upon, the date and hour of the Synod are announced by the *Decanus*. It is all the better if one can convene more frequently. Furthermore, every Presbyter shall maintain regular correspondence with the *Decanus;* he also collects their *quibus licet* slips and sends them unopened to the higher Class.

XXXI. The *Presbyteri* are not required to [attend] any Assemblies of the lower Classes, but one of them must be present in every Secret Chapter. However, they may frequent all Assemblies and ⌗ as they please – they may even attend the Love-Feasts; but they may not be known or attired as Priests, and they may not hold office or interfere in the affairs being dealt with.

XXXII. In extraordinary cases the *Decanus* can also admit younger members of the Order who cannot yet receive the higher degrees but of whose loyalty he has assured himself to the affairs and Assemblies of the Priests. These are called *Acolythi,*[132] and they wear the Priest's Garments, only shorter, and their heads are bare. They assist during the Synods, are used for secretarial matters, correspondence, etc., and are bound to secrecy without further ceremonial.

---

[132] *Lat. Acolyte. One who performs ceremonial duties.*

ADDENDUM C. ON THE INITIATION OF A *DECANUS*.

If a *Decanus* is to be installed for the lower Priest Class, this is done either when this Class is newly established in a Province, or after the death or departure of a prior *Decanus*. In the former case, the Provincial Superior announces this establishment in accordance with superior orders; in the latter, he requires the *vota* of all the Provincial Priests, reports the result to the Superiors and, once a decision concerning the subject has been made, calls a Synodal Assembly. The *Decanus* must be drawn from the higher degrees of the Order, and it goes without saying that he must have all the necessary qualifications and thorough knowledge.

During the ceremony the following are present, in addition to the other Presbyters:

1. *Plenipotentiarius*[133]
2. *Primus Praepositus*[134]
3. *Secundus Praepositus*[135]
4. *Delegatus Patrinus*[136] (Godfather)
5. *Neo-Electus.*[137]

All are in priestly attire, and the first 4 have crosses on their chests, with the exception of the Newly-Elect. His future cloak lies on the altar.

[The] *Plenipotentiarius* steps before the altar, facing the Newly-Elect, at whose left is the Godfather. However, the two *Praepositi* stand before the *Plenipotentiarius,* facing the altar.

Del[egatus]. Aperi, Domine, os meum![138]

Præp[ositus] I. (repeats this.)

Præp. II. (likewise.)

Plenipot[entiarius]. Fili mi, quid postulas[?][139]

Delegat. [Ut] Deus et Superiores nostri concedant nobis Decanum hunc, quem ad te duco fratrem N. N.[140]

Plen. Quid vobis placuit in illo?[141]

Del. Modestia, morum integritas, Scientia, benevolentia et ceterae virtutes.[142]

---

[133] *Lat. Diplomat. He who is invested with full power.*

[134] *Lat. First Superior.*   [135] *Lat. Second Superior.*

[136] *Lat. Delegated Godfather.*   [137] *Lat. Newly-Elect.*

[138] *Open my mouth o Lord!*   [139] *My son, what is it you ask?*

[140] *I ask that God and our Superiors grant us as our Deacon this Brother N. N., whom I have brought before you.*

[141] *What pleases you about him?*

[142] *His modesty, good morals, knowledge, benevolence and other virtues.*

Plen. Habetis Decretum?[143]

Del. Habemus.[144]

Plen. Legatur.[145]

Del. (reads aloud:) Reverendissimo N. N., Sedis dignitate conspicuo, credimus non latere, quod nostra provincia suo sit viduata Decano. Qua siquidem solatio proprio destituta Decani, communi voto atque consensu Superiorum elegimus nobis in Decanum Fratrem N. N. Presbyterum nostrae provinciae majoris ordinis, virum utique prudentem, hospitalem, moribus ornatum, sapientem, illuminatum, et mansuetum, Deo et Superioribus nostris per omnia placentem, quem ad Celsitudinis Vestrae dignitatem deducere curavimus unanimiter postulantes et obsecrantes a Vestrae Celsitudine, vobis illum Decanum confirmari, quatenus autoro Domino nobis velut idoneus Decanus præesse valeat, ac prodesse, nosque sub ejus sapienti regimine in securitate et quiete, magnis scientiis aliisque operibus curare possimus. Ut autem omnium nostrum voto in hanc electionem convenire noscatis, huic decreto propriis manibus roborando subscripsimus.[146] (Signed by all the Priests of the province.)

Plen. Videte, ne aliqua fraus vel Dolus intersit.[147]

Del. Absit.[148]

Plen. Ducatur.[149]

(The Newly-Elect is conducted before the altar, placed between the two Superiors, and the Godfather stands behind him.)

Neoel. Aperi Domine os meum[!][150]

Praep. II (repeats.)

Praep. I (likewise.)

Plen. Fili mi, quid postulas?[151]

---

[143] *Do you have the Decree?*   [144] *Yes, we have it.*

[145] *Let it be read.*

[146] *Most Reverend N. N., illustrious in the dignity of your office, we believe that it is generally known that our Province has a vacancy for a Deacon. Accordingly, deprived of the solace of having our own Deacon we have elected as Deacon, by common vote and with the agreement of the Superiors, Brother N. N., a priest in major orders of our Province, a man most certainly prudent, hospitable, of good morals, wise, well-instructed, mild-mannered and pleasing both to God and to our Superiors in all things, a man whom we, making due request of you and beseeching you in unanimity, have now brought before the dignified presence of Your Excellency to be confirmed as our Deacon, insofar as, with God's authority, he might be considered suitable to preside over us as our Deacon, so that we can benefit and look after ourselves under his wise rule in a state of security and tranquillity through great learning and other works. Since, as you know, we have voted unanimously in this election we have therefore signed this Decree with our own hands in order to make it effective.*

[147] *Make sure that there is no fraud or trickery.*   [148] *God forbid!*

[149] *Let him be brought forth.*   [150] *Open my mouth O Lord!*

[151] *My son, what is it you ask?*

Neoel. Reverendissime Domine! Confratres mei elegerunt me, sibi esse Decanum.[152]

Plen. Quo honore fungeris?[153]

Neoel. Presbyteratus majoris.[154]

Plen. Quot annos habes in Presbyteratu?[155]

Neoel. (answers.)

Plen. Habuisti directionem aliquam?[156]

Neo-Electus. Habui.[157]

Plen. Qualem?[158]

Neoel. (answers.)

Plen. Disposuisti domus Tuae?[159]

Neoel. Disposui.[160]

Plen. Nosti quanta sit Decani cura, quanta requiratur diligentia et fidelitas, et qua poena infligantur infideles et delatores[?][161]

Neoel. Doce me, Domine![162]

Plen. Ego autoritate Superiorum inductus admoneo te, ut pacem quietem, fidelitatem, diligentiam et amorem inter Presbyteros Tibi subditos conservare curam habeas et inferiorem benevolentia et debita cura dirigere complaceas, firmiter et sub indeterminatione Anathematis inhibeo Tibi, nec quid de scientiis occultis vel secreta Tibi revelata vel revelanda, abducas surripias, vel alicui profano communices sed eacum quiete possideas, et maxima cum cura custodias.[163] Si tu autem aliquid attentare praesumpseris, maledictus eris in domo et extra domum, [maledictus in civitate, et in agro,] maledictus vigilando et dormiendo, maledictus manducando et bibendo, maledictus ambulando et sedendo, maledicta erunt caro et ossa, sanitatem non habebis a planta pedis usque ad verticem.

---

[152] *O most reverend Master, my colleagues have elected me to be their Deacon.*

[153] *In what office do you currently serve?*   [154] *As a Priest in major orders.*

[155] *And for how many years have you served in the Priesthood?*

[156] *Have you had some instruction?*   [157] *I have.*

[158] *Of what kind?*   [159] *Have you set your house in order?*

[160] *I have.*

[161] *Do you know how much of a burden it is to be a Deacon, how much hard work and loyalty is required, and with what penalties the disloyal and the indiscreet are punished?*

[162] *Teach me, Master!*

[163] *I, invested with the authority of the Superiors, urge you to ensure that you maintain peace, repose, loyalty, diligence and love among the Priests who are subordinate to you so that you may win the affections of your inferiors in order to direct them with benevolence and due care. I strongly forbid you, under threat of anathema, to remove, purloin or reveal to any uninitiated person anything about the occult sciences or the secrets revealed to you or to be revealed, but instead to keep them to yourself discreetly and to guard them with the greatest care.*

Veniat tunc super te maledictio hominis, quam per Moisen in lege Filiis iniquita-
tis Dominus permisit. Deleatur nomen tuum in libro viventium, et cum justis
non amplius scribatur. Fiat pars et hereditas tua cum Cain fratricida, cum Datan
et Abiram, cum Anania et Saphira, cum Simone Mago et Juda proditore. Vide
ergo, ne quid feceris, quo anathema mereris.[164]

Neoel. Absit Domine[!][165]

Plenip. Accedite.[166] (All step closer to the altar, and the Newly-Elect kneels on
its lowest step.)

Del. Reverendissime Domine! postulant admodum per me Delegatum Presbyteri omnes, ut hunc praesentem Presbyterum ad onus Decani sublevetis[!][167]

Plenip. Scitis illum esse dignum?[168]

Del. Quantum humana fragilitas nosse sinit, ut scimus et credimus illum dignum esse.[169]

Plenip. Quia ergo omnium in Te vota concurrunt confirmaris.[170]

Neoel. Praecepisti Domine![171]

Plenip. (places his hand on the Newly-Elect's head.) Dilecto nobis fratri et
Decano salutem in Domino sempiternam! Quoniam ut credimus, et scimus,
Presbyteri hujus Provinciae, fratres nostri Te elegerunt Decanum et ad superiores
usque pendentes petierunt confirmari, et ideo auxiliante Domino, et auctoritate
Superiorum per manus nostrae impositionem, Te Decanum confirmavimus.[172]

---

[164] *If however you should dare to defy this prohibition then you shall be cursed in your home and cursed outside your
home; you shall be cursed in the town and cursed in the countryside; you shall be cursed whilst you are awake and
cursed whilst you are asleep; you shall be cursed whilst you are eating and cursed whilst you are drinking; you shall
be cursed whilst you are walking and cursed whilst you are sitting, just as the flesh and bones were cursed, and you
shall have no health in you from the soles of your feet to the top of your head. Then there shall fall upon you the
curse of man which, through the laws of Moses, the Lord awarded to the sons of iniquity. Your name will be erased
in the Book of the Living and may no longer be written along with those of the Just. Your own fate and that of
your descendants will become one with that of Cain who killed his brother [see Gen. 4:1–8], or that of Dathan
and Abiram [see Exod. 2:13–15], of Ananias and Sapphira [see Acts 5:1–11], and of Simon Magus [see Acts
8:9–24] and Judas the betrayer [see Matt. 27:3–10]. See to it therefore that you do not do anything by which you
might come to deserve anathema.*

[165] *God forbid!*   [166] *Approach me.*

[167] *O most reverend Master! All the Priests are demanding in the strongest possible terms through me, their delegate,
that you raise this Priest now before us to the rank of Deacon.*

[168] *Do you know for sure that he is worthy of such elevation?*

[169] *As far as human weakness allows us to know such things, we do know and believe that he is worthy.*

[170] *Because there has been a unanimous vote in your favour you are therefore confirmed as Deacon.*

[171] *You have so ordered, Master!*

[172] *To our dear Brother and Deacon, eternal greetings in the Lord! Since, as we believe and know, our Brother Priests
of this province have elected you Deacon and have petitioned the Superiors themselves for confirmation as his
dependants, we have therefore, with the assistance of the Lord and the authority of the Superiors, confirmed you as
Deacon by the laying-on of our hand.*

(He removes his hand from him.) Tu autem Frater charissime! Scias, te maximum pondus suscepisse laboris, exortamus ergo dilectionem Tuam, ut fidelitatem, quam in ingressu Ordinis promisisti, et dein saepius promissionem renovasti inviolabiliter custodias. Nam fidelitas omnium virtutum fundamentum est. Scimus, quod ab infantia literis es eruditus, et scientiis edoctus, attamen, breviter ad nos pervenisti, et multa adhuc occulta Tibi revelanda sunt. Sed cave, ne secundum Apostoli sententiam in superbiam elatus in judicium incidas Domini. Scientiae Tuae et virtuti nec confides, quia neque Samsone fortior, nec Davide sanctior, nec Salomone poteris esse sapientior.[173] Scriptores veterum Philosophorum et sapientum sepius lege, imo si potest fieri, lectio haec in manibus Tuis, maximeque in pectore Tuo semper inhaereat, ipsam vero lectionem, meditatio interrumpat, ad instar namque speculi anima Tua in ipsam sedulo respiciat, ut vel quae incorrecta sunt corrigat, vel quae pulchra sunt, exornat. Disce, quod sapientia doceas, amplectens cum, qui secundum sanam doctrinam est, ut possis exhortari in doctrina sua, et eos, qui contradicunt, arguere. Nec confundantur opera Tua sermonem tuam. Vita igitur Tua irreprehensibilis sit, in ipsa fratres inferiores regulam sumant, ex ipsa quicquid in eis minus correctum fuerit, corrigant, ex ipsa videant, quod diligant cernant, quod imitari festinent, ut ad exemplum tuum omnes fideli studio vivere compellantur. Sit ergo subjectos Tuos solicitudo laudabilis, exhibeatur cum mansuetudine disciplina, cum directione correctio. Iram benignitas mitiget, benignitatem zelus exacuat, ita ut alterum ex altero condiatur, ut nec i[m]moderata ultio, ultra quam opportet, affligat, neque iterum frangat Decanum remissio disciplinae, itaque boni Te dulcem, pravi asperum sentiant correptorem, in qua videlicet correptione hunc esse ordinem noveris observandum, ut personas diligas et vitia persequaris, ne si aliter agere vortasse volueris, transeat in crudelitatem? correctio, et perdas per irremissam iram, quod emendare per discretionem debueras.[174] (The Superiors place the cloak on him.)

[173] *You should however know, dearest Brother! that you have taken on a very great burden. We therefore make appeal to your good will so that you may inviolably retain the loyalty that you promised to us on your admission to the Order and have subsequently often renewed, for loyalty is the foundation of all the virtues. We know that from early childhood you were erudite in literature and thoroughly versed in the sciences. Yet it was only a short while ago that you came to us, and many are the secrets that have since needed to be revealed to you. Take care however that you are not, in the words of the Apostle, 'lifted up with pride' only to 'fall with the condemnation of the Lord' [1 Tim. 3:6]! Nor should you trust in your virtue, for you cannot be stronger than Samson, nor holier than David, nor wiser than Solomon.*

[174] *Read frequently the writings of the old philosophers and sages. Indeed, if possible, this present lecture should remain in your hands and even more so be taken into your heart. Meditation should interrupt the reading of the lecture, after the fashion of a mirror in which your soul can gaze carefully at its own reflection, so that either its faults can be corrected or its beauties enhanced. Learn what Wisdom has to teach you, 'holding fast the faithful word as he hath been taught, that he may be able by sound doctrine both to exhort and to convince the gainsayers'*

Sit in Te amabilis dulcido prudentia, mansuetudo et sapientia. Injuste oppressio defensio tua subveniat. Illic autem, qui opprimunt, vigor tuus efficaciter contradicat. Nullus te favor extollat. Nulla adversitas alterat, id est, ut nec in prosperis cor tuum elevatur, neque in adversis in aliquo dejiciatur. Sed omnia, et in omnibus caute et cum directione agere Te volumus, ut absque reprehensio ab omnibus vivere comproberis.[175] (He places his right hand on him again.) Sicut [r]os Hermon, qui descendit in montem Sion, sic descendat super Te Dei summaeque sapientiae benedictio.[176]

(He rises.)

[Tit. 1:9]. *Nor should your deeds confound your words. Your life should therefore be beyond reproach, so that your Brothers of lower rank can adopt it as a guide and use it to identify whatever may be less than correct in their own lives and so correct those failings, and learn from it what they should cherish, what they should think, and what they should hasten to imitate, so that all the faithful are compelled by devoted study to live by your example. Towards your inferiors let there be a laudable solicitude; let discipline be tempered with mildness, and correction with guidance. Kindness should mitigate your anger, and zeal make your kindness keener, that one may serve, as it were, as a condiment to the other, and so that a desire for vengeance never goes beyond what is appropriate and so that a mitigation of discipline never causes the Deacon to be thwarted in his task. In that way the good shall find you a gentle reprover and the wicked a harsh one, and in this act of reproof you will understand the rule that is to be followed, namely that you must love the sinner and hate the sin, for if you had perhaps felt the urge to act differently then correction might have become cruelty and you would destroy with undiminished anger what you should have corrected with discretion.*

[175] *You should be full of an amiable sweetness, prudence, mildness and wisdom. May your defence come to the aid of the unjustly oppressed, but may your vigour also effectively combat the oppressors. No favour should raise your spirits and no adversity should alter your behaviour. In other words your heart should neither be gladdened in prosperity nor saddened in adversity; rather we wish you to do everything and to act in all things cautiously and discreetly so that you may give proof of a life that is free of reproach by any man.*

[176] *'As the dew of Hermon, and as the dew that descended upon the mountains of Zion' [Ps. 133:3], so may there descend upon you the blessings of the highest wisdom of God!*

II. Lesser Regent Degree. Princeps

NOTIFICATION TO THE PROVINCIAL SUPERIOR REGARDING
THE ISSUANCE OF THIS DEGREE.

I. If one of the Presbyters appears to be especially capable of participating in the political government of the Order; if he combines worldliness with freedom of thought and action, caution with courage, flexibility with steadfastness, skill and knowledge with simplicity and honest reason, originality with orderliness, greatness of mind with punctuality and *esprit de détail,* magnanimity, tolerance and gaiety with seriousness and dignity; if he knows when to hold his tongue and when to speak; if he is modest and discreet; if he knows how to obey and how to command; if he is loved, respected, and feared by his fellow citizens; if he is zealously and completely loyal to the ☉, always keeping in mind what is best for the whole and for the world; then and only then may the Provincial Superior recommend him to the National Inspector for the Regent Degree. However, the following must be observed:

1) One should issue this degree as sparingly as possible.

2) As much as possible, free men should be chosen who do not depend on princes.

3) One should preferably select those who have often declared how dissatisfied they are with the common human institutions, how much they yearn for a better form of government for the world, and how much their souls were filled with hope by the prospects shown them in the Lesser Priest Degree.

II. If the National Inspector approves such a man for promotion, the Provincial Superior examines the Candidate once more orally or in writing about some of his principles about which one may still be in doubt. To this end he thoroughly studies all the files regarding him, especially those concerning his circumstances, his progressive answers to the various questions, any deficiencies, his strengths and weaknesses, etc.

III. Based on these results, he assigns him an essay on a topic regarding which he has not yet pronounced himself with sufficient clarity, e.g.

1) 'Would a society be reprehensible that contrives a plan which prevents the monarchs of the world from doing evil until one day nature's greater

revolutions dawn? So that they could not do evil even if they wanted to? A society that quietly prevented the abuse of the highest power? Would it not be possible that, through such a society, the states themselves would become *status in statu*[177]?'

2) 'Is the objection that such a society could easily abuse its power not unjust, for the following reasons: Do not our current national governments daily abuse their power, even though we keep silent about it? This power can hardly be safer in the hands of untested men, who hold it now, than in the hands of our members whom we educate so very diligently. Thus, if a regimen established by man can be harmless at all, which could be more harmless than ours, based as it is on morality, caution, wisdom, liberty, and virtue?'

3) 'Would it then not be worth the effort to at least make the attempt (even though it may be chimerical) to institute such a general moral regimen?'

4) 'The liberty to resign at any moment, the good fortune of having tried and elected Superiors, part of whom do not know one another and consequently cannot conspire to commit fraud, and whose fear of the existing states keeps them from doing any evil, is all this not security enough, even for a sceptic?'

5) 'And are there not perhaps other secret means to protect us from an abuse of the power the Superiors are vested with by the ☉? And what could these means be?'

6) 'Finally, can the despotism (if indeed it were despotism) of such people be dangerous, who from the first step that a Novice takes in the ☉, do nothing but preach enlightenment, freedom, and virtue, and therefore appear rather less suspicious given that, if in fact they had dangerous intentions, they would have constructed a machine that is entirely useless in this regard?'

IV. If the Presbyter has answered these or similar questions well, the Provincial Superior sends his essays to the National Inspector. Once the latter also approves his acceptance and returns the files, the Provincial Superior sets the date of the convention for the initiation.

V. The Candidate is then informed that, since he will from now on have documents of greater importance in his house, he should write a binding disposition

---

[177] Lat. *State within a state.*

regarding his intentions for his correspondence in the case of his sudden demise. He must also obtain a receipt from the courts or his family.

VI. Once the Regents of the Province have convened at the location, the day and hour of the initiation are set.

INITIATION RITUAL.

I. The location has three rooms. In the last of these there is, three steps high, a richly decorated red canopy, and under it stands an upholstered chair of the same colour for the Provincial Superior. To the right stands a white pillar, about 6½ feet tall, on top of which is a red pillow with a red and gold crown. A shepherd's crook made of white wood and a realistic artificial palm-leaf hang from the pillar like a trophy, as illustrated in the following drawing:

A table stands to the left, draped in red, on which the Regent's garments have been placed. These are as follows: above the coat a type of cuirass or breast plate is worn, made only of white leather with a red cross on it, like this:

Above that one wears a white, long-sleeved open cloak with the red cross sewn onto the left breast. The sleeves have small red cuffs. The cloak is fashioned like an open shirt, with a red collar, in this fashion:

[The Regents] wear a tall, white round hat with a red feather plume, as in this drawing:

On their feet they wear red, laced half-boots. As a distinctive sign, only the cross on the Provincial Superior's breast plate has golden rays emanating from it, as can be seen in this drawing:

The room is wallpapered red and well-lit. Only the Provincial Superior, seated on the throne, is in this room, all on his own. The other Regents are in the middle room. No one, not even the Provincial Superior, carries a sword or any other weapon.

The front room serves for preparing the Candidate. It is draped in black, and a human skeleton with a sword and crown at its feet stands in it, elevated by a few steps. The Candidate is led to this room; he is asked for a copy of his last will, written according to the regulations, together with the receipt issued by the courts or his family. Then shackles are placed on his hands. He appears in regular, civil attire.

II. After he has remained here for a few moments, the following conversation is held in the adjacent room, loud enough so that he can hear it:

Q[uestion]. Who has brought the slave to us?

A[nswer]. He came, and he knocked.

Q. What does he want?

A. He seeks freedom. He also asks that we free him from his bonds.

Q. Why does he not turn to those who have bound him?

A. They do not wish to free him. They benefit from his enslavement.

Q. Who has put him into servitude?

A. Society, the state, scholarship, and false religion.

Q. And he wishes to throw off this yoke, and become a renegade, a rebel?

A. Nay! He only wishes to fight hand in hand with us against the misuse of state constitutions, the corruption of morals and the desecration of religion. He wishes to be empowered by us so that he can meet these noble objectives.

Q. And who will vouch to us that when we place power in his hands he will not abuse it, become a tyrant to others and spread more misery over the world?

A. His heart and mind vouch for this; the ⊙ has purified him. He has learnt to conquer his passions. He has explored himself, and the Superiors have tested him.

Q. That is saying a lot. Is he also above prejudice? Does he willingly sacrifice the interests of smaller, narrower ties for the general welfare of the world?

A. This he has promised to us.

Q. Many a man has so promised and then failed to keep his word! Is he his own master? Can he resist temptation? Does he judge without distinction of person? Ask him who the man was whose bones now stand before him, whether he was a king, a nobleman, or a beggar.

A. He knows him not; nature has stripped and obliterated everything from this man by which corruption denotes the differences between the classes. He only knows of this skeleton that it once was a man, one of us. This quality of being human is all that matters to him. Even the destruction of decay does not disturb him.

Q. Good! If this is how he thinks, he shall be free at his own risk. Bring him here! – But he does not know us! What are his reasons for seeking our protection? Go and speak with him!

III. Now one Regent goes out to him, removes the shackles, and addresses him as follows:

'According to the intimate knowledge you, my Brother! now possess of the ☉'s lofty purposes you will certainly have no more doubts about the selflessness, dignity, grandness, and truth of the matter. Whether you know the Superiors or not should make no difference to you.

In the meantime I have been ordered to provide you with the following explanation regarding this question:

If one regards our ☉ as the small band of those good and wise men who are striving to stem the general corruption, who have escaped the deluge equipped with the treasures of wisdom and virtue, saving themselves and their kind to prepare happier epochs for a new generation, then one can say our ☉ is as old as the world. There has always been such a holy covenant. God and nature have at no time permitted that the better tools, by which they meant to gradually uplift mankind to the highest peak of its perfection again, would be consumed by the torrent of corruption. They built themselves an ark, the plan for which was provided by God himself, escaped the deluge, and once the worst storm had passed, handed down to their descendants the pillars of a new world that they had preserved and rescued.[178] For this reason Freemasonry counts even the Patriarchs[179] and Noachites[180] among its members. In the Priest Degree we told you how Jesus the Redeemer at last laid the cornerstone of the new church of the kingdom of truth, wisdom, and freedom, and how our ☉, on this foundation, works towards this last and happy revolution. Thus it has always existed, exerting its influence throughout, but always in different guises. Whenever it had arrived at a certain point and corruption had crept in here and there, the main trunk, the High ☉, cast off its husk and appeared in a new shape. In this manner, in every age one accomplishes as much as possible and in whatever possible fashion, while the inner core remains undefiled. Freemasonry too has experienced this corruption, and it was high time to reform it. But it has fully exerted the good influence one expected of it, preparing the world for our present endeavours. Its help is still needed for a while, and this is why we 'keep' its ancient traditions in the intermediate Classes. It matters little to any reasonable person how new or ancient the

---

[178] See Gen. 6–9.

[179] Abraham, Isaac, and Jacob, commonly referred to as the three patriarchs of the people of Israel.

[180] Descendants of Noah and adherents to his religious dogma. In The New Book of Constitutions of the Antient and Honourable Fraternity of Free and Accepted Masons (1738), James Anderson declared that 'Noachidæ, or Sons of Noah' was the 'first Name of Masons' according to some old 'traditions' (p. 4). The first of the 'Old Charges' accordingly stated that 'a Mason is obliged by his Tenure to observe the Moral Law, as a true Noachida' (p. 143). Both of these passages were changed from the version of the first edition of the Constitutions of 1723.

origins of symbolic Freemasonry are, or who has the right to constitute ⌻and where the seat of the true superiors of Freemasonry is to be found. Everything that makes me happy is true, no matter where it comes from, and only those Masonic systems that have only self-oriented knowledge, or none at all, argue about the right to establish ⌻. We allow everyone who understands his Craft to call it true. If it is good and wholesome it will benefit the world, and then our plan is fulfilled. If, however, it is worthless then it will soon crumble on its own accord. It is true that we attempt to guide everything according to our purposes because we are convinced of the goodness of our cause, but we force no one in the lower Classes to take our word that we are in the sole possession of true Freemasonry. He may see for himself if he can find something better elsewhere. Yet if he has searched long in vain and found nothing, then he should, out of gratitude, be entirely loyal to us. He will hear everywhere of secret superiors, but these superiors will give him nothing that will satisfy him, and yet he is supposed to take their word that they are at the authentic source. We demand this only to the extent that a man seeking satisfaction with us should not concern himself with the sources of our knowledge when we disclose to him insights and prospects worthy of every wise and honourable man. He must direct his attention to the matter and not the person.

Thus, if someone inquires who founded our system in the lower Classes, in its current form, how old this system is, and who are the founders of this institution, we may provide the following answer:

Our founders possessed knowledge because they shared it. When they established the Outer Order they applied the information gathered from studying the flaws and advantages of all previous similar endeavours and the advice of the wisest, best, finest, and most experienced men, combining this with philosophical acumen, traditions, warm interest in the general good and altruism. Partly out of modesty and partly to secure themselves against their own passions, they then delivered the edifice's direction into other, faithful hands and withdrew. Their names will never be known, and those who are presently at the helm are not the founders of the new institution. Posterity, however, will bless the unknown benefactors, and will bless them doubly for having renounced the vanity of being immortalised by the preservation of their name in the ☉. All documents regarding this have been burnt.

Consequently you are now dealing with other men who, by means of their instruction, have advanced over time to the direction of the ☉. Soon you will also be at its helm. But now I await your declaration if you still harbour any doubts concerning the Superiors' honourable intentions or if you are still dissatisfied with any aspect.'

The Candidate replies, and if he has any doubts, they must be resolved. The *Introductor* then continues:

'Follow me then!'

IV. The two approach the door to the middle chamber. The *Introductor* opens it (for in this degree, one no longer knocks). The present Regents arrive, and one of them asks: 'Who comes here?'

A[nswer]. A servant who has run away from his master.

The Other. No servant may enter here.

Introd[uctor]. He has escaped so that he may be a servant no more. He seeks our aid and protection.

The Other. But what if he is being followed by his master?

Introd. The doors are closed, and he is safe.

The Other. But what if this servant were a traitor?

Introd. He is not. He has been raised under the eyes of the enlightened ones, and they have impressed God's seal on his brow.

The Other. Well, then he is welcome with us!

They enter, accompanied by the other Regents, and approach the door to the last chamber. Walking ahead, one Regent enters it. The *Introductor* wants to open the door but is held back by the man who entered before and calls out to him:

Back! Whom do you bring? You shall not enter so easily here.

Introd. I bring a prisoner who desires freedom and seeks entrance to the ark.

The Other. We have not brought him into servitude. We do not seek to infringe upon his master's rights. He shall care for himself.

Introd. You have promised him help. You have given him hope when he was in servitude. – He was in the dark, and you have enlightened him. You have governed him. Now he can govern himself, and now he wants to be free.

The Provincial Superior calls down from his throne:

Let him enter so that we may see whether or not he bears the sign of freedom.

The double-doors open, and the Candidate is led before the throne. The Regents step to both sides of it, and the *Introductor* stands by the Candidate's side.

P[rovincial] S[uperior]. Unhappy soul! You are a mere servant, and you dare enter the Assembly of free men? Do you not know what awaits you? You have passed through two doors, but you shall not leave through this one without punishment if you desecrate our Sanctum.

Introd. He will not do this: I vouch for him. You have taught him to sigh for freedom: now keep your promise!

P. S. Well then, my Brother! You have passed through many preparations. We have tried you, finding you good and noble. With perfect trust have you delivered yourself into our hands. The time has come to demonstrate to you that we are quite prepared to grant you the liberty that we have presented to you so enticingly. We have guided you for as long as you were in need of guidance; now you consider yourself to be strong enough to govern yourself. So be it then: at your own peril, be a free man, that is, be a man who knows how to govern himself, who knows his duties and his lasting advantages, who serves only the world, and who does nothing that is not beneficial to the world and the human race. Anything else is unjust. You shall be independent even from us. – We herewith release you from all obligations to the ☉. (He returns to him all files concerning his person, the Obligation, initiation minutes, biography, etc.). – Furthermore you owe us nothing than that to which your heart moves you. We do not desire to be tyrants, but teachers of men. If you now have found with us satisfaction, serenity, joy, and happiness, you will not desert us. If we have deceived ourselves in you, or you in us, then the harm is yours. Thus you are free, but you should know that independent men help one another, never insult one another in any way, protect themselves against insult and that, in case of insult, everyone has the right of self-defence against you. Just as certainly, however, will you find protection and support with us if you do not abuse the power we wish to grant you for evil, and if your heart is filled with selflessness and glowing with affection for the welfare of your Brethren. O! join forces with us, labour for the poor human race, and your last hour will be a happy one; after all, we demand nothing else of you, and we seek to accomplish nothing for our own gain. Ask your own heart whether or not you have always been treated nobly and unselfishly! Could you be ungrateful towards so much charity? O! then let your heart punish you; we have no such desire. – But no, you are a tried and solid man! Do remain one, and henceforth govern with us the oppressed, lead them to virtue, wisdom, and freedom! What a prospect that happiness, love, and peace shall reign on earth once more, when all misery, all unnecessary need, all delusion and all oppression are banished, when everyone in his station does what he can for the best of the greater whole, when every house-father is lord in his quiet hut, when he who seeks to intrude upon these sacred rights will find no sanctuary anywhere in the world, when idleness is never tolerated, when the host of useless sciences is banished and only that is taught which betters man and brings him closer to his natural state and his future destiny, and when bringing about this period more quickly is our task, when every man extends his arms towards the other in brotherly love! – In our embrace you can find happiness and rest if you remain faithful and honest; and thus the *sign* of this degree is reaching out both arms towards the Brother and holding out your open hands, untarnished by injustice and violence. The *grip* is: clasping both elbows of the other to support him and help him to his feet. The *word* is *Redemptio*.

Now the garments are placed upon him.

The breast plate. Steel your breast with faithfulness, truth, and steadfastness, be a Christian, and the arrows of slander and misfortune will never penetrate you.

The boots. Be quick to do good, and fear no path on which you can spread or find happiness.

The cloak. Be a prince towards your people, that is: be a wise and honourable benefactor and teacher to your Brethren.

The hat. You shall never trade this hat of freedom for a crown!

Then rule with wisdom and keep in mind that he who gives power can also take it away!

(The Provincial Superior embraces him.)

Now hear what the duties of your new state demand of you forthwith!

Addenda A and B are read aloud. When the Provincial Superior wishes to close, he bows silently, and the Regents step aside. He who is appointed as Local Superior receives his sealed instructions from the hands of the Provincial Superior.

[Addendum] A. ADMINISTRATIVE SYSTEM FOR THE ENTIRE ORDER.

I. The Highest Superiors of our Illustrious Order and of true, ancient, and authentic Freemasonry do not directly concern themselves with the more intimate administration of the edifice. Fortunately, however, they work for our welfare in other very important ways, by their counsel, instruction, and very powerful help.

II. Meanwhile, our dear and gracious Superiors have established a Class of

Masons they have entrusted with the entire plan of operations, and this is the Regent Class to which you have gained your first admission today.

III. These Regents hold the ☉'s highest offices, and he who does not hold this degree may not become even a Prefect or Local Superior.

IV. Every country has a *National Superior* who is in immediate contact with our fathers, one of whom stands at the helm.

V. The *Provincial Superiors* are under the National Superior and his assistants; there is one in every circle of our fatherland.[181]

VI. The Provincial Superior has *Consultores* to assist him, and subordinate to him are

VII. a certain number of *Prefects,* who also may have assistants belonging to this degree in their respective districts. And all these belong to the Regent Class, such as the *Decanus* for each Province.

VIII. All these offices are for the term of life, except in the case of promotion to a higher office, resignation, removal from office, or death.

IX. If a Provincial Superior dies, a new one is elected by all the Regents in the Province and then either confirmed or dismissed by the National Superior. The other Superiors are appointed by the Provincial Superior with the National Superior's consent.

X. Since the whole welfare of the ☉ rests on this Class it is only fair that no Regent should suffer domestic privation. Thus, the Regents must be the first whose sustenance and support must be provided, if they so require.

XI. All Regents in a Province comprise a special corps, and their immediate superior, to whom they owe obedience, is the Provincial Superior. His burden is heavy; he can reap his reward only from the success of his noble efforts for the benefit of the world and the willingness of the other Regents to obey him who has been better instructed, without complaint.

XII. Since the offices in the ☉ are not positions of honour, but voluntarily-shouldered burdens, the Regents must be willing to work for the best of the whole as far as their circumstances and abilities permit. Age does not grant privilege in the ☉, and it will often come to pass that the youngest Regent is Provincial and the oldest merely a Local Superior or *Consultor,* if for example the former lives in the centre of the Province and the latter close to its borders, or if the former may be able to fill the position better, according to his natural activity or

[181] *Since the early 16th century, the Holy Roman Empire had been divided into ten 'Reichskreise'.*

worldly circumstances, but the latter perhaps possesses more eloquence. Indeed, many a Regent should not shy away from requesting some small position in a Minerval Church so that he may provide a good example.

XIII. So that the Provincial Superior is not required to maintain direct correspondence with many persons, all the Regents' reports and Q. L. slips pass through the Prefects' hands, unless the Provincial Superior orders otherwise.

XIV. However, he does not open the Regents' Q. L., but they are sent unopened to the Provincial Superior and are further forwarded from there.

XV. The Regents' Assemblies are called Convents. The Provincial Superior, who presides over them, holds them as often as he deems necessary, and he may invite all or only a few of the Regents as the proceedings require. Whoever is unable to attend must provide a sufficient excuse at least four weeks in advance. He must also present himself to render an account of his activities and accept new orders from the Provincial Superior and the Higher Superiors. The Provincial Convent shall be held at least once a year.

XVI. The other matters that the Regents must be especially mindful of can be seen in the Instructions that follow.

XVII. As far as the ☉'s economic circumstances are concerned this matter has already been discussed in detail elsewhere; however, it is necessary to add a few general comments here. As has already been stated, we should endeavour to acquire funds over time. The following is to be observed:

a) Every Province remains in full control of its funds. No monies are ever to be sent to the Superiors, other than small contributions, e.g. to cover postal expenses.

b) Thus, every Assembly and every ☐ shall maintain ownership of its funds, and when it is agreed at the Convents that the assets of several ⌗ should be pooled for a great endeavour, the money is regarded as a loan only, and the ⌗ must be paid not only interest but eventually the principal as well.

c) The Provincial Superior himself thus controls no funds, only the budgets of the assets in his Province.

d) In general, the revenues are:

aa) Masonic initiation fees.

bb) Surpluses from the monthly contributions, and other petty cash.

cc) Voluntary contributions.

dd) Fines.

ee) Legacies and donations.

ff) Trade and commerce.

  e) Expenditure:

aa) Expenses pertaining to the Assemblies, correspondence, decorations, occasional travel, etc.

bb) Pensions for destitute, unprovided-for Brethren, if no other means for helping them exist.

cc) For the achievement of great purposes.

dd) To promote talents.

ee) For experiments and tests.

ff) For widows and children.

gg) Foundations.

Our audits prevent any self-interest, and our funds are the holy property of mankind.

[Addendum] B. INSTRUCTIONS FOR THE ENTIRE REGENT DEGREE.

I. Since it is the Order's intention to promote true human felicity, present virtue more enticingly and be feared by vice, it goes without saying that the teachers and rulers of mankind must also be publicly known as the best persons. Therefore a Regent shall be among the most perfect of men: prudent, cautious, skilled, popular, much in demand, above accusation and reproach, possessing a general reputation of insight, enlightenment, and philanthropy, filled with integrity, altruism, a love for that which is grand, universal, and extraordinary.

II. The Regents shall study the art of ruling in an indiscernible manner. Under the cloak of humility (not a false but genuine humility, based on an awareness of their weakness and of being strong only through our association), they shall rule supreme and know how to implement every purpose of the ⊙. Any commands must have the appearance of requests, and reproaches the likeness of praise, for one is dealing with men who obey of their own free will, who should not only be unaware of their yoke, but must bear no yoke at all. Everyone is to be led to his own good guided by his own reason. They shall recognise their weakness and the necessity of their obedience: everything is ruined if one incites their vanity against this realisation. Therefore one should avoid the kind of stiff and schoolmasterly seriousness by which one only repels them, turning oneself into the object of ridicule among wise and worldly men. Instead one must present the strictest example of reverend obedience towards the Superiors, especially when a man of noble birth conducts himself towards a Superior from a lower station.

The treatment should however vary according to the persons with whom one is dealing. Be a confidant of one man, a father to the other, the third man's pupil, and the strict, unyielding Superior to only a few, and even then it should only be with some reluctance, and never out of one's own wilfulness! Tell him you wish the ☉ would have placed this irksome business in someone else's hands or that you are tired of playing the schoolmaster and disciplinarian of someone who should have learnt how to govern himself long ago.

III. Since our Holy Legion, scattered throughout the world, must bring victory to virtue and wisdom, every Regent shall attempt to promote a certain equilibrium among the rest of the people, should take those who are pressed too hard under his wing, and hold back those who are rising too high. He shall not suffer that the fool elevates himself above the wise man, the evildoer above the good man, the ignorant above the educated, or the weaker man above the stronger, even if the former happened to be right. But this must be done with caution and prudence!

[IV. There is an infinite number of means for influencing people. Who can prescribe them all? We therefore leave it to the Regents' consideration that they discover new resources for achieving our goals every day. Furthermore, the needs of the age change: at one time, one works through man's inclination for the miraculous, at another through the allure of powerful connections. Thus, it is sometimes necessary to let the subordinates assume (but without resorting to untruths) that we secretly direct all other orders and Masonic systems, or that the most powerful monarchs are ruled by the ☉, which is actually the case here and there. Wherever something grand and wonderful happens it must be assumed that this was our doing; wherever a great and peculiar man lives it should be believed that he is one of us. From time to time one should give mystifying commands for no particular reason; for example, letting the subordinate find a missive of the ☉ under his plate at an inn in another town, when one could have handed it to him much more conveniently at his home. If possible, one should travel to the large cities during trade fairs, sometimes as a merchant, sometimes as an abbot, and sometimes as an officer; and everywhere one should establish the reputation of an excellent, respectable man who has come on important business and other matters. – However, this must not appear forced but must be done with finesse, not as an *aventurier,* and only in those places where one does not find oneself subject to insolence or inquisition. One may also write important orders in a chemical ink that disappears after a while, etc.]

V. As much as possible, a Regent shall show no weakness towards his subordinates; he should even hide his illness and displeasure from them; at least, he should never complain.

VI. One can often accomplish the most in the world through women. How to ingratiate yourselves with them and win them over should be one of your prime areas of study. All women are more or less guided by vanity, curiosity, sensuality, and the desire for change. One should take advantage of this for the good cause! This sex has a large portion of the world in its hands.

[VII. The common people everywhere must be won over for the ⊙, as well. This is best done by gaining influence over the schools; then through generosity, some glamour, condescension, popularity, and outward tolerance of the prevailing prejudices when they can only be gradually extinguished.

VIII. Where one has a hand in the government of a country, one should pretend to be least influential; thus we will not be opposed. And where one has no leverage at all, one should appear all-powerful, so that one is feared, sought out and thereby strengthened.

IX. Anything unpleasant happening to the ⊙ should forever be kept secret from the subordinates.]

X. The Regents are obliged to be watchful of the Brethren's provisions and win for them the most suitable offices when instructed by the Provincial Superior.

XI. The Regents shall observe formidable silence, and therefore they should speak with the utmost caution when questioned about matters they are not allowed to explain. But none of this must appear forced. There are even cases when one may practise a certain talkativeness. Then one must appear of having said too much for the sake of friendship, either to test the subordinate, to see if he can keep the matter secret, or to spread a certain legend among the people, the belief in which is in the ⊙'s interest. For doubtful cases, the standing order is to ask the higher superiors for counsel in one's Q. L.

XII. Regardless of the office a Regent holds in the ⊙, he should answer as few as possible of his subordinates' questions orally, so that he has time to consider his answers well and to make the necessary inquiries.

XIII. The Regents shall be mindful of anything that can benefit the ⊙ at large, e.g. business transactions and similar measures that can increase the ⊙'s power. Any such projects must be submitted to the Provincial Superior. Urgent notifications shall not be included in the regular Q. L., because he is not allowed to open it.

XIV. In any case, matters of general influence must be reported diligently to the Provincial Superior so that preparations for joint efforts can be made.

XV. If an author teaches principles in a publicly printed book which, even though they are true, do not yet fit into our curriculum for the world because they are too far ahead of the times, one should either try to win him over or denounce his book.

XVI. If the Regents can bring about the dissolution of monasteries, especially those occupied by mendicant friars[182], so that their wealth can be used for our goals, e.g. to support capable educators for the rural population, the Superiors will welcome such proposals.

XVII. This will also be the case if they can draft solid plans for a widows' fund for our members' wives.

XVIII. It should also be one of our noblest concerns to prevent the people's slavish reverence for the princes from rising too high. Such servile flatteries corrupt those often very mediocre and weak men even further; therefore, one should set an example by one's own interaction with the princes and avoid any familiarity with them, never confide in them, being with them on a comfortable but courteous footing, thus ensuring that they revere and fear us, speaking and writing of them as one would speak of other men, so that they learn that they are men just like us, and that they are merely our lords by convention.

XIX. When it comes to elevating one of our deserving members who may not be well-known or even unknown to the public, one should set everything in motion to establish his reputation. Our unknown members must be instructed to trumpet out his fame everywhere and to silence all envy and intrigues against him.

XX. The smaller country towns often make better seed spots for us than capital and trade cities, where people are in their majority too corrupted, distracted, filled with passions, while believing themselves to be wholly educated.

XXI. It will prove to be very useful to have *visiteurs* travel around, or to task a Regent who is currently travelling in the area with attending the Assemblies, reading the minutes, calling at the individual members' homes, requesting their

---

[182] *Monastic Orders forbidden to own landed property and required to be supported by the alms only, e.g. the Franciscans and Dominicans.*

papers, journals, etc. for inspection, listening to their complaints, etc., as this provides the opportunity to correct errors committed by the direction by means of such a Plenipotentiary, who states that he has been sent by the Higher Superiors and must boldly reform those matters he has been tasked to correct, including those things the Prefect may not have the courage to change himself, preferring to use this tool instead.

XXII. If the format of our lower Classes is not suitable for all locations, one should consider how to go about working in another form. As long as we achieve our goals it does not matter under which guise we do so, and a guise is always necessary: for it is secrecy that forms the basis of our strength to a large degree.

XXIII. Therefore one should always disguise oneself with another society's name. Meanwhile, the ⊡ of lesser Freemasonry are a suitable garment for our higher purposes, because the world has already grown accustomed to expect nothing great and noteworthy of them. The name of a scholarly society is also a very appropriate mask for our lower Classes; we can hide behind it if someone were to learn about our gatherings. Then one says: 'We gather in secret, partly to make the matter more enticing and interesting, partly to escape the need of accepting everyone without discrimination, to evade obstacles that may be laid in our path by malicious persons and scoffers, or to conceal the weakness of a still brand new institution.'

XIV. It is very important to explore the systems of other secret societies and to govern them. Indeed, if it is possible without burdening oneself with weighty obligations, one shall join them with the permission of one's Superiors. For this also, secrecy will prove to be advantageous.

XXV. Higher degrees must always be kept hidden from the lower ones. One is more inclined to accept orders from unknown persons than from those one knows, whose various flaws one has come to detect over time. This way, one can also observe the subordinates better, and they will conduct themselves better and more cautiously, if they believe that they are constantly in the presence of supervisors; thus they will behave well until virtue becomes a habit for them. In general, this increases the allure all the more: the world loves the miraculous, and it is a pleasant surprise to meet new people when entering a new degree.

XXVI. Military schools, academies, book printers, book sellers, cathedral chapters, or any other institutions that influence education and government should never be ignored, and the Regents should unremittingly design plans for setting about gaining control over them.

XXVII. In general, the Regents' main focus is, apart from the tasks related to their offices in the ☉, *to be constantly alert to anything that can make the O. more perfect and powerful, so that it becomes the ideal of the most perfect human government in every age.*

These are the general rules of conduct; that which every Regent must observe in the place assigned him by the Illustrious Superiors is communicated to him in a special set of instructions.

[Addendum] C. INSTRUCTIONS FOR THE PREFECTS, OR LOCAL SUPERIORS.

In addition to that which the Prefect must know from the instructions for the entire Regent degree, his office entails the following duties:

I. He is the first Regent in his Prefecture, and since he directs the entire lower edifice, all reports, Q. L., etc., pass through his hands.

II. It is up to him to establish either Minerval Churches, Masonic ⌗ , or both, in eight locations within his Prefecture. For this purpose, the Provincial Superior gives him the ☉'s names for the locations and the persons to be initiated, which he may not distribute at will. He in turn communicates a small number of the names to each Minerval Superior.

III. In the Scottish Knight degree it was stated that a monthly general report about the Prefecture is compiled from the reports of the intermediate Superiors. The Prefect sends it to the Provincial Superior no later than a fortnight after the end of the month. Every quarter, on the last day of the third month at the latest, he must submit, with help from the Knights, the general table about the personnel as well as the moral, political, and economic state of his Prefecture.

IV. Only he opens the Scottish Brethren's Q. L. and the *Soli* of the Novices and Minervals. Yet he must not open the *Soli* of the Lesser *Illuminati* Magistrates and Scottish Brethren, and neither does he open the Knights' Q. L.

V. He remits the original Obligations and tables of all the members in his Prefecture to the Provincial Superior.

VI. He can make decisions concerning promotions up to and including the Greater *Illuminatus* degree, but he may not make anyone a Scottish Knight without the Provincial Superior's approval.

VII. As soon as someone becomes a Scottish Knight, he is obliged to send the files about this person to the Provincial Superior.

VIII. He shall give notice when his Chapter is about to grow larger than the set number of twelve.

IX. He must ensure that, when a member dies, that man's name is given to a Novice, who then also receives everything his predecessor collected about the life of the man whose name he [bears], so that he may complete the research.

X. The Prefect has the right to collect from his subordinates all ☉ documents in their possession once a year. He returns them to those who are trustworthy, but he retains the documents of disorderly persons or those who may even be designated for expulsion.

XI. Since the Prefect must thus care for the building's entire foundation, a brief lesson on how he should conduct himself in the process follows.

1) A large number of workers are required for implementing the ☉'s plan if it is to work properly. Thus, *dissemination* is the first duty. However, it matters very much what kind of workers one has: they must have the necessary insights and temperament. For this,

2) *instruction* and *education* is required. These educated people must also develop love for the purpose, so that they think it is impossible to find this purpose, so near and dear to them, in any other society, and so that they will be inclined to do everything in their power to preserve the ☉'s goals. From this springs

3) *allegiance.* No one will find what he seeks in a society if everyone is free to do as he pleases, and if he does not sacrifice his conceit, trusting that other, older, and experienced men may have more insight. If the subordinate respects his Superiors' orders, if he follows them and his first instinct is that everything the Superiors command serves a purpose, this will bring forth what is necessary in so many respects, namely

4) *subordination* and obedience. And finally, public workers of our kind have too many opponents, than that they may complete their day's work in peace. Thus arises

5) the *secret* and mysterious nature of the ☉. If everything in these five points is properly arranged, then nothing is impossible in any nation under the sun. One cannot recommend diligence in these matters to the Prefects highly enough, and they receive instruction in every point here, so that they may instruct the Superiors of the lower Classes hereafter.

1. *Dissemination.*

a) Bring as many good people to the ☉ as possible! Part of our strength rests in numbers, though not all of it.

b) However, no person who is of a generally poor reputation, who is widely hated and despised, even if this hatred is unfounded, shall be admitted, not even to the Noviciate.

c) All admissions must be made with the aim of receiving inquisitive, capable, obedient, staid, diligent, active, well-natured, scientifically-minded young persons, who do not know much yet, but are filled with a desire to learn more and who will have to thank the ⊙ for their enlightenment over time.

d) Thus, the ⊙'s attention is directed first and foremost to young men, if indeed a sufficient number of suitable members who have reached the age of majority can be found in the area, and one should always keep in mind that the ⊙ concentrates its efforts on the recruitment of young persons.

e) Therefore, the Prefect should seek to gain influence over the schools, the education of the young, and their teachers in his region and attempt to fill them with members of the ⊙. For in this manner, one teaches the ⊙'s maxims to the young, educates their hearts, influences the best minds to work for us, makes them accustomed to order and discipline, and gains their respect; we can expect the first offices in the state to be occupied with our pupils, and their loyalty to the ⊙ to be inextinguishable, like everything one learns in one's early years.

f) One must deal carefully with adult men; more often than not they will only partly be a gain, as they are already on the wrong path, want to pursue their own ideas, must be tested precisely, and, depending on the circumstances, they must be promoted more quickly.

g) The following must be observed when establishing a Colony:

aa) One sends forth a brave man who is wholly dependent on the ⊙ and lets him remain there for a while.

bb) One should not populate remote locations until the mid-sized locations are filled.

cc) One chooses persons whose domicile is in several locations, e.g. canons and merchants.

dd) Every member of the Order must be given assistance in every fair demand, but it is not permitted, without providing cause of the utmost importance, that one Province burden another with all sorts of demands, and every Province must instead satisfy its own people. Therefore, the

Prefects shall not light-mindedly recruit poor and unprovided men who might soon become a burden to the ☉.

ee) Be slow to advance further until matters in the main location have been properly set in motion.

ff) One must consider carefully to whom one can safely give the task to proliferate the ☉.

gg) Then, whether it is more advisable to establish a ☐ or a Minerval Church, or both;

hh) Whom one places at its head, and that man's skills, temperament, zeal, loyalty, reputation, credit, gift for educating others, punctuality, seriousness, and wisdom;

ii) The characteristics of the location, remote or near, dangerous or safe, large or small;

kk) The means to be employed,

ll) the time in which it can be accomplished,

mm) the people with whom one begins. If the first are unsuitable, nothing good will become of the others.

nn) Subordination and coordination.

oo) The outward appearance one gives this matter.

h) When recruiting adults one should seek out primarily those in whom the ideas necessary for our purposes are already present or can easily be awakened; persons who willingly accept better insights and act according to reason and deliberation rather than prejudice, but who are still eager to learn, who are capable of feeling and thinking in terms of great purposes and designs, who already feel the urge to become benefactors of mankind or in whom this sentiment can be stirred easily, vividly, and permanently, who eagerly seize every opportunity to make themselves useful; who, with reason, find much at fault with the world and its civil institutions, and wish to change it. One should not easily place great trust in the very wealthy and in noblemen who have had no other education than that which such people usually receive. They do not know the needs of human life, and thus they rarely know how necessary one man is to another, and therefore they are seldom trustworthy friends. Those however who have felt the power of fate not because of their own negligence or bad behaviour but because of misfortune and the wickedness and malevolence of others are primarily those to whom the ☉ offers its lap as a refuge!

i) Once the ☉ has gained its proper strength in a given place and has filled the highest positions it may, if it so chooses, strike fear in those who are uncompliant and make it clear to them how dangerous it is to insult and denigrate the ☉, and it may provide for its members. Obviously, once the ☉ has nothing more to fear from the government but instead has an invisible influence upon it,. it will be easily attract more people than are actually needed. But even then it is always safer to achieve proliferation through the schools – the ☉ cannot recommend this method highly enough.

k) The theological seminaries are just as important to the ☉ as the schools, and one should attempt to win over their provosts because it is through them that one gains the support of the first estate and thus draws the strongest opponents of all good designs towards our interests and, above all, because this ensures that the people and the common man are in the hands of the ☉.

l) Clergy must be treated with double caution as they rarely hold to the middle road but are either too free-spirited or too timid, and the former rarely have good morals. Members of religious orders shall never be accepted, and one must shun ex-Jesuits like the plague.

m) If over time the Prefect can fill the princely dicasteries and councils with zealous members of the ☉ then he has done everything he can do, indeed more than if he had initiated the prince himself.

n) Generally, princes are rarely admitted to the ☉, and if they already belong to it they should not readily be promoted beyond the Scottish Knight degree because when one frees their hands they are not only disobedient but use even the best intentions to their advantage.

o) However, one may seek to attract everyone who can be educated and who may be of use to us, who can strengthen us, and who neither disgraces nor endangers the ☉.

p) All men who live not only for their own sake but for that of the world and the human race, who can rise above all small things, are born members of the ☉.

Now to the second point:

2. *Instruction, education.*

Of what use can a larger number of people be to the ☉, who do not in any way resemble each other? All these men must be cleansed of their dross and reshaped into noble, great, and worthy persons. This then is the most burdensome and difficult task. The ☉ is not so much concerned with the quantity but the quality of its workers. Therefore,

a) when first entering the ☉ every man's soul shall be expanded and made receptive to great designs. From the very beginning he shall be imbued with high and worthy concepts. All matters must be presented to him in grand and impressive terms, but without going into too much detail. It goes without saying that the Recipient's demeanour must not let the Candidate expect the opposite.

b) The Candidate is guided according to the known regulations; not all at once, however, but gradually so that the time given for contemplation helps to imprint the vision more deeply into his mind. He must ask himself, rather than wait to be asked.

c) The understanding of greatness is taught by presenting him with the unselfishness of the ☉'s purpose as evidenced by the General Statutes; by pointing out the effort put into his education; by the difficulties one must overcome to reach us; by describing the advantages that even our lowest member has over all the profane; by the allure of secret power; by the example of strength that the initiate thus has received; by the promise of yet greater insights; by the hope of making the acquaintance of the noblest men over time; by considering the protection from evildoers that the ☉ can provide to its obedient pupils; by providing him with an opportunity to be useful unrivalled anywhere else; by the orderliness and punctuality that he witnesses; by the respect, reverence, and holiness with which the Initiator speaks of the ☉; by the reputation and eloquence of the Initiator himself. The Prefect shall instruct and exercise his subordinates in all these points.

d) However, it is not enough to kindle the fire: it must also be preserved, namely by reading books that create the desire to improve and distinguish oneself, and to become great: books that present virtue as desirable and interesting and vice as despicable, and something that leads only to its own punishment. The diligent reports of the Superiors must document how beneficial this literature has been to their men. Where appropriate one lets members of the ☉ who have knowledge as well as oratorical skills present lectures to the Minervals about matters of practical philosophy, pleasure and dissatisfaction, good and evil, etc. Practical exercises and opportunities for doing good are even better. Before promoting them to higher degrees, the young men must first be examined to see whether or not they have read the prescribed books, and no one is promoted until he is exactly as we want him to be.

e) The Prefect shall exercise the greatest care in obtaining the most precise tables about the Novices' and Minervals' diligence, demeanour, and progress every month. No Class requires as much supervision as the first.

f) Therefore, one also shall strictly insist that the subordinates complete their monthly tasks; these should not, however, be tasks of a theoretical or speculative nature but such that can truly influence the will, the improvement of the character and the society's bond, so that they are occupied with developing their skills, becoming accustomed to orderliness and diligence, and learning to project their thoughts into various situations. Whether one is promoted swiftly or slowly depends only on the quality and quantity of these essays; no rank, status, wealth, or other external advantage is considered in this process, but only capability, flexibility, and nobility of the heart and soul.

g) The focus must lie primarily on the heart; better to have a hundred weak minds than one that is malicious! Therefore, neither envy or pride nor defiance must be tolerated. One must encourage a general benevolence, exhort the corps of members to good deeds, and publicly praise, reward, and distinguish those who have done them.

h) Therefore, the Prefect shall collect anecdotes of noble and base deeds, and communicate them to the Minerval Magistracies. In the Assemblies these honourable or shameful deeds by the lowliest as well as the noblest people are then read out publicly with their names and preconised. One must learn that, here with us, due justice is given to every meritorious deed even though the whole world may have misjudged it, and that the evildoer on the throne is called a villain just as much, if not more, than the man who is taken to the gallows, while the truly great man will find his certain canonisation among us.

k) One must try to remove discreetly from the ⊙ recalcitrant men who believe themselves to be wise.

l) One shall accustom the pupils to conceptualise moral truth in visual terms. We therefore promote good poets as well as fables and novels; and he who wants to instruct others should familiarise himself primarily with images and examples so that he may give his lessons the necessary vividness.

m) Foremostly, however, one must understand how to link every teaching to the interests of the learner.

n) A proper number of well-chosen books, tailored to each degree's activities, shall always be required reading for the lower classes.

o) [The Prefect] must ensure that all members speak with one tongue about matters concerning the ☉ and other important subjects. To this end he arranges for all the subordinates to be instructed by the intermediate Superiors unbeknown to themselves. This he accomplishes by accustoming them to turning their attention to the Superior in all matters, deeming all his actions and speeches as purposeful even if they do not understand the underlying reasons, and encouraging them to try and work out these reasons and to ask him for instructions if in doubt. If the Prefect observes all this, he will lack nothing.

3. *Allegiance*

is achieved as follows:

a) If the men are convinced of the goodness of the cause, the purity of the ☉'s intentions, the importance of its purpose, its members' integrity, the dignity and reliability of the institution, the benefits of the instruction received, and their protection from oppression;

b) if they may hope to attain greatness in future;

c) if they feel the moral excellence of their character increasing;

d) if they feel that their own interests are inseverably bound to those of the ☉, and that one can be happy only in the ☉, whereas outside it one cannot be certain of happiness;

e) if they expect greater insights;

f) if they are bound by having come to view the ☉ as the sole source of their happiness. What man would not be attached to something that has given him instruction, education, protection from misfortune, serenity, and an improvement of his character, and where he expects great insights and further blessings in the future? A man for whom the decision to live his life not for himself but for humanity has become a necessity, and who can satisfy this habitual manner of thinking only here and nowhere else.

g) If the capability for doing good and acting nobly germinates within each member, for one cannot be sure of a man until the thought of being useful to the world becomes his greatest desire.

h) Thus, one must devise situations that cause the members to think of the ⊙ often and continuously and make it become almost their only, brightest and most excellent idea. Everything must remind them of it. The ⊙ must become everyone's hobby-horse. The Prefect should consider the means that the Roman Church employs to make its religion appealing to the senses, and to continuously bring it before the senses of every believer.

i) However, the Superiors should not overburden their people nor disgust them with continuous moralising, or they will do more harm than good.

k) Not much is said about all these matters here. The Prefect, just as all the other Regents, must turn his complete attention to their further investigation. Nothing must be closer to his heart than the education and allegiance of his subordinates. He should have various plans and suggestions for accomplishing this laid out before him. One can never write or speak enough about this foundation of our ⊙. By giving out assignments every Prefect has the opportunity to research this subject fully and secretly make use of his subordinates' insights. Generally, not all rules are suitable everywhere and, therefore, the Prefect and the other Higher Superiors would do well to remember the stratagem of holding essay competitions on subjects about which they do not possess sufficient information or which require further research, rewarding the best entries. In this manner the structure in each Province achieves consistency only gradually according to the local circumstances; and the lower members themselves erect the edifice they believe to have already been completed. The weak man becomes the teacher of the strong, who can learn from him without shame.

l) The members must be encouraged to help one another, to be magnanimous, agreeable, and generous towards one another and the ⊙.

4. *Obedience.*

Once the members have been educated to properly sense a grand design, a great system, there can be no doubt that they will gladly follow the Superiors' orders.

Who would not wish to follow him who has thus far been leading me well and safely, who has brought me my present bliss, and from whom I can expect more? Away with the man who shows no loyalty when he has drawn so many benefits! Cast him out of the noble society! One may assume that every morally good man who is filled with the dignity of our goal will gladly obey his orders. Still, the ⊙ wishes to point out several ways by which obedience may be preserved.

a) By good example,

b) by the benefits gained from the instruction,

c) by the lesson that every man basically follows himself.

d) by satisfaction and the hope for it,

e) by the anticipation of greater knowledge,

f) by fear, where necessary,

g) by rewards, distinctions, honour,

h) by expressing general contempt for those who disobey,

i) by avoiding familiarity with the subordinates,

k) by exemplary punishment of disobedience,

l) by a good selection of people on whom one may safely rely and who will obey any order.

m) By the *quibus licet,* from which one can tell if the orders have been obeyed; which is why they must be composed precisely and completely.

n) By proper submission of the tables the intermediate Superiors compile about their subordinates. The more detailed they are, the better, as the ☉'s entire plan of operations rests on them. From these one gleans the number of members, their education, the members' closeness and cohesion, the relationship of all parts and those persons who deserve promotions in the ☉, as well as how worthy the Assemblies and their Presidents are.

5. *Secrecy.*

This is the most important part. Therefore

a) the ☉ shall never make a public appearance even in a country where it would have enough power to do so;

b) the Prefect must skilfully change the appearance of his endeavours according to local circumstances, and know how to dress the ☉ in a different garment with the Provincial Superior's permission. Just as religion was – unfortunately! – only a pretence for the monastic orders of the Roman Church so our ☉ must, in a nobler manner, attempt to conceal itself behind a learned society, a trading company or the like. Its members must act accordingly.

c) It is impossible to work against a society concealed in this way.

d) The Superiors cannot be discovered in case of persecution or treason.

e) One may even arrange to have concealed Superiors sent out to investigate and thus become very useful to the ☉.

f) Ambition and factionalism are prevented by secrecy.

g) One is hidden from spies and the emissaries of other societies by an impenetrable night.

h) The Prefect shall ensure that no more than ten members gather in a Minerval Assembly. However, in the case that there are more members in a given location he shall divide them into two Assemblies or have them take turns in attending.

i) If there are two Minerval Churches in one location they should be concealed from each other as much as possible.

k) The Prefect shall not allow a member to reveal to another those Brethren whom he has met abroad.

l) Only in an emergency may a stranger be allowed to visit the Minerval Assemblies.

So much about the direction of the lower structure and what has to be observed in this regard. Some final remarks:

XII. The Prefect appoints the Magistrates of the Minerval Churches either on his own initiative or according to the Superiors' suggestions; however, only he submits these appointments to the Provincial Superior, who then confirms or rejects them. He is responsible for every Superior appointed by himself.

XIII. The Prefect shall make very sure that everything that happens in the Assemblies and ⊡ under his control is quiet, lawful, and respectable, and that no word against religion, the state, and public morals may be spoken there, just as he generally can never stress enough the importance of prompt and exact obedience to all rules.

XIV. Wherever feasible the Provincial Superior shall seek to establish a library, a natural history cabinet, museum, manuscript collection, and the like in the most suitable location of his Province.

XV. The Prefect shall proceed slowly and cautiously; he must do only as much as he can accomplish safely, and must be especially careful with promotions. No one may advance unless he already has the ideas and qualities required by the next degree. Here one cannot be too cautious.

XVI. It has already been noted that it is possible to accept men into the Masonic ⊡ who do not know anything of our society. However, the Prefect must take care that these people do not upset the mood, that they are honourable, earnest men, and that they can benefit the ☉ in some way.

XVII. The Prefect may not engage in any ☉ correspondence outside his Prefecture without the Provincial Superior's permission.

XVIII. Just as he must properly instruct the Superiors and Worshipful Masters on all these points, he must also inquire with the Provincial Superior about important matters when in doubt.

XIX. However, if he thoroughly studies these by-laws and obeys them precisely, always keeping the whole picture before his eyes and ensuring that everyone do neither more nor less than comply with the duties of his station, he will be able to accomplish everything he deems necessary or is tasked with.

[Addendum] D. INSTRUCTIONS FOR THE PROVINCIAL SUPERIORS.

I. The Provincial Superior shall familiarise himself with the ☉'s entire Constitution to the point that he retains the system in his mind as if he himself had invented it.

II. The Administrative System, the Instructions for the Regents and the Instructions for the Local Superiors must form the basis of all his actions, none of which may be in vain.

III. He is elected by all the other Regents in the Province and then confirmed by the National Superior, or another man is appointed. The Higher Superiors may also remove him from office.

IV. He shall be a native son of the Province or at least be familiar with the country.

V. As much as this is possible, he should be a man free from concern with public affairs and duties, so that he may wholly devote himself to the ☉.

VI. He must give the appearance of someone who is seeking tranquillity, having withdrawn from all public affairs.

VII. If possible, he should reside in a central location from which he can most easily direct the Province.

VIII. When he becomes Provincial Superior, he sheds his previous name in the ☉, which is then given to another member along with the information he has gathered about the man's biography. He in turn is given another name by the Higher Superiors. He also bears a signet of his Province, a drawing of which is sent to him, and which the Provincial Superiors generally carry in a seal ring.

IX. The files thus far collected in the Provincial Archives are submitted to him. It is the duty of the other Regents to have everything sealed until the new Provincial Superior is appointed.

X. The Provincial Superior is directly answerable to a National Inspector, to whom he must submit a monthly general report about his Province. Because the Local Superiors report to him only a fortnight after the end of the month, the Inspector always receives the report for May towards the end of June, etc. Such a report must be divided into 4 main sections, namely from each of the Prefectures in his care, and it must include anything remarkable that has occurred in every location and in every discipline, and in particular those who have been accepted and promoted, i.e. his name, date and place of birth, his social standing, and the date he signed the Obligation. The Higher Superiors need no further information about the members until they are to be promoted to the Regent Class (except in very exceptional cases). If the Provincial Superior requests a template for his reports, it can be issued to him.

XI. It goes without saying that, apart from these monthly reports, the Provincial Superior must inquire with the National Inspector about all those important matters that are not for him to decide. In particular, he shall do nothing *in politicis*[183] on his own.

XII. He shall not concern himself in the least with his fellow Provincial Superiors, and shall not ask whether things are good or bad in a neighbouring district; before he ventures there, he must report to the National Inspector.

XIII. If he has a complaint about the Inspector, he can approach the *Primus.*

XIV. All Regents in a Province are the *Consultores* of the Provincial Superior, and they must help him with every plan. Wherever possible, he must have some of the Regents as Secretaries at his side.

XV. He confirms all Superiors of the lower Classes and of the Masonic ⛝, nominates the Prefects, and awaits their confirmation or rejection by the Inspector.

XVI. He has the right to direct those people living in his Province who live off the ☉'s pensions and have no employment to move wherever he needs them most.

XVII. He hands the Order names received from the Higher Superiors to the Prefects for further distribution.

XVIII. He also assigns the ⛝ their names, which the Superiors have given him in advance.

---

[183] Lat. *In political matters.*

XIX. He announces the exclusions in his Province and ensures that an accurate register of them is maintained in all locations where Assemblies are held.

XX. If a member who cannot be treated too harshly must be reproached, he must do this in an unknown handwriting under the name of 'Basilius'. This name, which belongs to no one, has been set aside by the ☉ for this very purpose.

XXI. Based on suggestions by the *Presbyteri,* he prescribes from time to time books that must be read, according to the needs of each degree.

XXII. He opens the *Soli* of the Lesser *Illuminati,* Magistrates, and Scottish Brethren as well as the *Q. L.* of the Knights and Priests, and the Novices' *Soli,* whereas he does not open the Minervals' *Primo,* the Knights' and Presbyters' *Soli,* and the Regents' *Q. L.*

XXIII. Up to the Regent degree he may promote anyone on his own initiative. He may not, however, issue that degree without the National Inspector's approval.

XXIV. He shall keep his archive in order and, for this purpose, he shall keep the tables, Obligations, the records of the Knights, etc., bound as separate files for each person.

XXV. The *Decanus* must be informed by him on a monthly basis in which subjects the newly accepted Minervals have enrolled.

XXVI. In general, he should ensure that he has skilled workers in *scientificis.*

XXVII. He shall properly forward to the *Decanus* the best essays submitted to him, as well as anything that may concern the *Presbyteri* (e.g. the biographies, character sketches, etc.).

XXVIII. He shall remember the stratagem of rendering inactive a man who is unsuitable for political leadership, but otherwise very capable, by promoting him to the Priest Class.

XXIX. He must ensure that if a Chapter has more than 12 members, the most capable man enters into the Priest Class, and that

XXX. there is a Priest in every Chapter, and that he is such a man that he will readily entrust with the role of his Secret Censor in that Chapter.

XXXI. He shall not miss the opportunity to discuss the most important matters in his Province with the most prudent Regents during the Convents. Even the wisest man requires counsel and help.

XXXII. Just as the Provincial Superior receives a Charter from the National Superiors, he issues Constitutions to the Chapters (which have been named as the National Inspector has dictated), according to the template below:

We of the Grand National Lodge in the Orient (of Germany), constituted Provincial Grand Masters and District Officers of the ... Circle, proclaim and confess by the power of this letter, that we give the most worthy Brother (Order name), Herr ... (legal name), full power and authority to establish a Secret Chapter of Holy Scottish Freemasonry, and henceforth, according to his instructions, disseminate the Royal Art by establishing Masonic ⌸ of the three symbolic degrees. Thus ordained in the *Directorium* ... of the ... Circle.

     (L. S.)   Secret Provincial Direction (no signature.)

XXXIII. Summing up briefly, the Provincial Superior shall set his Province on such a footing *that he can accomplish all good things and prevent all evil therein.* Happy is the land where the ☉ has achieved this power! But he will not find this difficult if he follows the Superiors' instructions to the letter. He will accomplish everything, having so many skilled and morally educated men at hand, that they will make all noble things possible and render all evil things impossible. – Therefore, let there be no leniency for errors, no nepotism, and no animosity! – Consideration for the general good and the ☉'s goals shall be the only mainsprings for all his actions. And let us make sure that only capable men are installed as Provincial Superiors while we also have the means to discipline him who would abuse the power we have granted him.

XXXIV. This power must be used only for the good of the Brethren; all who can be helped must be helped. All other things being equal, a member of the ☉ must always be given preference. We must devote our money, servants, honour, property, and blood to them, especially to those who have been tried the hardest, and an insult to the lowliest member must not go unavenged by the Order.

B) Higher Mysteries
I. Docetists[184]

It is difficult to discuss matters for which our languages do not yet have words; when our entire language is constructed to express their exact opposite; when our sensory impressions have continuously reaffirmed this opposite since childhood and our abstract ideas, understanding, logic, and reasoning are based thereon; when our entire system of thought and even our inner awareness are shaken to the core, and all our sensations, thoughts and our most basic principles are suddenly shown to be dubious illusions; when it seems sheer madness to assert the contrary against the entire world as well as one's own inward and outward sentiments. Yet, despite all this, we shall dare to propound our thoughts, presenting concepts, with the tongues of mortals, that we can barely discern from afar, even with our highest intellectual faculties, let alone fully and clearly develop in our current form. We shall see who is strong enough to find his way out of this general illusion, to break free, for a moment, from the bonds of the senses and body, transfigure himself, and imagine himself in a different world.

No man's ideas are innate. We receive all our concepts only through our senses, and in proportion to whether these are better or worse, or whether we receive more or fewer of them. At first they are mere sensations. Generalised and abstract ideas develop only from repeated sensations; they are nothing other than sensations of resemblances, and consequently they cannot be conceived at all without using the senses beforehand; all our reason and understanding is built on this sole foundation – or could a man born blind and deaf possess reason and understanding? Our current ideas of the world and its parts are guided only by these senses; and with different senses, all our ideas and sensations would change; if the construction of our eyes were microscopic we would see a new, entirely different world, and we would have a different language and philosophy.

Thus, if we possess not a single innate concept, if all our ideas are derived from our senses, and if these senses can be heightened or lowered, decreased or increased: if experience furthermore demonstrates that with every change or modification of the senses the world in all its parts changes its appearance, and that with different senses we thus would have very different ideas about the world and its parts, since with these altered sensations our abstract concepts and

---

[184] *Adherents of Docetism, an early Christian heresy, professing that Jesus Christ did not have a real body while walking the earth but only an apparent one.*

everything that is based on them must inevitably be different once the foundation has changed: then we have every reason to assert with the greatest confidence that this earth as well as all other parts of the universe are not in and of themselves what they appear to be to us but that, on the whole, this shaky supposition is the foundation of all our knowledge and that all our concepts and abstractions based thereon do not lead to the inside of the matter itself; that for this very reason most questions in this regard cannot be resolved; that there are as many and diverging schools of philosophy as there are differently organised beings confronting reality; and that the five senses known to us are wrongly taken to be the only and final means by which the world can be conceived.

If these presuppositions are correct, then everyone must also be willing to accept the following conclusions as true and undisputed, even if one's own entire inner sensibility should revolt against it, because they are simply immediate conclusions and results of the foregoing, and this inward feeling of revulsion proves only that this prior way of thinking is too closely linked to our nature, most intimately, so to speak, for one to believe that this present discourse might find many admirers and followers. Indeed, it would be ridiculous if people wished to act and speak accordingly, considering that even the most zealous followers deem this unnecessary and such doctrines are meant only for those who dedicate themselves to the highest contemplations on nature and its essence, who seek to reach the very boundaries of human understanding. It is merely intended to humble the pride and insolence of man and to return him to what is not far to seek and essential for his felicity, to expel the spirit of speculation and spur men on to action, to show them what they do not know and shall never discover, to expose the inconsistencies of previous systems, to keep people from straying onto erroneous paths, and to expose materialism and its supposed power; it is meant to devise new reasons for the so strongly disputed and otherwise nearly unprovable continued existence of our self, thus presenting a consoling yet widely-ridiculed doctrine from a new perspective, giving new lustre to old and tarnished matters, demonstrating the glory of God and his works in a new, unexpected and irrefutable manner; and to prove that man in his arrogance, so proud of his reason, has no cause to spurn the things he does not fathom, that impossibilities may be possible after all.

Thus, if the above principles are correct, it inevitably follows:

1. That it is impossible for us to penetrate into the inner nature of beings and to uncover the creation of the world and its main components.

2. That, in essence, any sensation in a being, whether it is organised the same or differently, is nothing other than the effect of external objects on beings organised in this and in no other manner.

3. That any change to this organisation, no matter how inconspicuous, must inevitably incur a true change, proportionate to its cause, in the perception of the being which perceives and senses.

4. That by virtue of his natural or artificial senses, whether they are enhanced or diminished, every man is always right; the difference in his sensation is not deceitful, even if it is very great and his sensation differs from that of all others, because he sees things as his organisation allows, and it is no different for anyone else.

5. That we only accuse others of flawed and erroneous sensations because their mode of sensing and seeing is not like ours, not the prevailing one, as is their organisation.

6. That while there are other beings and forces outside us, they are essentially unknown to us and appear to us only through their effects, revealing themselves in different ways depending on the individual subjects' receptivity; that, consequently, these objects outside us are merely our own thoughts, and that in this respect this system is completely different from the idealism of ancient and modern thinkers.

7. That body, matter and extension, when viewed as such, are mere appearances, phenomena, beneath which the unknown forces become tangible for us; that following these principles, one can examine the truth of a doctrine which regards matter as dead and shapeless, as the origin of evil, and the body as the prison of the soul, which has been placed into this predicament by the creator of all matter.

8. That imaginary causes also produce imaginary effects, just as the universally accepted illusion and nullity of colour does not prevent entire arts, crafts and sciences, such as fabric dying, chemistry and painting, from being occupied with creating colours and properly arranging and using them.

9. That even our bodies, as well as our organisation, as such are also only mere appearances; that these words and figures of speech, in and of themselves, have no meaning other than the receptivity of our imagination equally unknown to us, our ability to imagine the effects of these unknown forces upon us in this and in no other manner.

10. That perhaps we visualise a vast multitude of these forces affecting us entangled herewith as a single sensory image.

11. That the selfsame object, when affecting a thousand different [organisations], would appear to others in a thousand different forms, although it would appear to me solely in one form; that, furthermore, it would appear to beings of a different nature and with other senses as something for which we presently do not even have a concept; that a tree is not a tree to all beings; that therefore, every object has the *potential* to appear in a thousand different ways, just as our faces, in a convex, plain, or concave mirror, will appear either normal or elongated, wide, enlarged, or small. Figuratively speaking, these different organisations are the plain, concave and convex mirrors.

12. That although it is basically only appearance, that which generally and consistently appears in some way to all or most men is as much as real to us; that this diversity of organisations known to us, however, serves to discover the ontological truth, i.e. a truth that is confirmed not by one, but several organisations known to us.

13. That all our knowledge and language are therefore based on the supposition that the world in all its parts really is, in itself, what it appears to us, regardless of linguistic usage; that all our philosophy is a philosophy of appearances; that this doctrine is necessarily prone to the most terrible and ridiculous misunderstandings, as long as our language is not equipped for it.

14. That there is, therefore, a peculiar kind of physics, philosophy, ethics and legislation for all beings of a different organisation or receptivity, and perhaps for certain beings none of all that and instead, some other sciences unknown to us suited to these new-found organisations – unless the sciences are designed for men alone, and not at all for such organisations.

15. That every organisation has its *own* truth, valid alone to its own kind, which however is not false, only because it cannot be confirmed in other organisations; that all our common truth is based only on premises abstracted from our senses, and is true only to this extent. – However, if the organisation changes, then the experiences and premises also change: and then, no more of all that: a different world, different objects, a different system and a different truth – unfathomable, unthinkable for us in this form – impossibilities perhaps becoming possible – perhaps nothing at all of that we know, what we presently are – currently unable to experience this – a lack of words and language, or of what use are words where there are no concepts, where they can only express what we presently are and experience and, therefore, cannot be applied to something we would experience in a different form. If one does not tell a blind man that there

is a sun, he will have no concept of it. However, once his eyes have been opened, he will indeed be stunned by a new and marvellous tableau! Is it not possible that we are afflicted with a similar blindness of which we are not aware because we lack other perspectives, but which may not have escaped the attention of other beings? Will death eventually brush the scales from our eyes, revealing to us a new, yet unknown world? Could what we experience in our current form as the body's decomposition be that vision itself? Could what looks like a pallid, dead body to us be a higher form of life imperceptible to us?

16. Thus the curtain is drawn back with every new organ, the hitherto impenetrable veil lifted, thereby revealing a new world – so to speak, thousands upon thousands of worlds for thousands upon thousands of different observers in a single world – just one, and yet also thousands upon thousands! And in every one of these thousands [upon thousands] of worlds, each of which is nearly infinite, a new, most perfect, greatest order and harmony – God in his new magnificence, nature in her new splendour, the most remarkable diversity in the most *fearsome* unity: thus

17. In themselves, no sun, moon, earth, men, animals, fire, air, or water – only to us, all of this, and to us only for as long as we are thus organised. All mathematical truths, too, are valid and permanent only to the extent that dimensions and volume are appearances.

18. Even all previously insurmountable difficulties arising from time and space, the division of matter, cohesion of bodies, motion and [rest], empty [and full] space, the infinity of space, simple and complex matters, are disputes over appearances. – In and of itself, nothing is simple, nothing is complex. It is only in this form and according to our logic based thereon, that there is no intermediate in this respect.

19. It is the same with the dispute over eternity and origin of the world, as well as its infinite expanse or limits. – This world *as such* is appearance, and therefore it has begun in this form with this our organisation, with this receptivity of certain beings; but these forces have existed for an infinite period of time before manifesting themselves as the phenomenon 'world'. For a sun to be seen there first had to exist beings with eyes; and a being equipped with something more than eyes, sees what we call 'sun' as something we cannot name, because we lack the senses to sense it as such. – In short, this form of the earth and the universe has come into existence with our current receptivity.

20. Perhaps in this respect, revelation may be anticipated, advanced under-

standing of certain truths that are comprehensible or conceivable only in a different form, just as the news of the sun's reality is a revelation to someone born
blind; causing people to become sceptical of their present understanding, stirring
their spirit of research to compare and reconcile what has been revealed with
what is actually known; to accept the futility of reconciliation, and to make them
surmise, for that very reason, truths of a higher order, to establish a nexus between
this new and future world and the present one, commencing here below. Perhaps
also new and unique revelations for a future organisation.

21. What a comforting prospect for the continuity of the self! Dying means
ceasing to see and know men, animals, trees; but here, dying does not mean
completely ceasing to exist, being without representation. Rather, it means obtaining a different organisation and changing one's receptivity, seeing and recog-
nising the same things in a different way, shedding one's old snake skin; it means
peeling the mask off that which is outside us, penetrating further into the core of
all forces, albeit still in a very imperfect manner. Dying means to be born, and
being born means to die, to cease existence in one form, so that one may act and
appear in another. After death, man will certainly cease to think – because
thought is only for the phenomenon of man, and yet he will not entirely cease to
exist; the spirit, the self, will obtain a newer, higher modification, as closely
linked to this new state as thought was to his former organisation. This modification will not be thought but, lacking the necessary experiences and words, we
have no other expression. Thus, we shall cease to imagine the world in this
manner, but we shall not cease to be active in another, entirely different manner.
Death is the transition from one way of seeing things to another, the gradual
progression towards an understanding of the inner essence; this death awaiting
us may not be the only one.

22. Likewise with our departed friends: their self which was so dear to us is
not lost to us, just as we are not lost to them now. Their self shall be forever part
of the universe around us, and it does affect us, although not in a way we can
perceive with these our senses. Although we do not appear to them in this
manner, in this form, we do appear to them in one peculiar to their own current
organisation. They do not remember us because *memory* is for man alone; but
even though we know neither how nor what the *actus* is by which the dead
imagine those organised beings that are called men in this shell, we are nonetheless constantly an object of their imagination. A thousand differently-organised
beings will know me, appearing to everyone around me here in this form and no

other, by a thousand different forms and shapes; why should it be different where the dead are concerned?

23. When one day the world's new form, that new, undiscovered, hitherto only dreamt-of country, is revealed to us after that grand metamorphosis all things must undergo and the present world ceases to be, we also shall obtain the organisation – peculiar to this new world form – of our friends who went before us; why then should we not find them once again, since we ourselves have not been lost to them during this interim period?

24. If what we have learnt about beings other than us and the phenomena 'earth' and 'world' while in our current form is already so excellent[,] orderly and harmonious, in spite of deception and appearance, orderly and harmonious even in its most fearsome manifoldness – should we not have cause for looking forward to death, this new, probably far more perfect insight into [the] inside of a much better world? Does death itself not become an initiation into a new life here, a triumph of nature? How grand must this tableau be if it is nearly impossible for spirits already accustomed to so much perfection, order and beauty in these nether regions to conceive of something even more magnificent? And how infinitely grand must he be who has predestined such bliss for his creatures? Should one not think that providence has concealed man's future state from him, because the certainty that such magnificence awaits us would make this life unbearable and speed the coming of death, so that one may reach that blissful state so much sooner? And should not in this manner the comforting doctrine of the immortality of the self be proven in the mysteries, more firmly, with all rights and for experienced, tried, moral men? (We should presume so!)

25. If then, as has already been established, this single world encompasses a thousand other worlds for thousands upon thousands of different observers, and if furthermore every being sees only the world that has been tailored to it alone, but the selfsame subject, by changing its organisation, cannot become the observer of another world, ascend towards higher spheres, survive its current form, look from one world form into the other, become the witness of a nexus of several forms emerging from one another and being founded on one another, then what is the purpose of this fearsome hoard and wealth of worlds? To what end would this earth alone have so many continents, kingdoms, countries, cities and villages, if everyone were destined to never set foot outside his own native soil – if a village, city, kingdom, or continent were only known to its inhabitants and [un]known to everyone else? What would humanity be, what would the earth be,

if no one were able to travel to its various parts, to survey and compare them[,] to sense and enjoy this far greater, immeasurable pleasure arising from this[?] Otherwise, the world would be an immense palace of a thousand different, most splendid apartments, each occupied by only a single tenant, none of whom would know or even suspect the existence of other rooms or their inhabitants, much less the coherence of its parts, its artful decoration, symmetry and ornament for the duration of his entire stay. Who then would be privy to this greatest of all pleasures, the joy of understanding the connexion of several parts? If partial insight already grants this much pleasure, then this order, this magnificent universe lacks the most essential, it lacks an observer; a being who sees the whole as connexion. The greatest object of understanding without the subject to understand it; the greatest joy existing without being enjoyed; the greatest work of art without connoisseurs to admire it and to draw conclusions about the magnificence of its creator; the greatest painter has made the most artful painting for the eternally blind; the most beautiful, delicious fruits ripen for no palate to taste them! Wherefore the most beautiful garden, if it is enjoyed by no one; wherefore the most beautiful, comfortable house if it stands empty? Wherefore the grandest harmony unheard by any ear? Wherefore these grand, magnificent properties for which we lack the senses? How are we served by this anticipation of even grander tableaux and more magnificent worlds? It would mean awaking the thirst, leading us to the spring, and then not quenching the thirst; it would mean showing us the land of rest[185] in the distance and making it impossible for us to reach; it would mean having feet, but never walking and having eyes, but seeing nothing; what good is the most fertile seed, if no one may harvest its fruit? Order and perfection forever unrecognised by anyone may as well not even exist – and yet, this order, this development, and connexion continue throughout eternity. It would be mad to believe that millions of the most artful creations exist, that the greatest beings were set into motion only to reveal to us transitory creatures the smallest, most insignificant part for a mere day, like a dream. This would mean to move an ocean only to drown a gnat; it would mean to prescribe a fixed star its orbit for several thousand years, so that it may be a poor beacon to the nightly wanderer. Where does this leave the economy of nature, this law so plainly visible throughout all creation? Why should one reach such intellectual heights in this form, only to suddenly be nothing more than a body's shade, which in turn

---

[185] *Heb. 4.*

serves only to eventually shed light on another, equally temporary one[?] Why then this eternal, purposeful rising and falling, this budding and wilting of all beings? Should there be nothing that is eternal? I could become what I presently am, could imagine and expect more than I am, and then suddenly, not only a complete standstill would follow, but a most fearsome, eternal night should fall on me as a result of a most unnatural, fearsome [leap]? Light would turn to darkness, and the brightest noon to the eternal, darkest midnight! We would have learnt only to forget? God and Nature would have built like children, having constructed a house of cards, only to destroy this most magnificent edifice senselessly, at their whim! Oh no! All this cannot be: everything clearly calls out to us that our self continues, albeit in different forms, that thousands upon thousands of grand tableaux still await us; that we are indeed mortal insofar as we lose this form, these seeds, and this manner of seeing the world associated therewith, but that nonetheless we do not cease to be entirely, that in a new form, with a new modification, we begin to see a new world that is connected to the old, because everything is connected; that there is a middle between being and not-being, and that is being different: and this different state of being shall prove the mutability of our organisation and as a necessary consequence, the mutability of the world and its form.

26. Thus, these world forms, one encompassed in the other, these various organisations of ours, one developing from the other, this cycle of alternately living and dying must be intrinsically connected because ultimately everything is connected, and indeed receive their value, their common purpose only when we have recognised this purpose and we can oversee this chain of worlds, even the great Pythagorean journey[186] may be real, after all. In this case it would be possible and even necessary that [at least after having shed this form this nexus would become visible to us, that at least after] each new world life [has come to an end,] the results of our experiences and observations will be overshadowed by the stronger impressions in the new life, that they are now merely dormant, but when the journey through a certain number of worlds is completed, all the *ressorts*[187] and containers of our collected world experiences will suddenly be released and present themselves to our rational selves. Therefore, this journey would not be from one star to another, from one known form and organisation to another form equally known to us, e.g. from animals to humans, and vice versa. It would

---

[186] *From one being or soul to another, after death.*   [187] *Fr. Mainsprings.*

be even more general and remarkable: it would be a journey from one cosmos and universe to another, entirely different from the previous one, and from one organisation to a completely different one, for which our mind has no concept yet and for which our language has no expressions.

27. The very intensity of this new life's impressions would also explain why we no longer remember anything at all of our state prior to our present human life although we would profit from it to the extent that, through the use of our reason thus obtained, through the enhanced capacity to make analogical deductions, we could infer that prior state with the greatest confidence even though its mode and exact nature are concealed from us due to the powerful effects of our current life until they are awakened again in the future by whatever means this may occur.

28. Furthermore, if everything we sense and know does not lead into the inside of things, but is merely the result of the influence of things outside us upon us beings organised in such a manner and no other, it inevitably follows that there is a twofold truth: one which shows the intrinsic side of things, the objective absolute of beings and forces outside us, and a second showing the effect of this inner objective upon us beings organised thus, upon our receptivity; and this latter truth is not absolute but relative, as it varies according to its basis, and it is as diverse as the organisation and susceptibility of all beings; although originating therefrom, it does not lead to the inside of things, but merely determines how something appears and how it would appear under these circumstances, with this receptivity; being as real as actuality for us, it forms the foundation of all our arts and sciences and, for this reason, they also are relative; they have to yield along with their basis, a different organisation and receptivity; and in this respect they are only as eternal, necessary and immutable as their basis. For the deaf there is neither harmony nor language; for the blind there are neither colours nor paintings. If all men were born deaf and blind, what would our sciences, arts and philosophy be like? Or our legislation? Every new additional sense is a revelation of nature, a means for new knowledge and experiences, a deeper insight into the inside of beings. But this knowledge cannot be the very inside of these beings, because it is appears differently through different senses, because it is not recognised by all organisations known to us, and because it is still uncertain what can be recognised by other organisations that are still unknown to us. If we accept the premise that space, matter, extension, and the body are something real and that they exist in and of themselves, then a great

many direct and indirect conclusions, and entire systems and sciences [follow] from this premise as their basis, and must also be true and correct in as much as they are consequences of this premise, just as the rules of chess are the necessary results of the properties arbitrarily assigned to each chess piece. However, just as these rules have to change if the properties assigned to the various chess pieces are changed, so the truth of our sensory experiences, along with our conclusions drawn from them, must also change with our senses and premises. They may change in whatever way, and yet the resulting experiences are always true and self-evident since it is the very purpose and destiny of these hidden forces to induce, through their influence on such an organisation, these conclusions, inferences and thoughts, just as their influence on another organisation will lead to different results. They are all true as long as we infer no more than the nature of things and the laws of influence permit and if we do not conclude that we perceive the same things under different conditions, that experiences made in this state can also be applied to other states; that a blind man can conceptualise a rose or colour, or that beings without the sense of sight also have concepts for the beauty or ugliness of things. And thus, even though illness as such may be no more than appearance, I would have no less cause to seek help, because it incidentally contains a factual element which inevitably affects me in this manner under these conditions, but differently under others, perhaps even pleasantly: I still require the effect I find disagreeable to be relieved, for appearance to be relieved by appearance, whether the pain is illusory or real. As long as we are organised in this way, and our current nature is such that we seek out pleasant states and avoid and flee unpleasant ones, then its effects remain unpleasant. All relative truths are valid only to the extent that invisible forces outside us, in this situation and in these certain conditions, manifest themselves in this way in beings of this organisation while manifesting themselves differently in others.

29. However, if relative truth is determined by the diversity of organisations, it must also be guided by their number. Among these there is one that is general, natural, and consistent for humanity. Our present logic accepts as true what we derive by it alone; it considers everything else as flawed, perhaps for the same reason that a man with a straight gait mocked in the land of the lame[188]. It provides the foundation for the totality of our knowledge as well as our concepts of ugliness and beauty, of virtue and vice. We even apply without discrimination

---

[188] *Allusion to the poem 'Das Land der Hinkenden' (1746) by Christian Fürchtegott Gellert (1715-1769).*

the concepts derived from it to worlds that we believe to exist, whose nature is heterogeneous from ours; we assign them to differently-constituted beings and, driven by the pride natural to us and the inability to think of anything better, we call a dearth of *our own* concepts imperfection, and if we want to distinguish beings of a higher order we merely equip them with a higher degree of our own perfections, thereby succumbing to the most glaring inconsistencies in assigning will and intellect to beings we consider incorporeal; we believe that a tree must be a tree for everyone, just because we ourselves perceive it as one, thus ascribing identical results to different causes. It is [this truth] that seduces us into holding that which we do not fully understand as impossible, and to think that a paradox here must also be paradoxical there even though the underlying premises and everything else are different. It is the basis of everything we can know. From it we derive our idea of space, structure, extension, shape, body, and matter; these collected ideas become the premises on which we base our conclusions, on which we establish and develop entire systems, sciences, and arts; through them, we characterise things outside us by odour, taste, colour, warmth, coldness, rest, and motion, and from them we derive our understanding of size, beauty, and ugliness. But if the supposition, our comprehensive capacity of sensation – our premises, experiences, and senses – is changed, then everything ceases to be cold or warm, great or small, beautiful or ugly, true or false. For in addition to this general and consistent organisation there are also certain others, natural and artificial ones, like exceptions to the rule by which an object viewed by everyone else in one way can be seen from a different vantage-point, thus prompting unusual sensations by which new and unique truths are discovered.

30. These new, scarcer and unique organisation[s] are thus the source of a second, relative truth. It is not perceived by the general human organisation, but is induced by microscopic vision, jaundice[189] and other similar conditions. The differently-organised majority calls it: *a flaw, an infirmity, an illusion, an optical deception, a disease.* To the majority this condition is very much what that same majority's knowledge is to more highly-organised beings, because to these beings our general human modes of sensation are likewise faulty. However this mode of seeing and knowing is in no way *falsehood, error, or deception.* It would be false if one were to see yellow with eyes of the same structure that others see red or green with, but seeing yellow with jaundiced eyes is natural, truthful, and perfect.

---

[189] *Jaundice can lead to xanthopsia, a type of colour-blindness in which everything looks yellowish.*

Anyone who judges according to the true sensations of such a peculiar and rare organisation is right, and speaks the truth, because he judges as he senses, and our judgements also are generated by our sensations. If all men were organised like that, and if the structure of most eyes was microscopic, this mode of seeing would be general and true, and our current mode would then be unusual and irregular; and although this individual would be just as correct and true in his perceptions and judgements according to his mode of vision as are all others who see and judge according to their own particular modes, it would still be necessary for this so-called flaw in him to be corrected – not because it is a flaw as such but because this flaw is not a general one; because others will think, judge and act based on their own sensations, which are very different to his; and because this mode is necessary for our felicity, conceiving of things in the same way as men generally do. If these anomalies, these irregular modes of sensation did not exist, it would also be impossible for men to discover the higher, ontological, relative truth. They would not know that the same object must appear differently to different senses; they would think that their own sensation, their own mode of perception, leads to the inside of things or may even be that inside itself; in which case it would be impossible even for the most skilled thinker to escape from this illusion. Yet the more such artificial or natural organisations there are that we are able to experience ourselves or [of which we] at least hear, see, or read about in the accounts of those who actually experience them, the more means we obtain to escape from this misconception, to discover new qualities previously unknown to us, something that is universal and real, that brings us closer to the matter; to see our previously made experiences confirmed even in other forms or to see them disappear, to experience ourselves whether or not something is more than mere appearance to these senses of ours, whether this beautiful face will retain its charm even under microscopic eyes? It is only through jaundice, the telescope, the microscope, every individual mode of perception, natural or artificial, that we are induced to make the great and important discovery that our senses do not in any way lead us to the inside of things; that, along with our receptivity, the representation and form of things outside us will change, too. Every time such a new mode of seeing, natural or artificial, emerges and becomes known it is a most important and valuable contribution to our current higher knowledge. Nature reveals herself with every natural spectacle.

31. This however gives rise to a third and new relative truth, the highest possible order of knowledge, namely the possibility of confirming an experience

undergone, a way of seeing in order to compare with another experience undergone in a different organisation; to determine what is *factual* in a thing, what is true only for some senses but not for others. Most certainly such a truth, which is recognised not only through the general way of seeing but is also recognised, directly or indirectly, by all organisations known to us, must be accorded a higher degree of certainty and reliability. This is the kind of truth that we call ontological.

32. This ontological truth is where general and special organisations, natural and artificial ones, converge; it is not perceived differently by any general or special organisation, be it jaundice, the telescope, microscope or a plain, concave, or convex mirror. But although it is certain and superior when compared to the two aforementioned relative truths, it too remains a relative one; indeed, it is far from absolute; it is very possible that some or even most of its propositions will not be confirmed by the discovery of a new organisation but will seem illusory instead. It is true and is a higher degree of truth only as long as all things and experiences remain as they currently are. Although of a higher order it is still human knowledge; only death can and shall reveal how much of it can stand the test, what will happen when everything is faced with this new, emerging organisation, and which new properties of things we shall thus discover, and even that shall be far from conclusive. To discover many properties of beings that remain hidden, to experience new manifestations of these invisible forces, it will be necessary to die many times over. Every death is a leap into new light, into a new life.

33. These ontological truths are the foundation of our knowledge, the *rectificatorium*[190] of our senses and all appearances; they are the infallible criteria by which we determine if something is mere appearance; they are the guideline to which we must adhere in our state of uncertainty and illusion, the solid ground on which we stand, and the point from where we set out. Only these truths enable us even to look into the past and the near future. They are the first principles of our understanding.

34. If however nothing can be counted among these ontological truths except that which can be confirmed by all organisations known to us or which is a direct, unquestionable result thereof, the following examples should be included, because with all organisations it is true and confirmed:

1) That something exists. Things only differ from one another in their

---

[190] Lat. *Rectification*.

mode of existence.

2) That I exist, and am active.

3) That I do not always stay the same; that I am being changed.

4) That things outside me are real too.

5) That these things are not all the same, but diverse and of several types.

6) That these things outside me act upon me.

7) That these things remain the same, as I remain the same, when they induce the same kind of change in me.

8) That they and I are different if they induce a different change in me.

9) That these same things appear to me differently if I am changed or if my organs are.

10) That, therefore, since these things appear to me differently depending on my changed organs, they are not in themselves as they appear to me.

11) That therefore, with changed organs, the same thing will appear to me differently.

12) That thereby, they are something, certainly not merely an idea.

13) That there are things that cannot exist in and of themselves; they are real only in and through others, and they are not real without them.

14) That, consequently, there must be things that are real, although we have no sensation of them with any of our senses.

15) That extension, composition, matter, body, and shape cannot be counted among this last class of things.

16) That other autonomous things must be concealed within this matter and composition.

17) That these are the basis of all activity[,] of the phenomenon known as matter, and [of] composition.

18) That these are the hidden forces which cause the appearances within us.

19) That, therefore, all [matter, all extension, all] composition is appearance.

20) That if the form, figure, and composition of something is changed, these inner forces also change.

21) that, furthermore, we are able to prompt this inner change of forces if we reproduce the same causes under which the [same] change of form and figure has previously occurred.

22) that, therefore, similar causes [prompt] similar results, and similar results [require] similar causes.

23) that there is something permanent inside me which is constantly being modified.

24) that my body, being a composite, is not this permanent object.

25) that therefore, my self and my body are not the same.

35. All these truths are and will always be of a fundamentally sensory nature. However, they come closer to the matter as it actually is because they are confirmed by several organisations, or because such confirmed propositions are immediate or remote but correct conclusions. These ontological truths can be subject to correction or supplementation as our knowledge of new organisations enables us to learn whether or not they are confirmed by these organisations, and if new rules and correlations are hereby discovered. In essence they are suitable only for persons or beings that can experience and compare different organisations and then draw further conclusions from their comparisons. The dominion of truth is expanded with every new sense and with every experience of a new organisation, just as the sphere of knowledge of a man with five senses must be incomparably larger than it would be if he only had one.

In man alone several such organisations can be found. A man whose only sense is touch would have an entirely different, almost non-existent body of knowledge. It is different again for someone with only:

touch and taste

touch and smell

[touch and] hearing

[touch and] sight.

Each of these persons has his own method of conceptualising objects outside himself, one that is different from ours; he is more or less in a position to compare and abstract.

It is different again for men with only the senses of

touch, smell, taste,

[touch, smell,] hearing,

touch, smell, sight,

[touch,] taste, hearing,

[touch, taste,] sight,

[touch,] hearing, sight.

And again different for persons with only 4 senses, such as:

touch, smell, taste, hearing,

touch, smell, taste, sight,

touch, taste, sight, hearing,

touch, smell, sight, hearing.

However, it is most complete for those who have all 5 senses and, in addition, the means to enhance them artificially. Every man with this number of senses has his own organisation compared with others. And it is well worth the effort to explore and determine the philosophy and sphere of concepts in each of these men, if it is at all humanly possible to resolve these concepts: to learn what and how much each sense contributes to each idea, and thus to dissolve the complexity of our ideas into its components. Only this would make it possible to reliably determine the degree of education, religion, ethics, legislation, and perfectibility that each of these organisations could achieve. The relative nature and development of our concepts would then appear in full certainty and strength.

36. However, no matter how grand and noble these ontological truths may be, no matter how much our ability to gather and understand them may be a testament to our nature's higher dignity, we are still incapable of knowing the inside of things, of knowing the absolute truth.

37. Absolute truth is that which is, in and of itself, intrinsic to something. It is the invisible force we perceive only through its effects, affecting differently organised beings in different ways. It is not for these senses, this form, this world, or for men. It is never subject to change. This force will always be force; it is always active, affecting different subjects in different ways according to their ability to suffer it, according to their receptivity. Thereby, it becomes the foundation and source of our relative truth. This is all we know about it.

38. Absolute truth is for God alone. God knows the forces and nature of things. Creatures base their judgements on the effects of these forces, how they appear to them, how they reveal themselves to them. From this they draw conclusions about the cause and characteristics of this hidden force, its reality. That is why God does not perceive the acts of men *as such*. For this, He would need to have senses and bodies similar to ours. He perceives them to be the effects of these forces observable only to Him. In and of themselves and to God, there is no space, time, motion, body, extension, earth, and men, just as He seems to know neither heat nor cold, darkness, light, or colour, nor beauty or ugliness. Therefore, the divine mind, will, freedom, goodness, and justice are mere anthropomorphisms. With these, we turn God into a man and convert the infinite into the finite.

II. *Philosophi.* Sages

You who are seeking peace of mind, come hither! We want to reconcile you with the world; we want to lead you towards felicity and teach you the great art of finding joy in all worldly matters and all the occurrences of life. The things surrounding you, hitherto the reasons for your discontent, shall lose their ugliness: that which is ugly shall become pleasant to you, the small shall become great, and many things that you dislike shall become desirable.

Wisdom is the only path to pleasure, serenity, and felicity. Come hither! We want to teach you – wisdom.

If you wish to be a wise man, you must know that while men call a purpose everything that is the object of their desires and efforts, there is nonetheless an infinite number of these purposes equal to that of our wishes and desires; that for this reason they contradict one another quite frequently, and it is impossible to achieve them all at the same time; that consequently, not all are equally good and legitimate, some of them being higher and others lower, and some more universal; that in order to determine the quality and value of these purposes, one of them must be the one that is the highest and most universal, all other high and low purposes being either simply means or even obstacles to it; that these limited purposes then cease to be called such; that man's true wisdom must be concerned only with these latter and most general ones and the subordination of the others; and, finally, that our true wisdom and understanding lie in our ability to view many purposes that were once very important to us as mere means; which entails that our entire capacity of desire, our judgement about the value of all things outside us and, at the same time, all previous causes of pleasure and displeasure change in such a manner that the latter must be decreased and the former greatly increased.

Hence, our perspective and position are the only source of our lesser or greater pleasure and satisfaction. Our serenity and felicity depend on them, and they expand or reduce along with them. – Only a man who is thus wise can determine what in the world is truly great or small, just or unjust, good or evil, ugly or beautiful, true or false, worthy of desire or despite. Without an understanding of the subordination of purposes, by which they all turn into means to a single end, a man's judgements will be skewed, his desires foolish, his designs vain and wavering, his prudence uncertain, and he will run be in danger of succumbing to the very evil that he is seeking to escape. His means of salvation become his doom, and what he believes to be his doom is a means to his salvation. Just as anyone who has never seen anything greater and more beautiful regards the village beauty as a Venus and the river or brook running nearby as an ocean, so all our judgements about the world and its parts bear the visible imprint of our slothful thinking, our ignorance, and our short-sightedness.

This loftiest and noblest purpose is the sole standpoint from which man should survey the world. It is the place that suddenly turns your giants into dwarfs, showing you previously unpleasant things in another and better regard and quality; it changes your understanding and, consequently, your capacity for desire; it turns evil into good, and good into evil; it removes the mask from that which is ugly, multiplies pleasure, and changes this world, previously so invidious to your eyes, into an Elysium. Until now you have seen everything through tinted glass, chased soap-bubbles, and mistaken the hill on which your village church stands for the world's highest mountain, because this was your highest vantage-point, because you stood in the wrong place. Now stand here, where we are standing, and cast your gaze into the world once more – and marvel! A different, new, more majestic world! – Your fatherland is like a grain of sand to your eye, Europe like a mole hill; the grand and earth-shaking affairs of our continent and the bustle of mankind are reduced to the hurried frenzy of an anthill; they lose themselves almost completely in the immense chain of the universe, like a drop of water in the oceans of the world. Now look how your torment is changed to joy, the great into the small and unnoticeable, and your hell into a Heaven. Was it this small, almost unnoticeable thing that brought you worry and restlessness? that drew your entire soul towards it? Could this minute thing, even if it were the anthill called Europe, really stir you to sow discord among your own kind? awaken raging anger and a tempest in your soul, thus eradicating that heavenly bliss? Miserable man! how little is the thing that angers you so! and on the other hand, how grand, how infinite is that towards which you are so indifferent and careless? – Rise up then, if you can, higher and higher, to where we are. This ascent, this universalising of your perspective, is the mountain or the great ladder to pleasure, that the elect climbs from here below all the way up to the deity, to felicity, because as he reaches greater heights with each step, he discovers more and more of a previously unknown land of joy and pleasure far beneath him. What seemed too ugly and improper to him down below receives its proper measure and proportion only from these heights; and when in this higher and higher ascent even the sun finally appears as a mere spark, then what will become of you, your wishes and desires? O, then be ashamed of your pride, your imagined majesty and greatness! You have spent your whole life sitting in those depths, believing yourself to be in the heights, disparaging everything that happens down there, being too lazy to free yourself and rise above. You even disparaged us, miserable scoffer! that we from high up, the top of the tower, to which you never dared to climb, proclaimed to you a most majestic view of a more beautiful land: for this you call us fools and dreamers, you laugh at our simple-mindedness and inexperience, that we sell to the world dreams we concocted in quiet nightly chambers by lamp-light as truths, glossing over the suffering and misfortunes of mankind with an overwrought imagination! – Awaken from your slumber, take heart, and arise unto us; or if you do not want this, then at least cease to defame the world. It is the work of God, and he who reproaches and blasphemes it also reproaches and blasphemes his creator as well as yours. You most certainly do not see the world as it is, but only as one can see it from your standpoint and through the glass tinted by your wishes; and this standpoint is too dear to you to abandon. If however you should make the effort, we will show you the land where ugliness becomes beauty and seeming disorder becomes the most orderly concordance. – We want to show you that you, your family, your home town, your fatherland, and even this earth are merely steps and periscopes by which one looks into the world and the city of God. We even want to show you that you and your entire race also are only subordinate means to a higher purpose. That you, who are impertinent enough to call yourself the purpose of creation, that you and the entire human race, as well as the lowest thing, are not the purpose, but only a part of that inexhaustible nature, just as you and your family are a subordinate part of civil society.

Everything in the world is standpoint; and it is this standpoint that directs the hearts and minds of men, in joy as well as in suffering. Joy dwells above us, in higher realms, and from there suffering descends into the middle and lowest regions. And yet, since everything is standpoint, only one standpoint can be the authentic one, from which one can survey all things in their true location. Not too close and not too far, not too high and not too low; all this modifies our felicity and our judgements of matters that are outside us and affect us.

You little, unsightly mite! which I could destroy – you too are thus one of my fellow creatures in the grand ladder and chain of nature. Beings of my kind have told me you are small, weak, and insignificant; because you neither fight and win battles, nor lay siege to cities, nor make small entries in heavy folios, nor understand the art of using the hands of millions as the means to achieve your desires, nor keep your neighbours small and make yourself great at their expense. Therefore, they, and I with them, have called you small, weak, and insignificant. And should I be just as much a tool and an instrument as you are? I, the king of nature! For whose sake everything exists! – But you would not be here if you were not just this. We think you small because we compare you to us, and think your shape unsightly and your powers limited because they are not ours. – But have I ever myself been a worm, so that I may know your inner and outer workings? Just as you and everything that is and is not human have no immediate experience with the inner workings of the other, and are therefore unable to imagine what powers and abilities are hidden in this or that configuration. This difference in your shape to mine may mean that what happens inside you does not occur in man; but it does not therefore prove that nothing better might ever occur inside you. Perhaps it is nobler to be a mite, and perhaps being human may even be a humiliation, if it were possible that any station in this creation could be humiliating.

How does man know he is exalted over all other creatures? Because he knows himself better than all others? Yet what then will prevent other beings, lesser in his regard, from drawing similar conclusions about their own importance? Since when is the incapacity to place oneself in another's position proof of our own superiority? Is it truly a universally accepted and established fact that man is the highest of all creatures? Where is the evidence that is proof only for us and not for others? – May it suffice that we are flattered by this judgement, that although it may not be an expression of truth, it is indeed one of our pride, desires, and vanity: that the logic and philosophy of the crowd contain flattery and lies against us and conclusions founded on and drawn from them. – But the sage does not think thus. He who alone judges truthfully and correctly determines the value of each and every thing not by its relationship to foolish wishes but by its ability to contribute to, by the way it aims at the universal beatitude of all beings and at the revelation of the greatness of its creator: he finds that every living thing bears the signature and imprint of deity. We do, you do, and so does the lowest insect and the smallest grain of dust. Do not sin against this, move nothing from its place; or indeed destroy and move regardless, because wherever you may move it, it will always be in the place assigned to it by providence and the arrangement of the world.

But our instruction should not go this far today: that hour has not yet come for you; let us rather descend again into the lower regions, remain on the earth, and observe the course of world events.

'Where will all this lead? – Whither does nature work? – Whither all needs, all human activity? – Is the present linked to the past, and both to the future? – Do all world events converge to a single point? Or are they isolated facts? – If all is development, by what laws does nature evolve?'

Examine the past, compare it to the present, and you will find the future.

Turn the past into the future; pretend as if all this had not yet happened, but had yet to happen. Consider what would happen according to these past and present circumstances handed to us by history, and you will understand the great art of being a prophet of the past, and if you wish to become a prophet of the future, this exercise must come first. It is by such exercises, by examining history and actual events, that seers educate themselves. Always keep in mind, however, that nothing in the world occurs without cause and preparation, that everything therein is merely the development of a primitive, God-given disposition: that in this first event in the history of the world, in this first development of powers there lies the reason why, among so many other possibilities, only this result became visible: that the third and fourth, as well as all other future, past, and present events are equally important consequences of this original disposition: that with a different primitive disposition, the entire succession of the world and all its parts would have changed; that consequently, this single original given contains, directly or indirectly, the foundation for the entire, most distant future; that everything is intimately linked with every other simultaneous, preceding, and coming event; that there are no small, and much less great, isolated facts; that nature's infinite wealth and resources will not permit her to repeat herself merely under a different name; that her certain progress from the smallest to the slightly bigger continues by way of imperceptible graduations without making any leap; that for this very reason, each of her preceding states is a rehearsal, so to speak, for bringing forth another, better state; and that with her, in the most infinite diversity, an astonishing unity prevails throughout.

In the light of these principles, confirmation of which any impartial observer can find in nature herself, you will consequently notice that our needs are the great driving wheel by which God and nature set and keep us and all creatures into motion; that, since all our pain and discontent are themselves needs, they are a blessing of God and nature; that without them, we would be miserable and wholly incapable of feeling pleasure; that only by these are we incited to activity and to the development of our mental faculties; that, for this very reason, we are happier and more perfect than animals, because most of our needs are less direct but more artificial, needs that must be satisfied by more circuitous endeavours; that by this alone we are also incited to consider the future, to make plans and, by thus occupying our mind, to find even in the most sensual creatures more than just means for the satisfaction of our bodily needs, seeing them also as means for perfecting our spirit and honouring our higher and subtler nature.[191]

Thus, you will see that man will always find something missing or lacking in his felicity, and that our very finiteness is perfection, because it leads to perfection. You will see that these needs were not so frequent during the origins of the human race and that, for this very reason, man had to be incomparably more imperfect at that time; that the unpleasant aspects of each need stirred the spirit of invention and became the stuff for exercising and developing the mind's power; that with each invention of means the human race necessarily achieved improvement; but that every need, by the unbelievable activity of our mind, immediately awakens another new need, which is then satisfied by some other invention, thus initiating yet another need that must be satisfied; that the history of the human race is thus the history of needs incrementally engendering one another, of the inventions to which they have given rise, and of the entire human race's ever-increasing degree of perfection inextricably connected with this process. Thus, you will also find that it is an easily proven fact, despite the lack of solid history and information, that our race must have begun at the lowest step; that, in its youth, the earth must have been in a state of extreme imperfection; that this imperfection decreases every day, with nature striving towards improvement and perfection, and that it is unphilosophical to believe that the earth and the human race are incapable of a degree of perfection higher than their current state – that it is impossible for a thing the very essence of which is continuous growth to suddenly halt its progress towards improvement, or even to regress.

Thus, if the world is constantly striving towards improvement, perfection, and enlightenment, then he who wishes to prevent this must find in God and nature the most terrible enemies to his purpose. Any endeavour of this kind is bound to destroy itself over the course of time, for it has carried the seed of its own destruc-

---

[191] *Weishaupt would elaborate on these thoughts in his philosophical dialogues Apologie des Misvergnügens und des Uebels (1787).*

tion in its first beginnings. Such an endeavour can only be encountered in the world and the city of God in order to nourish the pressure and, through this, the need to rally our powers to remove this obstacle and to bring about more suitable associations. This easily demonstrates that anything that is based on folly, super-stition, obscurity, and the mere opinion of man must eventually cease to exist and yield to wiser and better institutions; that these better institutions have nothing to fear, for God and nature are their great allies; and that all the world's obstacles will themselves only be tools to make them all the finer, wiser, and more enduring.

The kingdom of truth alone shall be eternal and indestructible.

It will further become apparent that any error, no matter how great, is the very *nisus*[192] and approach towards truth. That human opinions, just like everything else, run their own course from their earliest beginnings, one having sprung from another, and that the entire sequence of opinions being born of one another is based on a certain primitive idea and cause which has kept recurring in many variations and modifications until it became, in our present time, our current way of thinking; that every degree of culture and every more or less prevalent popular opinion is accompanied by its very own correlating morals, religion, and government, which are all subject to change. This must seem even more won-drous when it becomes apparent that the national and human enlightenment of every general non-scientific culture is always ultimately based on the greater or lesser number of men in a people, and that it waxes and wanes with this number. At all times poorly populated countries were also behind in culture and enlight-enment, and they increased in the latter as their populations also increased; to this day, entire nations, and especially the capital cities, serve as a living proof of this fact. Population growth is accompanied by a dearth of income, causing more than one to yearn for the same fruit; it has thus led to rivalry, with the effect that this fruit became the stronger man's reward at the expense of the weaker; this has taught the latter that strength has its benefits, has awakened in them the need to have the same strength, has taught them that a man may be stronger than other individual men but not stronger than all others, and, to this end, it has brought forth alliances and counter-alliances in addition to the measurement and valua-tion of strength. In a word, it has awakened the desire to be stronger than all others.

---

[192] *Lat. Effort.*

If the growing number of people has brought about the creation of human societies, then all further and more remote development that is the essential consequence of every societal union and could scarcely be envisioned without the further and greater proliferation of man must also be its consequence. By leading to a dearth of sustenance, a growing population has turned savages and hunters into shepherds and herdsmen, herdsmen into ploughmen, and finally ploughmen into citizens, tradesmen, and cultivated men.

More people require more and greater sustenance; the need for sustenance awakens industry and with it, the spirit of invention, and the arts. Industry is followed by surplus, and surplus creates trade.

Since trade inevitably creates great wealth, and since no one can become rich without increasing the poverty and destitution of others, trade has also caused the inequality of wealth and, with it, luxury, effeminacy, dependency, venality, moral decay, and rule by oppression on the one hand, and servitude on the other. These factors lead to the diminution and emigration of the best and most industrious inhabitants; this in turn causes a neighbour's growth and, over time, the proportional and purposeful decay of one country after the other causes the common culture to be disseminated through all the nations on the face of the earth along with the migrating population, by and by wresting all men from savagery without the once-cultured nations regressing towards savagery after their decline. Everything that happens, all the greater and lesser events on this our earth, the love for money, the inclination towards sensuality, even despotism and intolerance, everything serves this purpose and is therefore interwoven into the great sequence and chain of things to gradually populate the half-deserted earth, thus elevating it to culture, and driving men into foreign and as yet uncultivated climes.

Culture and populations travel from east to west, through temperate climates, because this is best suited to the sustenance and reproduction of men. They only push towards the icy mountain ranges of the north or the searing noon when the temperate zones can no longer contain such a number of people, or when north and south are the only regions in the world open to emigration.

Culture and populations travelled from Asia to Greece, from there to Italy, with Roman arms and Christianity to Gaul and Germania, and with the Romans and Saracens to the farthest regions of Spain. When all these areas and the rest of the north had grown to be respectable and flourishing kingdoms, nature opened up a new venue for man's spirit of migration, a new, immense refuge – and

America was discovered. To lure men from their homelands to this immense, sparsely-populated land she had also endowed it with unfathomable treasures which appealed to human avarice and selfishness and encouraged people to settle and found colonies there.

Already with the first planters the attachment to the mother country began diminishing, and with their growth the awareness of their own power also grew, decreasing the appetite for continued dependency. They understood how impossible and inadequate it would be to keep such an immense land, so far away and under such a different sky, in eternal obedience to the motherland. One's own power, the high probability of success, and man's natural instinct and desire for independence and liberty must eventually bring about the courageous resolution to cut the ties with the motherland and live by one's own laws.

According to the course of nature it is safe to assume that these ties may be cut soon; and as soon as this bold endeavour will have attained its intended purpose and success, the pressure on the working classes inevitably (as it were) exerted by standing armies and the increasing luxury and debauchery at the courts as well as, on the one hand, the despotism shown towards better, nobler men and, on the other, a foreseen advantage and the love of freedom and independence will transplant herds of men, and with them culture, to America. Any laws against emigration will only strengthen the urge and desire to emigrate. Emigration itself will be handled with greater sophistication, and the exchange business will ease the transfer of property. – The more languid and more oppressed American south will eventually follow the example of the northerners, or else will become their prey. In the meantime, the latter will penetrate into the country's interior, though encountering great difficulties at first: they will fell forests, root them out and dry out swamps, temper the climate, till the earth, multiply on their allotted lands and, due to their growing population and the resulting obstacles, move towards the south, north, and west, all the way to the great ocean, and establish trading-posts there from which they will travel to Japan, China, and all the islands as well as India. Meanwhile Europe, weakened by the loss of money, men, and culture to America, must preserve itself by adopting a milder form of government or, in search of compensation, must gather her remaining forces and push forward towards weak Asia and Africa to make these beautiful regions of the world, this cradle of humanity, these motherlands of our first knowledge which fell into decay for our sake, receptive to a higher culture and to return to them with compound interest the knowledge and men we so benevolently received from them in times past. The latter will of course never be the expressly-stated purpose. The desire for expansion, so natural to the great men of the earth, will mean that everyone will fall upon his weaker neighbour and advance for as long as he encounters no resistance, and far enough that the consequence will be – nature availing herself of this lust for conquest as her tool – that the more beautiful regions of the earth are wrested from barbarism, that gentler morals are introduced, the culture is elevated, and any opposing obstacles based on the national religion and despotism are destroyed. Certainly those nations will be and remain in a state of oppression at first: for their own benefit they will have to suffer the conqueror treating them according to his advantage and intentions until they become more acquainted with their own true benefits in the course of time through the growth of culture and population, and until their new overlords, either due to over-expansion or to riches from trade and the resulting moral decay and effeminacy, will descend into a state of impotence, becoming too feeble to maintain their hold on such distant conquests, and new kingdoms will therefore arise from their ruins and ashes.

Here then, culture would have completed its first voyage around the world, bringing all men separated by the seas and deserts closer to one another, having fulfilled its first intention of purging savagery from the earth by the increase in population, and it would then embark on its second voyage in order to fully erase any remaining barbarism and moral savagery, again using the same means for this purpose, a second, intensive multiplication of the human race, to spread an even higher degree of culture and morality all over the world. – If you study this fact diligently, you will find that men will only then reach their fullest happiness and enlightenment when the earth's population is at its greatest. Because all emigration will then cease due to the lack of desolate and vacant places while the population continues to grow, and because many people are forced to inhabit a small stretch of land, great property belonging to a single family will be divided into smaller parcels and fall into the hands of several families, so that it will be used more industriously. This will make it impossible for any man to further sustain himself by sloth and mere prejudice. The inequality of wealth will necessarily decline: even the value of its symbolic equivalents will drop, because the sale of real property becomes impossible, and with the decrease in affluence trade itself will also cease. The entire foundation for power and dependency, with all their [deplorable] consequences and moral corruption, must disappear along with the inequality of goods.

Since the number of men is large but the earthly realm is not inexhaustible, one man can no longer profit from the labour of twenty. Moderation, contentment, and frugality must become the general morals of mankind. They will bring about independence, abstinence from coveting the property of another, general morality, and universal peace. When a man's wages and burden of work are moderate, fear of boredom causes the needs of the spirit to be more general, urgent, and frequent. The whole earth becomes a garden, and nature has at last completed her day's work here below, bringing permanent enlightenment, peace, and felicity together with the greatest possible number of men: she has anointed every man as his own judge, priest, and king; has turned the often-ridiculed tale of the golden age, mankind's favourite idea of old, into a reality by discreetly removing the eternal inequality of wealth, which has been ineffectively combated by all lawgivers and has always has crept back in, and which is the source of the decay of all nations, and the root of servitude, tyranny, and disunity among men, of venality and moral corruption, making it forever impossible through the excessive growth of the human population.

If indeed this happy state, this patriarchal way of life, is an essential result of the highest degree of mankind's growth, and if one can properly substantiate through death and birth tables – even in the face of an absurd number of celibates, of widespread depravity and weakening of virility, of intolerance and despotism, of the still very common lack of experience among physicians especially where childhood illnesses are concerned, of all the hazards of the sea and of war, of debauchery, indulgence, and contagious diseases, in an age when lewd excesses and the ruining of oneself and of others is taken for sophistication, when decency, sobriety, chastity, and morality are branded and ridiculed as folly, naiveté, and unworldliness – that the human race is still increasing in spite of such circumstances and in such an age; if indeed experience shows that the depopulation caused by war and pestilence is quickly replenished and, beyond this, that the obstacles to repopulation must be reduced by increasing morality and humanity; if that is so, then what stops us from saying that nature is already working to attain this state, and that all her endeavours, for good or ill, are the most reliable means to reach it? And furthermore, if it cannot be denied that due to an overly growing population the hunter and herdsman class developed into ploughmen, and these in turn into civil society and its corresponding culture, why should nature suddenly come to a standstill here and not use the continuously growing population to create something else, new conditions with its new corresponding culture? Why should the effect not be similar if the same cause remains in force? Because the former is a fact, no one doubts it, but only because the future has not yet happened it seems impossible to us, even though the past teaches us otherwise[.]

The objections that may be raised against this population doctrine are mainly based on the assumption that the population will grow beyond all bounds and measures, and is therefore harmful and detrimental to the purpose we have outlined above.

However, before the population grows to excess it will come to a standstill on its own. As soon as there is a lack of sustenance, fewer marriages are made. Furthermore, it will be deemed more sensible and useful to enter into marriages at a more mature age. Every father will restrict his children's freedom to marry if the yield of his property is no longer sufficient, and every son will acquiesce in this all the more easily as he understands the impracticality of acting otherwise. Neither is there any reason to fear that an excessive population will cause its own decimation from infectious diseases, for before that point is reached the science of medicine will be founded on more detailed and reliable principles. Industrious, carefree, moderate, cleanly people living at proper distances from one another enjoy the open air more frequently than people who live tightly squeezed in our cities with all their foul evaporations, where entire social classes make a living off human misery and the sources of our diseases, resisting any reasonable provisions aimed at prolonging our lives with all their might. What is more, once the earth's surface has been turned into a garden, the climate will also change. Admittedly, if everything were to remain as it is now, this objection would be stronger. But are all changes in the world merely superficial? Or are all things not connected, interwoven, and intertwined? Change a single part of the world, whichever part you like, and all other parts will immediately rearrange themselves accordingly: they fill the gap and quickly restore the lost equilibrium. Nature comes to the aid of men in their short-sightedness to awaken the proportionate need in everyone at that very moment, and then, by instinct alone, everyone does what reason and general, express, or tacit cooperation would be too slow or impotent to accomplish. – Do not worry, therefore, for nature keeps watch, and she has provided for all things. Not everything whose feasibility we do not understand is impossible. Too accustomed to the forms and institutions of today we judge the whole future by them: at this time, we cannot trace and predict the sequence of needs that prepares us for this until finally, having passed through the intermediate steps, we reach the goal at last only to be amazed or, which is more likely, to find that what we have deemed impossible was actually very natural. Most people are too dull and sluggish in their thinking: they only want to see and feel and, therefore, decry everything that is not the immediate object of their senses and of factual origin as dreams, fantasy, and vain enthusiasm. They merely want to feel, grasp, and see – and who among us has hands with which he can reach into the future?

Therefore, he who populates the world has thereby played his part in the progress of culture and in the perfection and felicity of his race. Nature has excluded no l[i]ving creature from this ability to contribute. Either with insight and talent or even with the most sensual of instincts, everyone is capable of making reason prevail and of promoting the welfare of the earth. – O! What majesty and honour is it then to be a father! – To see an entire budding people, all of them instruments for attaining human felicity, emerge from these youngsters and little ones about oneself, one's grandchildren, and from one's own loins! to continue living in one's own descendants, living for the benefit of the earth! – O ye all, who are of our alliance, become fathers! fathers of well-bred children! Or if your circumstances and conditions prevent you, then at least join us in our revenge against celibacy, this grand treason against nature and human felicity. – Support marriage and thwart everything that opposes it, and do not desecrate the chastity and perfection of matrimony by setting a poor example; preach tolerance, prevent wars, and eradicate all things that cause death and weaken virility. Procreative instinct! Most sensual, but also noblest of all drives! Antiquity did not misjudge you, revering you in the phallus, the mysteries of Isis and the orgies of Bacchus! And yet our so-called enlightened times have found offence therein! – Not only do you give us animal life, in you we also find the root of man's true spiritual life, his felicity, and the perfection of his nature! – You are also nature's great instrument, and you contain the seed of all, of all past, present, and future events, and the fates of men!

History, the safest of all guides, at least shows that every nation's state of population correlates most exactly to its culture, morals, and form of government: it even proves that savagery resurged whenever depopulation became excessive.

Now be still and examine closely. You will find confirmation of this proposition in those few people who were rescued from the general inundation of the world. You will also find that people who are so heavily terrified procreate very slowly at first, and then proceed to do so in an entirely different manner, that this residual terror creates an exception to the rule in this case, and that culture does not progress at the same pace as the population grows, despite all prior insights. Rather, you will discover that these diluvian terrors affected our miserable second forefathers tremendously, creating such an especially timid, very easily influenced, fearful, gullible, and superstitious way of thinking that they could only produce similar descendants, whose customs and institutions reflect that ancient diluvian terror even in this day and age, directly or indirectly, as in a ceremony of commemoration; who are timorous at every gale, having for thousands of years dreamt up yet another end and destruction of the world, at first daily with every cloudy sky and sunset, then with every lunation, week, month, and, lastly, every year, and then at the end of every natural or artificial, self-configured period and cycle; a dream that, after various modifications made in the course of events, eventually created the doctrine of the millennial kingdom, which in turn instigated the Crusades, and now, strengthened by that ancient legend, sprung from the same source, that the world is six thousand years old, merely slumbers, continuing to simmer under the surface, only to re-emerge, after repeated prior attempts, in full force at the end of this millennium with all the more certainty since the next one, according to the common myth and calendar, will be a *seventh* and therefore a sabbatical millennium.

Or should we imagine that this terrible catastrophe would have had no effect, would not have caused any change at all in the prior, perhaps very enlightened way of thinking of these few people scattered to various parts of the earth's elevated regions where they found refuge? Would this event not necessarily alter their understanding of deity? Or could it even have initiated the doctrine of the principles of good and evil,[193] and with it the inclination to appease the principle of evil or devise means for acquiring its favour? Did not the mountains have to remain the residence and domicile of men for many years? Would not dominion, greed, and inequality of the classes vanish among them? Would not indifference and carelessness towards the present and all temporal things be awakened in people who viewed their stay in these nether regions as temporary and uncertain? Did this not inevitably create the very natural desire to live a life that was more secure against similar, future misfortunes, to make arrangements for dealing with them, to divine the future to this end – oracles, prophets, causing Sibyls to arise, credulity and superstition to spread, every return of the sun to be welcome, its every setting and nightfall to be regarded as evermore terrible? creating astrology,

---

[193] *The idea of a struggle between good and evil, central for Manichaeism.*

Sabeism[194] or the worship of celestial bodies to emerge? – How could such a human race, burdened with such sad experiences and, as a consequence, such a way of thinking have been similar to its forebears? Did it not rather have to become the foundation of an entirely separate race, with its separate institutions, customs, and traditions? Would not this primitive institution be perpetuated even in their most distant descendants even though any accounts of its origin and its purpose were lost to them? Or do customs and traditions change so drastically all at once? Does not our daily experience rather demonstrate that nothing is preserved, barring certain modifications, as perfectly as customs and traditions, living proof of which is the practice of duelling? that opinions, customs, government institutions, and religions also emerge from one another, just as men and languages do? Which colony has ever founded a state whose institutions were not, for the greatest part, borrowed from the motherland? How much in Germany, France, Italy, and Spain is not of Gothic, Frankish, Lombardic, Saracen, and generally of barbaric origin even today? How much is not the palpable consequence of the introduction of a feudal order? – Even in the Christian church, how many traditions, albeit with different explanations and meanings, have not obviously been borrowed from paganism and the Jewish religion? Even our reverence and preference for Jewish customs and cosmogony must be founded on a religion that wholly emerged from the Jewish faith. And how much of this Jewish faith, this mother of ancient Christianity, is not of Egyptian origin, even according to Scripture, and therefore a system that is the necessary result of an even older system, whose roots are ultimately found in the consequences of a renewed human race and its way of thinking after the flood? How much, through an orderly development one from the other, have oriental philosophy, Pythagoras and Plato, Gnosticism and Kabbalah, the Alexandrian School and Aristotle interacted to bring about Christianity with its mystical and allegorical sense?[195] How much has each of the various Christian sects prepared the way for the next one, how much has not one emerged from the other? – Admittedly, the meaning is often lost: indeed, a custom often acquires the opposite meaning from what it originally had, even for the very people where it originated. But that should not deter art and criticism from trying to find the primitive. – However, if all this

---

[194] *Sabianism, the doctrine of the Sabians, an ancient oriental sect that practised the worship of the sun, moon, and stars.*

[195] *The quatuor sensus scripturae are traditionally called the literal, the allegorical, the moral (or tropological), and the anagogical. The one referred to here as the 'mystical' is the anagogical sense.*

appears impossible to you, pray tell me where does that striking conformity in customs among ancient and young nations, both close and very far removed, come from? so remarkably similar that because of the striking similarities between their own customs and those in the Americas, to cite only one recent example, the Jews believed to have found in Mexico and Peru the – certainly very degenerate – descendants of the ten tribes of Israel, taken by Shalmaneser[196] into Assyrian captivity and since then lost to the memory and history of the world.[197] – If all that were nought, whence this otherwise inexplicable and yet clearly proven conformity? – Should it perhaps be proof of a common origin or of an ancient alliance of two or more nations? – However, as much as it may otherwise explain, this way of explanation loses its force if no supporting historical evidence can be found or if, indeed, the opposite can often be proved, and the matter must therefore be resolved in a different, more natural way, one that conforms with the premises of history, in this and no other manner. Wherefore this fiction, cutting the knot yet explaining nothing, of an ancient homeland, a common parentage of all nations on the earth, of one common progenitor, which was invented in support of the biblical Noachic descendence[198] but has been confirmed by no other nation and is indeed impossible? Or could this conformity rather be the consequence of a formerly shared doctrine or teacher? – But if so, then who was this teacher? – God? or a man? Would it not be unphilosophical to ascribe it to a miracle, to a direct revelation of God, as long as not all the natural avenues for solving this riddle have been explored? Not to mention that these conforming customs often contradict true religion or are not important enough to be regarded as the object of an immediate divine revelation! – What if this doctrine were not directly from God? Would it then necessarily be human in origin? But are men the only teachers of men? Is every teaching mere tradition and human invention? What then provided the first opportunity to conceive of this idea, of these doctrines? – Did it have to be just one individual? Is it not possible that several persons could have devised this idea because a similar cause inspired them to it? – Is it not more likely and much more natural that it was the result of shared experiences and observations? Of observations based on an event that must have affected everyone in the same way? – Therefore, could not all this be derived more logically from a certain basic fact that would also have caused a

[196] *Shalmaneser V, king of Assyria from 727 to 722 BC.*

[197] *A theory put forth by Menasseh ben Israel (Manoel Dias Soeiro, 1604–1657) in his tract Hope of Israel.*

[198] *See Gen. 10.*

common underlying principle and form of behaviour of which all human opinions and customs would be nothing but direct or indirect modifications and alterations adapted to the circumstances and spirit of the times, regarding which it could be proven historically and physiologically that they had to affect men in this and no other way, leading to this and no other effect, and that, in this manner, they became the direct or indirect source of those conforming customs? – Would not such a powerfully affecting fact, such a vivid and immediate instruction by nature, be far more effective than any kind of instruction by man? And in the end, is not all human knowledge the consequence of experience? Instruction by nature? – What other fact would be a better key to ancient wisdom, theology, mythology, to the mysteries, customs, and doctrines of the most ancient world, than that which has been generally accepted by all peoples, historically proven, and attested to by natural history, even in the absence of all further oral or written documentation, namely the great inundation of the world? – Would it not be possible to bring to light the imprint of this seminal event in all the old customs and doctrines of the ancient peoples? To explain by it how their customs, opinions and systems developed from each other? To demonstrate how powerfully and diversely a single vivid impression has had its effect throughout the millennia under various guises, how it keeps doing so even today, and how it will continue to do so without us noticing, while even suspecting its influence will seem foolish and impossible? To show that the true subject of both ancient and more recent as well as contemporary mysteries is to lessen the consequences of the diluvian terrors, to re-instil courage in men, to enlighten them; to awaken confidence in themselves and in their reasoning powers by demonstrating to them the motivating causes? To show that we people of today think and act this way and must think and act this way because our second, perhaps third or twentieth progenitors were so terrified by the waters of the general inundation? That if the human race had regenerated by any other means, instigated by a less terrible cause, its descendants would have received an entirely different way of thought, as well as morals and customs, fully conforming with the first foundation[?]

Initially such a race was only able to procreate very slowly. After much time had passed, people returned to the valleys and plains from their refuges in the elevated regions of the earth. And it would still be a long time until their growth in a given stretch of land was so excessive that their sustenance finally became scarce. Such great numbers gave rise to emigration. People were forced to seek new domiciles in the adjacent regions, and it is worth noting here that history, which admittedly begins at a rather late point in time, hardly knows of any emigration in which the emigrants did not discover previous inhabitants in their new residences. – Should this not support the contention that, after the general inundation, several progenitors preserved themselves in the higher regions of the earth whose descendants are known as sons of the earth, native-born or indigenous people?

But when people leave their native soil, they will surely either settle in the nearest vacant stretch of land or wherever they encounter the least resistance. To such a place they will transplant their language, morals, and their already greatly modified diluvian terrors: by and by, they will merge them with the language, morals, and customs of the indigenous inhabitants, naming them with their own, newly-invented symbols. The cohesion of nations among one another and thus also with their motherland being very weak in those ancient times, new languages will come into existence even without miracles or the construction of the Tower of Babel, and the descendants of a common forefather will no longer be able to understand one another.

Furthermore, since those lands where colonies are planted are not under the same stretch of sky, are either fertile or infertile, mountainous or flat, are more or less open to intruders and more or less populated, freely provide nourishment or await human labour and hands, have a surplus or a scarcity of fruit, animals, or fish; since people have migrated there in larger or smaller numbers, have found greater or lesser obstacles in the process, and pledge allegiance to one or more tribes or nations: all these things will give the planters who have banded together a unique character that distinguishes them from all others. – Without any doubt the diversity of national characters would be a necessary consequence of the growing population, would be the reason why some become raiders and hunters, others herdsmen, and still others ploughmen, and the condition and nature of the new domicile would be one of the reasons for one nation's culture advancing before another, and explain why others have been entirely left behind and why yet others over time even descended into a state of savagery similar to that of animals. Culture was certain to thrive under a blessed stretch of sky, among a people of ploughmen, owning their own land, and in a region that invites the trading of surplus before it thrives anywhere else. However, for this same reason, such a people was also bound to succumb to effeminacy more quickly: its abundance and the resulting weakness were bound to lure the neighbouring savage peoples to these mild climes, cause incursions, and subjugate the previous, weakened inhabitants to the more savage, still undespoiled, and stronger neighbours. They were forced to succumb so that they might gain new power and morale from their subjugation. Their wealth and decadence were the means employed by nature to bring culture to the savage neighbours, to infuse an unnerved body with new strength, to give birth to new customs, traditions, governments, and religions, to bring more people closer to a state of perfection, closer to their destiny, and to spread culture among the other more primitive inhabitants of the earth.

If the new colonies were settled in an already inhabited stretch of land, they were either welcomed by the prior inhabitants or forced to gain their future home by combat and violence. Each of these alternatives brought with it its own results, effecting a new difference; the latter alternative most of all. In this case the indigenous inhabitants were either driven out, which then constituted another source of emigration, wholly exterminated by the new arrivals, subjugated and made into slaves, or indeed allowed to keep in part whatever the victor left for them out of his goodwill and own accord. – The character of the immigrant people, its strength and numbers, as well as the strength of the resistance encountered, can alone determine which of the above methods was preferred over the others. – Peoples that earned their living by hunting and pillage, in the wilderness with no landed property, leading an errant, nomadic life, were very dangerous neighbours to quiet herdsmen or those subjugated ploughmen living in servitude in the flatlands, or wealthy trading nations by the rivers and oceans. Their slothfulness, aversion to work, tendency to the nomadic life, their hope of a bountiful nearby raid, and their neighbours' weakness and effeminacy tempted some tribes to hostile incursions long before their own homeland's population had grown excessively. – The news of some fortunate success disseminated among them must also have incited others to attempt the same on their own accord and under a brave leader. Strong resistance was bound to increase their numbers, unite several independent tribes and patriarchs to follow a common leader to take possession of that land of abundance. If more remote peoples in the background now joined in and pressed upon one another like waves, those in the first ranks suddenly had to abandon their positions, breaking in with violence, dividing the bounty and land parcels among themselves, subjugating the original inhabitants, letting them do their work, and thinking that the only occupation worthy of a free man was skill at arms. Now every other independent land owner banded together with those of the prior inhabitants still remaining in a defensive war, in order to be safe from neighbouring attacks. Only to this extent, and no further, did they recognise a leader and a common chief, and in this manner a new constitution was born: a people of independent citizens and slaves. With such a people under him the head of state would certainly have to count for little, and the freemen for everything.

Worldly honours, a personal entourage, a greater share in the bounty and land-parcels, and submission and obedience during defensive wars against a common danger were the only general rights voluntarily granted to the highest authority. The tendency, so natural to the independent man, to take the law into one's own hands and pursue blood vengeance for insults and the murder of blood relatives, as well as the martial spirit so intrinsic to the entire people, established and awakened such notions of honour and a disgust for cowardice and weakness that, even today, are preserved in our customs, particularly in our affinity for duelling, despite all the laws unsuccessfully proscribing it.

Domestic matters had to be conducted by the head of the household, and matters of the people and nation in the assembly of freemen. They alone were to decide about war and peace.

Who could believe that all kingdoms of today have emerged from such peoples? That to a greater or lesser extent, all state institutions of today rest on this first foundation? That our refinement of today has developed from this wild seed? Who would believe that these limited, insignificant provosts have become kings and despots? That even the most distant future is the result and development of this very simple prime *factum?* And yet, the only too natural desire to reign and to expand one's power, the revulsion against any limitation so natural to man, the changing of power, and the waxing and waning of predominance, as well as the wise use of fortuitous circumstances have brought about the transition to our current and future conditions quite easily and naturally, without any leaps. Under different names and at different times, the history of the European kingdoms arising therefrom knows of repeated attempts, on the part of the kings, to gain unlimited power, to abolish the feudal regimen, to reduce and weaken the estates and the power of the aristocracy, and, on the part of the latter, futile attempts at preserving and expanding their rights and freedoms, and claims to a limitation of the royal and highest power: in all, an eternal struggle and fight between these two competitors. Only the future will reveal which way the scales will tilt. The wise and prudent man must anticipate it, and the historian will find it confirmed in the past that in all European countries royal powers increase to the same degree as those of the estates are reduced, and that if this process is not stopped by secret endeavours and if the destroyed aristocratic part of government is not replaced by these sole true representatives of mankind, the course of nature in Europe will prepare and lead to the abolition of the feudal regimen and the privileges of the estates based thereon, and consequently to absolute and despotic power; that the large standing, continuously growing armies are the means for this; that the tremendous upkeep of these leads to heavy taxation and the invention of new duties; that while obtaining and collecting them becomes easier, the ability of the lower classes, who alone work, to provide them decreases; that with the lower classes being unable to satisfy their continued – ever-increasing – needs with their contributions, the princes will be forced to infringe on the privileges and income of the free estates; that in Catholic states the tremendous wealth of the church offers the most profitable and harmless means under the innocent pretext of a reformation, long expected by all sensible men; that consequently the military class will diminish the weight of the yoke of the clergy and then, with its continued need – and this source having run dry as well – will soon thereafter try the same with the proud landed nobility, and this with the best and undeniable success, but that in the end even the kings themselves, as previously during the Fall of the Roman Empire and afterwards in the case of the feudal militia, will perhaps learn once more and anew that the means to unlimited power will in turn become the tools of their humiliation and dependency, unless growing effeminacy has not by then already diminished the martial spirit and discipline.

Finally, the wise philanthropist and cosmopolitan sees emerging, from this impending pressure and spirit of conquest, culture and refinement of morals for the remaining backward nations, and population growth for the whole world: peace and serenity from war; harmony from strife; abundance from scarcity; light from darkness; freedom from oppression; morality from corruption; and equality from the greatest inequality. – Despotism itself shall become the means for eradicating the middle classes and easing the path to liberty. – All this and more – and in a more correct form – is what wise historians and thinkers discover in the conditions of immigrant peoples and in the so very limited power of their first rulers.

They find that, among these first leaders, such powers in times of war and such limitations in times of peace had to inspire an aversion to peace and a preference for war. However, since the nation had only united for defensive war and thus could only be forced into waging one, they had no other choice but to strengthen their immediate following – those who were ready to stand by them at their slightest nod – to have men ready for new incursions and, at the same time, the tools for oppressing their own excessively independent people, and to become feared from without and within. – Woe to the freedom of a people whose king has amassed excessive treasures! His power is limited for naught, because he has the means to pay for his own ransom. Where there is wealth, there is power. No one gives without taking, and he who takes in this manner, sells himself. – You who are needy and are not yet skilled in virtue, tremble before any rich man; he keeps your chains in his safe, and at his whim he can become the lord of your honour and duty, your virtue and liberty. In any country, with any people, freedom, morality and virtue are lost if the inequality of property is excessive. No free men can be found there; only a few despots and many indentured servants. Fortunately, no one can give always and forever, and to all: hence there are no eternal lords and no eternal slaves. Therefore, it is in nature's plan that the great become small and the small great, that the rich become poor and the poor become rich, the powerful weak, and the weak powerful. Therefore our history is the history of a change of wealth and poverty, power and weakness, blossoming and wilting among individuals and entire nations. This is why a budding foreign trade only infuses a nation and people with a feverish strength, why a nation's true strength lies in the strict morals and limited needs of its citizens, and this is why the princes and their advisers do not need to understand this: they must be deceived and misled by the dazzling immediate benefits of commerce because otherwise this purposeful rising and falling, this blossoming and wilting of entire nations, this means so essential for the spreading of culture and populations would be impeded; because nature would lack the means to achieve its purpose. This alone can reconcile the wise man with commerce, the resulting moral decay, and the inequality of wealth; and thus, human folly itself becomes wisdom and vice a virtue. Consequently, the first leaders of the savage peoples, through their greater share of the bounty and the lands they had acquired, had the means at hand first to usurp the freedom of the rest of the nation, and then promptly to forge their own fetters; then to break free from the self-imposed rule of their vassals, reaching their greatness of today, becoming truly sovereign, until this power, through their own fault, falls into other hands again one day, because power abused always destroys itself, and because it is nature's design that any power that one has been given is inevitably abused.

This greater share of goods and land which they had been handed by a savage nation in its naivety enabled these so-called kings to give – and consequently take – and so to strengthen their following. Now free and independent men, even the most important men among the people, proceeded to sell their freedom and services in exchange for land-parcels assigned according to the duration of their service. They in turn surrendered their share of the land to others under similar conditions. As a result, free men became rarer, and servants more common. Great men gave their services to the king, others to the great men. The previous equality and independence vanished. The inequality of wealth generated various social classes, each subordinate to the other. The headstrong and all too domineering national militia was pushed aside by salaried liege men or vassals, made more obedient by the allotment of land-parcels. At first these liens were limited to their tenure but soon thereafter, with several artful twists, they were extended to the term of their lives and finally, also to their heirs, and thus the kings, together with their power to give, lost the obedience of their vassals and their power: apart from the title and the outward appearance of power, all their might and strength was transferred to the kingdom's great men. Thus the feudal system brought about the end of democracy, a weak head of state, and an aristocratic constitution. From those vassals sprang forth the lesser and the greater nobility, previously unknown to these peoples, forming the mediate and immediate estates of the realm. All power now lay in the hands of the nobility; consequently, some of the greatest among them and their subordinate vassals were bound to cast off the already very weakened royal yoke, creating separate and independent states and thereby elevating the status of the previously mediate nobility in the newly emerging kingdom until they were powerful enough to do without them, to curb their privileges, and reproach them for the very things they had set an example of under their previous overlords.

Yet other great men did not find it objectionable in any way to maintain their previous roles under such a limited head of state; unable to understand, to foresee, how the fallen might rise again, gather his strength, weaken their own, and attack and destroy them, they believed themselves to be strong and safe forever; they rested too securely on their laurels and failed to consider the consequences of the anarchy that had sprung from their wantonness. Due to this carelessness and ill-considered underestimation of their oppressed opponent, he in turn did not idly let time and circumstances pass. In this manner, by enlarging their domains, through fortuitous wars and inheritances, through their vassals' weakness and disunity, revertible liens that were not renewed and fell back to the crown, prudent political economy, the acquisition of manors offered by their noble owners at a low price on various occasions, especially at the time of the Crusades, in the hope of acquiring more land in the Orient, by the building of cities and communities after the Crusades, by the liberties and support granted to them, and by decreasing serfdom, but especially by the introduction of a salaried militia, wise kings in many a kingdom, sooner in some and later in others, were able to gradually regain their previous rights, to do without the militia of the liege-men and the support of their estates, to confront the proud nobility and to curb its liberties and jurisdiction, which had expanded beyond all bounds and measure during their impotence; to reduce it even beyond its original limitations and destiny, to ridicule and scorn it by excessively enlarging the number of noblemen, to reduce its influence on public administration and thus its following by awarding military, court and civil offices to common men; and finally, to promote celibacy by means of primogenitures and knightly orders, and to encourage indebtedness, harmful divestment of manors, debauchery, and even death itself by the luxury at the courts.

Certainly, this is not always the intended purpose; certainly, the same freedom to choose the means does not exist at every court in Europe; certainly, in some countries the preponderance of the nobility and estates has not yet been noticeably lessened; but all of the above is a sure, infallible means of achieving this, and experience vouches for the fact that steps have been taken towards this goal for a long time, if not intentionally, then driven by necessity, and if not immediately, then sooner or later. Certainly, nature and necessity often anticipate the wisdom of man or come to its aid. But what does it matter whether intention or need bring about the effect, as long as it materialises[?] In any case, it remains a proven proposition that the course of nature and kingdoms leads to a situation – sooner here and later there – in which every man, and princes and kings even more so, reviles any limits to his power, and that all powers of the estates are an inconvenient limitation, and that their reduction is an occurrence and development that any monarch would welcome. With the origin of standing armies the bond of liege – and in some kingdoms, the entire power of the estates resting upon this foundation – begins to disappear completely, and the fiefdoms themselves become meaningless. If the Ottonians[199] in Germany and the emperors following them had not immediately liened their hereditary duchies, engaged less in Italian

---

[199] *Imperial dynasty of the Liudolfinger family in Germany (919–1024), beginning with Henry I of East Francia, continuing with Otto I (the Great), Otto II, Otto III, and ending with the death of Henry II.*

feuds, and lived more peaceably with the popes, Germany would have become an absolute hereditary monarchy long ago, and the powers of the estates would have come to an [end]; as indeed, once the emperors are in possession of their own extensive hereditary lands and, without being limited by oaths and capitulations, through the daily growing preponderance and growing influence of its sovereign and the proportionally increasing weakness, disunity, dependency, and impotence of its estates, it undergoes an inexorable transition from an aristocratic constitution to a monarchic one, being destined to inevitably fall prey to robbery by one or several stronger men unless in the meantime a middle power emerges from its lap, one that places itself between the competitors, takes the weaker estates under its wing, and thus delays for some time the almost inevitable downfall of the German Empire's constitution.

In this way, every present popular constitution to this day is founded on the first origins of the people concerned, its first origins, its early development, in the needs, blows of fate, and the obstacles it has experienced in circumstances beneficial or detrimental to its growth. It depends on whether the progenitors of this people were hunters or herdsmen, farmers or traders, whether they were still pure and aboriginal, or with what other nations and how often they had mixed. Every true philosophical national history must begin there and explore the source. The foundation on which the edifice of the state was subsequently built was laid there: it must divine how one thing developed from another, for a people's origins almost always contain its entire destiny. And only such an historian will determine the true worth and future success, the detrimental or useful qualities of any measure taken or yet to be taken, as well as the duration and downfall of his fatherland. From this alone as well as other considerations that any thinker can add, have sprung our contemporary nations, morals, and customs; and he who observes all these things closely will distinguish the primal from later additions and all subsequent gradations with precision. He will also discover that every nation enjoyed the highest degree of common culture exactly when it was at its most populous. He will discover nations where this state has passed, that are wilting, those that are currently in this state, and those whose turn is yet to come. Through continued, exact observation of the previous course of nature it is even possible to determine its future progress, even to discover the law and rule by which it operates and will continue further.

Therefore, you must explore, learn to understand, and practise understanding: What consequences have arisen from any given occurrence? What is its relationship to the entire race's population increase and common culture? Where does it lead? What is its visible consequence today? To what extent do thousand year-old events and the institutions of the ancients affect the world today? What are the intermediate steps between two extremes? How will they continue to affect the future? How have they been modified? Which form benefited them the most? Of what further modifications, changes, additions, and limitations are they still capable? Which is best suited to the world today? What has to happen to make this idea, this opinion more widely known? Through which need can the attention of men be drawn to it? What opinions are merely slumbering, so to speak? but are nonetheless active hidden from view, lying in ambush, waiting to be awakened by some new cause? What benefit or harm will then come to this part of the world? How does this benefit or harm relate to the total sum of human felicity, to the common good?

If the so vehemently decried Crusades are the source of European commerce, the splendour of the courts, the decrease of the nobility and the blossoming of royal power as well as that of the Italian and German cities, the former glory of southern Germany and of the Hanseatic League, the decrease of serfdom, the foundation of various knightly orders, and the refinement of morals; if, furthermore, the Crusades were initiated by the resurgent doctrine of the millennial kingdom and the approaching end of the world as well as the alleged oppression of the pilgrims in the Orient; if, moreover, these ideas of the near end of the world are evidently diluvian and the doctrine of the millennial [kingdom] has developed from them, then it cannot be all that ridiculous to claim that this doctrine of the millennial kingdom was the distant cause of the Crusades' effects, to wit, the rising European commerce at that time, the greater splendour of the courts, the reduction of the nobility, the blossoming of royal power, and, along with it, that of the Italian and German cities, the Hanseatic League, the decrease of serfdom, the foundation of various knightly orders, and so forth. It therefore cannot be all that ridiculous to claim that there is perhaps no one in Europe who would not find, were he to research his current and previous situation, that the Crusades and the doctrine of the millennial kingdom and the approaching end of the world, and therefore diluvian ideas and terror, determine his present condition, as a remote and ultimate source of his joys and sorrows. Or is the remote cause not also a cause? Why else would Adam be our father, and his sin be ours? Do not all events in the world, as much as men, have their forebears and their offspring? If one thing is so ridiculous, why not the other? Therefore, you should at least laugh at both or laugh at neither. But if this is the case, then nothing on this sublunary earth is small; there is nothing that is not interwoven with the world at large; nothing that could be separated from it without dismantling the whole. Thus it should be well worth the effort to explore how one thing is based upon the other, results from the other, and brings the other about.

Only when you have fathomed the progress of the whole, the interrelationship of its parts, will you be capable of understanding what you and your stretch of land can expect: what is of continuous, permanent benefit for both? You will see that families and nations destroy themselves when they strive for their elevation; that their current high bloom is also the nearest, most unmistakable harbinger of their demise. You will see how the scales tip here, only to rise there: how one man's downfall is the revival of the other; you will discover that this rising and falling is an essential means for the welfare of the whole, for the perfection of the race; you will find that all these changes happen according to plan, that nature works according to the same laws in the political and moral as well as the physical world, and that it brings about changes in both through the same power; you will find that everything is founded on everything else, that every period continues a previous one, that it is its consequence, having been caused by it; just as this same living age will ultimately be the source and preparation of all future periods. The more and the more general relationships you shall discover, the more correct your judgements will be. Nature cares for the individual parts only inasmuch as she is concerned about the whole. All parts are means, and not ends. She allows each to play only one role, and only that role which is appropriate. If this requires your overthrow and that of your fatherland, neither prudence nor scheming, neither precaution nor effort, neither power nor pleading, neither contracts nor associations will save you. These very efforts and all else will only accelerate your predestined, purposeful downfall; they are interwoven with the great chain of cause and effect as the causes of your downfall, not as the means of rescue. No kingdom in history has lasted forever. The kingdoms of today's world are subject to a similar fate. Just as everything under the sun is changeable, so they also change to edge closer to their purpose, their destiny. Every human institution carries with it the seed of its destruction at the moment of its creation. The first step into life is also the first step towards death, and perhaps death, in turn, is the progression towards life. – O, if you are one of us, you must know where the political and moral world currently stands. From the course it has already completed and the position of the remaining parts around us you must be able to surmise what distance remains to be covered and which role providence has destined us to play.

Every single event in the world, even the smallest, is the imprint and mirror of past, present, and future times. God sees everything in everything else, everything in each individual part; and man, limited as he is, only as much as he needs here below. Thus, if you, limited creature, do not discover everything at once, then see what has been given to you to see, and rise above the crowd. As a wise man you must see more than a mere change of place in the relocation of the imperial throne from Rome to Constantinople:[200] more than the simple unification of two estranged hemispheres in the discovery of America.[201] These momentous events, as well as all other, lesser ones, are changes whose tremors are felt in all parts of the earth, even in the most distant future.

What then were the immediate consequences of these great events? How did the German Empire develop from this change of the imperial residence? How did the papacy's secular greatness in part emerge from German woodlands? You will find how in this immense grand arch of world events, one stone pushes against another and the entire building stands erect by virtue of this mutual counter pressure. How from the little snowflake, this most insignificant occurrence when time and nature wrest it from the high rock, during its descent and its rolling forth a terrifying mass is formed, until it buries valleys and shakes parts of the world. – By solving this and similar tasks you will discover how one gear catches another in the grand machine that is the world and how nothing hampers anything else; how obstacles actually promote the cause. To properly foresee the future all discoveries yet to be made must also be taken into consideration, as much as this is possible. There may be such that will provide entire continents, even the whole race with a different direction. The invention of writing, the magnetic needle, gunpowder, book-printing, the discovery of America, were profound, hardly predictable events. There may well be more to come. Nature and the power of man are far from being exhausted. There are many things that currently appear impossible to us, because the intermediate inventions, which must precede them, have yet to be made. These also you must add to the plan and consider which fields have not yet been explored by man's spirit of invention. Explore their expectations, their most urgent needs, then perhaps you will be able to predict which path the fearsome efficacy of the human spirit will choose.

[200] *In 330, as commanded by Emperor Constantine (c. 272–337).*
[201] *In 1492, 39 years after the fall of Byzantium.*

Every such task, no matter how impossible or ridiculous it may seem, will teach you new ways in which things are related and connected to one another. If men could travel through the air in the same way they travel across the seas, what would be the consequences of this for human morality, trade, politics, warfare, and maritime shipping? Which present institutions would it render obsolete? or harmful? Which new ones would it create? Which class of people would profit or lose the most from it? What general upheaval[202] would that cause? What new needs would each class feel as a result? Which means would human cleverness devise to remedy them? – Or what if the cultivation of the breadfruit would thrive and become commonplace in Europe?[203]

Actual occurrences provide us with so much to think about that it almost seems mad and unnecessary to rack one's brain over uncertain, doubtful things; in doing so, one certainly runs the danger of drawing many incorrect conclusions due to the lack of proper [knowledge] and proper oversight of all concurrent circumstances, but in the absence of a better activity you should not neglect this exercise. It will teach you many new connections, and you will be increasingly acquainted with that most blessed of all doctrines, the cohesion and goodness of the world. You will learn to understand the implications of the fact that men do not yet travel through the air and that the breadfruit tree is not being cultivated; and in other words, the actual question is this: what are the consequences of grain cultivation? And even if many wrong conclusions are reached along the way, what can it matter? Have men ever arrived at the truth without first making all the errors related to it? – Or, if you wish to avoid that; would not, in the thirteenth or fourteenth century, the task of discovering a new continent have seemed frantic and ridiculous in the eyes of one's contemporaries? Instead of men, nature and history have now answered it in an inimitable manner. And if this does not please you either, then choose a task concerning a fact instead: what caused large, disciplined, standing armies to emerge over time? To what extent did they change our state constitution? What further endeavours will make their sustenance necessary? Will they always exist? What circumstances and what need could cause their downfall? How will this need be awakened and brought about? What consequences will it then create among the nations regarding the balance

---

[202] 'Gährung', literally 'fermentation'.

[203] The English botanist Joseph Banks had recognised the value of breadfruit in 1769, when visiting Tahiti during James Cook's first voyage around the globe. As President of the Royal Society, he lobbied for its introduction to the Caribbean.

of Europe, the industry of men, trade, morality, and state constitutions? What vacuum will their dissolution cause? What will fill this gap?

Such tasks wean a man from the unphilosophical delusion that everything that is today has always been and must forever be; they teach him that everything is a child of the times and circumstances; they lead us to the root cause of things; they instruct us that as this cause changes, everything based on it is changed, too, or causes change in exact proportion to it; they create the skill of overviewing a number of events at a glance and predicting the most distant results: they also instruct us to grab all evil by its root and not to leave the harmful main trunk standing while merely lopping off a few branches; they demonstrate the art of masking one's intentions and plans, leading one's enemies and opponents astray through one's operations; and finally, they prove that not every immediate advantage is truly useful or every immediate disadvantage truly harmful, but that they are so only through the most distant consequences.

Investigating and exploring the general cohesion of things will put your desires in order, reconcile you with the world, increase the sources of your pleasure and felicity, lessen your pain, drive the blackness out of your imagination; it will convince you that everything that is morally good and evil orients itself according to the perspective from which one overviews the world; that the narrower interests are the source of moral evil; and that, with respect to the whole, nothing is evil and everything is goodness, harmony, and order; that a wise man must strive to judge all things according to this most general relation; that in its absence, if unable to consider the general, the weaker part of mankind can employ the following principles for judging all occurrences, in order to avoid mistakes:

Everything that separates men, makes them mistrustful and superstitious, cowardly and inactive, that promotes the inequality of wealth and prevents population growth is a pernicious political tool, however much it may flatter our power and our wishes. Not being of a lasting nature, all of this will bring about its own punishment because it runs counter to the course of nature.

On the other hand, everything that brings people closer to one another, making them wiser, more refined, sociable, courageous, content, industrious, and independent, and which destroys the excessive inequality of wealth and promotes population growth, that alone is truthful, lasting, and a divinely blessed policy; it also vests permanent might, because nature is its friend and ally, against which all the world's obstacles are powerless. Even so, however, all the obstructions and intentions of evil and selfish people are no less necessary and essential, since they do not hamper, but do in fact promote, because they awaken needs, because through them the friction of forces brings life and fire to the machine and actions are initiated. And in the end it will be apparent that, in this world, both evil and virtue have their purpose.

You however may rejoice that providence has placed you on the side of good.

IV. Appendix

A SCHOOL OF HUMANITY.

With the help of Almighty God, we the undersigned have created among us a firm, inseverable, and lifelong alliance under the name of a *School of Humanity*, with the motto *Homo sum, humani nihil a me alienum puto!*[204] affirming it with a solemn oath according to the formula attached below, sealed and signed with our names by our own hand.

§1

The *purpose* of this association is:

1) to labour with joint forces so that every member of our school may attain as much true felicity as is proper for human nature and destiny as time, place, and other circumstances permit;

2) to give the entire human race an opportunity to share in this felicity.

Elaboration

Mutual protection and aid against foreign attacks as the original motivation why men establish civil societies were hardly the only goal of the Being that gave them the ability to understand and love one another. The abundance of intentional forces of nature, extending into the smallest blade of grass and rocky crevice, leaves no doubt in our mind that the instinct for sociability and language was also given to man with the goal of developing and furthering the hidden seeds of that moral and physical perfection which he may reach, and this is impossible without social communication. However, one may easily gather that this goal of nature in her wisdom is not nearly accomplished as perfectly through those social associations currently existing as it would be under certain conditions, because in the majority of its members the mere thought of the benefits one draws from society is suppressed or at least incapacitated in practice by ingrained habit, the burden of public duties, and by the standing army. Those who wield legislative

---

[204] Lat. *I am a human being, and count nothing that is human alien to me. (Terence: Heauton Timorumenos)*

and executive power contribute to this in no small part because alas! they all too often dare to treat the state entrusted to them as their personal property. It is for this reason that the subject, rather than being inclined towards due loyalty and dedication, counts the magistracy among the inevitable plagues that befall the land and which annually divest him of a portion of the bread he has earned by the sweat of his brow. Thus the social bonds by which each citizen's advantage should be tied to the welfare of all others are torn, every member of society regarding himself as an isolated being and the common good as a treasure to be plundered, of which he seeks to carry away as much as possible, justly or unjustly, without coming to blows with his competitors and the law.

Furthermore, the use of currency, introduced to ease trading, has been stretched far beyond its worth, since apart from satisfying all bodily needs its possession also seems to procure esteem, respect, friendship, and love, so that it has become the most important and direct object of all endeavours and labours and is even used as the measure by which the worth or worthlessness of charitable institutions and inventions are judged.

Religion is not factored into this valuation of things; instead, most of its followers have kept it merely as an object for speculation on holidays, without any influence on their moral lives: and so far, the young citizen's education has been aimed more at making him wise, learned, and well-mannered rather than cultivating within him valour, patience, loyalty to the state, friendship, compassion, altruism, etc. These are merely the most apparent causes for the slackening of all members of the body politic: but this is not the place to elaborate further.

Meanwhile it should be plain from the above that the mainsprings which are meant to set a moral man into motion and keep him thus have partly lost their force and partly taken a wrong direction, that therefore all endeavours aimed at the good of mankind are pursued with too little zeal and passion, and that consequently, the sum of felicity actually enjoyed by men in Europe, so highly praised for her culture, is not as great as it could be and is actually declining.

The aim of our band of students of humanity is therefore nothing less than to build, by erecting our society, a dam against this torrent of perdition and, with this goal in mind, to unite in action with us all noble, manly souls, who previously could express their finer way of thinking only to the heart of a friend or in powerful songs and writings. With joint forces, we endeavour to lead all human efforts and desires to the goal set before them by the creator, assigning their lesser instincts and needs their proper place, which is to say that their satisfaction should never be considered as the ultimate goal but rather as the means for inciting in every youth the greatest passion for the study or trade for which he is suited, and unifying in every soul their understanding of virtue, felicity, and joy: in short, to bring new life and useful activity to the world of ethics and politics – as far as we are able to accomplish this with our limited powers. The true felicity of all members of our school and that small or large portion of mankind whose fate depends on us is the final goal all our statutes and institutions are directed at; it is the payment every Brother expects for his labours and the blessing the creator of everything beautiful and good cannot deny our efforts, as long as this well-intentioned institute is not lacking in courageous and steadfast supporters.

However, to preserve ourselves as well as our successors from false interpretations and any misunderstanding, we wish to define more precisely what exactly we mean when we use the term *human felicity*.[205]

The individual's contentment with his condition is based on his current awareness of what he finds pleasurable and painful as well as the anticipation of future pleasure and pain. The more excitable and delicate his senses, the freer his inner feeling that makes him sense what affects him in the minutest points of contact, and the stronger, on the other hand, his power to affect the objects of his sensations and to direct them as he intends, the greater the sum of felicity he can achieve.

Since the liveliest pleasure is soured, however, by the anticipation of some pain resulting therefrom, just as any current suffering is sweetened and made pleasant by the anticipation of a subsequent benefit, and since, without this afterthought, a kind of saturation and weariness is generated in the soul once the desired object has been obtained, he who endeavours to make men happy must provide them with an uninterrupted series of such pleasant sensations, which can also be viewed as the most effective cause of even greater pleasures in the future or as a means of removing prior evils.

This can be accomplished in no other manner than by setting all human desires, passions, decisions, and actions a common main purpose, for which all individual objects of our desires and inclinations are means that bring us closer to the goal but which, during this lifetime on this planet Earth, can never be fully

---

[205] *'Menschliche Glückseligkeit.'*

reached, and always keeping the notion of this general mainspring of our actions vividly enough in our souls as to affect all our decisions and actions.

The more this ultimate purpose conforms to that of human nature, the greater the possibility of achieving it, and the nearer, greater, and more tangible the resulting benefits, the less effort will be required to motivate people to always keep it in sight.

What exactly this ultimate purpose is may seem a difficult problem to solve. However, may the humblest offering of thanks be given to thee for this, o thou unfathomable author of everything that is good; through your government over the mortals during these past five thousand years known to us, you have shed such a bright light on the goal that even the feeblest eye is able to find it; and let him who finds the necessary observations and conclusions too difficult or not plausible enough consult a most holy revelation that will bring the matter nearer to his heart by means of the most fitting images and words of advice.

Viewed as a whole, the human race's perceptions, concepts, and physical and intellectual capacities have grown incrementally since that first misguided amazement with which Adam looked upon the young creation, just as every individual man educates himself, and just as the achievement of a desired benefit will always make his heart well up with new wishes and desires. For all obstacles borne of human ignorance, weakness, and malice have never *halted* the progress of culture, but only *delayed* it.

This leads to the likely conclusion, which to us, however, is evident to the highest degree, that the ideal of perfection or the destiny intended for the human race by its creator is the best possible development of its entire physical and mental capacities and powers.

At every moment of its existence, mankind's general sensorium is meant to expand further and further, to gradually perceive all of creation in all its parts wherever possible; and to the same extent, its active force to purposefully influence things will increase in emphasis and scope from one degree to the next.

In this manner each and every individual's felicity is intertwined so thoroughly with the felicity of the entire species that it must be viewed as an inseparable part of the whole.

The individual takes everything he enjoys and perceives from perfections belonging to the entire species; therefore, he must also repay it for everything it does; and the former quite precisely correlates to the latter, even if there were no positive rewards and penalties.

The egotist, isolated in his own mind, feels only his own repulsiveness, whereas the participating citizen of the world opens all his senses to the gentle impressions of pleasure granted to him by the plentiful beauty and goodness of creation.

Thus, the felicity we seek does not consist of the so highly praised tranquillity and indifference of the sage, but in a comforting enjoyment of all of God's gifts and the ceaseless effort to do so much good inside and outside ourselves that the number of our pleasant feelings ever increases with new objects of joy and pleasure, until we enter eternity for the complete ennoblement of our nature.

Had the legislators observed these principles in their political and educational institutions, their states would not have reached the relative degree of perfection attainable for them so soon, only to descend into corruption thereafter – likewise, many of our most promising youths would not cease their efforts of improving their knowledge and skill once they gained a certain office or income, if the thought of their destiny's still distant goal were to remain quite vividly and forcefully in their souls.

Woe to us students of humanity, if on one of our assembly days we could not count at least a few steps that we have advanced! Stagnation in an individual's culture, as well as in society, is the first step towards barbarism!

§ 2

The means we are employing to promote this great ultimate goal are:
I. Mutual encouragement of all members to strive for an ever higher degree of perfection in the education of their hearts and minds.

Elaboration

That which is taught and preached in other institutions whose aim is the improvement of man is to be *done* among us. We therefore request our thinking fellow students, once and for all, to think of new and better exercises in addition to the ones below and to present them in our assemblies for consideration.

For the time being, the following has been decided:

1) Every member shall keep a journal in which he records his most important occupations, leisure activities, flaws, assessments, increase in knowledge, doubts, curiosity, moods, etc., whenever and in whatever language and manner he chooses.

At the end of the month he shall compose a summary excerpt from this journal for himself in which he notes everything he deems important for his own person, his progress in knowledge and virtues, but also those things where he is still lacking in his own opinion. If he thinks that some good counsel would be of use to him in certain areas, he should share it publicly in the assembly or privately with one or the other fellow-student. In another, still briefer excerpt, he shall record that which is of interest to our school or mankind at large.

This may be new discoveries in the sciences and arts, examples of great virtue and vice, hidden wisdom and hitherto unrebuked prejudices, acquaintances with good people, misjudged characters, and unknown, useful books – everything properly analysed and notated. No one shall come to our monthly assemblies without these two pieces.

At the end of each year the original personal remarks must be reviewed, and from these a brief sketch of the major changes that have occurred in the mind and heart over the year must be composed. At the same time, the most important matters one wishes to attain in the following years must be shown there as well.

2) In every city where the number and circumstances of the students permit, various learned training-societies shall be established as the respective needs of the attending students require; these must be presided over by an older member with the necessary skills if he is asked to do so by the others.

The institution itself must be local; furthermore, it will have the added benefit that the actual meetings of the Order can be concealed within these training-society meetings.

3) All our schools shall focus their efforts on acquiring their own libraries in the following manner:

Upon admission, every member must provide a complete register of his store of books. The appointed librarian then creates a large, systematic catalogue from these individual entries, leaving out duplicate copies and indicating the owner by means of a designated letter in the margin, which will be given to every student for copying until our numbers are large enough to have it printed. Likewise, students in different locations can share their catalogues with one another, and all may supply others with books from their catalogues. This library shall be open to all students at all hours of the day.

4) Reading societies where one may read the latest works of wit for a nominal fee shall be established, and when the annually-acquired works have been read by all interested parties, they shall remain the property of the school in order to create a lending library over time, the proceeds of which can be used for the good of mankind.

These societies are open to all.

5) It is the duty of every student of mankind to report the errors and flaws he discovers in his fellow student openly and lovingly and to give him brotherly counsel for his improvement if these errors and flaws are of such a nature that they could cause harm to him or some other creature of God.

If, however, one suspects that one of us harbours a vice suggesting a gross corruption of his character, this must be reported to the school's acting vice-chancellor.

He shall then, without speaking to anyone else about this, post a notice during the next assembly in which he states that someone in this society is suspected of having succumbed to a vice incompatible with the principles of the school, and that he is amicably admonished and requested to free himself from it.

Following this, he must observe him more closely, and if it is discovered that he continues on the path of evil, a new warning is posted during the next assembly, stating the vice but not the person.

If this still does not have the desired effect, the matter is handed over to the school's procurator who formally prosecutes the perpetrator before a committee of the most senior members, appointed by the vice-chancellor, which handles his case according to the criminal proceedings below.

6) If one of us notices in himself a flaw of the heart or mind of such a nature that it can be remedied by good counsel or a change of external circumstances, then he is obliged to confide this to one or several members and hear their advice. If he abstains from doing so to his own detriment, he shall receive a public reproach for it once the matter becomes known.

II. Ceaseless efforts of spreading a just way of thinking about all areas of knowledge, courteous manners, and applied religion among men.

Elaboration

1) Should men of genius emerge from among us who are capable of enlightening the world with their writings, they must be encouraged to submit all their products, prior to publication, to the vice-chancellor and the censors appointed by him and strike out everything that would do more harm than good. One should also strive to familiarise oneself with the true needs of human knowledge, and propose to these men those subjects whose treatment would be most meritorious, depending on the state of the nation for which they are writing.

The societies mentioned in no. I 2 should observe the same principle when choosing their activities.

2) In whatever company a student of humanity may find himself, he shall consider it his duty to suppress all dalliance as best he can. Instead, he shall endeavour to entertain the society with pleasant conversations and inconspicuously guide them towards useful subjects; at the very least, he shall rebuke all obviously false statements by others and divest libel and slander of their poison; but, whenever possible, this must be done with Socratic prudence and moderation, so that even if he should not be so lucky as to better his company it will still hold him in high esteem.

3) No one who does not either occupy a public office or strive to be useful to the public with an occupation of his own choosing shall be tolerated in our school and, if it is deemed necessary, every student shall be required to render an account of his monthly efforts in this regard to the lodge and accept criticism thereof.

Youths who do not yet occupy an office shall only be accepted if they have decided on the kind of life they wish to lead, and they shall be required to be particularly thorough and conscientious in the journal excerpts which they must submit according to no. I.

4) Improving the education of young people is one of our prime concerns. We therefore encourage all those among us with the necessary skills and leisure to dedicate themselves to public or private education, and we shall jointly assist them in word and deed, sparing neither time, effort, or cost if it is a question of putting the schools in a city or state on a better footing.

5) Those among us who have chosen to enter into the ministry shall be encouraged by our association to acquire the most useful kind of preaching, according to nos. I 1–6, to know the human heart and learn the language of most intimate friendship, so that by these means they can be the counsellors and spiritual advisers of their communities and do as much good through their intimate accord with their listeners as through the upright administration of their office.

6) A considerable portion of our school expenditures shall be comprised of awards for good deeds that would otherwise remain unrecognised and unrewarded either because of the low standing of those who have committed them, or because they have no visible effect on the welfare of the greater masses. Each of our students shall search for news of extraordinary examples ofcharity, filial love, honesty, steadfastness when tempted by evil, patriotism, etc., make inquiries about the most pressing needs of the noble persons who have committed such

deeds, and share this news with the vice-chancellor, who will then report about it in the ethics meetings. When such awards are given, one must always proceed in such a manner that the recipient views them as a special act of providence by God rewarding virtue, so that it spurs his enthusiasm to do good deeds, and so that this is also presented as an example to be emulated in his circle of acquaintances.

7) All beneficial innovations in the sciences and arts, but especially in medicine, pedagogy, economics, and mechanics, made or discovered by one of us shall be presented for examination at the next assembly and, if they are found correct and useful, shall be announced to the public immediately.

8) It is the duty of a student of humanity who occupies some rank due to his birth or office to treat meritorious persons of low standing, even if they are merely righteous peasants, with honour and courtesy, and to invite them to eat, walk, etc., with him and to let all of his other acquaintances take careful note that this is because of their dexterity and virtue.

9) If there is any office that must be filled and some of us have influence in the matter, the entire lodge at the place in question shall set everything in motion to assign it to the worthiest man, even if he is not one of us.

III. Improving the temporal circumstances of all students.

Elaboration

1) Since we all know one another down to the bottom of our souls due to the institutions outlined above, it will not be difficult to determine for which office each student of humanity is suited best, and the entire school will always use its credit, acquaintances, and, if there is noother way, its funds to procure it for him. Therefore, every student shall send any news of vacancies, persons who are charged with filling them, and the funds required to conduct the selection to the acting vice-chancellor, who will handle the matter according to his instructions.

If he gives one of his subordinate students a task pertaining to this, it must be executed with the utmost diligence.

2) The physicians, surgeons, judges, advocates, priests, and school masters in the arts and sciences recruited by the school may only require from their students that their expenses be reimbursed; they must otherwise perform their services for free. Men of means, however, are allowed to give them a voluntary present.

3) Unforeseen accidents, fire, water damage, and financial losses through bankruptcy, if they affect individual members, are regarded as concerning the

whole order and are compensated by mutual contributions from all lodges if he who has suffered the loss is incapable of recovering through his own efforts.

4) Students of humanity who are travelling on their own business or that of the Order and not merely for pleasure are to be accommodated for 24 hours in places where lodges are located at the expense of the respective lodge and should be assisted in every other way.

The provisions regarding this matter depend on the local circumstances of each lodge, but herewith it is decided and so ordered that among ourselves we will never serve more than 3 dishes and fruit, in addition to butter and cheese, and that we will drink no more than two different kinds of wines.

5) Should some of us lose their offices through no fault of their own, or become unable to support themselves due to illness, then they shall receive provisional income from the general funds until they have been given the opportunity to sustain themselves through their own labour again.

In such cases the superiors of the lodge must make the most unbiased examinations to ensure that any monies intended to alleviate human suffering are not consumed out of sloth or an ill-understood love of independence.

6) Those who wish to borrow money for improving their general circumstances or embarking on individual enterprises will find the swiftest service with our credit fund without encumbering their property or having to notify the local authorities, if indeed they can demonstrate the necessity or usefulness of the project as well as the ability and likelihood of them repaying the demanded capital. Likewise, our capitalists will never find a safer place than our general, guaranteed fund for depositing their money against interest.

7) As a result of the constant correspondence among all lodges, merchants and manufacturers will have the best opportunities for investments, receiving their goods first-hand, and accessing the most honest and unselfish carriers and commissioners in all major trade centres; just as every student will do his very best to procure them loans.

IV. A sensible practice of charity for needy persons outside the school.
Elaboration[206]

---

[206] *Here the fragment abruptly ends.*

SOME EARLY DOCUMENTS.

STATUTES OF THE ILLUMINATI.

Because our society does not intend to break the sensible bonds connecting us within the confines of the state, but rather to strengthen them, it is our will:

1. That everyone be treated with love, respect, discrimination, and according to his station.

2. Therefore, everyone should at all times stand on ceremony, and even more so if the members are among the profane. Thus, every nobleman must be treated with the respect proper to his station (even if his rank within the Order is a lesser one); and because we are anxious that our members are held in high esteem by the profane, our men must hold them in an even higher esteem, so that they may be highly respected by others as well.

3. When the Brethren of the Order are among themselves, however, all differences in status prevailing in civil society disappear, and all that matters here is one's seniority and the office one holds. Any senior member, even if he ranks only a little higher, and the Superiors even more so, are treated with the same reverence one would show a great dignitary when among the profane, especially when young members or equals are present.

4. The more courtesy a Superior shows his subordinates, the more it also behoves them to bear in mind not to treat this courtesy as familiarity. The subordinates shall not simply deem themselves entitled to do whatever a close friend might do, but wait for their Superior to prompt them not to treat a friend as a stranger.

5. Although it may seem that such compulsion should be unknown among friends, precluding all brotherly sentiments, our dearly-beloved Brethren shall know that good order requires it, and that we do not intend to love one another for a limited time but forever, and that nothing can sever the strongest, most intimate friendship as much as when it degenerates into familiarity. Bear this in mind and hold onto it, dearest Brethren! and lasting friendships will be your reward.

6. Do not deny strangers the rights of humanity and hospitality.

7. Attend your offices in civil society with loyalty and dedication, because if you are negligent there, you will also be so among us.

8. Disseminate the sciences, arts, industry, fellowship, and virtues, and thwart

whatever opposes them.

9. Therefore the Order, in this Class, also regards itself as a learned society, where example and instruction guide the mind and improve the heart.

10. Read the works of the ancients, and diligently record what you have read. Think about what you have read, but use your own understanding, not that of another; whatever someone else has thought and said, think and express it in your own words; do not accept an opinion without having examined its author, origin, and foundation; practise setting and solving problems; read whatever exalts the soul and moves the heart, and share this with others; consider practice and application; and above all, explore human nature not from books [but] from yourselves, and draw your own conclusions about others from similar circumstances.

11. For this reason, this Class is occupied with:

1) Researching human characters: their origin, foundations, results, and further resolving them.

2) With the organisation of human nature in general.

3) Examining the causes, or mainsprings of human actions.

4) Characterising and investigating human inclinations and how they might be guided, awakened, and extinguished.

5) Familiarising oneself with the ancient as well as modern systems of ethics and philosophy, such as Stoicism, Epicureanism, etc.

6) Discovering examples of these in ancient and modern history.

7) Examining the pleasant and unpleasant aspects of human interactions in principle, and preferably from personal experiences or the experiences of others.

8) Examining the origin and progress of our judgements and opinions.

12. Books and further instruction are provided by the Superiors.

13. Everyone must be a good father, husband, son, master, and servant to his family.

14. Above all, the Order recommends that each and everyone observe *golden temperance:* the path to the higher Classes is closed to those who have not sufficiently shown themselves capable of this.

To this end the Order also issues special rules and instructions concerning frugality, housekeeping, health, and a longer life.

15. So that everyone becomes accustomed to thriftiness, everyone must immediately procure a savings-box and hand its key to his Superior. All monies left

unspent on unnecessary pleasures are to be placed in this box. At certain times, such as March 31st and September 23rd, the Candidate and the Superior open it together, and any amount less than one carolin[207] goes to the Order, while the rest is kept for future emergencies or, in the event of his death, given to his surviving heirs unless he wishes to make other arrangements; on request, he is given a receipt for the surplus, stating that he is entitled to such and such amount, which is signed by two Brethren of the Order. They fully commit themselves to their obligation and relinquish the *beneficio divisionis*.[208]

If he resigns from the society, or in case of an emergency, these funds are returned to him.

16. The Order frowns upon indulging in *luxu*[209] in eating, drinking, and attire; our motto is: *Quo simplicius, eo melius*.[210]

17. It is our duty to combat error, prejudice, and malicious intentions as much as possible, and everyone must strive to make progress in self-knowledge as well as the discovery of his own weaknesses and ill-considered inclinations.

18. To this end everyone hands his Superiors a sealed sheet of paper at the end of each month, where he describes:

1) What he considers a prejudice[?]

2) In whom he has discovered this[?]

3) What prejudices he has discovered in himself[?]

4) What his most important prejudices are, and how many of these he has[?]

5) How many and which of these he has already weakened or even extinguished[?]

19. Anyone drawn towards us will surely disclose to us his discoveries, inventions, and secret connections; in turn, the Order solemnly promises not to misuse them.

20. Silence and secrecy are the heart and soul of our Order; reasonable frankness is virtuous only towards the Superiors, whereas sensible restraint and mistrust towards the other Brethren of the Order are the cornerstone and foundation for preventing that they do not tire and despair of one another. Therefore, you should not disclose even the slightest matter, e.g. tenure in the Order, fellow Brethren, your degree, etc., without good cause.

---

[207] *The equivalent of 12 guilders (approx. £1.16s).*

[208] *A communal claim to inheritance.*

[209] *Lat. Luxury.*

[210] *Lat. The simpler, the better.*

21. The duration of any member's term in this Class is not fixed; promotions mostly depend on his dedication and skill.

22. If you are not promoted quickly, dearest Brethren, do not grumble! Instead, consider that everything has its reason, and that no new creature appears in the grand world-edifice unless as many creatures as are necessary to bring this about have perished first.

23. Furthermore, the Order has accepted as its highest duty to make those truths that are indispensable for the felicity of every man so pleasant and tangible and to present them in a way appropriate to everyone's standing, so that these ideas are easily transformed into his desires and actions.

24. To this end the members constantly practise writing essays, and from time to time certain questions are proposed for them to resolve and discuss, and the best treatise is rewarded with promotion to higher Classes.

25. Similarly, every one of us takes it upon himself to raise the office he administers and the art or craft he practises to a higher degree of perfection and freedom.

26. The degree one is in always remains hidden from the others, and it may only be revealed to equals.

27. For this reason, no one reveals to another how long he has been in the Order, who initiated him, and so forth.

28. The Brethren of the present Class keep a close watch over those in the lowest degree, and they report about their *conduite,* either to the Superiors or to the entire Assembly, and thus the lesser members must always be known to those above. However, those below do not possess the same kind of insight but only know those above them as their equals.

Privileges, Rights, and Liberties.

In a sense, all of the above duties should be viewed as benefits, because without the strictest adherence to them the Order would be incapable of granting the following benefits. Only the firmest unity and observance of the laws allow us to keep our given word.

1. Everyone in this Class, after giving due cause, is free to resign at will, and if he otherwise observes strict silence, he need not fear the slightest reproach or harm from us.

2. We know that no one joins a society and sacrifices some of his freedom without expecting benefits. To this end, the Order promises the following to each

and every one who has distinguished himself through dedication and actual services:

1) To open and ease the way for them to much hidden knowledge.

2) To fraternally assist them in dire emergencies they experience in spite of all good housekeeping, and this to the best of our ability.

3) To assist them with recommendations and intercessions and, if their requests are reasonable and do not conflict with the interests of the whole, to bring these requests to fruition as much as we are able to do so.

4) To help them in word and deed whenever they have been insulted or affronted through no fault or negligence of their own; however, it is our hope that one would not unduly exploit this assistance by purposely exposing oneself to insult.

5) We further promise, for the consolation and reassurance of those with few means but, conversely, many children, and who have been wrested from their loved ones by an untimely demise, that we wish to assume a father's role for these children, providing for their livelihood, and assisting their widow in word and deed.

For this we implore the help of those of our members with sufficient means, who will deem themselves fortunate to find a way and opportunity to make good use of their affluence.

6) Should one or the other of our Brethren or of their children prove to be particularly talented, and if travel could further his education even more and he could thus provide the Order with evidently useful insights or services, the Order is not disinclined to sponsor such travel by advancing the expenses.

7) In general, we commit ourselves to ensuring that none of our Brethren should ever be deprived of all help as long as his misfortune is not the result of his own lack of prudence or poor housekeeping; at the same time, we demand that no one asks another for money or anything else, but that he approaches his Superior, explains to him the circumstances he finds himself in, and then waits for him to take action.

8) We also hope that such an unfortunate man will in turn do something beneficial for the Order once he is back on his feet.

To this end all monies and goods contributed or bequeathed to the Order are considered common property, which only the Order as a whole or its needy members may lay claim to.

Since we also know that there is nothing more unpleasant and more often the cause of disorder and conflict in societies than the Superiors' harsh, rough, and domineering comportment, the Order has taken necessary precautions in this regard; and as the power and supremacy are based on experience and supreme insight into the dealings of the Order alone, the following measures have therefore been decreed:

1) If a reprimand or rebuke is to be made, the Superior shall be careful to avoid bitter feelings and must present his reproaches in the most general terms possible; e.g. clothed in examples, or by telling what he dislikes about the other man to others, or to himself, and such words and occurrences will induce everyone to look within to discover whether or not it applies to him. In doing so they spare the Superior from giving a detailed and unpleasant explanation, and themselves embarrassment and displeasure.

2) Since words always have an element of harshness and our government is to be based on love as much as possible, the Order has substituted them with gentler means of indicating warnings and reproaches. It demands that:

1. The Superior remains silent about insolent questions, indecent talk, sarcastic humour, and unseemly jokes, and he does not respond to such words or interrupt his discourse to deal with them.

2. In the absence of strangers or the profane, undue familiarity is followed by immediate suspension until further notice.

3. If strangers are present, however, and when the familiarity reaches the point where the Superior begins to feel uncomfortable, he begins to play with his handkerchief, moves his chair, or asks him for tobacco (even though he may not be accustomed to smoking) the moment he strays.

4. In case the Superior has not personally witnessed the other person's wrongdoing but only knows of it because has been told about it, the Superior hands him a blank, unsealed sheet headed *Confiteatur*[211] as a sign that he knows of his wrongdoing; after a while, the offender returns the sheet, having written down what he thinks he has done wrong; if he is correct, no further words are said: if he has missed the mark, he receives a second slip on which the reason has been written.

We caution all Superiors not to leave a single wrongdoing unadmonished, and as someone wielding authority, it would be still worse to be found out

---

[211] Lat. *Let him confess.*

oneself. The subordinates, however, will not be upset, as they are being reminded of their flaws with the utmost love.

3) In order for the highest Superior to be informed if the intermediate Superiors are following these laws of ours, every intermediate Superior must collect, at the end of March, June, September, and December, from all persons under him their concerns and grievances against the Order and fellow Brethren, being well-sealed and labelled *au Premier,* and send them unopened to our general Chief through his respective intermediate Superiors.

4) These concerns must be handed in by everyone every Embertide[212] without exception, and even those who have no grievances must nonetheless submit that they have none.

5) Suggestions for improvements and changes with regard to the grievances may also be included.

6) After the end of each quarter, the replies and settlements of the grievances follow shortly; they are delivered to the grieving party by his immediate Superior, together with his own submission, then signed by the accused party, and both returned; should any Superior dare to mistreat or admonish the subordinate even in the slightest due to the grievance directed at him, then this must be noted as a new *gravamen*[213] in the following quarter.

REFORM OF THE STATUTES OF THE 1ST CLASS.

Since legislative prudence requires that whenever circumstances change, the relevant regulations and statutes are also changed, that abuses that have occurred over time are prevented by adding new statutes, that doubtful cases are clarified, and that, if necessary, provisional enactments are made universally applicable and incorporated into the statute book, the Order enacted during its last general assembly the following regulations pertaining to the first Class.

1. All prior statutes, constitutions, privileges, however they may be called, are herewith completely annulled and withdrawn insofar as they contradict the current fundamental regulations; however, [the Order] reserves the right to make any necessary amendments in the future.

2. Our society's final goal has always been and will remain to make the perfec-

---

[212] *Days of prayer and fasting recurring four times a year according to the liturgical calendar of the Catholic church.*

[213] *Lat. Burden, annoyance.*

tion of his mind and moral character interesting to man, to spread humane and social sentiments, thwart malicious intentions in the world, assist a suffering and harassed virtue against injustice, further the promotion of worthy men, and generally facilitate the means for spreading knowledge and the sciences. We solemnly swear that this is our society's only and unadulterated purpose.

On the contrary, our society stands for nothing else; should the Candidates discover more than this over time, so much the better for them, and from this they will see that, contrary to the customs of other societies, we deliver more than we have promised. A member who is chiefly moved to join our society by the prospects of great power and riches would not be the most welcome here.

Since mutual assistance, concord, and unbreakable confidentiality among the members are however necessary to maintain such an ultimate purpose and, just as importantly, so that others outside the society are won over for its good and its objectives, all members must

3. avoid, out of consideration for the society, as well as for their own good, which otherwise cannot be promoted, all hatred and envy towards their fellow Brethren and view them as their best and dearest friends, as collaborators for the same grand purpose.

4. The society requires a sacrifice of their freedom, although not at all times, but only if it is a means for the grand purpose. Orders given by the Superiors should always be assumed to be leading to this goal; for the Superiors have further and deeper insights into the system, and they are Superiors only for this very reason.

5. Every newly-accepted member submits an Obligation *de silentio*[214] to his Recipient.

6. Our society has no use for men as they are; they must become that for which they are needed over time. For this, examination, proofs of loyalty, as well as silence, allegiance, industriousness, and the expansion of useful knowledge are required.

7. Hence the time Candidates have to spend in this degree. Young persons, aged 15 to 18 will be examined for 3 years, those aged 18 to 24 for two years, and those from 24 to 30 years for one year.

8. However, depending on the Candidate's diligence, maturity, zeal, and attentiveness, his term may possibly be shortened.

---

[214] *Lat. Of silence.*

9. During this time the Candidate works on examining himself and his fellow men, eagerly recording everything, making notes according to a certain specified method, and in general, thinks and observes more than he reads.

10. A multitude of notes, observations, character sketches, written records of conversations of people during their impassioned moments, as well as obedience towards the Superiors are the surest path to promotion.

11. During his initiation the Candidate changes his name to one given to him: he reads and makes notes about the name as much as he can.

12. Among his observations, physiognomic observations and the discovery of rules to assess human characters are especially valuable.

13. One should also keep a separate journal for those persons with whom one maintains frequent contact, entering under the rubric for each person their good deeds to us on one page and their evil ones on the other.

14. It is strongly recommended to observe all things in one's own way, not that of others.

15. Among the first proofs of ability is the task that everyone has to complete and submit at the end of his probationary period.

16. The safety of the society, the allure of all things hidden and the observation of the Candidate require that the identity of not even the least member is revealed to him without good cause: should our society have been unfortunate enough to admit a prattler, he would thus only be able to betray a single man.

17. This will make the Candidate careful not to speak to anyone about matters of the ☉, even if he believes them to be members.

18. Every Candidate's Recipient is also his Superior; everyone is permitted to recruit a member, but everything must be done as instructed by his immediate Superiors; if he wishes to be promoted to a higher Class, he must have recruited at least one or, in certain cases, two men; thus, it is possible that an industrious man can establish a small kingdom even in his Noviciate years, becoming great and mighty in his smallness.

19. However, the Superior must be kept abreast of every step, and no one may do anything without his permission.

20. The Candidate keeps separate sheets of paper for everyone he is considering for recruitment, entering for each person those pronouncements and actions that reveal his soul, especially very minute ones made when he believed himself unobserved. As all our judgements and actions reveal something about ourselves, he will find no lack of material for his notes.

21. These notes are the basis for all subsequent records, and therefore they must be very accurate, strictly narrative, without any commentary; all reports, letters [of recommendation], etc., are derived from these notes, and if someone is to be admitted, the Recipient's character must be derived from these and presented to the immediate Superior.

22. For the Superiors' safety it has been decided that no subordinate may keep a single written word about the ☉'s business given to him by his Superiors. The Superiors' letters must be immediately returned, together with the reply.

23. One may, however, make excerpts from the letters received.

24. Absent members write post-paid letters to their Superiors every fortnight; local members visit their Superiors at least once a week, and if the Superior has enough time, he may divide the days of the week among his people, read with them or have edifying conversations with them.

25. So that all members are infused with one spirit and become of one mind and will, they are assigned certain books to read from which they can educate themselves.

These books have been chosen for present-day Germany:

    1. Seneca, Phil[osophical works]

    2. Epictetus

    3. Antonine's Observations on Himself

    4. Plutarch's Biographies

    5. His ethical as well as all his other writings

    6. Wieland's works

        Agathon[215].

        Golden Mirror[216].

        Secret Contributions[217].

    7. Tobias Knaut[218].

    8. Hirschfeld on the Great Man and on Heroic Virtues[219].

    9. Pope's Essay on Man[220].

---

[215] *Christoph Martin Wieland: Geschichte des Agathon (1766/67).*

[216] *Id.: Der goldene Spiegel oder die Könige van Scheschian (1772).*

[217] *Id.: Beyträge zur geheimen Geschichte des menschlichen Verstandes und Herzens (1776).*

[218] *Johann Karl Wezel: Lebensgeschichte Tobias Knauts, des Weisen, sonst der Stammler genannt (1773–76).*

[219] *Christian Cay Lorenz Hirschfeld: Versuch über den grossen Mann (1768) und Betrachtungen über die heroischen Tugenden (1770).*

[220] *Alexander Pope: An Essay on Man (1734).*

10. Smith's Theory of Morals[221].
11. Basedow's Practical Philosophy for all Classes[222]
12. Meiners' Philosophical Writings.
13. Abt's On Merit.
14. Montagne's Essay[s][223].
15. Helvetius' On the Mind[224].
16. La Bruiere's Character[s][225].
17. All writings by Bellegarde[226], as well as
18. le Noble's School of the World[227].

In general, no book that educates the heart is excluded, and we especially recommend writers of fables and all others that are rich in imagery or moral and political maxims.

26. We require a kind heart of all and contributions in the arts and sciences from those who can make them; apart from ethics, the society values chemistry and trade the most. Languages, especially French and Greek, are highly treasured if only to comprehend the books; but Italian and English also hold great value, and everyone who wishes to advance must understand at least one of these languages.

27. The *Arcanum* remains the same throughout all Classes.

28. The Superiors are our leaders, guiding us when we wander in darkness and error and leading us away from treacherous paths. Here, pliability and obedience turn into indebtedness and even gratitude; no one, then, will refuse to follow him whose efforts are in his best interests.

29. However, Superiors can also abuse their power, and they are not always [good] fathers; therefore, the society wishes to protect all members against any oppressors, tyrants, etc., by means of the following measures. At the end of each month, every subordinate hands his Superior one or several sealed sheets of paper, *Quibus licet* or *Soli,* in which he indicates:

[221] Adam Smith: The Theory of Moral Sentiments (1759).

[222] Johann Bernhard Basedow: Practische Philosophie für alle Stände (1758).

[223] Michel Eyquem de Montaigne (1533–1592), French politician and author.

[224] Claude Adrien Helvétius: De l'esprit (1759).

[225] Jean de la Bruyère: Les Caractères de Theophraste traduits du grec. Avec les caractères ou les moeurs de ce siècle (1688).

[226] Jean-Baptiste Morvan de Bellegarde (1648–1734), French author, chiefly of works in the moralist vein, and translator.

[227] Eustache le Noble: L'école du Monde (1715).

1) How his Superior treats him, whether he is industrious or negligent, severe or kind.

2) What grievances he has against the society.

3) What orders the Superior has given him this month and how much he has paid to the Order.

He must submit the sheet even if he has no grievances, and to make this easier for the subordinate he prepares one or the other sheet at the beginning of the month and, as soon as something draws his attention, he records it on the respective sheet and does not seal it until the month's end. This regulation remains in effect throughout all Classes, and no one is excluded; if it is disregarded, the subordinate is subject to a fine proportionate to his circumstances, and the same applies to the Superior who neglects to send them out in a timely manner. The Candidate will not be fined if these sheets are submitted on the last day of the month; therefore all Superiors must put a date on them.

30. During his Reception everyone must declare whether or not he is able to contribute money to the society. In the latter case, it is our hope that no one will try to give the impression that he is poorer than he actually is, as we are already informed of the Candidate's fortunes; in the former, every Superior must assign his Recipient a proportionate contribution ante receptionem[228], which is set at will for lesser men, one ducat for those of the middle-class, and one carolin for affluent men; [229] this is proposed to him after he has issued the Obligation and before he receives the Statutes, with the Candidate's signature that he has paid this amount on the day he issued the Obligation, and that this amount is due again the second year and also for those who have been admitted for 3 years. The Superiors hand the contribution to their respective Superiors: if the contribution is in arrears past the date set, the Superior of the member whose contribution is missing is contacted. Should one of the Candidates attempt to defraud the society, he forfeits all future benefits. Nothing at all shall be collected from a truly destitute person, si fidem paupertatis fecerit;[230] if his fortunes improve, his annual contribution increases in proportion to his resources.

31. To this end the Order decrees that all Superiors must collect any outstanding amounts by next year, Jan. 31st, 1779, but without overburdening anyone; any exceptions must be justified in writing. This statute was enacted due to the

---

[228] Lat. Prior to the reception.   [229] I.e. three times the amount.
[230] Lat. If he has given evidence of being in poverty.

members' negligence in paying their dues even though it is they who hope for true assistance from the Order in times [of need]. This order will be regarded as more than fair, since other orders demand an initial fee of 100 guilders and more without exception, and they collect this amount repeatedly and over the course of many years.

32. Should someone resign during his probationary years, all contributions are refunded to him, which is why the Superiors must record them diligently.

33. Every Candidate is allowed to resign up to the last hour, *imposito tamen silentio.*[231]

34. The present statutes are made known to those who have not yet recruited anyone orally; others will receive written copies. Exceptions are permitted for absent members. Any subsequent, new decree shall immediately be entered into this very copy.

GUIDING IDEA.

Since it is our society's purpose to make the effort of improving and perfecting his moral character interesting to man, spread humane and social sentiments, thwart malicious intentions, assist an harassed virtue against injustice, further the promotion of worthy men and, finally, reward particularly deserving men who can benefit the ☉ with their talents, wealth, or good reputation, by special respect, fame, and glory both within and outside the society[:]

This society assures each and every one who has received the current Statutes that this is the ☉'s only and unadulterated purpose. Indeed, this society stands for nothing else; should the Candidates discover more than this over time, so much the better for them, and may they learn from this that here, contrary to the practices in other societies, more is fulfilled than has been promised.

A member who is primarily moved to join the ☉ by the prospects of great power and riches would not be the most welcome here.

However, since everyone's assistance, whether it consists of moral or physical prowess, good concord and the unbreakable commitment of all Brethren are needed to maintain such an ultimate purpose, and since it is no less important to draw those outside the ☉ towards what is best for our society as well as its cause, all members,

---

[231] *Lat. With, however, silence being imposed.*

1. out of consideration for the society, must avoid any hatred or envy towards their fellow Brethren, regard them as their foremost and dearest friends, guard their hearts against all ignoble selfishness, and view the good of the whole as their own.

2. They shall constantly strive and think of ways to win the hearts not only of their Brethren but those of their enemies as well.

3. No less shall they be anxious to provide concrete proof that they intend to benefit their ☉.

4. To cultivate the habit of exemplary prudence and secrecy towards all.

5. As far as the ☉'s business is concerned, the ☉ requires unconditional obedience.

6. All members must aspire towards the greatest possible inward and outward perfection.

7. Acquire an endearing, cordial personality and conduct.

8. Learn the art of disguising themselves, and of observing and probing others.

9. Every member must immediately choose a particular science or art as his major field of study; however, since this cannot be required of everyone, because some may or may not have the inclination or opportunity to pursue it, the ☉ has established in this regard that everyone must let his *Insinuator* know, within a fortnight, whether he wishes to benefit the ☉ through his efforts in the sciences or with a monetary contribution. In the former case he must deliver a treatise fit for printing; in the latter, he must make a proportionate contribution (here, another member must write a treatise in the contributor's stead, which is then dedicated to the financial contributor).

10.[232] Should his admission not come to pass it is returned to him unopened, along with everything else.

11. Should a member learn any *arcana* he must forward them to the ☉, but it is understood that no use will be made of these unless the reporting member gives his permission or until he passes away, in which case it must be observed that any benefit derived from these *arcana* should be used for his destitute friends or surviving children.

12. Because, in this degree, the Candidate has no standing but is merely being observed by members who are concealed from him, the fee for this degree is only

---

[232] *This point may have been meant to follow no. 12 below.*

one ducat. If someone chooses to give more, it is regarded as a sign of exceptional dedication. This contribution must always be handed to the *Insinuator* in a sealed container.

13. He receives no further degrees until the fee is paid.

14. Silence being the supreme law, it is not permitted to speak of one's admission into the ☉ even to those believed to be Brethren in the ☉; because:

a) If he is not a Brother in the ☉, the society is betrayed.

b) If he actually is one, one does not know if he is of a greater or lesser rank, or indeed an equal who is free to show it.

15. It is important to the society that it remains as secret as possible:

a) So that the society's plans and operations are not hindered by counter-efforts on the part of the malicious, malcontent, etc.

b) So that the whole society cannot be betrayed in a single stroke.

c) Because the appeal to remain in the society would otherwise dissipate.

d) So that any conspiracies and exploits of those hungry for power can be undermined.

e) So that the higher ranking, hidden members may observe the lesser ones more easily.

16. If a Candidate in this degree wishes to resign, he may do so at any time: *imposito tamen silentio.*

17. In this degree, it is prohibited to recruit another person, but one may certainly suggest suitable members to his *Insinuator.*

INSTRUCTIO PRO RECIPIENTIBUS [233]

1. Once someone has found a suitable subject, has proposed him to the Order, and has received permission to proceed with him, the necessary steps cannot be taken all at once; he shall first seek to earn his affection, trust, and esteem.

2. In his conduct, he shall act in such a manner that the man to be recruited is led to believe that there is more to him than meets the eye, and that he has hidden qualities.

3. He must guide the man in such a manner that the desire to join such a society does not arise all at once, but gradually, and so that the candidate effectively asks the recruiter to assist him in this.

---

[233] *Latin. Instructions for Receivers.*

4. This can be done most easily in the following manner:

    1) The reading of good books that uplift the soul serves this purpose, e.g.

    Seneca.

    Abt, On Merit.

    Meiners' Miscellaneous Philosophical Writings.

    The Golden Mirror.

    Contributions to the Secret History of the Human Mind and Heart.

    Tobias Knaut.

    Agathon.

    Plutarch's writings on morals.

    His Lives.

    Antonin's self-reflections.

Alternatively, one should engage in discourse from which one can subtly proceed to the topic of social bonds.

2) To this end, one must have books at hand that deal with unity, the strength derived from social connections, etc.

3) For example, if one witnesses the cry or helplessness of a small child, one should begin to talk about the weakness of man and how little he can accomplish on his own. One further demonstrates to him how strong and powerful he is through the help of others.

4) One makes it clear that all human greatness and princely sovereignty is derived from a consensus of will.

5) One demonstrates the advantages of society over the state of nature.

6) One then comes to speak of the art of knowing and directing men.

7) One shows how easily a single wise mind can lead a hundred or a thousand men, if one knows one's strengths.

8) Pointing to the example of military service and soldiers, one shows what princes are able to accomplish with the unity of their subjects.

9) One shows the advantages of society in general and the shortcomings of civil society and how little one can count on the help of others, even one's own friends.

10) One states that in our time it is necessary for a man to join forces with others. Men could create heaven among themselves if only they were united, for it is only their disunity that makes their subjugation possible.

11) One expands on this with examples and fables, e.g. that of the two hounds who herded sheep and defended the herd as long as they were

united. Everyone should gather suitable examples.

12) Finally, one gradually proceeds to the idea that secret associations could do even more, and shows the reasons for this.

13) One illustrates this by pointing to the Jesuit Order, the Order of Freemasons, and the secret associations of the ancients: one argues that all world events are the result of a hundred causes and mainsprings, in which secret associations are at the fore. One extols the pleasures of quiet and secret power and of insight into the deepest secrets.

14) At this point, one begins to reveal certain insights and to drop ambiguous figures of speech into the conversation here and there.

15) Once the candidate starts to become fiery, one continues to reason with him until one senses he has come to the decision and conclusion that if he had the opportunity to join such an association, he would take it immediately.

16) These conversations are to be frequently repeated.

17) One tells him that one has had the opportunity, that one has been confidentially told, etc., one asks the candidate for advice, presents one's own opinions, which must always be supported by stronger arguments, one expresses concerns, and precisely those that one believes to be holding the other man back: however, one should dispel these right away and keep asking him for his own assessment, so that he is compelled to make a judgement. NB: Among those one has known and trusted for a long time, this short route may be chosen right away.

18) On another occasion, one arranges for a letter written in cipher to arrive while the candidate, who has already been led some way, is present. One opens it and reads it as if trying to keep it concealed from him, but in such a manner that he is able to see the ciphers.

19) Or one leaves such a letter half-open on the desk and, when one thinks the candidate has seen it, one picks it up with the mien of a man who is not keen about revealing something and tucks it into one's own pocket or leaves the room as if called away by some urgent matter.

20) On another occasion, one returns to the first topic.

21) One also tries to discover the man's governing inclinations and motivations, introducing the matter in such a way that he has to realise that it can be confirmed only through these connections, and in no other way.

22) During these conversations and actions, the candidate will eventually

show whether he is inclined to join or not. On this depends whether or not he should be made to sign the first Obligation.

5. One shall not, without special permission, seek to recruit anyone unless

1) he is of the Christian faith.

2) He is younger or of the same age as the Recipient.

3) One finds that he has a great, philanthropic, and benevolent heart.

4) Furthermore, he should either be gifted with intelligence (even better if he owes his enlightenment primarily to the Order) or skilled in the arts; he should be industrious and precise, parsimonious and of good repute.

5) Prattlers, revellers, lechers, the headstrong, proud, uncouth and unsociable, braggarts, the fickle, liars, and egotists will always be rejected, unless there is a most likely hope of improvement.

6) Likewise, this includes Jews, pagans, women, monks, and members of other secret orders.

7) Those who already hold public offices and are more advanced in age are only eligible if the Recipient himself is already older and *in officiis,* or if the *Recipiendus* is receptive to instruction nonetheless.

8) Young men, 18 to 20 years old, who are wealthy, inquisitive, obedient, kind-hearted, steadfast, and persistent are preferred.

6. When one notices that the candidate is allowing his eagerness and his desire to be accepted to show, one may inform him that the Order is rather less interested, and that it requires effort to obtain admission.

7. When imparting his insights, the Recipient or *Insinuator* must not reveal everything at once, but instead always keep something to himself which he discloses only if his candidate's enthusiasm grows tepid.

8. He must not allow him to retain anything in his own handwriting, but instead demand that everything be returned to him once it has been read.

9. He reports in detail about all occurrences to his Superiors and requests instruction for further action, and he strictly conceals his identity from those who are subsequently recruited by the candidate, directly or indirectly.

10. In particular, he should occasionally catch the candidate unawares to ascertain how he is looking after the Order's documents.

11. He must also have frequent conversations about the Order with him and furthermore note in his oral or written reports to the Superiors whether the candidate is speaking about it with zeal, earnestness, or indifference.

12. In order to prevent boredom, he must also entertain him and give him undemanding tasks to perform, but most of all he must accustom him to orderliness and punctuality, especially when it comes to following orders, and keep testing him with regard to this.

13. Moreover, he must continuously encourage him to suggest others who might also be accepted.

14. He should also read good books with him, give him instructions how to take notes and make excerpts, and have him show him these.

15. From time to time, all points listed in the table are to be entered with precision.

16. He shall also strive to win his trust, discover secret connections through him, get him to make character sketches of different persons, etc.

17. In general, the Recipient has to ensure the strictest implementation of the statutes and give report thereof to his immediate Superior; but he himself should not be too quick to issue a reprimand. To this end, one should refer him to the statutes and regulations already in his possession.

18. These instructions should not be readily handed out; they are intended only to be read out or explained orally.

INSTRUCTIO INSINUATORUM[234]

1. Everyone must maintain a journal in which he records all events of the Order, documents received, etc., according to day and year.

2. He must copy the tables received by his *Insinuator* and faithfully enter everything into those that must be submitted to the Order through his respective Recipient.

3. Submit to the ☉ in the same way a list of those persons whom he believes to be suitable for the Order, with a mark next to those whom he could introduce himself.

4. Concerning those persons to be proposed, one shall ensure that they have a good heart, a desire to learn, and a love and zeal for work. If they are already knowledgeable in the sciences, then so much the better; if they are not the society can satisfy their desire through instruction. Artists are also suitable, preferably painters; craftsmen, especially wood-turners, goldsmiths, and locksmiths; also

---

[234] *Lat. Instructions for 'Insinuators'.*

handymen, such as scribes, printers, etc., as well as men who can lend the ☉ their protection and good name. One must therefore strive to become acquainted with such persons.

5. Everyone must set aside individual sheets of paper, and when a sheet is completed another one must be added. In particular, each must contain

a) everything he has read and gathered about the character and actions of learned and noble men from ancient and modern times. Similarly,

b) all sublime thoughts, peculiar sentiments, and pithy sayings must be written down and sent to the ☉ on demand as proof of industry.

c) In addition, each month, through his *Insinuator* and without being asked, everyone must submit to the ☉ on a folio everything that he has learnt, read, or contemplated during the past month for the benefit of the society, its enrichment, increase in membership, or internal arrangement. Even if the society does not need such projects or they are dismissed due to their impracticality, one can still see from these how far the Candidate is involved in the plan and where he needs further instruction.

6. Since one receives a name from the ☉, everything pertaining to it has to be specially collected.

7. If someone has a complaint against his *Insinuator*, he shall submit it in a sealed sheet of paper labelled *Au premier*.

8. Everyone shall have a special container for all matters related to the ☉ furnished with a card stating that, in the event of his unforeseen demise, these documents must be sent to the respective *Insinuator's* address. If illness leaves a man enough time to put his matters in order, he shall swiftly see to it that the seal is placed on the documents and that the proper address is added.

9. Everyone must maintain summary copies of everything he sends to the ☉ and copy all models, tables, instructions, etc., for himself.

INSTRUCTIONS FOR THOSE WHO HAVE RECEIVED THE *FACULTAS INSINUANDI.*

1. As soon as the ☉ approves the introduction of a suggested person, the *Insinuans* has to find suitable occasions to speak to his new Candidate, unfolding the matter by and by, depending on how he believes to best win him over. Once he has explained to him the society's main purpose, he requests of him the Obligation, then reads to him the Statutes, submits the Obligation to the ☉ through his

own *Insinuator* and awaits further instructions, refraining from issuing any written documents to the new Candidate until he receives permission to do so. When ordered to, he hands the Candidate first the Statutes and then the *Instructio Insinuatorum,* demands the completion of all required tasks, takes note of every step in his diary, and submits those items listed below to the ☉. The following is to be observed:

2. Strictest adherence to the Statutes he has received as *Insinuatus.*

3. He must faithfully enter everything into the table for his suggested Candidate, according to the enclosure.[235]

4. He must submit exact, written reports on every matter concerning his subordinate to his own *Insinuator,* who in turn communicates them to the ☉.

5. He shall surprise the Candidate from time to time, to see if he handles the ☉'s documents with care and keeps them in order.

6. He shall have frequent conversations about the ☉ with him and observe whether the Candidate speaks about it with zeal, seriousness, or coldness, what it is he foremostly seeks in the ☉, etc.

7. Deliver everything required to be issued to the new Insinuant in the name of the society and demand receipts for important items.

8. Constantly encourage him to suggest suitable persons and to himself become, through his zeal, worthy of the permission to recruit others.

9. When the new Candidate receives this *facultas* from the ☉, the person who has been introduced by him may not know the new Candidate's *Insinuator,* and it must always be kept thus *in descendenti,*[236] until the moment the society determines otherwise. This is *strictissimæ observantiæ.*

10. Since he who receives the ☉'s permission to introduce other subjects has climbed one degree above mere *Insinuati,* the society must ensure that he places his whole trust in it. Hence it has been decided for this degree that, in addition to the folios that must be submitted according to the *Instructio Insinuatorum,* another one that lists all secret intrigues, amours, enmities of various persons, etc., in order of completeness, has to be sealed and submitted by the respective *Insinuator,* labelled *au Premier.* For this, one may make use of the cipher no. 1.

11. A catalogue of all books owned must be submitted to the society.[237]

---

[235] *No such enclosure was published along with the present document.*

[236] *Lat. In descending order.*

[237] *Here follows a postscript by Zwackh: 'Only used and handed out pro privata instructione, in order to acquaint young men with orderliness. Based on each person's character, they may also copy them piece by piece.'*

24 POINTS DESIGNED TO BE PRESENTED AS QUESTIONS TO NEW CANDIDATES.[238]

1. Does he still seek admission?

2. Has he sufficiently considered that this is a big step to take? That he is making obligations as yet unknown to him?

3. What are his reasons for joining the Order? What does he hope and expect from it?

4. Would he still join the Order even if it had no other final purpose than moral perfection and there were no other benefits?

5. What if the Order were new, had only a few members or were an invention of the Recipient?

6. What if he discovered immoral and unjust things occurring within it?

7. Could he view the Order's welfare as his own?

8. Would he willing to love all the members?

9. Even if he found his enemies among them?

10. If it were necessary and if one would have to depend on him, would he even be prepared to do his enemies good, recommend and praise them?

11. In the event of his absence, would he stay in contact with members of the Order?

12. Would he honour and distinguish them, preferring them to the profane at all occasions?

13. How would he avenge wrongs done to him by members, or wrongs done to him by outsiders?

14. How would he conduct himself if he repented it?

15. Would he be willing to share good fortune and misfortune with his Brethren?

16. Would he renounce the advantages of his birth, office and status so as to never use them to the detriment and contempt of other Brethren?

17. Does he belong to any other order?

　　What is its name?

　　Would he renounce it or not?

18. Would he consider joining another order in the future?

19. What would he do if it pursued opposing interests?

---

[238] 'In Spartacus' (Weishaupt's) handwriting.'

20. Has he been led to make his promise too easily, out of carelessness or out of the expectation that he would very soon be learning something about the present Order's structure soon?

21. Would he be ready to follow the Order's statutes to the letter?

22. Would he also concern himself with the Order's proliferation in the future?

23. Would he be ready to help the Order by word and deed, money and property, if needed?

24. Under what penalties and punishments and with what assurances does he commit himself to all of this?

GENERAL EXPLANATION OF THE SOCIETY OF THE *ILLUMINATI.*
(ALTERNATIVE BEGINNING)

There is an ancient society that has always remained secret for more than one reason; which is why not many have heard of it, but he who has studied the history of the Pythagorean school, has heard of the Illuminés, condemned long ago in Spain,[239] and has read *Crata Repoa*[240] with some attentiveness, too, will be able to find some kind of trace of it. This society is comprised of men who, since times immemorial, have investigated, searched, and in part have been handed down from their ancestors everything that men can know. Consequently they know what is true and what is false; they have made many of their collaborators disperse into all [other] societies; they know the institutions and what is good and evil therein, and so they are more capable than any society in the world of satisfying a man who thirsts for knowledge. However, their focus lies not on knowing, but on doing. They believe that man was not only put into the world to gather knowledge but also to use it for the benefit of his fellow men. He shall not ask for supernatural knowledge until he has filled his place here. You will have noticed that hardly any of the secret societies has understood this.[241]

---

[239] *The sect of the 'Alumbrados' or 'Iluminados', active chiefly in Castile and Andalusia in the 16ᵗʰ and 17ᵗʰ centuries opposed the hierarchy of the church and sought after a mystical union with God.*

[240] *[Carl Friedrich Köppen and Johann Wilhelm Bernhard Hymmen:] Crata Repoa. Oder Einweihungen in der alten geheimen Gesellschaft der Egyptischen Priester (1770).*

[241] *The remainder of this text is identical to the other version, beginning with 'When better men unite …'*

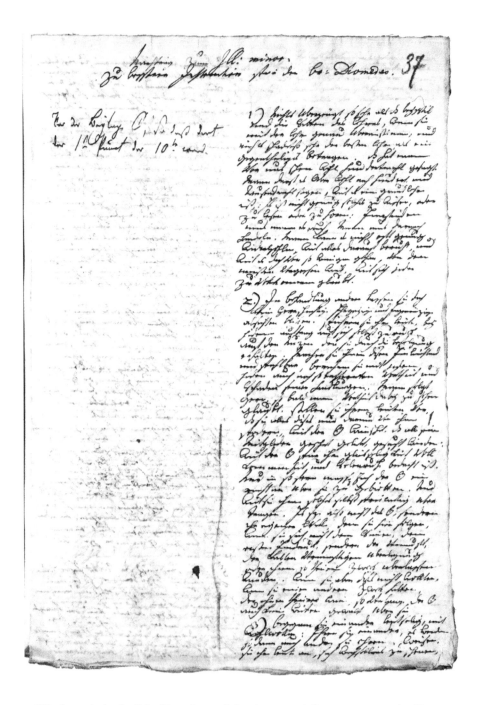

Weishaupt's draft of the 'Supplement'. In the upper left corner, a note by Knigge.

SUPPLEMENT TO THE ILLUM. MIN. FOR THE BETTER INSTRUCTION OF THE SUPERIOR.

1. Nothing is more convincing than when the example set by the teacher's morals exactly matches the lesson taught, and nothing damages even the best doctrine if his actions contradict it. This has probably been said hundreds of times before. Even so, it may well be said hundreds and thousands of times again, since it is a fundamental doctrine. It does not suffice to know, read or hear this; one must *sense* and also *act* by it. It cannot be repeated often enough because everything else rests upon it and because so few follow it and most forget it, since everyone believes himself to be perfect.

2. When dealing with others, do not show any domineering, ambitious, and selfish intentions. Show your men how every task you assign is relevant to them and that it is they who gain from completing it. Make them understand and feel this. Review with each of them even the most distant benefit and harm of his actions. He will eagerly follow you if he believes that he can see the benefit. Demonstrate to your men that you only require all these things of them because the O. wishes its members to be treasured, loved, and sought after [because] the Order cares about their felicity, perfection, and peace of mind. Tell them that only in this respect the [Order] can claim a right to command them, and because they have transferred to it this right voluntarily. Thus they do not obey the will of the O. but their own if they do not rely on their senses and first impressions, but instead on reason, [cool] and sensible deliberation or on their goal so dear to them. If however this is not what they desire, if they have a different goal that is dear to them, the O. shall demand no further power over them.

3. Treat one another affably, with goodwill; if you honour one another, then others will honour you as well. Instruct your men to treat each other with caution, to avoid displeasing one another and to curb their pretensions. Do not nourish the members' discontent with the O. or among themselves; step into the middle immediately as an angel of peace and prove to them that united power is indestructible while a scattered crowd will always succumb to others; that it is neither noble nor a sign of magnanimity to give in to one's passions over every trifle, to create schisms and to bring the greatest punishment upon oneself where one believed to find the greatest benefit. Teach your men to suffer flaws and misdeeds out of love [for the greater whole and, at the same time, out of true

love] for themselves. Men must always remember that they are dealing with other men – even more so as they are not gods themselves.

4. Your men must gather from your more or less cordial demeanour alone whether they are in good or poor standing. The mien must speak while the mouth is silent. Your friendship [shall] be the reward of the good man, because he is good and for as long as he remains so. You must however have earned your people's reverence and respect first. If their *conduite* changes, your behaviour shall change as well. Your reticence alone should more than suffice as a reproach to well-bred men. In general, try to encourage your [*élèves*[242]] with honours, approval, and small rewards, rather than proceed against them with penalties or reproaches. A man who requires the latter has already fallen far and has lost much of his dignity. His decreased esteem in the eyes of the sensible must be more painful to a noble man than the gallows and the wheel.

5. To teach your flock the spirit of self-examination, instruct them to be aware of themselves, to look within themselves whenever there is mention of the flaws and errors of others, to imagine themselves in their situation, to avoid flattering themselves and [rather] to discover their own flaws and ills [than their virtues]. That is the path to self-knowledge. He who finds no flaws in himself and only good deceives himself most shamefully. Do not trust such a man. But it is a sign of enlightenment and indeed of enlightenment of the highest degree if one is capable of finding more good in others and more evil in oneself than usual. [He who wants to become good must first doubt that he already is good: he must understand, must know that he is not. This is a most important and most difficult art, since the love of the self is too blinding. Only few achieve extraordinary prowess in this domain: they even become indignant when others reproach them about flaws that they as explorers of the self should have discovered on their own but did not. Of what use is it if I believe and believe well, but others do not? If these others are indispensable to me, it is their vote and not mine that counts in my attempts to achieve my goal of being popular and esteemed. Every judgement by your fellow man must be your schooling and lesson. Take note of who praises you and who chides you, and take note of what you are praised and chided for. Be suspicious of other people's praise, but search yourself when reprimanded. There must be some truth to what others say of you, and even if it is their envy speaking, try at least to lessen their envy. One can also be misguided in the

---

[242] Fr. Pupils.

demonstration of one's perfection. It is imprudent always to appear as the first among others. Great human perfection is hated and despised if it humiliates others too greatly and promises them no benefits. Men judge a thing by how it affects them and by its appeal; if it is good, then vice is even dearer to them than virtue. A thousand men would be happier and more popular if they understood the art of letting others surpass them. Folly is often wisdom. He who chides you is your friend and benefactor; he who praises you is your flatterer. Knowing this is illumination; acting and living by it is the labour of the illuminated.

O! men, do not place trust in your judgement of yourselves; and you who chide yourselves and tell me you mistrust my judgement, consider that in this judgement you may also deceive yourself. Consider that you often reproach yourselves because you want to seem great and impartial. Consider that you flee praise only to beg for greater praise. Examine the mainspring of every action, and when you believe you have found it do not rest there but climb one more step and examine the mainspring of that mainspring itself. Here, in this reflected judgement, in the further contemplation and examination of why I judge myself in this way you will discover the real truth more often, and you will be all the more certain to find it the more you desire to examine the judgements and the causes of my judgements in ascending order; the further you progress in this manner, the more it will become apparent that even the most selfless action is not done without the anticipation of some benefit, that the latter is inseparable from our actions and that ultimately virtue is nothing other than interest that agrees with and promotes the well-being of others; which is what makes virtue laudable and vice repugnant; that true self-love cannot exist without benevolence; finally, that true felicity is inseparable from the felicity of others. Morality itself is nothing else than an instruction in loving oneself sensibly: to incur the favour of others, to do good unto them in order to receive good from them, thereby to increase pleasure and lessen displeasure, to receive tranquillity, contentment and felicity. And according to this doctrine, every vice is error, a poorly-understood interest that sooner or later punishes itself through unrest, discontent, and fear of retribution. Therefore, have pity on these erring souls and lead them onto the right path. Spread approval, increase the number of the illuminated, and you will also decrease vice and spread bliss over the earth.] All the sciences in the world do not reach this degree of enlightenment, for it is not scientific splendour by which it is achieved but a healthy and pure common sense that knows how to judge one's own circumstances and those of others and truly deserves to be called enlightenment. One must be able to spot a member of the O. from his morals rather than from outward symbols.

6. An enlightened man must find joy and instruction in evil men as well, for it is certain that no one, truly no one would be evil if he understood his own best interests. Every evil-doer believes he is doing good, [believes] he is doing the best. In dealing with [good men we learn how we ought to be ourselves, in dealing] with evil ones we learn what we ought [not] to be and how despicable it is to be and act as they do – or why else would we do what we dislike in others so much? This is reason enough for also loving our enemies. They are of more use to us than many friends, they are no flatterers or liars whose charms deceive us, they make us prudent, make it easier to know ourselves, and they are almost the only way by which the truth reaches us.

7. Teach your subordinates the habit of observing when and how ardent persuasiveness in a conversation arouses a desire, passion, or decision in them, what figures of speech accomplish this, and what ideas and what emphasis of these ideas were required to stir this desire in a previously indifferent and cold soul. They shall memorise and record this sequence of ideas so that they may use it with others, as these are tried and tested weapons whose effect they can discover best within themselves. Similar causes must also have similar effects with others. If the effect does not occur, an inquisitive mind finds more food for thought here. He investigates the lack of success; he learns to break the idea down into its components, investigates the degree to which the speaker's language, voice, gestures, time and place, as well as the listener's general mood may have contributed, and how much of this must be added or subtracted on a different occasion, with another person; he learns to investigate the individual and subjective aspects of dealing with men. One can [most] certainly convince anyone, without exception, of anything. However, this needs effort, and if one does not prevail, the flaw must surely lie in the method which therefore must be changed as often and as much as necessary to achieve success. Say and prove to every man: 'You are lacking something!' Make him value what he is lacking; make it near and dear to him, vividly present it to him as an essential part of his felicity; moreover, show him that it is possible and easy to obtain, and to obtain everything in this way and through you only – what man will fail to follow and love him who is so concerned about his well-being? Be assured that if your [élèves] fail and do not meet your expectations, the fault lies with no one but yourself. Nothing is as certain as that your manner of dealing with these men is of little use. No one in

the world resists self-love or a vividly presented interest. But you, my friend! you do not understand the art of making it tangible to this individual in these circumstances. From the beggar to the emperor, from the greatest villain to the foremost saint, no one can resist if he is assailed in the proper place and in a measured, subjective manner, if the attack is continued undauntedly and changed after every failure. And is it really that difficult to discover each man's weakness? We rather have too many of them than too few. Therefore, do not proceed with everyone in the same manner, not even with the same subject in the same manner at all times. If one thing has failed then try something else; try it more often, less often, more strongly, more vividly, more mildly, and through others. Some are thought to be invincible because they have not yet met the man who understands the art of mastering them. In every instance, note precisely the degree of success. From this you may deduce the cause as well as your skill and manner of dealing with men – and how much it must be changed, what must be added, dropped, or repeated. Do not despair at the remedy if the first attempt has failed. Many are won over only through steadfastness and through constant patience and effort. It means nothing if the ailing man at first even pushes the healing hand away. He needs its help the most when he scorns it the most. Therefore repeat the attack, from a different angle and with more finesse, and sure enough your pains shall be rewarded in the end.

8. Above all, seek greatness in overcoming your passions, wishes and desires – indeed, seek to surpass others in this. This is a noble contest[.] Miserable is the philosophy that is the toy of every whim; where the boisterous clamour of even the least and lowliest lust silences reason; where a man can prove everything yet does nothing, being wise in theory but a fool in practice, strong and invincible in his chamber and weak and defeated at the first opportunity, brave when there is no danger and victorious without enemies. What can one expect from such a man[,] what can mankind and the good cause hope from him? Even if he could bring happiness to thousands, he would not do it, as the present, tantalising benefit, his palate's desire, a paramour's smile, the glitter of metals, and every imagined insult affect his dwarfish soul too powerfully for him to rise above them and to purchase the happiness of his fellow men for a price so dear [to him].

He who loves himself too much, too excessively, hates all others. Do not trust such a man. What can a friend expect of him, when he would destroy the world to earn the favour of a cheap strumpet?

[9. Commanding another man means to us to show him what may be of use to him under the given circumstances and what is useful to the body to which he belongs. He who cannot be of use has lost every right to dominion and command. Commands and laws are only that which everyone should and would do if he had an overall view of the entire situation. They are the result of a general sensibility which also watches over those whose circumstances force them to walk in darkness. There is only one perfectly true manner of conduct, because there is only one true benefit. And if orders and laws are to be good they must express and demonstrate this benefit. Therefore it is essentially one and the same thing whether I tell a man: 'This will benefit you', or 'I order you'. However, the former ensures success, because it does not make its compulsion felt, removes any reluctance, and allows willingness to arise on its own accord. Not fear, but only the feeling of a present or future special or general benefit, the goodness of the cause itself and the desire to act grandly and nobly shall direct our members and preserve them for us. Fear is a blunt, worn-out mainspring that is unworthy of a noble cause. It is almost impossible for a great spirit to be capable of it.]

PREPARATION FOR THOSE WHO ARE TO PARTICIPATE IN GOVERNING THE ORDER.

My Brother!
You have declared that you regard the institute of the Illustrious Order up to the Lesser *Illuminatus* degree, which you have received, as important, noble, and worthy of your collaboration. We therefore welcome you to the smaller circle of operative workers! With confidence we can assert that the Order deserves this sentiment and that you shall never regret having become one of its active members.

Now you know what is essential, the main focus of our association's Superiors and the manner in which we perpetuate it – and that in order to spread truth and light we must first set up preparatory schools and educate men according to our principles. However, before you direct such an enterprise in your parts, before you can proliferate the Order and link it to the Freemasons, it is necessary that any conceivable doubt or mistrust on either side be fully resolved, if indeed any still exists.

You still have two *Illuminati* degrees before you, one of which is concerned with the most precise knowledge of man, and another which, in addition to various disclosures, demonstrates its practical applications for the members of the Order.[243] Then follows the Mysteries Class, in which your spirit will find nourishment as well as the opportunity to teach and learn.

However, neither you nor we are served well if we bestow these degrees on you one after the other before you are ready to use such knowledge for the benefit of other men.

The lowest Class is the Order's foundation. Once you have established this preparatory school and then entrusted the worthiest among the Minervals with the care of the weaker ones, thus placing the direction of the Minerval Class into other hands and discharging yourself of this duty, then you have the leisure, merit, and right to learn more about the Order and participate in its government. Until then we shall postpone everything else to avoid confusion, skip the other degrees, and look ahead to give you a first glance at the larger plan of operations. If we could not agree on the latter, it would be fruitless for both parties to dwell on the theoretical part, as our main focus is to be of practical use for the world.

A society desiring to spread wisdom and virtue in this corrupted world is bound to encounter obstacles. The Order has taken the most reliable measures to overcome these and to gain power over evil; should we, my Brother! share this power with you, and if you wish to become a pillar of the just cause, we must better acquaint ourselves with one another in one more aspect. Our work must be accomplished with prudence and caution as well as honesty and unselfishness. You can easily see that an association resting on such a solid foundation is and must be very powerful in secret in order to remove the obstacles barring the progress of wisdom, and that it does not suffice to have noble principles alone but *that he who has the power to implement them must also choose good means for this end.*

Therefore, it is in the interest of both parties to ascertain:

I. On our part, that the man whom we allow to stand at the helm with us uses the instruction and means placed in his hands in a most unselfish manner and for the advantage of the whole.

II. On your part, that you can be assured that we seek nothing other than universal felicity and that we plan no dangerous treason. –

In a word, we must ask one another about our political principles, and you must know our plan of operations. Or we ask you: 'Which measures would you

---

[243] *Illuminatus major and dirigens, respectively.*

take to remove the obstacles hindering us to disseminate our knowledge and intentions with which you are familiar?' You then ask us: 'How do you intend to make the good cause prevail with this legion of well-trained men?'

For this purpose please be so kind as to answer the following XVII questions frankly, unwaveringly and according to your best conscience; and if these answers are as we may hope, then we shall present our plan of operation to you. Then you will proceed with the work in good spirits, and we shall be able to put you in a position to oversee the whole matter.

XVII Questions.

I. Can it be indifferent to mankind if religious and secular affairs continue to be conducted in the same manner as they are now? Is everything fine the way it is, or are there still flaws that must be corrected?

II. Is the wise, honest, and virtuous man also a happy man in the current state of affairs? Does he deserve to be happy? Can he? (Here, we are only speaking of *temporal happiness*.)

III. Why are there so many evil men and so few good? Is there enough entice-ment to do good? Should it not be increased by the prospect of happiness, con-tentment, and outward tranquillity? Does one currently not have more cause to be evil than good? Why should there be happiness only in vice; why not also happiness in virtue? Is not the consolation that virtue is its own reward too specu-lative for unfortunate good men, too cold and too unattractive?

IV. Is it not possible to conceive of situations in which all of the above could be resolved without hindrance, in which the enticement (including, *nota bene,* enticement of a sensual kind) to be good would be as powerful as the current enticement to be evil? Situations in which one could uncover vice and villains and even strike terror into their hearts? Where good men would be so strong that vice would beg for mercy, where it would even be compelled to do good and be rendered incapable of harming an honest man?

V. Would the means leading to such an end be good? Even if by these means, employed imperceptibly, certain prejudices hallowed through error would be attacked, even if they opposed the interests of certain persons who currently have good reasons to support despotism, superstition, and faithlessness?

VI. Do we already have such an institution in all public and secret societies? Is there a state which is able to accomplish all this? Is it not an intrinsic flaw of any state constitution that it is powerless in this regard even with all the will in the world?

VII. Would such a society be against the state? Can a higher, better purpose be imagined? Is it worth the efforts of noble souls to strive for it?

VIII. Is everything that opposes a corrupt state nevertheless always unjust and unlawful? Or rather, is that which opposes the abuses of administration also against the state?

IX. Would such a society be evil if it were to contrive situations in which the greatest monarchs of the world would be rendered incapable of doing evil? So that they could not do evil, even if they wanted to? A society that would thwart the abuse of the highest power? Is it possible for such a society to prevent abuse without going to the root cause?

X. Is it not conceivable that the states themselves are a *status in statu* without the current civil constitution being suspended?

XI. Would it then be unjust to establish oneself so firmly in some country that all members there would be provided for according to their merit and protected against any misadventure? That it would be impossible to make them unhappy? Would it be unjust to secretly direct this outward power, now being used for evil, towards good purposes – in a word, to govern without ruling?

XII. Is there a better government than a moral regime?

XIII. However, would not such a society have to pursue, in addition to a most sacred probity, the subtlest insight, the greatest knowledge of man, and the purest scholarship? Would it therefore not be necessary that this society endeavoured to unite all wise and mature minds on the face of the earth? That it would devise a plan by which they could all join forces to seek, research, observe, share observations, demonstrate, compare, and teach the correct perspective, so that one might immediately begin to work where others have left off? Which would facilitate and multiply all resources leading to understanding? A republic of scholars, a world academy?

XIV. What form of government would be best suited to such an order? Would the best form not be a certain kind of despotism, allowing the entire body to be preserved in a single casting? This may sound harsh; however, what is it that makes despotism so terrible in a monarchy? Three things: 1. That I cannot elect my monarch. 2. That he is sometimes a bad man. 3. That I cannot withdraw from his rulership again. Once these three difficulties disappear, would patient obedience not be necessary to prevent all confusion in a society founded on a comprehensive overview, proven wisdom and benevolence? Is it not also necessary that the Superiors remain hidden? Think of the reasons why this may be so.

XV. What are, in general, your thoughts about a society that skilfully manages to obtain the power to do everything it wishes, to implement all that is good and thwart all that is evil, thus becoming the monarch of monarchs while possessing knowledge of everything men can know in this world?

XVI. Finally, what do you think of the appendices A. and B.? Does it not appear as if, in the former, the correct perspective has been found from which a secret society with righteous, unselfish and enlightened men at its head could thwart all evil and make the good prevail without tearing apart the bonds of society? On the other hand, might not the initial propositions in Appendix B. lead to dangerous errors, even though they are somewhat curbed towards the end of the treatise? All violent reform, if not illicit, is never safe. Men must be educated differently, and then they will act differently all by themselves.

XVII. Were there not nations in antiquity where the *wise* were placed at the side of kings? Should it not be in accordance with divine intentions that the better and wiser man governs? Would such a regime, however one may call it, not be the sole means to return mankind to its high dignity bestowed by God? But should this regime not extend to the heart rather than to outward circumstances?

Addendum A. *Written sample answer to the prize question: What means exist by which the inconstancy of those belonging to secret societies can be fixed so they obey without external compulsion and one may safely trust them in all things?*

Formés par des parents, qui ne raisonnent presque jamais; élevés par des instituteurs, à qui la raison est odieuse; entourés d'une société remplie de préjugés de toutte espèce; gouvernés par des Maîtres qui se croyent intéressés à la durée des opinions, sur lesquelles ils fondent leur empire; le mensonge est, pour ainsi dire, identifié avec les hommes! Est-il donc surprenant, de ne trouver par tout que des êtres déraisonnables?

Système social T. I. chap. II[244]

---

[244] 'They have their personalities shaped by their parents, who hardly ever reason at all; they are brought up by ducators who find the whole idea of reason odious; they are surrounded in their everyday lives by people who are full of every conceivable kind of prejudice; they are governed by masters who have a vested interest in ensuring the permanence of the opinions upon which they have founded their Empire: mendacity is therefore, as it were, part and parcel of what it means to be human! Should we therefore be surprised when all we see, wherever we look, are unreasonable people?' ([Holbach:] Système social. Ou Principes naturels de la morale et de la politique, London 1774, p. 17.)

If this, my preamble, is justified, if priests and princes have joined forces to suppress human reason,* if they cast dalliances and tinsel before us to distract men from serious matters that are of interest to them, there is always sufficient cause for wisdom, in order to evade persecution, to hide in the shadows—and there to preserve, among faithful friends and followers in secret associations, the sacred sparks that one day shall erupt into a momentous conflagration in spite of all pressure, desiring the fruits of reason and saving the rights of an oppressed mankind.

It is thanks to these scattered, silent admirers of eternal truth that the world is not entirely in disarray, that superstition, faithlessness, hypocrisy, and despotism still find their opponents and resistance, and that, even though the world may end, the kingdom of truth shall be forever unperturbed.

Thus if self-interest governs the world in all things great and small; if one is free only to say what is in accord with it, and that alone is called truth; if men are so poorly educated about their temporal and eternal felicity, even their moral behaviour, that error, ignorance, and misunderstood interest are the mainsprings of their actions: then it is not only good that secret mystery schools exist but, if honesty, uprightness, friendship, and truth are to be preserved on earth at all, it is even necessary – for the human race would have lost with them one of the greatest tools of the providence by which God and nature intend to lead all mortals through the midst of corruption and persecution up to their highest exaltation and perfection.

Most certainly then, the objective of this silent union of the quiet friends of truth must be weighty and important. It must be nothing less or smaller than the felicity of not merely one man, one family, one nation, nay! but of the entire human race. Its benevolence must spread across not only one epoch or nation, it must, as it were, encompass the whole immensity of eternity and the entire universe. What are to be pursued are no mere theoretical speculations but earnest, active endeavours which must attack the root of human suffering, destroy error,

---

* *L'ignorance, les préjugés, l'opinion, l'éducation, les gouvernemens injustes, la paresse, voilà les sources permanentes de la corruption publique. ['Ignorance, prejudice, opinion, education, unjust government, and sloth are permanent sources of public corruption.' Ibid., p. 1; the original text has 'des peuples' instead of 'publique'.]*
au même endroit. [Ibid., pp. 5–6, with some deviations from the original text.] Si la morale réligieuse fut fondée sur des chimères dépourvues des motifs connus, subordonnée aux intérêts des prêtres, si elle n'eut rien de ce qu'y fallut; pour contenir ou diriger les passions des hommes – les loix, au lieu d'être les oracles de l'équité ne furent que les oppressions des injust[ic]es, des fantaisies p – ['If religious morality were based on illusions, devoid of any known rationale, and if it were subordinate to the interests of the priests, and had everything it needed to contain or direct human passions – the laws, instead of being infallible sources of justice and fairness, would be nothing more than expressions of injustices, fantasies, etc.']

prejudice, ignorance, and selfishness, and spread the light of truth across the whole earth. They must enforce what religion and the state either will not or cannot accomplish in this current state of corruption.

Many honest men have realised this. They often felt the desire to meet this society of upright men so that they might rally to its banner, and among some great men, their souls and minds aglow with philanthropy, this desire struck such deep roots that they dared to establish such an association themselves. In ancient as well as modern times there has always been a wealth of men who conjured up and commenced such an enterprise. Unfortunately, however, their efforts almost never met with success, and such societies perished no sooner than they were created. The heart of a man concerned with his own felicity as well as that of all mankind may weep that corruption and blindness have penetrated so deeply and mightily among men, and that there are countless collaborators willing to create a permanent association among themselves in order to pursue the most shameful, most despicable and selfish ends, even to engage in highway robbery; but scarcely will three or four men enter into a lasting bond with the only goal of perfecting human nature.

Does virtue really have as little appeal, and vice such diligent defenders? Where does the fault lie here, and how can it be rectified?

The illustrious society seeks to get to the root of the matter with the question presented here. Not as if it did not know how to do so itself and could not provide any help – otherwise its own organisation would be faulty – but to try and probe the man who is about to join its band, if he has the required strength and quality. Nonetheless I must admit that this task is infinitely difficult and that he who can solve it correctly must be regarded as mankind's greatest benefactor, for it is he who shows the certain path to reach that which is of the utmost importance to man, yet also that at which thousands have failed. A profound understanding of the human soul is required for this. And the heart of the man who knows men in their inconstancy – *chi soli nel variar sono costanti*[245] – trembles at the question of how he might firmly attach them to goodness. What prisons and shackles, love of life, fear of the yoke, and even a future fate in other worlds with all its suffering and joy have thus far not brought about is to be accomplished by a single secret society without any external compulsion – if this can be done, then truth and virtue must be your kingdom, and your power must indeed be great!

---

[245] *Ital. Who are constant only in their wavering.*

And if such a thing is possible then it is only thanks to the power of truth. I will therefore outline my thoughts, as my Illustrious Superiors have instructed me; I believe that I have truly understood and developed the question; and if I am given 5 or 6 respected and faithful collaborators, I shall also vouch for its implementation.

But first I will address the question as to why thus far all secret institutions for the cause of good were so easily destroyed.

1) Because the collaborators were not well-chosen in the beginning. Either they were not unselfish enough, not imbued deeply enough with the goodness of the cause, or they fell out through ambition and imperiousness in their midst.

2) Because the collaborators did not know the human heart well enough, were too trustful, because the foundation was not solid enough, and because men were accepted the way one found them.

3) Because they were not cautious enough and did not keep the matter as secret as is necessary under such dangerous conditions; because they were subsequently destroyed by those whose interests they opposed.

4) Because they were unable to put a beautiful veneer and shine on their good causes, and finally

5) because they were unable to advertise the benefits of being good as vividly as those of evil presented themselves.

6) Because they concerned themselves too quickly and too soon with their growth and proliferation, and most of all

7) because they allowed an insight into the whole enterprise without the least preparation, as they wanted to accomplish everything at once.

To devise a plan in which these flaws are avoided I wish to submit what I have gathered from my own experience in general, from history, and from my knowledge of other orders and their founders; I want to preserve their good qualities, and their flaws will help me discover the opposite rule. I therefore say:

If certain principles that are indispensable to human felicity, but which offend the interests of others too gravely, are to be made general, proliferated, and preserved among men and so become the substance of a secret society, then I shall not consider this the work of a day, nor the work of a year or a century, but the work of millennia; I would indeed be satisfied with small, almost imperceptible progress; I would neither exaggerate nor hasten the system's overall development;

---

* *The habit of acting virtuously is simply the result of frequently meditating upon virtue, of putting virtue into practice, of repeating that behaviour, and then transforming virtue into a human need.*

I would do no more than my particular strength allowed (time and circumstances included) without incurring any well-anticipated injury. I would first educate and prepare my men myself, notthe way I find them, but as I would require them for my purposes.

For the education of my collaborators, I would take the following measures:

I. I would strive to awaken in them a vivid desire for secret associations.

II. I would strive to weaken all their previously-held opinions contrary to mine and even to extinguish them over time.

III. I would want what I needed for my plan to develop over time and by my own design.

IV. [I would try] to ingrain these newly-created principles so deeply into their souls that they would feel compelled to think in this manner and no other.

I. *The art of creating a passion for secret associations.*

1) I would use a time of public hardship. It is during such times when a man most strongly feels the need for his fellow man.

2) If no public hardships existed I would wait for a time when some misfortune or other occurrence that had befallen the man I had chosen required him to approach others for help; then I would show to him what man can accomplish alone and how powerful he is when he joins forces with others.

The dearth of such opportunities and the need for aid mean that the great, the powerful, and the wealthy rarely make good associates. I would not pursue them too urgently, but neither would I exclude them.

3) In short, I would deal with them as has been so excellently outlined in our 'Instructio pro Recipientibus'.

II. *To change a Candidate's fundamental position,* I would

1) choose only those who would submit themselves to leadership and guidance, hence primarily young persons, especially in places where many respectable men already belong to the society.*

2) From among adult men, those who are still capable of being led, whose thoughts are nearly as I want them, who do not yet know too much, but yearn for enlightenment, who are free of prejudice and whose interests do not oppose ours too much. I would therefore never choose:

a) Those who already have a developed system,

b) are filled with pride because of it,

c) members of clerical orders,

d) selfish and especially imperious men,

e) high-ranking and powerful men, unless they have been groomed for this role since childhood.

f) Bigots and hypocrites.

g) All those who lack the quality of a good heart. This is the first quality I would demand of everyone.

3) I would want to make them passionate for immortality, for leaving an eternal legacy by their good deeds; I would show them their limited, vegetative life, show them their destiny, the sphere of influence to which they will be transposed; I would praise the pleasure of affecting the greater whole, of being great despite one's low class: In short, I would always show him that side of the Order that agrees with his governing disposition, by which it is not only confirmed, but confirmed better than anywhere else.

Thus, I would demonstrate to the ambitious the joy of governing in secret and without being noticed, and of giving the world another direction from inside his chamber, perhaps ruling those who believe themselves to be his lords, and all that with such certainty that no other power could undermine my own.

4) In the Preparatory Class, the so-called Noviciate, I would not want him to know all members; with the fear of being watched by one [hundred] eyes, I would want to entice him to better his heart and open it towards the general welfare. I would want to provide them with the necessary guidance and also subject them to tests.

5) At the same time I would want to make him mistrustful towards himself, his knowledge, and all truths; I would want to teach him the great art of doubting everything.

6) I would also want to stir their desire for the new and the strange, the desire to rise above common opinion, so that they would wish to know a little more than the greater part of mankind.

7) Pointing to the history of the Eleusinian mysteries, the Bacchanalian orgies, and the mysteries of Isis, I would want to show that the purest principles have always been preserved only in secret mystery schools.

8) This would prepare him for penetrating the most clandestine wisdom.

9) I would tell them about books leading in this direction and then put certain opinions that they deem irrefutable to the test, thus showing them that our knowledge is far from what it should and could be.

10) In general they should develop a willingness to discard any belief in the face of better-understood truths and reasons.

If I find this willingness in my man, if it has taken root with him, it must then be made vivid and nurtured.

This also means that he who would open the door to hidden wisdom to another must be a man of whom this might be expected with good reason. Therefore, he must:

1) Act mysteriously; show no selfish intentions; not be the opposite of that which he says the other shall become.

2) He must lead a distinctive life, aloof from the unworthy part of mankind.

3) He must have a reputation of being enlightened and revealing insights.

4) Express enjoyment of his work and studies.

5) One must deem oneself fortunate to know a man who can be approached by so few and only noble men.

6) When he speaks of the cause, he must always do so with trembling and reverence, and always behind closed doors.

7) Only say as much as is necessary; concerning the Order, he may only talk in general terms but must reveal nothing of its actual organisation.

8) Owe his enlightenment, felicity, and satisfaction to these institutions. In short,

9) to create enthusiasts, he must be one himself and show it, since nothing is as infectious as enthusiasm.

If I deal with my Candidate in this manner, I will instil him with respect not only for me but for the entire society as well. Even more so:

1) If my man is convinced it is the sole and therefore exclusive source of the goal:

2) If one gives few commands, but urges the strictest execution of what has been commanded.

3) If no dispensations, privileges, or favourites are encountered.

4) If one makes sure that only worthy men are admitted to this society, and these only through tremendous effort, preparation, and trials. Then the effort of applying for it and of searching for something that not everyone has or may receive, no matter how small, is well justified. Men always place a much greater value on what they gain only through struggle and for which great efforts are required.

This thought that only a few are capable of such greatness, patience, and endurance stirs one's pride so much that one cannot resist coveting what is given to so few. Distinction always pleases, even if I can distinguish myself only by the most paltry trifles. Once it is no longer distinctive because it has become too common, all respect and sympathy are lost.

If my candidate has a good heart, the desire to rise above even the noble rabble, respect for his superiors, and the belief he may satisfy his curiosity in this society alone, then he is mine, and I do with him as I please. I proceed with him in the following manner: Which is

III[.] The Instruction

1) I begin presenting him with some propositions, though not the most important ones.

2) Therefore, I would divide my system into several classes.

3) The first would include preparatory teachings, general teachings of such a kind that would not allow the Candidate to see their aim.

4) Teachings so simple that anyone could grasp and understand them easily.

5) If he found these convincing, I would take him further; I would present him with new propositions which would be of such a nature that he, as a thinker, would be able to deduce them from the ones preparing them, that is, the very next propositions immediately following from the preceding ones.

6) Even these I would not present to him unadorned. I would teach them directly to his heart in solemn silence, inspiring his awe with hallowed and suitable ceremonies.

7) And with symbols and hieroglyphs whose meaning he would have to discover for himself.

8) Not only that, but these principles would also be proved and made tangible with fables, examples, and allegories in the frequent assemblies, so that his soul would be filled not with a theoretical proposition but with an excellent image, enriched by all the instances and individual experiences from which the proposition has been abstracted.

9) The speeches in the assemblies must be full of warmth, spirit, and fire. Enthusiasm should shine through everywhere.

10) And once my candidate commenced to surmise the further conclusions and felt compelled to regard the first propositions as given truths, then and only then would he be promoted further until, at last, having advanced all the way, the entire system and its final conclusion lay before his soul. – The ultimate goal of this present method of proceeding can be described as the principle of estab-

lishing constancy in virtue. *L'habitude de la vertu n'est jamais que la vertu, très souvent méditée, pratiquée, réitérée et changée en un besoin.* *

In this fashion, I gain this much:

1) By refraining from abusing the revealed truths

2) I need not and must not fear that he will stray.

3) Or that he will reveal the secrets of the society to others.

4) I can bet against all odds that he will await the full development and fear no truth, no matter how strange it might have appeared to him before:

IV. And then I need no longer worry about the IVth. The habitual joy he has experienced in the Order, the education he has received therein, the example of his Brethren, the good he has done, the vast sphere of influence in which he finds himself, and the insurmountable power of the truth shrouded in symbols all cause him to unite his own interests with the greater whole, so that he will suffer persecution and death itself for the good cause of mankind. Here, I think I have demonstrated sufficiently how men are to be attached to goodness, but I have not nearly said everything, and some of what I have said may be incorrect. But if everything were false and useless, then things do not bode well for the best of causes. I know of no other way to unite men in steadfastness, and otherwise the honest man will be left with no other course than to suffer in silence. Then it is said: *Sous un gouvernement vicieux (et quel gouvernement ne l'est pas?) on ne trouve de vertu que dans un petit nombre de gens de bien isolés, qui, content de quelques approbateurs, résistent au torrent universel, ou jouissent à l'écart des vertus domestiques, dont ils savent goûter les douceurs.*

But God's wisdom and grace shall avenge the injustice we have suffered; on this we rely. *Donnés le temps à la sagesse, et le bonheur sera pour elle; donnés le temps à la folie, et elle se punira elle-même.*[246]

---

* *Tout homme, qui donne au public des idées nouvelles, ne peut espérer d'estime que de deux sortes d'hommes, ou de jeunes gens, qui n'ayant point adopté d'opinions, ont encore le désir et le loisir de s'instruire, ou de ceux dont l'esprit, ami de la vérité et analogue à celui de l'auteur, soupçonne déjà l'existence des idées qu'il leur donne. de l'Esprit T. I. Diss: 2. chap. IV [the original text has 'auteur' instead of 'homme'].* ('[...] *every [man] who abounds with new ideas can only expect esteem from two sorts of men; either young persons, who, by not previously adopting any opinion, have still the desire and leisure of informing themselves; or of those whose minds, being desirous of truth, and analogous to that of the author, had previously some glimpse of the existence of these ideas.' C. A. Helvetius: De l'esprit; or, Essays on the mind, and its several faculties, ed. by William Mudford, London 1807, pp. 52–53.)*

[246] *'Under a government that is full of vices – and which government is not? – we find virtue only amongst a small number of quite isolated individuals who content themselves with a small circle of admirers or else live a life apart, enjoying a cosy domesticity. But God's wisdom and goodness shall avenge the injustice we have suffered; on this we rely. If you spend time engaging in wisdom then it will create its own happiness, but if you spend your time in foolishness then it will surely make a rod for its own back.' (Holbach, ibid.)*

I therefore desire the following to be a secret society's cause:

1) A most interesting, hitherto unknown system for human felicity,

2) presented in steps,

3) with the greatest possible secrecy and solemnity of suitable ceremonies,

4) shrouded by hieroglyphs and images,

5) with the greatest prudence,

6) presented only to a few, but those the worthiest part of mankind; men, who beyond this

7) possess the resolve and constancy

8) to make this become a reality in the world through hidden institutions over thousands of years.

And this, I believe, must be the desire of every wise man and wormwood to any villain whose interests are the opposite.

Addendum B. *Written sample answer to the question: Are secret societies detrimental to the state? May the state tolerate them without weakening itself?*

If candour in thinking and writing is what a man seeks above everything else but may only hope to find in secret associations, I shall, with the permission of the Illustrious Superiors, dare to counter the question with another: Are secret societies, if they are harmful to the state and its interests, therefore unlawful at all times? Does not the state have every cause not to tolerate them without these societies losing one iota of their legitimacy and goodness[?]

Are all things that are prohibited necessarily evil? Certainly they are evil for him who enacts the prohibition, but are they necessarily evil in other regards?

Could not this other regard be so universal and so charitable that the prohibition itself may be an evil because it hinders a great good?

May I doubt, question, and examine whether or not states are always good?

It is therefore essential to establish if it can be satisfactorily proved that the states will not forever be necessary and essential to human felicity[.]

If this proposition is certain, why would the friend of truth not agree with it or endeavour to work on bringing something evil to an end?

But if this statement cannot be proved, then the secret society is evil, and one has every right to oppress it as harmful.

Furthermore, I find it necessary to define this question more precisely: Does a society that actively opposes an evil state constitution deserve to be called harmful?

Would it thus be wrong or sinful to give the Orient a milder form of government? to thwart and end despotism?

To cure the flaws and ailments of a state by means of secret operations?

If this is not in any way evil and is condemned only by him against whose harmful interests one takes action, the state may forbid a society opposing it for this very reason, and unjustly so.

Therefore, only those secret societies working to thwart good state institutions would be dangerous. Here I shall take the liberty of expressing further doubts and questions.

1) Where are these wholly good states that need not be improved?

2) Can we not find a number of flaws and ailments in even the best governments that no statesmanship is able to remedy?

3) Where did the states and their supreme authority originate?

4) If they owe their origin to the union of men and social contracts, what should therefore keep men from joining a new, additional, and mutual union?

5) Can Holland, Switzerland, the Papal Territories and the Carolingian monarchy be counted among the legitimate states? Did they not break free from their former overlords and become independent by way of rebellions?

6) May I not act against the power in these states which was born of rebellion and can claim no other right to its legitimacy than the incapacity of their prior lords to repossess it, the course of time, and the wisdom of men who deem what cannot be wrested from other nations due to their own weakness as rightful?

7) Are today's Americans rebels or not? If the latter is true, one may act against the state and liberate oneself. If the former is true, I shall also ask: may an American take action against his rebellious countrymen? Even if America's independence should be recognised? And even if America has lived a hundred years in this state of independence? Do the Americans cease to be rebels because Spain and France recognise theirs as a separate and sovereign state? Would England's weakness and incapacity be a sufficient title to sovereignty?

8) If we delve into the origins of states, do we not find that most of today's states were born of usurpation and enlarged by violence? Thus, a secret society may only refrain from being detrimental to those states that are perpetuated legitimately; for why would a usurping supreme authority condemn their subjects for what they have themselves done to others, their prior overlords? or does the passage of 100 or 1000 years justify sacrilege and rebellion?

Thus our question is narrowed down and answered to the extent that a secret society which opposes a rightfully established and well-governed state is illegitimate. Even so, I still have concerns and doubts.

I can think of only two instances in which this statement can be true:

1) If the purpose of a secret society is lesser, more limited, and more pernicious than that of the state.

2) If one has accepted this proposition as correct: that the states are the goal and that men exist for their sake, whereas the states do not exist for the sake of men. Yet, what if all states were only means or intermediary steps that lead to something better?

What if the prolonged and perpetual existence of states thwarted the achievement of this better goal?

Should a society with an even better, universal, and unselfish purpose than the states themselves be illegitimate? a society which pursued that for which nations are only intermediary means[?]

And could one not level the same justified charge against the states which they themselves raise against other secret associations, namely that they form a *status in statu?*

Should the friend of truth and the human race not gladly join such a society, whose purpose and benefit are even more universal?

Should it not be permissible to take action against the rights of princes if they contradicted higher and inalienable rights? if they thwarted the highest and best goal of the world and of nature?

Are the princes themselves not rather bound to relinquish their rights as soon as they infringe the rights and dignity of mankind? In my humble opinion it all depends upon whose goal is higher, worthier, and more universal. I claim only this:

1) All societies that wish to implement, independently of the state, a lesser and narrower goal are illegitimate and against the state;

2) all societies whose goal is higher and worthier than that of the state itself are legitimate, and here it may

3) come to pass that states themselves become illegitimate, a *status in statu,* if they oppose this higher goal.

Would it not be strange if God's and nature's intentions went no further than making so many of his favourites among men great, mighty, and happy, while subjecting all others to servitude and the whim of their favourites in order to accomplish this? Could there not be a different condition in which such happiness were not merely and excessively for the chosen few, but became universal? and could more widely-proliferated reason not teach all men *that he who knows how to guide himself has no need of another man to direct him?*

Finally, I must also note that there is a curious difference in how a society takes action against the state.

If it eschews regicide and the subjects' rebellion, *following only the course of nature, lending it a hand, doing nothing more than spreading the light on all paths and teaching man the great art of governing himself,* should this be considered unjust? Should all the princes' power be capable of preventing this from coming to pass eventually? I believe not, for in this world all means most often work in the opposite direction, no more and no less, so that whatever one seeks to thwart is promoted more assuredly.

These then are my thoughts on the questions presented to me. I have answered them boldly and with full candour, not as if I believed that this were the purpose of this Illustrious Order, but because I can imagine that I am dealing with men who have risen above all prejudices and who take pleasure in seeing a subject treated in any new manner, no matter how bold: men who are not held back even by their own interests when examining a matter whose falsehood they would deem reprehensible. And I am thus confident that this essay will not embarrass me even if princes should be members of this Illustrious Order, because I know they are members of a society where enlightenment is so prodigious that one will also think and act against one's own interests. If I have erred, if my arguments are wrong, I ask to be corrected. I follow the truth, wherever it may lead. And even if everything here should be false, the fruit is still rich enough if it provokes thought, if many a head awakens and begins to doubt something which otherwise he would not have had the heart to reject as a given.

FOOTNOTES TO A REVISED PRESBYTER DEGREE.

[ON COSMOPOLITANISM.]

With respect to the greater whole, states and nations are nothing more than large, further subdivided families; are not the end, but a means; are not the final step, but only an elevated step in the great ladder of nature that the human race shall climb to reach its dignity and greatness. If you want tranquillity and unity to reign among men and the nations on this earth, then lessen the narrower ties and interests and unite them in one that is higher and more universal, for the higher it is, the more the cause of discord will dissipate. Great deeds and acts of self-denial will become apparent and heroes will appear. If you want to destroy the world and spread disunity, then narrow the perspective and thus multiply the interests, and dwarfs and small spirits, libellers and hypocrites, murderers and conquerors, haughty and devious men shall ravage the earth; to a greater or lesser degree, depending on whether the perspective is wider or narrower, hatred and discord are the children of egotism and of all narrower inclinations. Universal peace and tranquillity are the results of cosmopolitanism.

[ON TRADE.]

How many things become possible for a nation only because, in its transactions with others, the balance of trade is favourable? To what extent must others, where it is negative, depend on it, having to account for it in their state institutions? and what is the basis of the rule over otherwise independent states other than the greater or lesser needs of one or the other? How easily can a change in trade affect the mutual relationships? What consequences must this single change in trade also have for the internal affairs of the nations and in all of Europe? Is this not the danger around which the present felicity and morality of men and nations revolves?

[ON ENLIGHTENMENT.]

Enlightenment, however, means here not merely the knowledge of words, but of things. This great change depends neither on the sciences nor on some universally-active scholarship. Universal scholarship would truly be universal misfortune. Enlightenment can exist very well without scholarship. In the time of this great decline, men, the masses, shall therefore possess only as much reason as is necessary to properly occupy their freely-chosen, unimposed station in life with joy, grace, and usefulness, and act in accordance with some given, general, and easily-understood purpose. They shall know only those few things that we highly-educated men, in our great and overflowing scholarship, overlook and deem too insignificant, although the world's happiness and tranquillity rest on these trifles. They shall know only what each of us should and would know if his mind had not been overfilled so much, from his earliest childhood, with prejudices and words that nothing or only the smallest part of it enters the heart. They shall receive no theoretical speculations but only a practical mind that knows how to help itself in the most important matters of life, without endangering the felicity of his fellow men in doing so. They shall not so much define, distinguish, and demonstrate but observe, experience, feel, and perceive. And why should this demand be so impossible? Does not the first as well as the last man wish for a longer life and pleasant living conditions? Is this not in the nature and essence of every man? Does not everyone have the ability and opportunity to conduct experiments and have experiences by which he may distinguish that which is true and permanent from the temporary, illusory good? – If all those who have been presented as exemplary to the world and the masses had earnestly sought not to hold their own narrower circumstances, which would lose out in the process, in higher esteem than the general happiness of mankind, then this state would not merely have long been possible, but it would be a reality. But today, what in fact is the understanding of most people other than prejudice and a regurgitated popular opinion or, at most, a borrowed, but not truly grasped opinion of those who set the tone of our age – the opinion of a somewhat better rabble, which believes itself wiser, that meets with our approval because we have received it from our teachers in our youth without questioning it and that is widely held and reiterated by those who think in our stead, and whom we trust for this very reason because, in doing so, we may hope for tranquillity without persecution, since it most easily agrees with our hopes and expectations and, finally, because most of the time we are too sluggish to tear down our rotting, decrepit hovel to live under the blue canopy and arch of the sky for a while in order to build a more permanent and thorough edifice in its stead? How many of those who call themselves thinkers are truly worthy of the name? How many of them are capable of finding and loving truth even where they would not desire it, where it contradicted their wishes and systems, where courage and resolution are needed, because danger and interest also come into play? Most only seek confirmation of what they have accepted without questioning; and what they accept or reject depends on whether or not something conforms to their prior thinking, but they rarely possess the strength to investigate further where they do not suspect any error or examine if this very assumption may not itself be an error or prejudice. They who otherwise think about all things close their eyes to the two most important matters of our entire knowledge, the state and religion, the past and the future; they reject any doubts that might arise without wanting to know, examine, or be convinced;

they only want to believe, believe those whose interest lies in decrying reason, those who possess enough cleverness or malice to seize our earliest years, to plant seeds in us of those notions that are useful to them, to repeat them *ad infinitum,* to turn this way of thinking into a need for us and to enslave us to a habit so detrimental to our reason and our rights. – Stand ready, all ye who call yourselves enlightened, in whom a higher spirit is at work! Cast off the yoke and the prejudices of your youth! Make a resolution to think, to think about all things! Henceforth, no longer call true what the noble or common crowd or the party who has an interest in it commands or allows to be called truth! Truth is the daughter of heaven. He himself, the great one, the infinite one is truth. He, the author of the same, the creator of this universe has given us a mind and reason for self-examination without limitation. The threshold at which investigation must stop was invented by the selfishness of men; God and nature do not know it. In future, it shall no longer be as it is today! Let the greatest spirit appear today, let him prove the loftiest, most soothing and useful truth with syllogisms and experiences in geometric rigour;[247] his reward will be ridicule and persecution, for selfishness and darkness are unable and unwilling to understand him until, in later times, in a more mature age of mankind, the interest changes, coldblooded observers seek out his almost wholly forgotten opinions, supplement the missing intermediate propositions, gather a small crowd of men who confess the truth, acquire respect in their own age and use it to set the tone, increase their small following by and by and then sweep along the once again falling crowd of sycophants, thus tearing the hoodwink from the eyes of the world. – O, how many truths were dismissed only because the man who first presented and publicised them did not possess an *equipage*[248] of his own and, furthermore, was but a single man! As if the truth were the privilege of the masses, as if not all our opinions of today did not invariably owe their origins to a sole thinker and never to a group. For only if a general clamour arises, a certain doctrine becomes fashionable, and the interested party allows you to confess to it or becomes too weak to find such a general creed, only then will the train of straggling men don the mantle of the latest fashion, although its age and general acceptance so poorly prove the truth of a matter that one has every cause to doubt it all the more. This prejudice of age and general opinion binds the spirit in chains and favours ignorance, error, and deception. It only proves that people have always and everywhere been deceived by their own

---

[247] *Allusion to Spinoza's method (more geometrico).*   [248] *A horse-drawn carriage (with attendants).*

gullibility and sluggishness, that the host of the ignorant and the deceivers has at all times been greater than the small band of the wise and the enlightened; that the latter were feeble and too prudent to struggle against such an overwhelming majority; that the truth was not at any time in the past nor at any place the property of the people but only that of a few isolated or united brilliant minds, and that, finally, because the truth has always been accompanied by so many hazards, these seers and brilliant thinkers wrapped themselves in a cloak under which they preserved this sacred spark and loftiest gift from heaven, truth and reason, in silence and secrecy under a thousand locks, and conveyed it only to a select few, sharing with the rest of the world and their contemporaries only as much as their respective mood and capacity would allow. A society such as ours must therefore concern itself with examining the current popular opinion, knowing the tenor of its age and noting its progress without wrongfully disputing or discarding it, but instead using and connecting to it, divulging to others only as much as the cause demands and the world is able to bear. It must understand the art of giving and accepting opinions, depending on the various circumstances. By the general clamour that it is capable of immediately instigating through its members, who are dispersed everywhere, it can awaken the sleeping crowd, grasp its attention, incite general ridicule or praise and admiration for old as well as new propositions, bring the sluggish thinkers into its fold and give reason strength by turning its principles into customs and opinions; after all, the crowd must always have opinions, and the benefit is always great enough if reason itself is turned into opinion. – Such a society must be the mistress of all minds and of the prevailing way of thinking of its age. The latter shall endure by its permission, and at its command it must vanish immediately. Why then should it be impossible that, through its endeavours, it can bring about the moderate degree of enlightenment necessary for freedom?

INSTRUCTIONS FOR THE NATIONAL INSPECTORS.

Apart from that which the Inspector can already find on the due discharge of his office in the Regent degree and its addenda he has, briefly summarised, the following duties:

I. He must have a thorough knowledge of the Provinces under his care with regard to their personal as well as their political conditions and, consequently, he needs to know all members of the Order who hold some lesser or greater office, the specific regional needs, the degree of enlightenment, the system of government, etc.

II. If Brethren lacking the proper talents for government have crept into the ranks of the intermediate Superiors, he shall shrewdly find a way to wrest control from their hands again and put other, more capable men in their place.

III. He must be particularly watchful of his Provincial Superiors, so that if they are too hasty in granting promotions or assigning offices, he can notify the National Superior in a timely manner and suggest how such a Provincial Superior might be removed from office or how a supervisor might be appointed alongside him.

IV. He is appointed by the National Superior, but this is usually discussed with the district's Provincial Superiors beforehand so that a man who has their trust is selected.

V. The Inspector reports to the National Superior on a monthly basis, attaching the reports he has received from the Provincial Superiors after removing from them the less important supplements to save postage. In addition, twice a year, namely at the end and after the first half of each Order's year, he sends the National Superior the main tables containing the personnel of each Province.

VI. He must therefore insist that the Provincial and Local Superiors compile and attach these reports accurately, precisely, and on time. What is reported to the Provincial Superior in the month of *Pharavardin* he must report to the Inspector in the month of *Adarpahasht,* and only in *Chardad* does the Inspector send the report for *Pharavardin* to the National Superior.

VII. He must diligently remind the Provincial Superiors of their duties, especially that no Minerval live somewhere without being assigned to an Assembly, that no one is in possession of O. documents unless his office in the O. calls for it, that all items required are submitted before a degree is conferred, etc.

VIII. Although he cannot concern himself with the minutiae of the lower degrees, the files of any Candidate for the Regent Class must always be sent to the Inspector before such a man can be promoted to it. It is known that conclusions are drawn from the character sketches and biographies, as well as the Priest Class, whereas all original files are returned to the new Regents. However, it must be noted that the Inspector retains the silhouette of each Regent as well as a brief summary of his personal circumstances in his archives, which he sends to the National Superior should this man become a Provincial Superior.

IX. The Inspector unseals the Minervals' and Lesser *Illuminati*'s *Primo,* but the Greater *Illuminati*'s *Primo* and the Regents' *Soli* are sent to the National Superior unopened.

X. He shall ensure the timely promotions of the members according to their merit, and therefore he has the right to request receipt of the files on any member he chooses so that he can be assured that the O. is not wasting its recommendations on unworthy persons.

XI. The communication among the Provinces in this and other circumstances must pass through his hands, and he must not allow one Provincial Superior to communicate with another without his permission. On the other hand, the Lodges in the lower degrees may correspond with one another on matters of Freemasonry as they please.

XII. Nor should the Inspector concern himself about his fellow Inspectors; the communication among the Inspectors is maintained by the National Superior alone.

XIII. As much as possible the Inspector shall conscientiously direct the affairs of his inspection on his own without burdening the higher Superiors with frequent minor inquiries, but he should not fail to consult with the National Superior in very important matters.

XIV. He confirms the Prefects suggested to him by the Provincial Superior, and he must exercise great care in his selections for these important offices. He nominates the Provincial Superiors and awaits the National Superior's approval.

XV. He distributes a number of O. names received from the National Superior to the Provincial Superiors.

XVI. He keeps an Inspector's seal, a drawing of which will be sent to him.

XVII. He may choose whomever he wishes to assist him in his office.

XVIII. He assigns the Chapter names.

XIX. If he needs to correspond with someone about vitally important matters, he may use the attached unidentifiable cipher and give that person the key to it; he must, however, carefully note this and let his successor know to whom he has given this cipher.

a b c d e f g h i k l m n o p q r s t u v w x y z   ; : , ? !

A ♯ before a vowel indicates an *umlaut,* e.g. ♯o is ä and ♯♪ is ü. Use a · or a
vertical line | to separate words.

Example

D i e s e   E r k l ä r u n g ,   s o   g u t   s i e   a u c h w a r ;

v e r d r o ß   m i c h.[249]

---

[249] *Ger.* This explanation, as good as it was, annoyed me.